The Classic Chinese Novel

PREPARED AS ONE OF THE *Companions to Asian Studies*

WM. THEODORE DE BARY, EDITOR

THE
CLASSIC
CHINESE
NOVEL

A CRITICAL INTRODUCTION

BY C. T. HSIA

Columbia University Press

New York and London

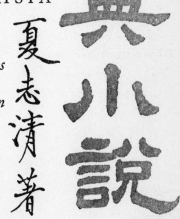

中國古典小說

夏志清著

C. T. Hsia is Associate Professor of Chinese at Columbia University and a Fellow of the School of Letters at Indiana University.

Portions of this work were prepared under a grant from the Carnegie Corporation of New York and a contract with the U. S. Office of Education for the production of texts to be used in undergraduate education. The material so produced has been used in the Columbia College Oriental Humanities program and has subsequently been revised and expanded for publication in the present form.

Portions of Chapter VII reprinted in revised form from C. T. Hsia, "Love and Compassion in *Dream of the Red Chamber*," *Criticism*, V, No. 3 (1963), by permission of the Wayne State University Press.

DEDICATED
TO THE MEMORY OF
MY BROTHER
TSI-AN HSIA
(1916–1965)

FOREWORD

The Classic Chinese Novel is one of a series of Companions to Asian Studies sponsored by the Committee on Oriental Studies. The series includes bibliographical guides, syllabi, and manuals introducing different aspects of Asian civilization to general education and the general reader. Assisted originally by the Carnegie Corporation of New York and more recently by the U. S. Office of Education, this series is intended to complement basic texts and translations appearing in the Introduction to Oriental Civilizations and the series of Translations from the Oriental Classics, also sponsored by the Committee.

In any study of Chinese literature the classic novels stand out as major expressions of the Chinese cultural tradition, and some of them merit consideration as major works of world literature. Professor Hsia's approach to these works is primarily interpretive. He does not seek to settle the many textual and historical problems which surround them in scholarly literature, but to draw from such studies the information most needed for a basic understanding and appreciation of the works themselves. In other words, he seeks to do for the classics of Chinese fiction what Burton Watson's *Early Chinese Literature,* in this same series, has already done for the early classical literature of China.

WM. THEODORE DE BARY

PREFACE

This guide to six major Chinese novels is intended for several kinds of readers: specialists in Chinese literature, nonspecialist teachers and students having occasion to discuss these works in the classroom, students of Western and comparative literature desirous of enlarging their knowledge of fiction, and others similarly impelled by curiosity. Accordingly, while I have provided for the unprepared reader pertinent information concerning the evolution and authorship of each novel, I have mainly undertaken the kind of inquiry that should prove of equal interest to the specialist and the student of Western literature—critical exploration of the art and meaning of the six novels and of their genre. In adopting this critical approach, I am of course fully aware that the specialists commanding the highest respect in the field have been invariably those primarily concerned with bibliographical and historical scholarship. But it seems to me obvious that we cannot indefinitely neglect the critical study of classic Chinese novels until all puzzles concerning their composition and publication have been solved. Problems of authorship and textual corruption have similarly plagued modern students of Elizabethan drama, but this handicap has not deterred the best critical minds among them from significantly enriching our understanding of that drama as literature.

The main text of this book was completed just before the full-scale launching of the Proletarian Cultural Revolution on mainland China in the summer of 1966. The six novels under study, which had hitherto been proclaimed as national classics, are now dismissed as relics of the feudal past totally incompatible with the thought of

Mao Tse-tung. I have not thought it advisable, however, to change my references to the affirmative Communist attitude toward traditional Chinese fiction to the past tense since it is most likely that this earlier position, though officially repudiated, still claims the silent allegiance of mainland scholars seriously concerned with the nation's literary heritage.

With the exception of *The Scholars,* I have translated most of the excerpts from the six novels myself either because they are missing from the available English translations or because the corresponding passages appear to me unsatisfactory. I have translated the longer excerpts with especial care in the hope that they may bear scrutiny as Arnoldian touchstones by readers who cannot read the novels in the original. Beyond serving the immediate context of my critical discussion, each of these passages possesses an intrinsic literary interest deserving of further exploration.

The preparation of this study was made possible mainly through the support of funds granted by the Carnegie Corporation of New York to the Columbia University Committee on Oriental Studies and, additionally, through a contract with the United States Department of Health, Education, and Welfare, under the provisions of Title VI, Public Law 85–864, as amended, Section 602. To Professor and Mrs. Wm. Theodore de Bary, who kindly read the manuscript upon its completion, I am deeply grateful for their great interest in my project and their constant encouragement. In translating passages from *Chin P'ing Mei,* I have benefited from the treasured advice of Professor Liu Ts'un-yan of the Australian National University, though any remaining errors in the translated excerpts are entirely my own responsibility. I also want to thank Dr. Hsin-cheng Chuang of the University of California at Berkeley for repeatedly arranging the loan of materials available at his university and at the Hoover Institution. The Chinese characters adorning the title page are in the distinguished hand of Professor Chiang Yee, who includes among his various inimitable accomplishments that of a master calligrapher.

Portions of Chapters III and VII have seen earlier publication, in somewhat different wording, as articles in the *Yearbook of Com-*

parative and General Literature (No. 11, 1962) and *Criticism* (V, No. 3, Wayne State University Press, 1963), respectively titled "Comparative Approaches to *Water Margin*" and "Love and Compassion in *Dream of the Red Chamber*." I wish to thank the editors of these journals and the Director of the Wayne State University Press for giving me permission to incorporate these articles in the present work. Chapter IV developed from a paper I read in March, 1964, at the annual meeting of the Association for Asian Studies. That paper and a companion paper given by my late brother T. A. Hsia at the same meeting have subsequently been accepted for inclusion in *Wen-lin: Studies in the Chinese Humanities* (University of Wisconsin Press, in press) under the joint title "New Perspectives on Two Ming Novels: *Hsi-yu chi* and *Hsi-yu pu*." To Professor Chow Tse-tsung, the editor of that volume, I owe a special debt of gratitude for allowing me to quote and adapt portions of the forthcoming article. The Appendix originally appeared in *The Kenyon Review* (XXIV, No. 3, Summer, 1962) under the title " 'To What Fyn Lyve I Thus?'—Society and Self in the Chinese Short Story." Thanks are due the editor for permitting me to reprint the article in its present revised form.

The name of my beloved brother appears on the dedication page —a feeble commemorative gesture that suggests nothing of our deep attachment to each other while he was alive and of my abiding loneliness since his passing on February 23, 1965.

C. T. H.

November, 1967

CONTENTS

The Classic Chinese Novel

CHAPTER I

INTRODUCTION

A student of the traditional Chinese novel who has been at all exposed to Western fiction is sooner or later struck by the sharp contrast between the majority of unrewarding works composing that genre and a number of titles which, while sharing the literary conventions of these works, possess enough compensating excellences to appeal to the adult intelligence. The most severe modern reader would endorse at least one work of that tradition, *Dream of the Red Chamber* (*Hung-lou meng*), and most would include among the classics of the Chinese novel the following five, as well: *The Romance of the Three Kingdoms* (*San-kuo-chih yen-i*), *The Water Margin* or *All Men Are Brothers* (*Shui-hu chuan*), *A Record of the Journey to the West* (*Hsi-yu chi*), *Chin P'ing Mei,* and *The Scholars* (*Ju-lin wai-shih*). Not all these are among the finest Chinese novels ever written; even if we exclude the modern period, I believe there are a few traditional titles which are superior in artistic merit to the poorer works among the six though their importance has not yet won general critical recognition. But without a doubt these six are historically the most important landmarks of the genre: each had for its own time broken new ground and appropriated new areas of interest for the Chinese novel and had deeply influenced its subsequent course of development. To this day they remain the most beloved novels among the Chinese. In the absence of an over-all revaluation of the Chinese novel from its beginnings to the late Ch'ing period, one cannot go far wrong in focusing critical attention on these books as works representative of its strength and diversity.

Indeed, judging by the prodigious amount of scholarly industry expended on these titles in the last four decades, they would appear to constitute the *tradition* of the Chinese novel. Not only Chinese scholars but also Western sinologists now approach with the utmost seriousness the minutest problems connected with their authorship and texts.[1] In Communist China, though important reservations have been made about the pornographic and pro-capitalist natural-ism of *Chin P'ing Mei*,[2] the six are invariably acclaimed as works expressive of the genius of the people, as classics in every sense of the term. Their enhanced prestige partly reflects the increasingly chauvinistic fervency with which the vernacular literature of old China has been affirmed in recent years. The new designation for traditional novels, "the classic Chinese novel" (*Chung-kuo ku-tien hsiao-shuo*), signalizes conclusively a change of national attitude. It was not too long ago that these works were dubbed "the old novel" (*chiu hsiao-shuo*), to underscore their difference from "the new novel" (*hsin hsiao-shuo*) being consciously created under the Western influence. Or else they were more objectively called *chang-hui hsiao-shuo* (the chapter-divided novel), but the term retains a tinge of condescension, implying that the traditional method of composition—to divide a novel into a large number of chapters without caring whether each is a coherent unit of narrative—is no longer fit for modern imitation. Though the leaders of the New Culture Movement championed the vernacular novel in support of their literary reforms, they were at the same time West-orientated scholars never completely at ease in that genre of writing.

A new beginning in the criticism of the Chinese novel was in-evitably made under the Western impact. Toward the end of the Ch'ing dynasty enlightened scholars and journalists had become concerned with the social influence of popular literature and, in particular, of the novel.[3] They reasoned that, if traditional novels were indeed to be held partly responsible for the unpreparedness of the Chinese people to face the modern world, then they had to be replaced with popular works of educational import designed to foster patriotism and propagate new ideas. Liang Ch'i-ch'ao himself, who was among the first Chinese to promote new fiction, wrote rousing accounts of Western patriots which were highly influential at the time, and other concerned writers increasingly turned to the novel as a medium of social and governmental criticism.[4] Their growing awareness of the novel as a living social force, however, entailed the recognition that earlier novelists had not lived up to their educative role.

Among the writers of the May Fourth period this feeling of dissatisfaction with the traditional novel had persisted, but at the same time the enlistment of a few major titles in the battle for *pai-hua* had given rise to the contrary impression that it was indeed a national heritage to be cherished with pride. As a champion of *pai-hua*, it was Hu Shih who made high claims for such works as *The Water Margin* and *Dream of the Red Chamber*: according to him, their authors should be placed in the company of Dante, Chaucer, and Martin Luther as progenitors of a national vernacular literature and their language should prove a seminal influence on the new writers in the *pai-hua* idiom.[5] Following the success of this persuasion and the universal adoption of the colloquial language among the younger writers, the stock of the traditional novels rose high. Among the most welcome endeavors of Hu Shih were his newly punctuated editions of several major novels, duly prefaced with long introductions inquiring into the historical and biographical circumstances of their creation and essaying somewhat tentative revaluations of their worth.[6]

But the new vogue for these works notwithstanding, it was generally felt at the time of the Literary Revolution that despite its use of a colloquial language traditional fiction had little to offer on artistic and ideological grounds.[7] In his influential essay "Humane Literature" (1919) Chou Tso-jen lists ten kinds of deplorable literature, all of which are identifiable primarily with popular fiction and drama rather than with the classical genres of poetry and prose.[8] Despite his zeal for research in the Chinese novel, Hu Shih himself recognized its artistic inferiority even though he appeared much less perturbed by its "feudalistic" thought. In his prefaces to novels as well as in his more general essays on vernacular literature we find a series of asides expressive of his critical attitude.[9] Because his prefaces and essays are usually affirmative in tone, these asides had understandably attracted little attention until Communist critics exhibited them a few years back as proof positive of Hu Shih's pro-capitalist denigration of Chinese literature.[10] But if Hu Shih is to be condemned on that score, then the whole generation of the more serious scholars and writers who had blossomed after the May Fourth Movement should be condemned. One could say that, like Hu Shih, they were very fond of traditional Chinese fiction in their early youth, but once exposed to Western fiction, they could only acknowledge, implicitly if not explicitly, the greater technical proficiency of the latter along with its far greater moral seriousness. Until the outbreak of the Sino-Japanese War in 1937, among the most dedicated students of traditional fiction as well as the most talented makers of the new fiction, few defended the old novel for its intrinsic literary excellence even though these two groups should have been far more objective in evaluating its worth than most earlier champions of the new culture with their manifest anti-traditionalist bias. Thus, though a great historian of vernacular literature with a passion for acquiring rare editions of old novels, Cheng Chen-to would occasionally confess his disgust with these works:

Some six or seven years ago I had the ambition to prepare a whole series of summaries of Chinese novels and did contribute twenty-odd such précis to the *Appreciation Weekly* (*Chien-shang Chou-k'an*), a Shanghai publication. But after writing continually for five or six weeks, I felt really discouraged and could not continue. All those shallow and stupid novels of interminable length, they really couldn't get me interested. And I haven't written about them since.[11]

This feeling of impatience was shared by other conscientious students of Chinese fiction.[12]

The modern Chinese novelists are no different. Until the outbreak of the Sino-Japanese War, when Chinese writers were urged to adopt older forms of fiction for the manufacture of patriotic propaganda and when a few serious authors were beginning to explore the resources of the old fiction on their own, few novelists, though in their nonage they had all read the old novels, were consciously indebted to them. Instead, they turned to Western fiction for inspiration and guidance. Among the major novelists, Mao Tun consistently deplored the old novel and declared that he had no personal use for it. He even regards the narrative techniques of *The Water Margin* and *Dream of the Red Chamber* as too elementary for modern imitation.[13] The influence of *Dream of the Red Chamber* and also of *The Scholars* is of course quite noticeable in the sentimental and satiric fiction of the twenties and thirties, but what is of interest is the novelists' conscious repudiation of that influence despite its actual presence in their work.

Though as a rule exceptions are made of the greater novels, usually including the six to be discussed here, modern scholars and writers of the pre-Communist period are generally agreed that the traditional novel as a whole is profoundly disappointing. This feeling was at first inseparable from a sense of national shame which they shared, but it soon matured into an honest recognition of the artistic inferiority of the old Chinese novel in comparison with the Western novel. It was the Communists who eventually rejected this modern view of the old novel by insisting on its national importance. Capitalizing on wartime patriotism and the propaganda potential of folk entertainment, Mao Tse-tung affirmed in 1939 the "national forms" of literature and art and enjoined writers and artists to make use of them.[14] Traditional popular literature was now upheld in opposition not only to the Western tradition of critical realism but also to modern Chinese writing nurtured in that tradition. While a reaffirmation of popular literature coincided with a new militant nationalism, it is nevertheless symptomatic that such a reaffirmation was made possible only by the active repudiation of the Western influence. The novels and other works of literature written under this self-conscious cultivation of propaganda and naïveté have consequently shown a drastic decline in quality, and one may even wonder whether the obligatory praise of certain classic novels along expected lines of ideological criticism has advanced our understanding of these works. The periodic denunciation and punishment of ranking Communist literary theorists and critics who have clung to "revisionist" views of Western humanism indicate that even in a totalitarian regime a modern preference for honesty and sophistication in literary understanding dies hard.[15]

Whatever the critical fashion in Communist China, it seems to me self-evident that we cannot accord the Chinese novel full critical justice unless, with all our due awareness of its special characteristics that can only be fully understood in historical terms, we are prepared to examine it against the Western novel. (Except for isolated masterpieces like *The Tale of Genji,* all non-Western traditions of the novel appear negligible by the side of the Chinese, and in modern times they have all taken new directions under the impact of the Western novel.) The modern reader of fiction is brought up on the practice and theory of Flaubert and James: he expects a consistent point of view, a unified impression of life as conceived and planned by a master intelligence, an individual style fully consonant with the author's emotional attitude toward his subject-matter. He abhors explicit didacticism, authorial digression, episodic construction that reveals no cohesion of design, and clumsiness of every other kind that distracts his attention. But, of course, even in Europe the conscious practice of fiction as an art was a late development, and we cannot expect colloquial Chinese fiction, with its humble oral beginnings, to have been designed for the cultivated modern taste.

Though, in a sense, the art of storytelling had flourished in China since the age of the pre-Ch'in philosophers, it was the Buddhist monks of the T'ang period and earlier who first turned professional storytellers to edify and convert the laity. Many of their stories, told either in verse or in prose intermixed with verse, were discovered in the Tun-huang caves some sixty years ago. A selection of these *Ballads and Stories from Tun-huang* made by Arthur Waley comprises legends of Buddhist saints; fairy tales in a Chinese setting but showing the unmistakable influence of Persian, Arabic, and Indic folklore; highly fictionalized accounts of such beloved Chinese figures as the sage-king Shun, Confucius, Wu Tzu-hsü, and Emperor Kuang-wu of the Later Han dynasty.[16] Many stories of the latter two categories contain no explicit Buddhist propaganda, and even in the retelling of Buddhist legends traditional Chinese ethical motives are emphasized. Thus the Buddhist saint Mu-lien has characteristically become a filial son in his undaunted attempts to save the hungry ghost of his impious mother.

Since there are several good accounts in English of the rise of colloquial Chinese fiction,[17] I shall not attempt to summarize the story here but shall rather dwell upon a few essential historical facts with crucial bearing on a critical understanding of the Chinese novel. In T'ang literature we first come across references to professional lay storytellers in the capital of Ch'ang-an. These storytellers, who could have arisen as a class to capitalize on the popularity of Buddhist entertainers, in turn stimulated the growth of the classical tale known as *ch'uan-ch'i*.[18] (I shall not go into the other historical circumstances that led the T'ang writers to cultivate that genre.[19]) In the early Sung period, public storytelling by Buddhist monks was prohibited. With their competitors out of business, it is little wonder that, according to contemporary records, storytellers were flourishing in the capital of Pien-liang during the last years of the Northern Sung and that they continued to thrive in Hangchow, the new capital of the Southern Sung, following the loss of North China to the Chin invaders. Of the several kinds of storytellers, each organized into a guild, the specialists in *hsiao-shuo* or short stories (with such divisions as love stories, ghost stories, crime stories, and stories of chivalry) appeared to be the dominant group though the reciters of dynastic history, especially those specializing in the Three Kingdoms and Five Dynasties periods, were not far behind in popularity.[20] Several abbreviated accounts of dynastic history first published during the Southern Sung and Yuan times, known as *p'ing-hua,* were apparently based on the prompt-books of the latter storytellers, though their eventual expansion into full-length novels was often the work of individual authors not necessarily compiling from these promptbooks. In the early seventeenth century an enterprising Ming author and publisher, Feng Meng-lung, printed three collections of *hsiao-shuo* of forty stories each (known collectively by the abbreviated term *San-yen*) which would seem to represent the full vitality and range of the repertoire of the reciters of short stories during the Ming period. Many of these tales (also known as *hua-pen*) are obviously of Sung origin, even though both the earliest extant collection and the first surviving comprehensive catalogue of such tales (*Ch'ing-p'ing-shan-t'ang hua-pen; Pao-wen-t'ang shu-mu*) date only from the mid-sixteenth century.[21]

The indubitably Sung tales give us a clear idea of the formal and rhetorical features of a story as actually told by a professional story-teller, but I would hesitate to use these written versions as a criterion for judging his individual art. Even in such a well-written story as "The Jade Worker,"[22] which has a long preamble and clearly marks the point where the storyteller pauses to collect donations from his audience or leaves them in suspense until they return the next day to hear the second half, the skeleton narration of the main story of the jade worker and his wife would seem to be too brief to make full use of the art of oral presentation. Already during the Southern Sung nostalgic guidebooks to the capital cities refer to several storytellers by name, and these performers must have excelled in their art by their ability to amplify and elaborate upon the promptbooks, to add comic and topical remarks of the kind that would establish rapport with their audience. One may presume by modern analogy that a performer who faithfully recites his prompt-book would get nowhere with his audience. In the pre-Communist period a storyteller of the Soochow school, whether he specialized in *p'ing-hua* (historical narratives unaccompanied by music) or *t'an-tz'u* (romantic and domestic stories requiring singing accompanied by simple music), would have learned from his master at most two or three stories, and many were known for just one story, although that story would last many months and usually over a year, as parceled out session after session in the teahouse. In such elaborate retelling, the plot as such becomes almost irrelevant; at each session the storyteller attends to a fraction of an episode, with vivid impersonations of characters and free-ranging comments on manners and morals.[23] The oral recital of the Wu Sung saga by the foremost contemporary *p'ing-hua* artist in the Yangchow school, Wang Shao-t'ang, has been preserved in print: it runs to over 800,000 characters and 1,100 pages.[24] By its side, the same story as given in *The Water Margin* seems a brief chronicle even though the ten chapters devoted to the exploits of Wu Sung constitute the longest story of a single hero in the novel. And what has been recorded in the Wang Shao-t'ang version is the actual story, without the asides and topical comments that would have further swelled its volume.

It is unlikely that a Hangchow storyteller in the Sung period could have developed a tale with as much elaborate skill as his latter-day descendants in Soochow or Yangchow. But the signal contrast between the sketchy promptbook version and an actual recital by a famous storyteller can be safely assumed. The gap appears minimal in some of the longest and also finest stories preserved in Feng Meng-lung's collections, such as "The Oil Peddler" and "The Pearl-sewn Shirt," [25] but the publication of these collections seems to have marked the end of the vital influence of the oral tale upon the development of the colloquial short story, for the subsequent compilations in the same genre, all by literary men in conscious imitation of Feng Meng-lung, owed little to professional storytellers of their own time. On the other hand, the earliest promptbook versions of what eventually became the major novels appear to have been least faithful to the art of the storytellers despite their adoption of its rhetorical formulas and ideological premises. As early as the late T'ang period the poet Li Shang-yin alludes to the

popularity of the story-cycle of the Three Kingdoms in the following couplet about his five-year-old son who delights in making fun
of his father's visitors:

> And he would mock someone for his Chang Fei-black face
> And ridicule another who stutters like Teng Ai.[26]

Though Chang Fei appears as the principal hero in the *p'ing-hua*
version of *The Three Kingdoms,* its clumsy compiler, while delight-
ing in the foolhardy exploits of this hot-tempered warrior, makes no
use of his black complexion or other facial features as a source of
comedy. And Teng Ai, one of the two Wei generals responsible
for the conquest of the Shu Han kingdom, remains in the *p'ing-hua*
a minor figure hardly individualized. In the standard and much
longer version of the novel, at the first mention of Teng Ai's name,
the editor Mao Tsung-kang has supplied the historical information
that he stutters. The newly defected Wei general, Hsia-hou Pa, tells
the Shu commander Chiang Wei: "Teng Ai stutters. When he
memorialized at court, he would stutter, 'Ai, ai.' Ssu-ma I once
asked him in jest, 'Since you *ai-ai* so often, how many *ai*'s have you
got inside you?' Ai promptly replied [quoting a line from the
Analects], '"O phoenix, O phoenix!" There is actually one
phoenix.'"[27] But in the subsequent narrative Mao Tsung-kang
merely follows the compiler Lo Kuan-chung's original version,
which records Teng Ai's speeches in a simple literary style without
any indication of stuttering. If Li Shang-yin's couplet justifies the
inference that late-T'ang reciters of dynastic history were already
so good at impersonating at least a few of their characters that even
children found it a source of fun to mimic the latter, then it would
appear by contrast that the Sung and Yuan compilers of these
reciters' promptbooks had not begun to aim at this high reach of
visual and verbal comedy. And given the noncolloquial character of
the classical literary tradition, it is also understandable that even the
far more literate Ming compilers of dynastic novels could not have
encompassed the vivid realism of the storytellers.

While the colloquial short story stems directly from the oral tradition, the colloquial novel is additionally tied to the tradition of historiography. So strong is the latter influence that many Ming historical novels could be considered works written in conscious reaction against the oral tradition, as I shall demonstrate in the next chapter. If the storytellers achieved the immediacy and amplitude of realism, they were at the same time vulgar didacticists interpreting history and legend in strict accordance with the concept of moral retribution. This concept will receive fuller treatment later in the chapter; suffice it to say for the present that it encouraged the story-tellers to reward the virtuous and punish the wicked, if not in their present lives, then surely in their future reincarnations. Turning against this simplistic attempt to rectify the injustices of history, the compilers of better historical novels were more inclined to follow the official historians and to share their Confucian view of history as a cyclic alternation between order and disorder, as a record of the careers of great men engaged in a perpetual struggle against the periodically rampant forces of anarchy and sensuality. They show a greater respect for fact so that, while they lack the narrative ampli-tude of the oral storytellers, they are able to convey a sense of com-plex reality less circumscribed by a rigid moralism. In the present study, only *The Romance of the Three Kingdoms* is a full-fledged example of the novel whose declared intent is to retell official history and make its meaning clearer (*yen-i*) in a more plain language. However, it must be remembered that during the formative period of the novel the *yen-i* type of historical chronicle was clearly domi-nant while all other types of the novel at least pretended to be his-tory. Next to the oral storytellers, therefore, the historians provide the most important literary background in the making of the Chinese novel. Until the novelists became more proficient in the arts of fiction, their reliance on dynastic histories assured them of an abundant supply of characters and events whose reality could be suggested even in a bald narrative of little artistry.

Because the Ming novel has inherited the traditions of the story-tellers and historiographers, its language can be called vernacular only if we are aware of the diverse forms of style and rhetoric subsumed under that label. During the May Fourth period it was generally believed that with Yuan drama and Ming fiction Chinese literature had entered into a vernacular phase because the classical language was found wanting for these more complex literary forms of lower social origin—a notion which then served as a very persuasive historical argument in favor of the general adoption of *pai-hua* in writing. But in reality both Yuan drama and Ming fiction employ a popular language of which the literary idiom remains an essential ingredient. While the dialogue in Yuan drama is to a large extent recorded in the vernacular, its operatic passages retain a strong literary character despite their liberal inclusion of colloquial expressions. A student of Yuan drama unschooled in T'ang and Sung poetry would not be in a position to identify the countless lines and phrases either borrowed or adapted from that poetry. Even in passages meant for recitation the Yuan playwright feels no compunction in adopting the clichés of the literary language (as when he describes weather or a landscape, for instance). It would seem that he made as much use of classical literature as was practicable for mass consumption instead of consciously devising a vernacular language stripped of all literary associations. It is only in the rendering of the speeches of men and women of lower social station that a striving toward vivid racy speech is in evidence. This is the case partly because it would be inappropriate for these low and usually comic characters to mouth literary phrases. But by Ming times the trend toward democratization of language in the theater was actually reversed: as a genre cultivated by literary men, the Southern drama is far more elegant than the Northern drama of the Yuan dynasty.

To a lesser extent, the language of colloquial fiction also reflects the prestige and dominance of the classical tradition. Not to mention such novels as *The Romance of the Three Kingdoms* and *A Chronicle of the Many States of the Eastern Chou Period* (*Tung-Chou lieh-kuo chih*),[28] which were composed in an easy literary style in conscious opposition to the storytelling tradition, even stories and novels more or less based on promptbooks possess a stereotyped elegance because of their ample inclusion of songs, poems, and set pieces of description. The language at the disposal of the Sung storytellers had already become so overladen with stock phrases culled from the standard authors of *shih, tz'u, fu,* and parallel prose that it was actually far easier for them (and this is also true of Yuan and Ming storytellers) to use the classical phraseology at hand than to forge a vernacular prose that could render with precision an actual landscape or human face. One could almost say that among the scores of beautiful girls and handsome young men to be seen in the *San-yen* tales there is hardly a face one can sharply visualize, because its description usually consists of a cluster of conventional metaphors. In composing descriptive prose or verse, the Ming novelists of course differ widely in skill and ambition: some, like the compiler of *The Romance of the Three Kingdoms,* shun ornate description while others, like the author of *Journey to the West,* delight in weaving tapestries of exotic landscape. But it remains true that the long passages descriptive of a person or a scene are usually distinguished by an allusive classical vocabulary and a neat compositional structure suggestive of poetry or parallel prose. If our six novels give us a fair idea of the evolution of the Chinese novel, it is only during the Ch'ien-lung period (1736–95) that we find in *The Scholars* and, to a lesser extent, in *Dream of the Red Chamber* an impressive descriptive prose in the vernacular.

Until the eighteenth century, then, the novelists made strong use of the vernacular only in the speeches of their characters. While a literary quality still persists in the speech of the educated, tradition had early assigned to certain heroes of coarse vitality[29] and to the lower classes in general the use of the vernacular. This tradition, which first blossomed in *The Water Margin,* culminated in *Dream of the Red Chamber,* where nearly all the major characters reveal themselves through their speech, each with an individual idiom and way of talking. That novel also marks the unprecedented success with which the colloquial language registers the psychological conditions of characters. P'an Chin-lien, the principal heroine of *Chin P'ing Mei,* speaks a most racy language studded with slang and billingsgate; but when the author describes her mental conditions, he invariably uses the language of the popular song to dress her in the borrowed elegance of studied languor, anger, or frustration.

Because the Ming novelist usually reserves the poetic language for descriptive occasions, his prose narrative is very matter of fact. Except when he resorts to dialogue, he relates a temporal sequence of events in straightforward fashion. The narrative techniques employed by the major Ch'ing novelists are somewhat more sophisticated. In *The Scholars* one actually comes across scenes which are observed through the eyes of a particular character: when the scholar Ma Ch'un-shang takes a stroll by the West Lake, only those items of interest which have caught his attention are described.[30] But, by and large, the Ming and Ch'ing novelists pay little attention to mood and atmosphere so that narration, dialogue, and description are rarely integrated into an organic whole. To introduce a new scene, the novelist may describe the place quite elaborately, but in the subsequent narration few of the descriptive details will again be hinted at, so that the characters in that scene go about their business virtually detached from their setting. These characters may have a conversation, but, as the author reports their speeches, again he provides only the most rudimentary stage directions, which means in effect that we can not see the characters while they talk. However frequently interspersed with description and dialogue, a narrative that is almost expository in character speaks for the novelist's lack of ambition to define a scene and unfold all its potential drama.

Except for works like *The Romance of the Three Kingdoms,* it is hard to say whether the matter-of-fact narrative style of the classic novel reflects the conscious influence of the historians, who usually wrote in far more terse classical style. But, in praising individual novelists, traditional commentators always stressed their economical style as well as their serious didactic intent, another virtue associated with the historians. As the noblest monument of classical narrative prose, the *Records of the Grand Historian* (*Shih chi*), especially, was frequently invoked as the standard by which to judge the excellence of novels. Even *Dream of the Red Chamber,* a work little sug-

gestive of official history, was compared to it.[31] Interestingly, when
Lin Shu, the first Chinese translator of Western fiction, tried to inform his public of the genius of Dickens, he compared him to Ssu-
ma Ch'ien,[32] much as the seventeenth-century critic Chin Sheng-t'an
ranked *The Water Margin* with the *Shih chi* in order to secure for
the novel a high place among the masterpieces of Chinese literature.[33] All evaluative criticism implies an act of comparison: until
Chinese critics became acquainted with Western fiction and informed of its high literary standing, traditional historiography was
for them the only body of narrative prose whose unquestioned
respectability could be enlisted in the cause of advancing the claims
of the novel. In comparison with such outspoken defenders of the
novel as Chin Sheng-t'an and the late Ming intellectual Li Chih,[34]
it would seem that the novelists who were their contemporaries were
far too modest about their art or far too diffident to speak out in its
behalf: their preference for anonymity (hence the large number of
Ming novels of unidentified authorship) indicates to a certain extent
their perfect contentment with the hybrid form of the novel. They
made no attempt to depart from those formal and stylistic characteristics of the novel that betray its historical ties with the storytelling
and historiographical traditions and its eclectic reliance on other
forms of literature. If we adopt the modern definition of the novel
as a form of narrative distinct from the epic, the chronicle, and the
romance, then we could say that the Chinese novel found its true
identity only belatedly in an eighteenth-century work which also
happens to be its supreme masterpiece. Though still eclectic in form
and style, *Dream of the Red Chamber* is artistically contemporaneous with, if not ahead of, the Western novels of that century, judging by its realistic concern with manners and morals and its psychological depiction of characters placed in an actual social setting. *The
Scholars* has anticipated these tendencies, but in form it is a collection of short stories rather than a novel in the narrower sense of
the term.

The classic Chinese novel spans a long period of European literary
history stretching from the late Middle Ages to the nineteenth cen-

tury. Even judging by its finest titles, it differs from the modern Western novel not only because it shows no comparable concern with form but because it represents a different conception of fiction. A modern reader regards a novel as fiction whose truth can be vindicated by the author only through an elaborate process of demonstration. In Ming and Ch'ing China, as in a comparable stage of Western culture, author and reader alike were more interested in the fact in fiction than in fiction as such. The barest story would do as long as the fact contained therein proved sufficiently arresting: little wonder that through the centuries Chinese men of letters had compiled strange stories and anecdotes, and that readers seemed to find this type of writing perennially interesting. The professional storytellers always honored the convention of treating fiction as fact: there is not a single *San-yen* tale which does not place its main characters in a particular locale and time and vouch for their historicity. Most of these characters, if not famous figures in history and folklore, were once upon a time involved in a murder or scandal, though their stories must have been altered in the process of retelling. Dynastic novels were, of course, written and read as popular history, and even fantasies flimsily based on history were probably taken by the less educated readers as fact rather than fiction. When the domestic and satiric novels arose, therefore, their obviously fictitious content often led readers (and qualified readers who were themselves men of letters) to guess at the real identity of their characters or the peculiar biographical circumstances which had led their authors to adopt the mode of fiction. *Chin P'ing Mei* was read ·in this fashion, and so was *Dream of the Red Chamber,* which was supposed to be a veiled allegory of many high-placed persons in the Manchu court.[35] Their intensive study of the Confucian classics had of course conditioned the Chinese to the habit of allegoric reading. But far more important, their distrust of fiction indicated that stories and novels could not justify themselves as art alone: they must justify themselves as truth, however allegorically disguised, to inculcate the kind of lesson which history teaches.

In his fascination with fact, the Chinese novelist seldom feels the challenge to concentrate on one major episode until all its potential meanings have become dramatized. Instead, he crowds his pages with scores of characters, some only names, and piles incident upon incident, climax upon climax. Though novels of pornographic intent and sentimental novels about a talented young scholar (*ts'ai-tzu*) and a talented beauty (*chia-jen*) are usually much shorter,[36] most other types of novel are quite long. Five of our six novels contain 100 or 120 chapters, and even *The Scholars,* with its 55 chapters, is a big book by modern standards. But, whether short or long, whether literate or illiterate, nearly all traditional novels observe in their episodic structure the storyteller's mode of narration. It was customary for the narrator of dynastic history to end each day's recital on a note of suspense so as to induce his audience to return the next day to listen to the sequel. In like fashion, every Chinese novel is divided into chapters, each chapter except the final one ending with the formula, "If you want to know what happened next, please listen to the next chapter [*hui,* literally, a round of recital]." Since the late Ming period, moreover, it has been the convention to prefix each chapter with an antithetical couplet, summarizing its contents. The novelist is therefore too easily tempted to include two episodes in a chapter when its normal length does not allow the full treatment of one. For social realism and psychological insight, *Dream of the Red Chamber* is a work to be placed alongside the greatest novels in the Western tradition, but the author achieves his success in spite of laboriously maintaining the episodic convention, which entails the invention of many subsidiary stories that could well have been removed so that their space could be given to fuller elaboration of the major episodes.

In calling attention to the Chinese novelist's failure to utilize fully the arts of fiction, it has not been my intention to equate elaboration of treatment with artistic excellence: the prior critical question remains whether a given story or novel has something interesting or important to say about the human condition. In such works of antiquity as the Old Testament, the *Tso Commentary* (*Tso chuan*), and the *Records of the Grand Historian,* each event may be briefly narrated, but since it is about real people (real in the sense that their motivations and actions are entirely credible) engaged in an enterprise of some magnitude, the cumulative moral weightiness of these events more than compensates for their inchoate realism, their lack of circumstantial detail. *The Romance of the Three Kingdoms,* which soberly recounts an exciting period of Chinese history, enjoys the same kind of solidity. But, once he outgrows his dependence on historiography, the Chinese novelist faces the problem of providing a version of reality that can vie in human interest with the events of history. The authors of *The Water Margin* and *Journey to the West* still appeal to the authority of fact, but they have now to contrive the fact in the absence of reliable historical sources or in their unwillingness to use them. Their task is not only to engage our interest in their stories but to convince us of their human importance. By this double criterion we may say that the comic fantasy of *Journey to the West* captures a sense of complex reality while, with all its initial vigor of realism, *The Water Margin* eventually bogs down in an implausible plot little suggestive of a momentous historical event. Like a good historical narrative, a good fantasy tells us something vital about the actual world. One doesn't have to believe in devils, for instance, to enjoy the irony of the following brief tale written in the Eastern Chin period:

Chin Chu-po [Ch'in Chü-po] of the principality of Langya was sixty. One night after drinking, as he passed Pengshan [P'eng-shan] Temple, he saw his two grandsons coming towards him. They took his arms and helped him along for about a hundred paces. Then they seized him by the neck and threw him to the ground.

"Old slave!" they swore. "You beat us up the other day, so today we are going to kill you."

Remembering that he had indeed beaten the boys some days ago, he pretended to be dead, and they left him there. When he got home he decided to punish them. Shocked and distressed they apologized to him.

"How could your own grandsons do such a thing?" they protested. "Those must have been devils. Please make another test."

He realized they were right.

A few days later the old man pretended to be drunk and walked past the temple again. Once more the two devils came to take his arms, and this time he seized them so that they could not escape. Reaching home, he put both devils on the fire, until their backs and bellies were scorched and cracked. He left them in the courtyard, and that night they escaped. Sorry that he had not killed them, about a month later the old man pretended to be drunk and went out at night again, taking a sword, unknown to his family. When he did not come back though it was very late, his grandsons feared the devils had caught him again. They went to look for him. And this time the old man hacked his own grandsons to death.[37]

A disciplinarian and self-righteous do-gooder, the old man is fooled the second time because he is too eager to punish and too much carried away by his sense of power. His failure to tell appearance from reality indicates his moral condition, and in a sense the devils have picked him as their victim because they know it would appear to him quite normal that his grandsons should retaliate against his harshness. One could have developed this tale into a long story or play and fully explored its comic-tragic implications. But with its minimal amount of dialogue and narrative detail, the tale is intrinsically satisfying because of its adult embodiment of a moral problem.

While the Western concept of realism has been in recent years profitably applied to the study of traditional Chinese fiction, every title must be first tested against the broader concept of reality, irrespective of its adoption of a primitive or advanced realism. Precisely because it has captured a real problem, the tale of the old man seems to me superior to many a longer story whose more circumstantial realism actually adorns a thesis too stale or childish to deserve elaboration. Whether a tale or novel is able to encompass a complex reality, of course, finally depends upon the author's intelligence, his understanding of man and society. But even for the most intelligent novelist, his depiction of reality is inescapably conditioned by the moral and religious assumptions of his cultural tradition. He has the freedom to choose diverse elements from his tradition to compose his own world view, but he cannot totally reject that tradition. For a proper appreciation of the classic Chinese novel, we have to turn next to the beliefs and attitudes underlying its ideological structure.

By Yuan and Ming times Confucianism, Buddhism, and Taoism had long enjoyed government support and popular reverence as the "three teachings" (san-chiao) of the nation, and no form of popular literature could have entertained and edified the public without drawing upon these teachings. The novel was certainly no exception. But in China as in the West, the premodern novelist reveals himself as much through his covert sympathies as through his public didactic stance: in a sense, his relative inattention to matters of form is symptomatic of his unconcern with philosophical coherence, his proneness to embrace incompatible values. The Western novelist, however, was less liable to incur serious ideological inconsistency since he was confronted with one established teaching rather than three. Until the late Victorian period an English novelist usually professed to be a Christian, and his was the relatively easier task of accommodating his private sympathies to a system of beliefs and morals still commanding general assent. The Ming novelist could with equal respectability declare himself a Confucianist, Buddhist, or Taoist, but he seldom did so because, except for the idealistic school of Neo-Confucianism which is little reflected in fiction,[38] all three schools were actually in a state of intellectual decline. Their doctrinal distinctions had become blurred, and popular Buddhism and Taoism, especially, inculcated the same type of teaching and observed similar forms of ritual. Whatever his private sympathies, therefore, the novelist tended to embrace an uncritical ideological syncretism. With the exception of the more reliable historical novels which reflect by and large the Confucian world view of official history, no Ming novels are ideologically pure in the sense of *The Pilgrim's Progress,* a purely Christian work. But this syncretism could be turned to good account by authors with a personal vision of their own: some of the best Ming and Ch'ing novels are intellectually exciting precisely for their embodiment of various attitudes in a state of unreconciled tension.

While the storytellers and novelists share many beliefs and attitudes that could be labeled Confucian, Buddhist, or Taoist, we may first attend to the two major premises guiding their depiction of reality which are not readily identifiable with the three teachings: their total acceptance of life in all its glory and squalor and their strong sympathy for the individual's demand for self-fulfillment not unmingled with a sense of horror over his penchant for self-destruction. This dual affirmation of life and the self reflects the coarse vitality of the market place where storytelling first flourished, though the market place itself had not been uninfluenced by certain types of classical literature partial to the romantic and heroic self. Inevitably, too, the storytellers and novelists would disproportionately stress those aspects of the three teachings consonant with their major premises, with the result that in certain types of fiction Confucianism appears primarily as a form of individual heroism.

Chinese fiction shares with medieval European hagiography a regard for life as an inexhaustible supply of wonders. To our sophistication these wonders often appear flat, especially when their depiction merely serves to prove the efficacy of Buddhist-Taoist piety and Confucian virtue. But the Chinese storytellers and novelists are interested not merely in the patently miraculous, but in all aspects of life, including those whose depiction would offend good taste if we observed the conventions of American publishing of only a few years ago. In spite of the severe moralism it ostensibly upholds, Chinese fiction is notable for its lack of Victorian prudery. But this tolerance, originally stemming from the low culture of storyteller and audience alike, indicates not so much modern broadmindedness as an unsqueamish delight in sex, filth, and disease. These are just as much a part of life as the ghosts and divinities that frequently intervene in human affairs, and they claim as much fictional attention as the politer forms of social intercourse. Aldous Huxley once made a useful distinction between "tragedy" and "the whole truth" as two modes of depicting reality. "To make a tragedy the artist must isolate a single element out of the totality of human experience and use that exclusively as his material," whereas the "wholly truthful" artist—and Huxley cites Homer as his primary example—responds to the totality of that experience.[39] In this regard, the Chinese storytellers' and novelists' indiscriminate fascination with life can be seen as a form of unself-conscious attentiveness to the whole truth. At least no Chinese novel attempts to be consistently tragic or comic: even *Dream of the Red Chamber,* famed for its poetic sensitivity, does not shun the physiological aspects of life and moves from low comedy to sheer pathos with the greatest of ease. But the novel is a great tragedy precisely because it encompasses the sordid and the sublime, the bestial and the celestial, in its vision of humanity.

Because of their fascination with life, Chinese novelists are almost incapable of noticing the condition of ennui, which is so commonly depicted in modern Western literature. Characters of extreme heroism and villainy abound in the Chinese novel, but both kinds pursue their chosen courses with gusto. In the domestic novels, of course, we frequently encounter women characters deprived of their proper sexual happiness. The destructiveness of these frustrated creatures can be truly frightening, but none arrives at the conclusion that life is meaningless and settles for an existence of amused boredom. They will fight for their happiness: even if they finally elect a life of Buddhist renunciation, they are at least hoping for their eventual rebirth in the Western Paradise. With all its rapacious and lecherous characters, Chinese fiction could not conceive of a monster like the Stranger of Camus, not to say the Underground Man of Dostoevsky, who has lost connection with all values. A Hemingway hero has given classic expression to the modern Western disease of disillusion and fatigue: "Abstract words such as glory, honor, courage or hallow were obscene beside the concrete names of villages, the numbers of roads, the names of rivers, the numbers of regiments and the dates."[40] Even in Chinese novels pointing a Buddhist moral, words like glory and honor nevertheless retain unquestioned reality because the hero's quest for personal salvation does not cancel out the other characters' equally admirable pursuit of mundane goals.

The hero or villain who elects to live his own kind of life is an individualist. The Chinese may have been a practical nation sensibly abiding by the Confucian doctrine of the mean, but their fiction tells a different story: while moderation and prudence are always explicitly stressed, its characters actually take the road of excess in reckless pursuit of love, honor, and pleasure. Even to seek selflessness —to renounce the world and become a Buddhist or Taoist recluse— is itself a deliberate act of self-commitment. The storytellers' delight in extreme forms of heroism and villainy reflects to a large degree, of course, the primitiveness of their art and the naïveté of their audience: there would be simply no stories to tell if the element of sensationalism were removed. And this sensationalism certainly implies an insensitivity to certain finer aspects of traditional Chinese culture. The hero of extraordinary courage or endurance, to be sure, exemplifies praiseworthy Confucian conduct, but there are other types of Confucian behavior that could have equally merited the storytellers' attention. The man of moral introspection, for example, receives much more space in the *Four Books* than the man of sheer physical courage. Had proper attention been paid to the first type of hero, Chinese fiction could have early arrived at psychological realism: a character who habitually examines his conscience and watches out for incipient evil thoughts when alone (*shen-tu*) would be much closer to Stephen Dedalus than to the stereotyped Confucian heroes.[41]

But if, through their inattention to certain psychological aspects of Confucianism, the Chinese storytellers and novelists made no ambitious attempts to explore the world of the interior consciousness, their depiction of the absurd Confucian hero suggests another kind of affinity with modern fiction. The Confucian virtues most frequently celebrated in the colloquial stories are loyalty, filial piety, chastity, and selfless friendship (*chung hsiao chieh i*). Ideally, the cultivation of these virtues should be a reciprocal affair: the minister is loyal because his emperor is just, the wife is chaste because her husband is faithful and considerate, and so forth. But in these stories the virtuous person shows his stamina precisely in the absence of appreciation: the minister remains stubbornly loyal to an unworthy emperor and often courts martyrdom to impress upon him the enormity of his wrongdoing; the wife remains faithful even if her husband proves a sadist and after his death she espouses chaste widowhood so as to rear his young and preserve his family name. Though such behavior is usually deplored today as blind compliance with the dictates of "feudalism," it actually defines the absurd hero who overcommits himself to a cause in order to assert his individual dignity.

In the Confucian scheme of basic human relationships, however, there is no place for the unmarried lover, and yet one would suppose that even in traditional China far more men must have found their deepest emotional fulfillment in love than in serving their parents or emperors. In speaking out for the lover in the absence of Confucian sanction, therefore, the storytellers and novelists turned for support to a tradition whose eventually belletristic character could hardly disguise its vital connections with popular literary expression —the tradition of romantic sentimentalism composed mainly of *shih, tz'u,* and *ch'ü* poetry and the classical tale.[42] (It is generally known that *tz'u, ch'ü,* and certain types of *shih* had their origins in the popular song and therefore embody the common sentiments of man denied adequate expression in the more orthodox types of Confucian writing. I have already referred to the fact that the T"ang tale grew under the stimulus of popular storytelling.) Just as colloquial fiction has borrowed from the descriptive and allusive vocabulary of classical literature, so it has appropriated its concern with romantic sentiment and extended its sympathy with the instinctive self. Furthermore, by the late Ming period a few individualistic thinkers, themselves much influenced by vernacular literature, had lent their intellectual prestige to the commercial exploitation of the erotic so that we find in the fiction of that period a strong note of sensuality, conspicuous in *Chin P'ing Mei* and other kindred works.[43] But, of course, neither the booksellers eager to meet the public demand for the salacious nor the heretical elite countenancing that trend could confer upon sensuality the moral respectability of the major ideas of the three teachings. The storytellers and novelists had little choice but to stress these ideas even while their unmistakable sympathy for the lovers was being affirmed in language of increasing boldness. In the Appendix, "Society and Self in the Chinese Short Story," which should be read as an integral part of this chapter, I have discussed at length the dual allegiance of the storyteller, mainly with reference to the love tales in the *San-yen* collections.

Yet sensuality raises the moral problem of license and aggression. Even in the *San-yen* tales the innocent passionate lover, who is invariably treated with sympathy, is quite a different person from the hardened sensualist bent on self-destruction, who deserves punishment for his crime against his victims. The archetypal sensualist in Chinese historical and pornographic fiction is the bad ruler who indulges his lust in his harem and counts on his relatives, eunuchs, and fawning ministers to abet his tyranny and satisfy his every whim.[44] The Chinese novelist details this character's career of limitless license with evident fascination, but at the same time is truly appalled by the extent of his degradation. His sympathy for the individual quest for happiness notwithstanding, the novelist can only side with traditional morality by exposing the bad ruler's wickedness and denouncing his tyranny. Without intending any paradox, one may say that the Chinese novelist is a champion of both individual liberty and social justice.

Traditionally, China has been a land governed without benefit of the Western concept of law. This absence of law would not have mattered if each person had been able to exercise Confucian self-control. But in fiction, as in history, the Chinese cultivation of interpersonal relationships had actually encouraged those entrenched in power to abuse their influence and neglect their responsibility. If the emperor could do what he liked in the absence of parliamentary controls, the local magistrate and the head of a family could also tyrannize, each within his sphere of influence. A beginning student of Chinese fiction cannot help being shocked by the way a magistrate settles lawsuits and solves murders and robberies. Unless he is a scholar with an academic degree and therefore socially on an equal footing with the magistrate, the defendant is always subjected to beatings and other forms of torture until he confesses to the crime charged against him. Quite often the innocent sign a false confession merely to avoid further intolerable punishment. Many falsely accused die of brutal beating on the spot, and many die of infected wounds in their subsequent unsanitary incarceration.[45] And the magistrate, unless he is the type of exceptionally sagacious judge understandably celebrated in fiction and drama, is usually in league with the powerful gentry to perpetrate injustice, out of cowardice, greed, or sheer laziness that keeps him from exercising his own judgment. The head of a family, too, can be a despot since his wives and children usually have no redress against his harshness and all bond servants are his property to be abused at will. Under his domination, the women in the house have no choice but to intrigue against one another at all times: unless they are resigned to what fate has in store for them, it is their imperative task to seek to possess or regain his love, to domesticate his instinct for roving, to outshine their rivals, to gain the approval and respect of their elders, to have male issue so as to guarantee their respectability and financial security in old age. This relentless struggle, whether in the form of the outwardly polite cunning of Wang Hsi-feng, a heroine of *Dream of the Red Chamber,* or that of the undisguised ruthlessness of P'an Chin-lien, constitutes the tragedy of the Chinese woman. It is her tragedy that she has to become mean and cunning in order to cope with male domination, a condition of injustice to which she is nevertheless resigned.

Against these manifold conditions of injustice, however, the ideological orientations of the characters in Chinese fiction take on dramatic significance. Though of the three teachings only Confucianism is supposedly concerned with worldly values, as seen in fiction, both Buddhism and Taoism stress moral and philanthropic conduct as a prerequisite to worldly success. Except for the true devotees, who will choose the path of Buddhist enlightenment or Taoist immortality, good Buddhist-Taoist laymen observe the same Confucian virtues and expect the same mundane rewards: rank, wealth, longevity, and the continuation of the family line by distinguished offspring. But despite their reiteration of the moral lesson that virtuous deeds bring material rewards, the storytellers must have been at the same time aware that in real life one does not always get his just deserts and that, given the prevalence of injustice in China, it is more likely that the virtuous will suffer while the wicked continue to prosper. They had therefore to resort to moral retribution or *pao-ying* as a plausible theory to account for apparent injustice. Although, as popularly understood, *pao-ying* is primarily a Buddhist concept because it demonstrates the workings of karma, it could be regarded as an article of faith subscribed to by all Chinese with the exception of a small minority of Confucian rationalists. By the Ming period the Taoists had long appropriated it as their own and extolled its efficacy in their canonical works,[46] while the average men of Confucian outlook, who could cite from Chinese history and the pre-Ch'in classics and philosophers numerous instances of moral retribution, had been too much under Buddhist-Taoist influence to resist its appeal. The storytellers shared the general belief and vindicated its truth in a great many of their tales.

Yet precisely because the theory of *pao-ying* is applied to all human situations in the colloquial tales, it may be seen as a conventional element of the plot largely responsible for giving them an air of childish unreality. If we believe the storytellers, then we will naturally ascribe the success of a virtuous person to moral retribution. But if this person remains miserable despite his virtuous conduct, the theory still holds because we can adopt any one of the following explanations: that he once harbored some evil thought, however transient that thought may have been; that, though he himself is virtuous, his father or grandfather or any of his other ancestors has done evil deeds; or that he himself has accumulated bad karma in his earlier lives. He can alleviate his lot, of course, by continuing to be good in the Confucian fashion and to practice philanthropy and perform rituals according to Buddhist or Taoist prescriptions. He can also comfort himself with the thought that his oppressors and enemies, if he does not live long enough to see them punished, will surely suffer torment in hell and in their future incarnations. The theory of moral retribution is therefore foolproof: whether a man's good deeds are rewarded or not, karma is always vindicated provided the storyteller is able to weave an ingenious tale linking that man's present existence with his past and future lives.

In effect, however, the theory justifies the *status quo* and confesses the failure of simple virtue or heroism to triumph over evil and rectify injustice. In conformity with the elementary desire to see virtue triumph and prosper, the Western fairy tale always rewards the good at the end and punishes the evil, and in a great many Chinese tales justice is meted out with equal dispatch. That there should be a special type of Chinese story and novel where the road of justice is too circuitous to be negotiated by simple valor or innocence certainly reflects the prestige of the karma concept, but it may also mean the presence in traditional Chinese society of insuperable obstacles to the simple expedition of justice. An emperor may kill the most loyal minister or general for sport; a landowner may dispossess a peasant on the slightest legal pretext. In neither case is the wrong likely to be avenged, but if the storytellers find it worthwhile to make stories out of these events, they will have to provide each with a sequel in which the villain, either in his present or future existence, meets his due punishment.

The note of moral retribution is most insistent in the colloquial tales. It is heard in most novels, though very few great ones make it their main business to demonstrate the efficacy of karma.[47] Of our six novels, only *Chin P'ing Mei,* a work steeped in the storytellers' tradition, fully endorses this belief. It is generally true that the further removed from that tradition a novelist is the less likely is he to make serious use of moral retribution. By the Ch'ing period, moreover, the novel had increasingly attracted practitioners of superior intellect, such as the authors of *The Scholars* and *Dream of the Red Chamber,* who could be said to be above that type of superstition. On the other hand, since men of undoubted culture and scholarship continued to compile brief tales of moral retribution throughout the Ch'ing period, the relegation of the karma theme to a decorative position by the novelists may have been indicative less of their intellectual maturity than of their artistic awakening. They may have realized that, while this theme may be effectively embodied in a tale or anecdote, it only makes for melodramatic or pietistic contrivance in a novel.

Far from reconciling the reader to an imaginary scheme of reward and punishment, then, the better novelists are actually much more concerned with two other types of response to injustice that promise greater fictional possibilities. The hero can combat injustice and disorder with all his might without caring whether he succeeds or not, or he can resign from the human order and choose the path of enlightened detachment, but, whichever course he adopts, he is a man of moral courage little concerned with worldly happiness or the state of his karma.

The Confucian hero differs from the lover and the sensualist in that he seeks self-fulfillment through selfless dedication to the cause of justice and order. A defiant individualist with a passion for service, he is the dominant figure in historical and chivalric novels. In these novels we find, on one hand, the familiar types of individual license: the bad emperor, the foreign chieftain determined to contest China's power, the minister consumed with jealousy and hatred of a meritorious colleague, the corrupt magistrate, and the highwayman bent on murder and robbery. On the other hand, we find their counterparts: the rebel leader given the mandate of heaven to overthrow a decadent dynasty, the maligned general who defends the Chinese border against great odds, the minister of outspoken loyalty, the judge who solves case after criminal case, and the swordsman who rescues the innocent and punishes the evildoers. These latter types all exemplify the Confucian hero fired by the ideal of service though, at first glance, the affinity of some of these types with Confucianism may not seem apparent. In his unconcern with legal and institutional safeguards against injustice and disorder, the novelist sees these heroes primarily as bulwarks against the ever-present threat of anarchy at the national and local levels. Conditions may immediately worsen when they are removed from the scene, but, while they are at their tasks, they provide the novelist with instances of courage and dedication, of sagacity and prowess, in which Chinese readers have always taken the greatest delight. It is not too much to say that all dynastic novels are concerned with the restoration of order and all chivalric novels with the restoration of justice.

Of these traditional types of heroes, the swordsman (*chien-hsia*) continues to enjoy great appeal among Chinese readers outside the mainland. In its broadest sense, the term *hsia* applies to all men and women of a chivalrous temper, but in fiction it additionally denotes a person of considerable prowess, usually a swordsman with or without magical skill.[48] He could be a boss of the underworld, a good outlaw of the Robin Hood type, a bodyguard or officer in the service of a conscientious prefect, or a lone wanderer roaming over the country to rescue the innocent from oppression. Whatever his mode of operation, he appeals to our strongest instincts for good as an embodiment of individual heroism in behalf of the wronged—hence his great popularity in recent decades when all other traditional types of fiction have been modified beyond recognition under the dominant influence of Western literature. In Hong Kong and Taiwan, new novels and stories about swordsmen (*wu-hsia hsiao-shuo*) are being continually published and avidly read.[49] Probably, in their impotence to relieve the suffering of their compatriots under Communist rule, these readers have turned to a simpler world of fantasy where the champions of justice have never failed to punish the oppressors.

While justice always triumphs in novels about sagacious judges and mighty swordsmen, in certain historical novels the Confucian heroes themselves have become the victims of tragic injustice in their very conscientiousness to serve the throne. The most beloved military heroes in China—it is most likely that they would not have become so beloved if their careers had not been portrayed in fiction and on the stage—are nearly always those who have done their best to repel enemy aggression and quell civil rebellion even if by doing so they have to suffer calumny, disgrace, and death. Yüeh Fei, the Southern Sung general sentenced to capital punishment despite his smashing victories against the Chin forces, is historically the most prominent of these, but to readers of fiction the martial families of Hsüeh and Yang, respectively of the T'ang and Northern Sung dynasties, are at least his equal in fame and approach something of his tragic grandeur.[50] Chu-ko Liang, the principal hero of *The Romance of the Three Kingdoms,* is an even better-known case of tragic devotion. Forsaking the life of a recluse to serve Liu Pei out of his undying gratitude for the latter's sincere friendship, Chu-ko spends the remainder of his untimely shortened life in fighting the usurping power of the Wei. But during the weak reign of Liu Pei's son he eventually enjoys little success and his life's work collapses with his death. A statesman attempting the impossible to preserve a right cause, he exemplifies the highest type of selfless service to have been commemorated in Chinese fiction.

In the face of injustice and disorder one may also embrace the Buddhist-Taoist alternative of renunciation. After experiencing his due share of disappointment and suffering, the spiritually gifted sooner or later becomes disenchanted with pleasure, ambition, or even Confucian service, and feels the urge to leave behind him the contentions and beguilements of the world and go into the forests and mountains to enjoy the untrammeled freedom of contemplation. Fluctuations of fortune are but waves on the ocean of being, and one's duty, after being tossed around in that ocean, is to return to the depths. Chuang Tzu has defined the attitude of all Chinese contemplatives in a brief parable: "When the springs dry up, the fish are all together on dry land. They then moisten each other with dampness and keep each other wet with their slime. But this is not to be compared with forgetting each other in a river or lake."[51] The crowded human scene of the Chinese novels, with men and women desperately craving love and pleasure and fighting for power and position, surely reminds one of so many stranded fish trying to keep themselves wet with various kinds of slime: it would be so much better to return them to water, to their proper element of Tao, discontinuing completely their petty expedients for survival and comfort. It is quite inevitable that the two Chinese novels which have shown most powerfully the condition of stranded humanity keeping itself wet with the futile slime of love and lust should have turned to Buddhist-Taoist philosophy for consolation: the hero of *Dream of the Red Chamber* eventually renounces the world, and so does the posthumous son of Hsi-men Ch'ing in *Chin P'ing Mei,* thus canceling out his father's career of profligacy and crime.

Philosophically, the Buddhist-Taoist message enjoys the last word in Chinese fiction. But, being stranded fish themselves, the novelists can only point to the path of renunciation while their active sympathies are with men and women engaged in their often contradictory schemes for a more just mundane order and a fuller life. Thus, whatever its consciously upheld scheme of justice or salvation, we find in each of our six novels heroes of an assertive individualism whose energies could be as well directed toward the fulfillment of that scheme as toward its negation. *Chin P'ing Mei* is ostensibly a Buddhist novel which features a self-destructive sensualist as its hero. In *The Water Margin,* which upholds a Confucian utopian vision, we have the violent hero—typified by Wu Sung—whose sexual puritanism actually heightens his vengeful aggressiveness. Traditional critics take Wu Sung to be a great hero and Hsi-men Ch'ing to be an unqualified villain. But, if we ignore the conventional distinctions between good and evil, both hero and villain can be seen as primarily anarchic men seeking after autonomy and power: one is as much out of place in a just Confucian order as the other in a community of Buddhist devotees. Despite their eventual submission to Buddhism, the heroes of *Journey to the West* and *Dream of the Red Chamber* are both rebels, Monkey with his quest for immortality and defiance of established authority and Chia Pao-yü with his romantic nonconformity and distaste for bureaucratic success and pseudo-Confucian scholarship. In *The Scholars* the stated ideal is fully embodied in the hero Tu Shao-ch'ing—an uncompromising individualist who asserts his Confucian integrity by refusing to look after his self-interest and succumb to the inducements of an official career. In *The Romance of the Three Kingdoms,* whose every major hero is fired by the ambition to achieve fame, the hero that has most inspired national reverence—Kuan Yü—is also the proudest and the most assured of his own greatness. It is certainly not an accident that in our six novels the heroes all exemplify an individualistic temper as they pursue their various courses of sensual abandon, chivalric action, Promethean defiance, romantic and Confucian nonconformity, and sheer proud egotism.

In this section I have isolated some of the major elements composing the ideological substance of traditional Chinese fiction. Each of the following six chapters will take up a novel and discuss among other things the degree of success it enjoys in translating the varied elements of its thought into the actual conflict of its characters. How successful each work is in this regard, of course, ultimately depends upon the intelligence, taste, and skill of its author. But the very fact that the novelist should draw upon the contrarieties of his culture in his depiction of reality suggests at least that he will be dealing with the fundamental problems of man and society. In China, as elsewhere, the novelist has no choice but to record the dilemmas of civilized man as he concomitantly tries to indulge his appetites and build a more just social order, alternately seeks his destiny in the permanent illusions of love, power, and fame and anchors his hope in the possibly illusory permanence of God or Tao. Despite their great disparity in artistic achievement, therefore, even the beginning student will soon find that at least six of the major Chinese novels, like the great novels of the Western tradition, study these dilemmas with power and insight.

CHAPTER II

THE ROMANCE OF THE THREE KINGDOMS

The Romance of the Three Kingdoms is by design a historical narrative rather than a historical novel as we understand the term in the West. Hardly a single character in the book is ahistorical, and there is no plot to speak of beyond the plot of history. Though it borrows from the oral tradition of storytelling, it is clearly far more an epic than a romance (to borrow the distinction maintained in W. P. Ker's still useful book, *Epic and Romance*), in that its drama of human motivation is rarely adulterated by other independent kinds of narrative interest to be found in knightly and amatory adventure, in pageantry and fantasy.[1] Finical scholars from the Ch'ing historian Chang Hsüeh-ch'eng to Hu Shih, it is true, have complained that it is neither sufficiently truthful to be good history nor sufficiently fictionalized to be good literature.[2] To complain so, however, is to disregard the peculiar strengths and limitations of the *yen-i* type of fiction of which *The Romance of the Three Kingdoms* is the first and greatest example: it attains the condition of good literature precisely because its slight fictional elaboration of history has restored for us the actuality of history. The work contains, to be sure, occasional minor episodes patently fictitious and unworthy of the name of history. Yet in comparison with a great many other Chinese historical novels or with the pseudohistorical epics of the Renaissance, *The Romance of the Three Kingdoms* is remarkably chaste in its supernaturalism and restrained in its use of folk material. By and large it is a sober drama of political and military contention of about a hundred years' duration (A.D. 168–265) among rival power groups bidding for control of the Chinese empire.

Long before Lo Kuan-chung (*ca.* 1330–1400) compiled *The Romance of the Three Kingdoms* in the late Yuan or early Ming period, its major characters and events had been romanticized by poets, storytellers, and playwrights so that their influence could not but be felt in his work. Yet Lo's main intention was to abide by history as he knew it and to reject palpable fiction. Though for the earlier attempts at historical fiction, which are nothing but inept compilations of oral material, we should properly emphasize their popular, folk quality rather than their individual authorship, *San-kuo-chih yen-i* represents a major breakthrough for the Chinese novel in that it is a unified piece of work by a single author which is intentionally corrective of the narrative crudities and superstitious excesses of the storytellers. The Three Kingdoms period had been a major subject for historical storytellers at least since the late T'ang. Though they followed the main events of the period, in catering to their unlearned audience they must in time have exaggerated the traits of certain beloved and detested characters and added a wealth of fanciful and interpretative fiction until the retold cycle of stories departed quite far from official history. There is an extant compilation of such stories dating from the Yuan period entitled *San-kuo-chih p'ing-hua.*[3] This version is atrocious in style and often transcribes the names of places and persons in wrong characters. Events are narrated most sketchily and history itself is reduced to a contest in magic, cunning, and prowess. Insofar as other preserved *p'ing-hua* are less illiterate, it is possible that the publishers in this instance had entrusted the task of compilation to a hack of little learning and less writing ability. Based on promptbooks of provincial storytellers, it could not have represented the art of storytelling among its famous practitioners in the capital cities. But with all its uncharacteristic crudities, this version must have conformed to their repertoire in one respect at least: the application of the theory of moral retribution to the workings of history. According to this source, the ultimate split of the Han empire into three kingdoms is directly traceable to the founding emperor Kaotsu's unjust execution of his three able generals: Han Hsin, P'eng Yüeh, and Ying Pu.[4] In time these three are reborn as the founders of the three kingdoms: Han Hsin as Ts'ao Ts'ao (Wei), P'eng Yüeh as Liu Pei (Shu), and Ying Pu as Sun Ch'üan (Wu). Kaotsu and his cruel wife, Empress Lü, also return to earth as the last Han emperor Hsien-ti and his consort Empress Fu, to suffer endless torment in the hands of Ts'ao Ts'ao.

Lo Kuan-chung does away with all this kind of didactic nonsense. In fact, he is so intent on retelling history that the earliest preserved version of his *San kuo* (the so-called Hung-chih edition, actually published in the Chia-ching period, 1522–66) begins without rhetorical flourish of any kind:

Upon the death of Huan-ti of the Later Han, Ling-ti succeeded to the throne. He was then twelve years old. At court Grand General Tou Wu, Grand Tutor Ch'en Fan, and Minister of Public Instruction Hu Kuang gave him counsel and assistance. The ninth month of that autumn, the palace eunuchs Ts'ao Chieh and Wang Fu arrogated power. Tou Wu and Ch'en Fan plotted their death, but their plot leaked out and they themselves were killed by Ts'ao Chieh and Wang Fu. From then on the palace eunuchs became powerful.[5]

In its complete independence of the oral conventions, the passage recalls the terse style of official dynastic history and makes few concessions in the direction of a more popular narrative. By contrast, the *p'ing-hua* version begins as follows, after four lines of introductory verse:

> In the days of long ago, there lived Liu Hsiu of White Water Village, in Teng-chou of the commandery of Nan-yang. His courtesy name was Wen-shu. His posthumous title was Emperor Kuang-wu. "Kuang" indicates the light of sun and moon illuminating all under heaven; "wu" indicates his winning an empire by military force. Hence his posthumous title was Kuang-wu. His capital was erected in Loyang. During the fifth year of his reign, one day in a moment of leisure, he visited the Imperial Park. . . .[6]

The passage betrays its oral origin by its attempt to explain the title "Kuang-wu." In a text specifically prepared for reading, these two simple characters would have needed no explanation; moreover, an educated reader would have been insulted by the author's officiousness. After laboriously establishing his identity, the *p'ing-hua* version then tells how Kuang-wu meets at the park one Ssu-ma Chung-hsiang, who is later transported to hell to preside over the case of the three wronged generals. Ssu-ma Chung-hsiang, in turn, becomes Ssu-ma Chung-ta, better known as Ssu-ma I, the founder of the Chin dynasty. We are given a typical folk tale with no pretense to being serious history.

The Lo Kuan-chung version as revised by Mao Tsung-kang and his father Mao Lun, which has been the standard version of *San kuo* for over three hundred years, also begins differently. A summary of Chinese history now precedes the story of the powerful eunuchs at Ling-ti's court:

> Empires wax and wane; states cleave asunder and coalesce. When the rule of Chou weakened seven contending principalities sprang up, warring one with another till they settled down as Ch'in and when its destiny had been fulfilled arose Ch'u and Han to contend for the mastery. And Han was the victor. . . .[7]

Thus in conformity with the style of popular historical novels, the editors have introduced a preamble to lessen *San kuo's* dissimilarity to that genre of fiction.

It has been the fashion among modern Chinese scholars to question the information given in prefaces to most editions of Chinese novels. Actually, in the case of carefully printed editions, this skepticism is often uncalled for: the baffling nature of some prefatory statements merely reflects our lack of more accurate knowledge about authors, editors, and printers. The Chia-ching edition of *San kuo* was prepared with extreme care, and its bibliographical and prefatory material accordingly deserves our close attention. Its full title is *San-kuo-chih t'ung-su yen-i* (An explanation of the *San-kuo-chih,* done in the popular style). Ch'en Shou, the compiler of the official *San-kuo-chih,* is given equal credit with Lo Pen (courtesy name, Kuan-chung), the author who has prepared this popular version from Ch'en's history. There is a 41-page name index of all historical characters appearing in the book. Though by Lo Kuan-chung's time Shu Han had long supplanted Wei as the legitimate successor to the Han dynasty and appropriately occupies the place of honor in the index, the personages of each state are listed in the order observed in the table of contents for that state in Ch'en Shou's history. Most important, this edition has a preface by Chiang Ta-ch'i, which gives the *raison d'être* for Lo Kuan-chung's popularization:

The former dynasties saw the rise of *p'ing-hua* based on unreliable history and recited by blind storytellers. Such *p'ing-hua,* characterized by their contemptible and erroneous language and their retelling of wild fiction, were detested by gentlemen-scholars. Lo Kuan-chung of Tung-yuan, however, basing his account on Ch'en Shou, consulted official history and carefully adapted and expanded its chronicle of events from the first year of the Chung-p'ing reign of Han Ling-ti to the first year of the T'ai-k'ang reign of the Chin dynasty. He called it *An Explanation of the San-kuo-chih, Done in the Popular Style*. Its language is neither too difficult nor too vulgar. It records events truthfully so that it should be properly deemed history.[8]

Even though not all scholars are prepared to accept this quotation at face value, yet the sharp contrast between the illiterate *p'ing-hua* and the eminently readable and reliable *yen-i* version would support the conclusion that Lo Kuan-chung was writing in conscious departure from the tradition of the storytellers rather than in imitation of them. His novel was popular literature with a difference, compiled by a scholar and carrying forward the historiographical tradition of Ssu-ma Ch'ien and Ssu-ma Kuang. As a matter of fact, several Ming publishers of *San kuo* and other *yen-i* novels announce these works as adaptations from Ssu-ma Kuang's comprehensive history, with the phrase *an Chien* (According to *Tzu-chih t'ung-chien*) duly incorporated in their titles.[9]

Lo Kuan-chung is extremely fortunate in that his source, Ch'en Shou's *San kuo chih,* is rich in historical and biographical detail. One is used to the idea of the voluminousness of Chinese dynastic histories; yet, with all the records at their disposal, most official historians are actually too concise to fully capture the personalities of the historical figures they are dealing with. Though superior to later histories, Ch'en Shou's *San kuo chih* is less copious in detail and less dramatic in style than Ssu-ma Ch'ien's *Records,* but its relative terseness is early complemented by a lengthy commentary by P'ei Sung-chih of the Liu Sung period (420–78), who sees as his task the inclusion of all relevant passages from other sources to illuminate the text. Drawing upon some 210 titles, most of which have long since been lost, P'ei Sung-chih therefore preserves twice the amount of material included in the history proper; most of this material dates from Ch'en Shou's time (the third century) and has as much claim to reliability. Some of these sources are written from a definite point of view; thus, the biography of Ts'ao Ts'ao known as *Ts'ao Man chuan* includes many interesting episodes that are derogatory in intention though their maliciousness does not necessarily preclude their truth. In compiling his novel, Lo Kuan-chung draws as much from P'ei as from Ch'en, apparently proceeding on the assumption that all this material is worthy of elaboration. It may appear as a weakness that he does not have the modern historian's sophistication or passion for consistency. Yet, whereas a modern biographer like Lytton Strachey inevitably introduces a note of falsity in his ironic concern for a consistent image, Lo Kuan-chung, in his apparent failure to discriminate among his sources, ultimately attains a remarkably impersonal objectivity in his re-creation of a complex age.

In compiling his novel, Lo Kuan-chung had also to accept certain myths that were too well entrenched in the popular mind to be rejected, such as the sworn brotherhood of Liu Pei, Kuan Yü, and Chang Fei; the extraordinary nobility of Kuan Yü; and the super-natural wisdom of Liu Pei's chief counselor, Chu-ko Liang. These myths, however, were themselves developed from hints in the offi-cial history, and their inclusion in the novel dramatizes the history without falsifying it to any serious extent. Thus the sworn brother-hood of Liu, Kuan, and Chang confirms rather than contradicts the genuinely fraternal relations between the Shu leader and his com-rades-in-arms; Kuan Yü's undoubted nobility lends poignancy to his folly and arrogance; and, with the possible exception of one important episode, Chu-ko Liang's supernatural powers only em-bellish his career without contributing to the impression that his wizardry is essential to his success.

Because of the compiler's eclectic inclusion of a diversity of ma-terials, it is very easy to misread *The Romance of the Three King-doms*. Careless readers would form their impression of the major characters, say Ts'ao Ts'ao and Kuan Yü, on the strength of a few dramatic and unambiguous scenes and then maintain that it is in-deed the compiler's conscious intention to vilify one and ennoble the other. While agreeing with this simplistic view of the major characters, more careful readers would notice scenes where they are presented in a different light. Thus Hu Shih, who, incidentally, subscribes to the view that the novel came about through a slow process of evolution, maintains that *San kuo* is an inconsistent nar-rative:

The authors of *San-kuo yen-i,* its revisers and final editor were all pro-vincial Confucians of ordinary intelligence; they were not literary geniuses or exceptional thinkers. They did their level best to portray Chu-ko Liang. But they had a preconceived notion that Chu-ko Liang's great forte lies in his "resourceful plotting and strategy"; so in their hands he eventually became a Taoist magician of divine intuition and wonderful calculation who could summon winds and propitiate the stars. They further wanted to portray Liu Pei as a man of benevolence and righteousness but ended in making him a coward of no ability. Again, they wanted to portray a Kuan Yü of divine prowess, but he was reduced to an arrogant and stupid warrior.[10]

What Hu Shih seems to be doing here is testing the book against the popular conceptions of three beloved characters and deploring its lack of success in embodying these conceptions. While, in line with Chu Hsi and the succeeding historians, Lo Kuan-chung shows evident sympathy for the cause of Shu and regards it as the legitimate successor to the Han dynasty, it would be extremely naïve to suppose that he had indeed preconceived its founding heroes in a simple-minded fashion. For most Chinese, of course, it is very easy to misread the novel since they have been conditioned by the popular theater and the storytellers to accept unquestioningly the benevolence of Liu Pei, the wizardry of Chu-ko Liang, and the divine bravery of Kuan Yü. Furthermore, in the version then available to Hu Shih—the standard version edited by Mao Tsung-kang—minor stylistic changes have been introduced to ensure the reader's sympathy for these heroes. But even in that edition the version of Lo Kuan-chung has remained substantially intact and no one should have been misled by the thin veneer of flattery.

Take Kuan Yü, a most misunderstood character. To any unbiased reader it must be quite apparent that Lo Kuan-chung has adopted, not inadvertently or perfunctorily but deliberately, Ch'en Shou's view of the hero as a haughty warrior deficient in generalship. Lo Kuan-chung was writing at a time when Kuan Yü was already an object of national veneration (he was to become a god in Ch'ing times) and so he accords him all the reverence merited by a saint. He duly notes his imposing looks and martial stature, his long beard and mighty sword, and, whenever justified, impresses us with his surpassing bravery and extreme nobility. But at the same time he gives history its due by noting in instance after instance his sheer ignorance of policy, his childish vanity and unbearable conceit.

And this conceit, abetted by general credulity, eventually brings about his downfall. He dies a shattered idol deserving some pity because of his invincible belief in his own sagacity and prowess.

Far from producing a discordant impression, as Hu Shih would suggest, the mythical and historical strands of Kuan Yü's character are consistently interwoven to produce an impression of organic unity. The author makes it quite clear that both his strengths and his weaknesses stem from his extreme pride and self-confidence. He underscores this point in describing Kuan Yü's initial deed of valor that so impresses the assembled nobles and rebel leaders in their expedition against their common enemy, Tung Cho. They are temporarily at a loss before the unexpected might of Tung Cho's general, Hua Hsiung:

Yuan Shao said, "What a pity that my top generals, Yen Liang and Wen Ch'ou, are not here. If one of them were here, we shouldn't be afraid of Hua Hsiung."

He had not yet finished when a man strode from the last row of the assembly to the front, facing the leaders on the platform. He cried loudly, "May I volunteer to take Hua Hsiung's head and present it to you!" They all looked at the speaker. Standing there was a man nine feet tall with a two-foot-long beard. He had phoenix eyes and silkworm eyebrows. His face was the color of a jujube, and his voice had the resonance of a large bell. Yuan Shao wondered who he could be. Kung-sun Tsan replied, "This is the younger brother of Liu Hsüan-te, Kuan Yü."

"And what kind of position does he have?"

"He is in the train of Liu Hsüan-te as a mounted archer."

From his place Yuan Shu roared, "What effrontery to suggest that we nobles have no able generals! A mere archer, how can he speak like this before us? Throw him out of here."

Ts'ao Ts'ao hurriedly intervened, "Kung-lu, cease your anger. Since this man has made this boast, he must be skilled in arms and strategy. Let him try. If he fails, then you may punish him." Yuan Shao said, "Hua Hsiung will surely laugh at us if we send a mere archer to fight him." Ts'ao said, "He looks no common person. How could Hua Hsiung know he is an archer?" Kuan Yü said, "If I fail, you may behead me."

As Kuan Yü was getting ready for the battlefield, Ts'ao Ts'ao poured a cup of hot wine and offered it to him. Kuan Yü said, "Leave the cup here; I'll be back and drink it soon enough." Then he left the tent with his long sword in his hand and vaulted into the saddle. The nobles soon heard from outside the pass the fierce roll of drums and the loud yelling of troops as if the sky were falling and the earth were shaking under the impact of the tearing down of mountains. They were all seized with fear. They were about to send messengers out to get the news when, amid the tinkling of bells, Kuan Yü rode toward the center of the tent, the head of Hua Hsiung held aloft in his hand. He threw it on the ground, and the wine in the cup was still warm. In later times it is sung:

> His might impressing heaven and earth, his first deed of valor
> Was heard at the tent gate amid the roll of battle drums.
> Yün-ch'ang declined the wine cup until he should have displayed
>   his might
> And the wine was still warm when Hua Hsiung was slain.[11]

In this scene the author has refrained from describing the actual encounter between the two warriors so that Kuan Yü's celerity in making good his boast may make a deeper impression upon the leaders assembled at the tent, as it does upon the reader. Initially, the leaders are divided in their reactions to his boast: his impressive features and carriage are definitely in his favor but his humble position speaks for his extreme insolence. The exchange of words among three of these leaders—Yuan Shao, Yuan Shu, Ts'ao Ts'ao— may not seem impressive until one realizes that each speaks entirely in character and that it is these small scenes of dialogue that build up the cumulative impression of the realness of the major characters. A vain aristocrat, Yuan Shu shows his utter contempt for the plebeian upstart. Yuan Shao is not as rude as his younger brother; in fact, he has always cultivated an image of hospitality so that, until he suffers utter defeat in the hands of Ts'ao Ts'ao many years later, he enjoys the reputation of a great leader with a following of distinguished counselors and generals. In the present scene his characteristic weakness is shown in the fact that, while he himself is willing to try Kuan Yü, he fears the ridicule of the opponent. Ts'ao Ts'ao eventually vanquishes the Yuan brothers, and in this scene his superior judgment is already apparent in his confidence in a man of ability, whatever his origin.

But Ts'ao Ts'ao may have been overimpressed. If in the present scene the author secures for his hero a strong impression of self-confidence and bravery, he at the same time may have hinted at a possible weakness in his eagerness to impress people. As we read on, we are introduced to more tableaux of this sort, with Kuan Yü keeping night vigil outside the bedchamber of Liu Pei's wives to avoid any hint of a scandal, charging down a hill to kill a general who under normal circumstances would have been his superior in armed combat, swiftly dispatching another enemy general to prove his innocence before the incredulous Chang Fei, and calmly playing a game of *go* while a physician operates on his poisoned arm.[12] With his undoubted courage and his long streak of good luck, he acts with increasing arrogance and haughtiness to sustain his public image, not realizing that even in his prime there are at least a dozen generals who are his equal in armed combat and that in military strategy and statesmanship he is a mere bungler. It is his tragedy that he eventually takes his appearance for his reality.

Few in the novel are indeed privileged to see behind Kuan Yü's appearance—so great is his fame and so impressive his long string of heroic deeds. Ts'ao Ts'ao, who was initially so taken by his valor, remains his lifelong admirer. During Kuan Yü's temporary stay with him, he tries his hardest to win his friendship and alienate him from Liu Pei, but his efforts only provide our hero ample opportunity to prove his unshakable loyalty to his elder brother. But among all his awed spectators there is one dispassionate observer: Chu-ko Liang. And this makes all the difference in our understanding of Kuan Yü. If Ts'ao Ts'ao, a shrewd judge of character and talent so far as his own men are concerned, often appears as a romantic admirer of Liu Pei's top generals—Kuan Yü, Chang Fei, Chao Yün—Chu-ko Liang is their commander who has to evaluate their abilities realistically. The glamor of their heroism can not win battles for him. Moreover, to Kuan Yü and Chang Fei, Chu-ko Liang initially appears as an intruder into the intimate circle of the sworn brothers, and he has to humor their peevish acts of noncooperation to win their confidence.[13] From the first, then, he sees Kuan Yü and Chang Fei as spoiled children jealous of his sudden eminence rather than legendary heroes, and in his own mind there is no doubt that he prefers Chao Yün—brave, cool-headed, nontemperamental, and a military strategist in his own right—as the ablest general under his command. He keeps him by his side on every military expedition and entrusts him with the most delicate or difficult assignments. After long years of distinguished service, Chao Yün dies in his old age, and on hearing the news Chu-ko Liang stamps his feet and cries, "Alas, Tzu-lung is dead! The state has lost one of its pillars and I have lost an arm." [14] (Chao Yün is such a beloved character in the novel that one is shocked to find in Ch'en Shou's history that he was actually ranked the last of the five "Tiger Generals" in the Shu state—after Kuan Yü, Chang Fei, Ma Ch'ao, Huang Chung. He is so ranked in the *p'ing-hua* version, but in the Mao Tsung-kang edition he is ranked third.)[15] For a contrast, upon the death of Kuan Yü, Chu-ko Liang merely advises the grief-stricken Liu Pei, "My lord, please restrain your sorrow. It is said that birth and death are all controlled by fate. Kuan Yü brought this disaster upon himself by his harshness and haughtiness. You must now take care of your health and slowly deliberate revenge." [16] Any sign of personal emotion is conspicuously absent.

Yet the phrase *kang erh tzu chin* (harsh and haughty) is not of the novelist's coinage; it is taken from Ch'en Shou's final evaluation of Kuan Yü's career[17] and is here dramatically attributed to Chu-ko Liang to reinforce a point which the novelist has been making all along despite his deference to popular esteem for the hero. In one of the subtlest scenes (chapter 63) Chu-ko Liang scrutinizes Kuan Yü's fitness for the vital post of governor of Ching-chou. Even before Kuan P'ing, the foster son of Kuan Yü, brings the news, Chu-ko Liang has foreknown from a star's fall from the sky the

untimely death of the counselor P'ang T'ung, which would necessi-
tate his departure for Szechwan:

A few days later, while Chu-ko K'ung-ming was sitting with Kuan
Yün-ch'ang and a few others, it was reported that Kuan P'ing had arrived. All present were alarmed. Kuan P'ing came in and submitted a
letter from Liu Pei. K'ung-ming read that on the seventh day of the
seventh month this year Counselor P'ang was trapped by Chang Jen at
Fallen Phoenix Slope and fatally shot with arrows. K'ung-ming wailed,
and not a one present did not shed tears. Then K'ung-ming said, "Since
our lord is hemmed in at the P'ei Pass and can neither advance nor retreat, I must go there to help him." Yün-ch'ang asked, "If you leave,
who will guard Ching-chou? Ching-chou is a vital region and concerns
us all." K'ung-ming said, "Our lord has not written plainly, but I know
what was in his mind." Then he showed the letter to the others and
said, "The letter entrusts me with the defense of the region and I am
to find one equal to the task. But since he asked Kuan P'ing to be his
messenger, I understand him to have Yün-ch'ang in mind as the man
to take over this important job. And I know Yün-ch'ang will do his
best to safeguard this area to honor the pledge taken long ago at the
peach garden. But the responsibility is not a light one, and may you
always do your best."

Yün-ch'ang accepted with alacrity. Then K'ung-ming ordered a special banquet at which the seal of office was to be handed to him.

"All the future rests with you, general," said K'ung-ming as he raised
the seal to hand it over to him. Yün-ch'ang replied, "When a man of
honor accepts such a task, he is only released by death." The word
"death" displeased K'ung-ming. He was thinking of not handing the
seal to him, but then his word had gone forth. He went on, "Now if
Ts'ao Ts'ao attacks, what would you do?" Yün-ch'ang answered, "Repel him with all my strength." "But if Ts'ao Ts'ao and Sun Ch'üan both
attack you, what then?" Yün-ch'ang replied, "Repel them both." K'ung-
ming said, "In that case Ching-chou would be endangered. I have eight
words for you, and if you remember them, Ching-chou will be safe."
"What eight words?" asked Yün-ch'ang. "North, repel Ts'ao; south, ally
with Sun Ch'üan." "These words I will engrave in my heart," replied
Yün-ch'ang.[18]

One notices here the extreme reluctance with which Chu-ko Liang hands over the seal of office. Blinded by love, Liu Pei cannot see Kuan Yü's unfitness for the post, but as a counselor with no personal ambition, Chu-ko Liang cannot but agree to his choice. Despite the advice that is supposedly engraved in his heart, Kuan Yü soon spurns friendly overtures from Sun Ch'üan and incurs his enmity. Under the combined attack of Sun and Ts'ao, he eventually forfeits his life and loses the region of Ching-chou. His tragic folly spells the beginning of the downfall of the Shu state.

Soon after being appointed governor of Ching-chou, Kuan Yü becomes highly incensed over the fact that Ma Ch'ao, who has only recently joined the Shu forces, has been made a top general with the title *P'ing-hsi* (Pacification of the west). So he sends word to Liu Pei through Kuan P'ing that he is desirous of entering a tournament with Ma Ch'ao to test who is the better warrior. This episode is found in Ch'en Shou's biography of Kuan Yü, and Lo Kuan-chung has only slightly enlarged it. On receiving the message, Liu Pei is naturally shocked:

K'ung-ming said, "Don't worry. I will personally compose a reply." Afraid that Yün-ch'ang would get impatient, Liu Pei asked K'ung-ming to compose one right away. Then he gave it to Kuan P'ing and made him return to Ching-chou without delay.

P'ing returned to Ching-chou. Yün-ch'ang asked, "I want to have a contest with Ma Ch'ao, did you mention that?" P'ing replied, "Here's a letter from our military commander." Yün-ch'ang opened it and read:

"I understand you are anxious to have a contest with Ma Meng-ch'i. In my estimation, though Meng-ch'i is unusually brave, he is but of the class of Ying Pu and P'eng Yüeh. It is fitting that he should compete with Yi-te [Chang Fei] but surely he cannot approach your unrivaled excellence. Now you are given the grave charge of Ching-chou. If you come to Szechwan and if in the meantime something happens in Ching-chou, would you not be guilty of a terrible crime? I think you will see this."

After finishing the letter, Yün-ch'ang stroked his beard and said with a satisfied smile, "K'ung-ming knows me thoroughly." He circulated the letter among his retainers and thought no more of going to Szechwan.[19]

This episode, like the preceding one, adds immensely to the portrait of Kuan Yü. It is only his extreme vanity that could have prevented him from detecting the palpable flattery in the letter. He really believes that Chu-ko Liang sets him apart even from his brother Chang Fei.

Kuan Yü's downfall and death are recounted in some of the finest chapters of the novel (chaps. 74–77). An aging warrior, he is reaching the pinnacle of his fame but also exhibiting the most impossible haughtiness and folly. Luck once more prevails in his vanquishment of P'ang Te, a fierce Wei general determined to destroy his reputation and expose it as a lie, and in his capture of P'ang Te's cowardly commander, Yü Chin. But Kuan Yü proves no match for a man of true cunning, the Wu commander Lü Meng. His forces disintegrate under the combined attack of Wei and Wu, but he remains a hero of desolate grandeur as for the last time he breaks out of the enemy's encirclement to face his capture and death.

In my presentation of Kuan Yü's character, I have tried to demonstrate the care with which Lo Kuan-chung has used his sources to compile his novel. It is simply not true, as Hu Shih has alleged, that he conceived a Kuan Yü of "divine prowess" and then bungled the job by turning him into an "arrogant and stupid" warrior. The arrogance and simple-mindedness are essential to Lo's concept of a hero cursed with the tragic disease of hubris; without this flaw, a storybook hero of divine prowess would have been insufferable. By the cumulative use of telling detail, Lo Kuan-chung has blended the historical and folkloristic concepts of the hero and made him into something truly memorable.

Not all characters are as self-conscious about fame as Kuan Yü, but even the minor heroes are determined to play a part in history. Roy A. Miller has rightly called *San kuo* "a fascinating novel whose chief theme is the nature of human ambition."[20] But in their own eyes, the major protagonists are concerned not so much with ambition as with the achievement of fame. Theirs is a secular world conditioned by the Confucian and Legalist philosophy of public service in which a man's greatest satisfaction is to achieve the kind of fame commensurate with his ability and talent and thus earn a place in history. In periods of dynastic stability, ambitious men can do little more than climb the ladder of bureaucratic success. But in turbulent times, such as the period of the Three Kingdoms, opportunities for men of ambition are limitless; hence nearly all the more interesting historical novels are about periods of dynastic transition when the ultimate prize for success is nothing less than the imperial crown.[21] In *San kuo,* one watches during the earlier stages of the historical struggle the ruthless elimination of the unqualified leaders until there remain only three, the founders of Wei, Wu, and Shu. They have succeeded because they have attracted the best men to their service, but at the same time men of equal talent who could have risen higher if they had chosen the right leader often go down with their fallen master. When Sun Ch'üan succeeds to the throne of Wu upon the untimely death of his elder brother Sun Ts'e, Chou Yü persuades Lu Su to serve the new ruler by quoting the words of a famous general, Ma Yuan, to Emperor Kuang-wu, "At times like this, it is not only the ruler who seeks his ministers, but also the ministers who seek their ruler." [22] In *San kuo,* therefore, one watches the ups and downs of many a man of ability who seeks to advance his fortune with his chosen master. In his untried years he may transfer his allegiance but, once committed to a lord, his honor dictates his faithful service to the bitter end. For many potentially great counselors and generals, their fate often lies with their initial choice.

Ch'en Kung is an obvious case. He is a local magistrate who, impressed by Ts'ao Ts'ao's courage and nobility, gives up his post to follow him. But, immediately disillusioned by the latter's unscrupulousness, he later joins his lot with Lü Pu, an unprincipled weakling who, though the greatest warrior of his time, decisively lacks leadership. Also under him are a pair of traitors who eventually deliver him to Ts'ao Ts'ao. Ch'en Kung is captured, as well:

Then Hsü Huang led in Ch'en Kung. Ts'ao Ts'ao said, "I hope you have been well since we last saw each other, Kung-t'ai?"

Kung said, "I left you because your ways were crooked."

Ts'ao said, "I may have been crooked, but how could you have chosen Lü Pu, of all people?" Kung replied, "Though Pu is a fool, he is not deceitful and crafty like you." Ts'ao said, "You regard yourself as an able and shrewd man—how come you are reduced to this?" Turning to Lü Pu, Kung said, "To my dying regret, this fellow did not follow my advice. If he had done so, we would not have been caught." Then Ts'ao asked, "What shall I do with you now that you are captured?" Kung gave a loud reply, "There can be only death for me." Ts'ao said, "Very well, but what about your mother and family?" Kung replied, "I have heard that he who rules with due regard for filial piety does not harm a man's family and he who governs with benevolence does not cut off the sacrifices at a man's tomb. I place my mother and family therefore in your hands. But since I am your prisoner, please kill me quickly. I have no regrets."

Ts'ao Ts'ao had the intention of saving his life, but Kung walked straight down the stairs, repulsing the attendants who would stop him. With tears in his eyes, Ts'ao rose and followed him. But Kung never looked back at him. Ts'ao instructed his attendants, "Let his mother and family be taken to Hsü-tu and looked after. Those neglectful of this task are to be punished with decapitation." Kung heard him but still uttered no word. He stretched out his neck for the blow. All present shed tears at his execution. Ts'ao gave orders that his remains be honorably coffined and buried in Hsü-tu.[23]

Not only scholars, but military men also undergo tribulations in their quest for a master properly appreciative of their ability. At first a minor officer in the service of Yuan Shao, Chao Yün later joins Kung-sun Tsan, who is also not much of a leader. Then Liu Pei, while a guest at Kung-sun Tsan's place, spots Chao Yün, and they take to each other. When Liu Pei has to depart from Kung-sun's headquarters, he says farewell to Chao Yün:

They held each other's hands. With tears streaming down their cheeks, they could not bear to part. Yün said with a sigh, "Formerly I mistook Kung-sun Tsan for a hero. Judging from his actions, I can now see he is no different from the likes of Yuan Shao." Hsüan-te said, "For the present serve him with patience. We shall surely meet again." They parted in tears.[24]

Soon afterwards Liu Pei borrows Chao Yün from Kung-sun Tsan and further cements their bond. After the death of Kung-sun, therefore, Chao Yün wanders about in search of Liu Pei, then down on his fortune and leading a most unsettled life. They finally meet, soon after Liu Pei's reunion with Kuan Yü and Chang Fei:

Hsüan-te was overjoyed and told Chao Yün all that had happened to him since they parted and so did Kuan Yü. Said Hsüan-te, "Tzu-lung, I was drawn to you the first time I saw you and did not want to part from you. I am very happy indeed to be with you again." Chao Yün said, "In all my wanderings, trying to find a lord worth serving, I have seen no one like you. Now that I am privileged to serve you, my life's ambition is fulfilled. I shall have no regret even if in serving you my brains are to be dashed out on the ground." [25]

Yet although his amiability and benevolence have attracted some able men to his side even during his darkest hour, Liu Pei is as yet no match for Ts'ao Ts'ao, who soon inflicts upon him a crushing defeat and reduces his forces to a mere thousand. Liu Pei feels keenly his repeated humiliations and confides to his followers his sense of shame that he should have involved them in his misfortune:

All of you have talents fitting you to be chief ministers to a king; unfortunately you have followed Liu Pei. And my miserable fortune has involved you all. Today I have not a spot to call my own and I am afraid I have indeed ruined your chances for success. Why don't you all abandon me and go to some illustrious lord where you may be able to achieve great deeds and fame? [26]

It is at this juncture of events that Liu Pei begins his quest for Chu-ko Liang. Leaders have sought men of talent, and men of talent have sought leaders since the reign of Han Ling-ti. Yet no man of talent has been sought in as courteous a style and with as much desperate sincerity as Chu-ko Liang by Liu Pei. By the time Chu-ko arrives on the scene, Ts'ao Ts'ao has eliminated most of his rivals in North and Central China; though he has not yet embarked on his expedition across the Yangtze River against Sun Ch'üan, he is practically assured of wiping out the puny forces of Liu Pei. Yet Chu-ko is to thwart the grand design of Ts'ao Ts'ao and establish the power balance of the three states. With sure artistic instinct, therefore, Lo Kuan-chung slows the pace of his narrative to introduce *the* hero of his book. His account of Liu Pei's three visits to Chu-ko in chapters 36–37 is justly celebrated.

Two aspects of Chu-ko Liang deserve special attention: his initial reluctance to serve and his undying loyalty to Liu Pei and his cause once he has so committed himself. I have mentioned that most protagonists of the novel are seekers after fame, but there is a special class of marginal characters—magicians, sorcerers, fortunetellers, physicians, and unconventional intellectuals too clever or too superior for their own good—who regularly tease and mock the fame-obsessed heroes. It may be that in compiling his romance Lo Kuan-chung feels duty-bound to include all men worthy of note who, though not directly involved in the political and military events of their time, have won reputation of a kind in official history and anecdotal literature. But it seems to me more a matter of design that the author periodically introduces these odd characters to provide a sardonic commentary on men immersed in politics. Like Oedipus, the ambitious heroes are all rationalists who disbelieve in supernatural signs and scorn prophetic mockery. Thus the dying Ts'ao Ts'ao would rather cast Hua T'o in prison than suffer having his brain operated on—he suspects that the wonder physician has been suborned to kill him.[27] Thus, even though the recent victim of a near-fatal ambush, Sun Ts'e takes vindictive pleasure in persecuting a rain maker and physician of divine efficacy simply out of contempt for his supernatural powers. He succeeds in having Yü Chi decapitated, but he himself is soon hounded to death by the unavenged spirit of the magician:

That night there was a very violent storm and by morning Yü Chi's body had disappeared. The guards assigned to watch the corpse reported this to Sun Ts'e. In his wrath he wanted to kill them, but suddenly he saw someone calmly walking toward him in the hall, and on closer view it was Yü Chi. Highly enraged, he was about to draw his sword and slay him but all of a sudden he fainted and collapsed on the floor. His attendants hurriedly carried him to his bedchamber; eventually he recovered consciousness.

His mother, the Dowager Wu, came to visit him and said, "My son, you have wrongly killed the holy one and this is your retribution."

Ts'e smiled, "I have gone to battles with my father since I was a boy and have chopped down people as if they were hempen stalks. When have I received any retribution for this? Now that I have slain a sorcerer and put an end to his evil, how could I suffer any retribution on that score?" She said, "This has come about because you disbelieved in him. Now you must perform proper ceremonies to appease him." Ts'e replied, "My fate rests with heaven. A sorcerer cannot harm it, why appease him?" [28]

(In Ch'en Shou's history, Sun Ts'e dies solely of the wounds suffered during the ambush; another popular source tells of his being hounded to death by Yü Chi.[29] Lo Kuan-chung combines these two sources to produce a memorable portrait of a man who is fey. With his belief in fate Sun Ts'e is almost a stoic, but what he doesn't realize is that it is fate itself that has provoked his murderous rage against the popular rain maker.)

Even more interesting are the vignettes of intellectuals and writers who tempt fate with their futile display of wit and their open mockery of the powerful. As is well known, neo-Taoist "pure talk" was in fashion among the poets and wits at the Wei and later the Chin court. Though, as retainers to various members of the royal family, they are often involved in court intrigue, they at the same time affect a pure scorn for politics and politicians. San kuo has not given us a complete gallery of these intellectuals, but it does give glimpses of such men as K'ung Yung, Ni Heng, Yang Hsiu, Chang Sung, and Ho Yen.[30]

Among them, the most popular figure with readers of the novel is certainly Ni Heng, a scholar of high repute recommended to Ts'ao Ts'ao's attention by K'ung Yung, who is himself the senior member of the "Seven Wits of the Chien-an Period." During his initial interview with Ts'ao Ts'ao, Ni Heng calls his best-known generals and counselors by scurrilous names and dismisses the rest of his followers as "clothes trees, rice baskets, wine caskets, and meat bags."

Ts'ao said angrily, "What abilities do you have then?" Heng answered, "I know all about heaven and earth, and am conversant in the three teachings and nine schools. Above, I could assist a king so that he may become Yao and Shun; as for myself, I match virtue with Confucius and Yen Hui. How could I be classed with ordinary scholars?"

There was only Chang Liao with them, and he was about to pull out his sword and kill him. But Ts'ao said, "I am just in need of a drummer to perform at court receptions, dinners, and sacrifices. Ni Heng may fill that post." Heng did not decline, said "yes," and left. Chang Liao asked, "This fellow is insolent, why don't you kill him?" Ts'ao answered, "He enjoys an undeserved reputation far and wide. If I kill him, the world will think that I am not hospitable to talent. Since he is so vain about his talent, I have made him a drummer to humiliate him."

Soon afterwards, Ts'ao was having a big banquet at the reception hall and the drummer was ordered to entertain. The former drummer told Heng, "When beating the drum, you must wear new clothes." But Heng arrived at the hall in his old clothes and beat the drum to the tune of "Three Variations on Yü-yang." The tone and rhythm were exquisite; the drum had a resonance like the notes from metal and stone. The audience was all moved to tears. But the attendants shouted at him, "Why didn't you change your clothes?" Facing all these people, Heng stripped his worn and tattered clothes and stood in his nakedness. His entire body was exposed to view. The guests all covered their faces. But Heng slowly put on his trousers, without changing color.

Ts'ao rebuked him, "In this ceremonial hall, how dare you be so insolent?" Heng replied, "To hoodwink and deceive the emperor, that's insolence! I expose the body my parents gave me—that's showing my purity." Ts'ao said, "If you are pure, then who is foul?" Heng said, "You cannot tell the virtuous and stupid apart—your eyes are foul; you haven't read the classics of *Poetry* and *History*—your mouth is foul; you don't listen to good advice—your ears are foul; you are ignorant of the past and present—your whole person is foul; you can't abide the other nobles—your belly is foul; you harbor thoughts of usurpation—your heart is foul. I am a scholar known all over the world and you use me as a drummer. This is like Yang Huo slighting Confucius and Tsang Ts'ang vilifying Mencius. You want to establish the work of a king or hegemon; then how could you so belittle me?" [31]

In Peking opera, Ni Heng is usually portrayed as a thoroughly sympathetic Confucian who rails at Ts'ao Ts'ao as a usurper and villain.[32] The same sympathy is observable in the present scene, but nevertheless the novelist also sees him as a comic figure with his completely naïve egotism and contempt for others. No Chinese in his right mind would compare himself to Confucius and Mencius, and yet Ni Heng unblushingly does so. He is a sort of Confucian beatnik whose scorn for Ts'ao Ts'ao hardly disguises an essential boorishness stemming from self-conceit.

Chu-ko Liang may seem a far cry from the likes of Yü Chi and Ni Heng. Yet initially, he and his friends at Nan-yang offer another, and more serious, kind of critique of the contending world of ambitious heroes. For they are the Taoist recluses, engaged in simple farming, singing songs of their own composition, visiting one another at leisure, or roaming among the hills. Their world is the traditional antithesis to the bureaucratic world—what every Chinese poet-bureaucrat longs for when overburdened with the cares of office. In describing Liu Pei's three visits to Chu-ko Liang, the novelist for the first and last time pays conspicuous attention to idyllic nature. When a good friend broaches the possibility of his serving Liu Pei, Chu-ko Liang dismisses him curtly with a Taoist question reminiscent of Chuang Tzu, "So you want to make me into an animal to be slaughtered at a sacrifice?" [33] Whereas other men of talent and ambition are eager for service, Chu-ko Liang shares with the marginal intellectuals and men of prophetic wisdom a mocking detachment from the political world. He seems extremely reluctant to leave his hermitage.

Or does he? So challenging are the times for men of talent that Chu-ko Liang, the supreme genius of his period, could not but be drawn to the call for personal achievement. He has early compared himself to Kuan Chung and Yüeh I, two eminent statesmen of the pre-Ch'in period, and all his friends attest to his potential for un-rivaled greatness. Oversubtle readers have read his slow response to Liu Pei's call as an elaborate preparation to enhance his own im-portance and win his future lord's complete trust. But, while his years at Nan-yang can be viewed as a period of preparation for the great task ahead of him, Chu-ko Liang is genuinely reluctant to embark on an active career because he knows that the times are against him and that his accomplishment, however great, cannot alter the course of history. During his first visit to Nan-yang, Liu Pei is told by Ts'ui Chou-p'ing, one of Chu-ko's bosom friends acquainted with his ambitions:

"You, sir, wish to restore order, and this shows your benevolence. But, since the earliest times, order and disorder have always succeeded one another. . . . Now we are entering a period of disorder after a period of order and the present disorder cannot be immediately rectified. You, sir, wish K'ung-ming to change the decrees of heaven and earth and regulate the workings of yin and yang, but I am afraid this task is not easy and to attempt it would be a vain expenditure of energy. Have you not heard that he who complies with the decree of heaven has an easy time and he who works against it has a hard time? What the science of numbers has foretold reason can not alter; what fate has decreed man can not change.[34]

When Chu-ko Liang finally agrees to serve, therefore, he is in large part touched by Liu Pei's sincerity. As a practical man, he must know that he could not earn the complete trust of either Ts'ao Ts'ao or Sun Ch'üan, both men being staffed with competent counselors, and as a Han loyalist, he will not want to serve them. But in the service of Liu Pei, he will enjoy a free hand and the challenge of building something from scratch. Though, as presented in the novel, he is a man of prescience able to predict the outcome of events, his acceptance of the stupendous task of restoring the Han dynasty through Liu Pei's legitimate succession to the Han throne speaks for his Confucian convictions. In the official history he is presented as a Legalist administrator,[35] in popular imagination he is seen with the trappings of a Taoist magician, but in the novel he must be seen first of all as a Confucian statesman who attempts to achieve the impossible out of his friendship for a man who reposes complete trust in him. His youthful preference for Taoist reclusion and his command of Taoist magic, however exploited by the novelist in concession to popular taste, only accentuate the poignant tragedy of his Confucian devotion.

But no friendship, however binding, can be the sum total of one's emotional obligations. If Liu Pei and Chu-ko Liang are united in their ideal of a Shu Han kingdom that will someday inherit the Chinese empire, they are set apart by their regard for other imperatives that determine policy. If Chu-ko Liang loves Liu Pei as a friend, he eventually places a higher value on what he stands for—a united China under the rulership of the Liu house. If Liu Pei places complete confidence in his minister, he nevertheless has his own reputation to care for and his other emotional obligations to meet, especially those to his sworn brothers. In his humbler years he has long cultivated an image of kindness and benevolence to offset his political disadvantages, and now under the efficient guidance of Chu-ko Liang he will nevertheless demur at policies of expansion that would tarnish that image. He heartily agrees with his minister about the necessity of occupying Ching-chou and Szechwan, but he is reluctant to dislodge from these regions their rightful rulers who happen to be his distant kinsmen, Liu Piao and Liu Chang. Chu-ko Liang has to honor his scruples and eventually gains these two areas after much delay. Ching-chou, in particular, is not taken until after Sun Ch'üan has already established his claim over it. The subsequent dispute over Ching-chou, as we have partially seen in our account of Kuan Yü, weakens Shu considerably.

Liu Pei and Chu-ko Liang are completely at variance following the death of Kuan Yü. Lo Kuan-chung, who has hitherto treated Liu Pei's scruples and indecision as something for Chu-ko to triumph over in his continual exercise of amazing resourcefulness, now arrives at the climactic point in their relationship, with due awareness of its explosive dramatic possibilities.

We have seen Chu-ko Liang's reaction to Kuan Yü's death. In order to thwart the designs of Wei and ultimately bring about its downfall, he has long upheld a policy of alliance with Wu. Since Kuan Yü's conduct has worsened the relations between the two states, he deems it imperative that friendship be restored, especially since Wu is willing to make huge concessions to compensate for its crime. If another general had been slain, Liu Pei perhaps would have agreed to this cool-headed rationalist policy. But since the victim of Wu's treachery is his sworn brother, he brushes aside the counsel of Chu-ko and of all others who have the best interests of the state at heart to pursue private vengeance. A politician long used to prudence and dissimulation in his slow climb to prominence, Liu Pei finally turns into a man of passion, a roused Achilles intent on punishing a whole state for the crime of the murder of his beloved Patroclus.

While Kuan Yü and Chang Fei (who is murdered by his underlings soon after the death of Kuan) are still alive, their complete loyalty to their sworn brother has only served to bolster his political fortune so that for Liu Pei the claims of private friendship are never in conflict with the claims of political ambition. But, with their death, the former claims now dictate his state policy. It is a mark of his tragic dignity that Liu Pei should decide in favor of private vengeance; at the same time he appears the doomed hero of Greek tragedy, elated with overweening pride. Ever since Chu-ko Liang became his chief minister, Liu Pei has entrusted to him the conduct of major military campaigns, his own experience as a military commander having been mostly disastrous. But now, to punish Wu, he insists on leading personally a major expedition, which ends in the almost total annihilation of his forces camped by the bank of the Yangtze to the length of 700 li. He despises the young and obscure Wu commander Lu Sun and scorns to seek the advice of Chu-ko, who is stationed in the capital. When Ma Liang, a competent adviser, urges him to do so, he gives the proud answer, "I, too, am well versed in strategy, why should I consult the prime minister?"[36] Ma

Liang, however, finally exacts his permission to consult Chu-ko
Liang:

Reaching Chengtu, Ma Liang lost no time in seeing the prime minister and presented him the map detailing the deployment of the army.
. . . After examining the map, K'ung-ming tapped the table and cried
out in distress: "Who advised our lord to adopt such an arrangement?
He ought to be put to death!" Ma Liang answered, "It is entirely our
lord's own work; no other had any hand in it." K'ung-ming lamented,
"The fate of the Han dynasty is sealed!" [37]

Chu-ko Liang, who does not share Liu Pei's passion for vengeance, sees the impending disaster primarily as a crushing blow to
all his hopes for the renewal of the Han empire. With all his unfeigned devotion to his prince, he nevertheless impulsively calls for
his death because Liu Pei the man now stands in the way of Liu
Pei the politician-idealist. Yet, though his folly will create insuperable difficulties for his prime minister, Liu Pei is seen in his last reckless act as a man of *i* (righteousness, selfless friendship) obeying a
higher kind of duty than that enjoined by the ordinary dictates of
prudence and success. In the peach garden he and his newly sworn
brothers had vowed, "Though we were not born on the same day of
the same year, we wish to die on the same day of the same year." [38]
Now, although his death wish urges him to commit folly on an
extravagant scale, yet his political failure spells his human success.

After his disastrous defeat, Liu Pei is too ashamed to go back to
his capital. While at his temporary quarters in Pai-ti-ch'eng, the
dying emperor recalls Chu-ko Liang from Chengtu to entrust the
future to him, in one of the most moving passages in the novel:

K'ung-ming arrived at the Yung-an palace, and, seeing that his lord
was critically ill, he prostrated himself at the foot of his bed. The First
Emperor bade him sit by his bed and patted his back, saying, "It is
thanks to you that I became an emperor. How could anyone suspect
that I could become so stupid as not to follow your advice, and therefore
reap this harvest of failure? I have fallen sick with remorse and shame
and now I shall not live long. My heir is a weakling, and I cannot but

entrust the future to you." His tears were streaming over his face as he concluded his speech. Also in tears, K'ung-ming said, "May Your Majesty meet the hopes of the people by a speedy recovery."

The First Emperor looked about him and saw that Ma Shu, the younger brother of Ma Liang, was present. He bade him retire. When Ma Shu had left the chamber, the First Emperor asked K'ung-ming, "What do you think of Ma Shu?" K'ung-ming replied, "He is one of our ablest men." "Not so," said the First Emperor. "I have observed him and his words exceed his deeds. He cannot be trusted with heavy responsibilities. May you ponder my words."

Having said this, he gave orders that the high officers of the state be admitted to his presence. Taking paper and brush, he then wrote his testament and handed it over to K'ung-ming. "I am no scholar and only roughly informed of the basic principles," said he with a sigh. "But a sage [Tseng Tzu] said, 'When a bird is about to die, its cry is sad, and when a man is about to die, his words are good.' I had hoped that we could all see the destruction of Ts'ao and the restoration of the Han house, but unfortunately I am now called away and this last command of mine I ask you, prime minister, to give to my heir Ch'an. Tell him not to take my words lightly, and please guide and instruct him in all things."

K'ung-ming and all those present wept and prostrated themselves, saying, "May Your Majesty not overtire yourself. We will do our utmost whereby to prove our gratitude for the kindness we have received." Then the First Emperor bade the attending eunuch to raise K'ung-ming from the floor. With one hand he brushed away his tears while with the other he grasped K'ung-ming's hand and said, "The end is near; I have something confidential to tell you."

"What command has Your Majesty to give?"

The First Emperor wept, "You are ten times as able as Ts'ao P'i. I am sure you will pacify the empire and complete the great work. If my heir can be helped, then help him, but if he proves unworthy, then take the throne yourself in Chengtu."

As K'ung-ming followed the speech to the end, a cold sweat broke out all over his body and he almost lost the use of his limbs. He fell on his knees and wept, saying, "How could I dare harbor any other thought than to wear out my limbs and serve your son with the utmost faithfulness and loyalty until I die?" Having said so, he knocked his head against the ground until it bled. The First Emperor then asked K'ung-ming to sit on his bed and called Liu Yung, the prince of Lu, and Liu Li, the prince of Liang, to come closer to receive his instructions: "My sons, remember my words. After my death you three brothers are to treat the prime minister as you would your father and not be remiss." Having said so, he bade the two princes to bow to K'ung-ming on their bent knees. They did so, and K'ung-ming said to the First Emperor, "Even if my brains were spilled on the ground, I could not hope to repay your kindness."

Turning to the assembled officers, the First Emperor said, "I have confided my orphan to the care of the prime minister and bidden him to treat him as a father. You too, sirs, are not to be remiss in performing your duties. This is my dying request and charge to you."

Then he charged Chao Yün, "You and I have gone together through many dangers and difficulties, but now we are to part. For our old friendship's sake, please look after my son. Remember my words." Yün wept and said, "How could I dare not to do my best at all times?" Then the First Emperor turned to the others, "Sirs, I am unable to speak to you one by one and lay a charge upon each of you. I trust you will all do your best." These words were his last. He was sixty-three, and he died on the twenty-fourth day of the fourth month, in the summer of the third year of Chang-wu.[39]

In his dying hour, the chastened Liu Pei is keenly aware that his last act of rashness has grievously disappointed his prime minister. But, if he has failed him, he is sure that his heir apparent will do even worse. For the good of his kingdom and to assure him complete freedom as a statesman, would it not be better if Chu-ko Liang should succeed to his throne? But if his alternative injunction to his minister—to supplant his son if he proves unworthy—betrays an impulse of idealistic generosity, Chu-ko is surely right in interpreting it as a harrowing trial of his loyalty. Liu Pei does not press his offer again in face of Chu-ko's dramatic demonstration of his devotion. With a man of dynastic ambitions, it cannot be helped that his sons should stay uppermost in his mind.

And with all his deference to Chu-ko's wisdom, Liu Pei does not entirely abdicate his superiority: his evaluation of Ma Shu proves for once that he is a sounder judge of character than his minister. The novelist has planted this little scene here so as to anticipate the one major miscalculation in Chu-ko's career, when his misplaced trust in Ma Shu leads to military disaster.[40] On that occasion Chu-ko will cry as he belatedly recalls his master's words. Never again in Chinese history has there been a comparably touching farewell between emperor and minister, and Lo Kuan-chung has properly presented their relationship as one of abiding friendship fortified by a common ideal. But at the same time he does not overlook the political overtones of this pathetic scene, and, in doing so, he has made Liu Pei into a memorable character of historical credibility.

In the preceding sections I have focused my attention on three of the major characters, Kuan Yü, Chu-ko Liang, and Liu Pei, and several lesser ones, such as Chao Yün, Sun Ts'e, Ch'en Kung, and Ni Heng. In doing so, I have demonstrated the subtleties of Lo Kuan-chung's seemingly simple art and introduced some of the major themes of his book. This critical procedure is justified because, unlike a modern novel, *San kuo* does not exhibit an imagistic or symbolic structure, and its language, while always functional, is plain, in the tradition of Chinese historiography, with rhetorical flourishes introduced only in the longer speeches of the characters. In Ni Heng's tirade against Ts'ao Ts'ao we have a specimen of this type of rhetoric, but otherwise I have only quoted excerpts whose dominant feature is the exchange of short speeches among various characters. Such dialogues are very difficult to translate because the ubiquitous character *yüeh* (in more colloquial novels, this would be replaced by *tao*), which introduces every speech, becomes obtrusively and monotonously emphatic when rendered into English as "said." For all Chinese traditional novels, perhaps the best way to transpose short scenes of dialogue is to cast them in the form of a drama, with *yüeh* or *tao* reduced to a colon and with the accompanying verbal adjectives, such as *hsiao* (smiling) and *ch'i* (weeping), placed in parentheses. So rendered, these scenes may gain the rapidity and liveliness of comparable scenes in *The Pilgrim's Progress* and Boswell's *Life of Johnson*.

I have presented *San kuo* primarily as a novel of character with its continual preoccupation with human motivation. Yet a young Chinese reading the work for the first time will inevitably be engrossed in the story itself, in its countless military campaigns and political intrigues. But for the mature reader even the cleverest stratagems of Chu-ko Liang, however they may overawe the young, are nothing beside the cunning of a Western detective, and few scenes of armed combat are as vivid as those in *The Iliad,* where the duel of champions is inevitably presented in sharp and grim detail. Like most other Chinese historical novelists, Lo Kuan-chung is often merely content with summary narration, giving us the number of strokes exchanged between two generals until one flees or is killed. Occasionally we come upon scenes of combat that stick to our memory, such as the following one in which the hero is the brave Wei general, Hsia-hou Tun:

Advancing with his army, Hsia-hou Tun soon encountered Kao Shun [a general of Lü Pu's] and his men. He rode forward, his lance poised in his hand, and challenged Kao Shun to battle. Kao Shun accepted the challenge and they fought forty or fifty bouts. Then Kao Shun began to weaken and he fled. Tun pressed him hard and Kao Shun rode around the area where his troops were arrayed. Undaunted, Hsia-hou Tun also circled the area. There stationed among the troops was Ts'ao Hsing who secretly stretched his bow and fitted the arrow, aiming straight. As Hsia-hou Tun came closer, he shot the arrow right into his left eye. Tun shrieked and straightway pulled out the arrow. But the eyeball was also pulled out. He cried, "This is the essence of my father and blood of my mother: I cannot throw it away!" He put it in his mouth and swallowed it. Then he again leveled his lance and galloped toward Ts'ao Hsing. The latter was caught unaware as the lance ran through his face, and he was hurled from his horse a dead man. Both sides were struck dumb with amazement.[41]

Hsia-hou Tun's encounter with Kao Shun is a routine duel done in the routine manner, but when Ts'ao Hsing shoots an arrow into his eye, Hsia-hou Tun becomes no longer a mere warrior, but a brave man rising to the challenge of a great test. His subsequent

words (adapted from the *p'ing-hua* version) and actions are eloquent with defiant courage.[42]

In like manner, the battles and intrigues in *San kuo* are interesting to the extent that they are informed with human purpose. As in
the *Tso Commentary,* the first major Chinese chronicle to describe
battles in detail, human interest resides far more in the preparation
for battle than in the battle itself.[43] This is true of the most celebrated long episode in the novel—the Battle of Red Cliff, during
which the combined forces of Sun Ch'üan and Liu Pei smash
Ts'ao Ts'ao's ambitious design to cross the Yangtze River and subdue the Wu kingdom. It is the pivotal event upon which hangs the
eventual equilibrium of power of the three kingdoms, and Lo Kuan-
chung rises to the occasion by giving it the most elaborate fictional
treatment of any event in the novel.

Initially, as the threat of invasion strikes home, most of Sun
Ch'üan's counselors advise surrender since the untested mettle of
Wu is conceivably no match for Ts'ao Ts'ao's proven might. It is
the eloquence of Liu Pei's emissary, Chu-ko Liang, and the brave
determination of Sun Ch'üan's two farsighted commanders, Chou
Yü and Lu Su, that change the defeatist attitude at the Wu court
and turn imminent doom into proud victory. Basing his account on
Ch'en Shou and Ssu-ma Kuang, the author properly exploits the
dramatic possibilities of this tense situation and makes out of it an
exciting narrative of great credibility.

Unused to naval battle, Ts'ao Ts'ao has in the meanwhile followed the advice of spies who recommended the linking of his ships
by iron chains to provide greater stability for his land soldiers. He
is so pleased with his armada that about a week before the naval
encounter he gives a banquet for his civil and military staff:

It was the fifteenth of the eleventh month, the thirteenth year of
Chien-an. The day was sunny and the winds were quiet on the river.
Ts'ao ordered a banquet with music to be set up on the commander's
ship, saying, "This evening I am going to entertain my generals."

The day turned dark and the moon rose from the eastern hills,
bright as the sun. The Yangtze River shone like a wide swath of white

silk. Ts'ao sat on the deck of the commander's ship, flanked by several hundred attendants, all splendidly attired and wielding either javelins or tridents. The civil and military officers were all seated in their proper order of precedence. Ts'ao looked around and saw the hills of Nan-p'ing outlined as if in a picture. The city of Ch'ai-sang lay in the east while the river showed west as far as Hsia-k'ou. He gazed south at the Fan Mountain and descried in the north the woods of Wu-lin. The view stretched far on every side, and he was filled with joy, saying to the officers:

"Since I raised my righteous army to remove all traitors and insurgents in the country, I have vowed to pacify all the land within the four seas, and the only area that has not yet submitted to me is Chiang-nan [the region south of the Yangtze]. With my million sturdy troops, and with you gentlemen doing my bidding, how could I fail to take it now? Once Chiang-nan is subdued, there will be no more fighting, and you gentlemen will share prosperity and high honors with me, to enjoy the peace."

The civil and military officers all rose to thank him, saying, "May the trumpet of victory sound soon! All our lives we shall repose in the shadow of Your Excellency's good fortune."

By midnight Ts'ao was in high spirits. Pointing to the south bank of the river, he said, "Chou Yü and Lu Su, they know not heaven's design. Fortunately, some of their men have surrendered to us and will wreak havoc upon them. This is indeed heaven's opportune help to me!" Hsün Yu advised, "Your Excellency, please say no more. This might leak out." Ts'ao laughed loudly. "You gentlemen drinking wine with me and all my guards and attendants here, you are very close to me. What's the harm if I talk about such matters?" Then, pointing to Hsia-k'ou, he said, "Liu Pei and Chu-ko Liang, you don't realize that you have only the strength of ants and yet you want to shake Mount T'ai from its foundations. How foolish can you get!" Then, turning around to his generals, he confided, "I am now fifty-four. If I get hold of Chiang-nan, there is something I would like to possess. Formerly, Ch'iao Kung and I were good friends. I know both of his daughters are great beauties, though Sun Ts'e and Chou Yü married them some years ago. I am now building my Bronze Bird Tower by the Chang River. If I take Chiang-nan, I'll have both of the Ch'iao sisters married to me, and place them in the tower to amuse my old age. Then all my wishes will be fulfilled."

He concluded with loud laughter. The T'ang poet Tu Mu has a poem about this:

> A broken halberd buried in the sand, its iron head uncorroded by rust—
> When washed and sharpened, it tells of a great battle in a former dynasty.
> Had the eastern wind refused aid to Chou Yü,
> The Bronze Bird Tower would have imprisoned the daughters of Ch'iao.

While laughing and making merry, Ts'ao Ts'ao suddenly heard the cawing of crows as they flew toward the south. Ts'ao asked, "Why are the crows cawing at night?" Those around him replied, "The moon being very bright, they thought it was dawn. So they left their trees and cawed." Ts'ao again laughed. By now he was intoxicated, and he took his lance and stood by the prow. He poured a libation into the river and drank three full goblets of wine. Then, lowering the lance, he told the generals, "With this lance, I smashed the Yellow Turbans, captured Lü Pu, destroyed Yuan Shu, vanquished Yuan Shao, and went deep into the North until I reached the Liao-tung Peninsula. I have conquered the length and breadth of the land and have not left unfulfilled my ambition to be a great hero. Now, facing the moon, my heart is full. I am going to improvise a song, and you gentlemen harmonize with me." And he sang:

> Facing wine, you should sing accordingly—
> How long is your life-span?
> It's like the morning dew
> Soon vanishing under the sun.
> A burdened soul needs release,
> Too often oppressed with sad thoughts.
> What's the best cure for sorrow?
> The choicest brew of Tu K'ang.
> You scholars with your blue collars,
> Always and ever I think of you;
> Because of you gentlemen
> I've been sighing and singing;
> *Yu, yu,* cry the deer

Nibbling southernwood in the fields—
I have worthy guests.
Let's play the zithers and blow on the *sheng!*
Bright, bright is the moon,
Unending its glory:
Yet sorrow rises in my heart
Over my unceasing quest for talent;
Over narrow farm roads
You have come to join me—
After a long separation, we carouse
And talk, thinking of our old friendship.
The moon is bright and the stars are few,
Black crows fly south.
They circle the tree three times
And find no branches to perch on.
One never complains of a mountain being too high
Or a river being too deep:
Oh, to seek talent with the selflessness of Chou Kung
So that the world turns with contentment toward me.

After he had sung, all harmonized with him and joined in the merry mood. Suddenly, a man rising from his seat remonstrated, "Our great army is facing a critical battle, and all the officers and troops are risking their lives for the occasion. Why does Your Excellency utter such inauspicious words?" Ts'ao looked at him and knew he was Liu Fu, *tzu* Yuan-ying, the governor of Yangchow. He was a native of Hsiang, of the region of P'ei-kuo, and he had begun to receive notice while in Ho-fei. When first appointed to Yangchow, he had resettled the refugees there, established schools, set up land for cultivation by the military, and raised the moral tone of the place. He had long served Ts'ao Ts'ao and had a distinguished record. At once Ts'ao asked, with his lance still poised horizontally, "What words of mine are unlucky?" Fu replied, " 'The moon is bright and the stars are few,/ Black crows fly south./ They circle the tree three times/ And find no branches to perch on'—these are inauspicious words." Incensed, Ts'ao said, "How dare you ruin my good mood?" With one thrust of the lance, he killed Liu Fu. The rest were all frightened, and the banquet was over.

The next morning, again sober, Ts'ao was filled with unending remorse. The son of Liu Fu, Liu Hsi, requested leave to bury his father. Ts'ao said with tears, "Last night I was drunk and killed your father by mistake. I am filled with remorse. Your father shall be interred with the honors of a minister of the highest rank." [44]

For Lo Kuan-chung, this is a scene of supreme fictional realization. The official history gives no record of this banquet,[45] but it is entirely in keeping with Ts'ao Ts'ao's character that he should have given a party like that in anticipation of a crowning victory. During that period of history, in China as elsewhere, a man of fifty-four is considered no longer in his prime, and Ts'ao Ts'ao has led an active life of unceasing campaigning. His speeches at the banquet, therefore, express his sense of satisfaction that he has indeed been an unparalleled hero in his time, and looks confidently to his victory. But along with it there is a note of fatigue in his feeling that he may, with the vanquishment of Wu, look forward to a time of happy retirement in the company of his two captured beauties. (In his *fu* on the Bronze Bird Tower, Ts'ao Ts'ao's poet-son, Ts'ao Chih, does mention these two beauties. Earlier in the novel, pretending that he doesn't know whom the Ch'iao sisters married, Chu-ko Liang has quoted this poem before Chou Yü to steel his determination to fight.[46] In both instances the author has made expert dramatic use of a well-known poem.)

But, above all, in his enjoyment of the moonlight view, Ts'ao Ts'ao appears enraptured with wine and the prospect of a victory. The song he is made to recite is the most famous of his extant poems; it is a banquet poem in which Ts'ao Ts'ao laments the transience of life, quotes verses from the *Book of Poetry* to indicate his yearning for talent and his enlightened statesmanship. In all probability, it was composed for a more intimate occasion when the poet expressed mingled sorrow and joy over his reunion with some old friends. Though the poem does not entirely fit the present occasion, it nevertheless serves to introduce a startlingly beautiful scene of crows awakened from their slumber and flying south. And for the novelist the crow is a rare instance of a symbol. Though not as much detested in China as in the West, it, especially in contrast to the magpie, has its unpleasant and unlucky associations. The crows' failure to find a perch in their southward flight signifies the doom of the expedition. Ts'ao Ts'ao is fully enraged when Liu Fu spells out the ominous significance of his poem, and in his murderous wrath against the man as in his subsequent remorse we are shown further facets of his character. What Lo Kuan-chung has given us in the banquet scene is, then, the fascinating portrait of an unpredictable poet-statesman of enormous self-confidence, at once expansive and violent and not untouched by certain signs of age and weakness. Readers who persist in regarding the Ts'ao Ts'ao of *San kuo* as an arch villain show a lack of appreciation for masterful scenes like this.

But because the Battle of Red Cliff has been much elaborated upon by the storytellers, Lo Kuan-chung, in his enlargement of the episode beyond the accounts of Ch'en Shou and P'ei Sung-chih, also resorts to time-sanctioned fiction that represents a false simplification of history. If, in the scene just discussed, he has enhanced the historical reality of Ts'ao Ts'ao through his use of fiction, elsewhere he has reduced some important protagonists of the battle to caricature in his attempt to glorify Chu-ko Liang. Nearly all critics have praised the author for his fictional elaboration of the Battle of Red Cliff, but Hu Shih is surely right when he deplores his handling of Chu-ko vis-à-vis the Wu statesmen during the battle and afterwards. Official history has recorded many conversations among Chu-ko, Lu Su, Chou Yü, and Sun Ch'üan, and whenever Lo Kuan-chung reproduces these conversations in his novel both Lu Su and Chou Yü appear as farsighted and courageous statesmen in contrast to Sun Ch'üan's other cowardly advisers. But in the more fictional scenes they become mere comic foils to Chu-ko's genius. Thus Lu Su, historically a great and astute commander in his own right, becomes Dr. Watson to Chu-ko's Sherlock Holmes, forever naïve and forever astounded by the latter's foresight and cleverness. In like fashion, Chou Yü becomes Chu-ko's ineffectual rival, consumed with envy and obsessed with the desire to trap the latter and kill him. Of course, Chu-ko easily eludes every trap, only to infuriate the Wu commander and bring on his own death. Although the Chinese find all this delightful reading, in such episodes history itself appears frivolous and lighthearted, in marked contrast to the gravity of the rest of the novel. Since the Battle of Red Cliff takes place during the springtime of Chu-ko's success, long before his futile expeditions against Wei have robbed him of all gaiety, the author is certainly justified in adopting a gladsome comic mode. But, as a great adapter of historical sources gingerly embarking on the path of fiction, Lo Kuan-chung can achieve this comedy only by caricaturing the historical reality of Chou Yü and Lu Su.

The victory of the Wu forces ultimately depends on the fire strategy agreed upon by Chou Yü and Chu-ko Liang. But Ts'ao Ts'ao is no fool: he chains his ships together because he correctly reasons that a successful attack by fire on his fleet will require the assistance of winds blowing in its direction and that since in the dead of winter there are only winds blowing from the north and west, the fire strategy if adopted by the Wu forces will boomerang. To enhance his role as the architect of the victory, Chu-ko Liang is therefore forced to assume the garb of a Taoist priest to summon the southeastern winds.[47] I have earlier said that Chu-ko's magical arts and accurate predictions never seriously affect the course of events —they are either inconsequential or nullified by chance or fate— but in the present instance the wind-summoning ritual is both crucial to a decisive battle and carried out with astounding success. Despite its perennial popularity, one may object to this scene of magic not because one objects to supernaturalism as such but because the novel is predominantly a human drama of cunning and courage unfolded in the absence of supernatural aid.

After calling attention to the childishness of some of the most celebrated scenes in the account of the Battle of Red Cliff, Hu Shih draws the conclusion that, if these most fictionalized scenes are obviously weak, then the rest of the novel which is little fictionalized must enjoy even less literary success.[48] But Lo Kuan-chung, at least while he was composing *The Romance of the Three Kingdoms,* had no pretension to being a novelist. Occasionally he rises to the challenge of fiction, but his habitual strength lies in his role as a popular historian. He exhibits little talent for that full-bodied kind of fiction which calls for the invention of character and plot in the absence of historical documentation. Where his sources have misled him—as in some of the episodes in the Battle of Red Cliff—his further elaboration of these sources only enhances their naïveté.

The habitual strength of the work is therefore far more impressively present in the little fictionalized battle at Kuan-tu between the armies of Ts'ao Ts'ao and Yuan Shao than in the battle at Red Cliff.[49] In hewing to the line of the historical chronicle, Lo Kuan-chung has preserved intact a gripping story that could have been fitting material for Greek tragedy. Yuan Shao's indecisiveness and lack of leadership, his passionate partiality for one of his sons, his failure to make use of a group of individually brilliant but feuding counselors—these are some of the factors in the easy victory scored by Ts'ao Ts'ao over an amply provisioned army of numerical superiority. Lo Kuan-chung does not elaborate on any of the episodes building up to the battle at Kuan-tu and the subsequent rapid disintegration of Yuan Shao's forces, but the reader nevertheless feels caught in the web of a weighty historical event fraught with deep human significance.

Yuan Shao has already amassed a large army and sent an ultimatum to Ts'ao Ts'ao, who in the meantime is preparing a campaign against the puny strength of Liu Pei. Understandably, Liu Pei sends an emissary to Yuan Shao asking him to launch an attack on Ts'ao Ts'ao while his main strength is occupied elsewhere. The emissary, Sun Ch'ien, asks one of Yuan Shao's counselors, T'ien Feng, to arrange an interview for him with Yuan:

Feng then brought Sun Ch'ien to see Yuan Shao and presented the letter. To Feng's surprise, Shao looked haggard and was carelessly and improperly attired. Feng asked, "My lord, what happened?" Shao said, "I am about to die." "But why do you utter such words?" asked Feng. "I have five sons," answered Shao, "and the youngest pleases me most. Now he is suffering from a scabby skin disease and his life is doomed. How can I have the heart to think of other matters?" Feng said, "Now

Ts'ao Ts'ao is attacking Liu Pei in the east, and the capital Hsü-ch'ang is undefended. If you send a righteous army to raid the city, you can at once protect the emperor and save ten thousands of people from Ts'ao's tyranny. This is a rare opportunity; please think it over carefully." Shao said, "I also know this is the best course, but I am worried and distressed and I am afraid this expedition will bring me bad luck." "What's there to worry about?" asked Feng. Shao replied, "Of my five sons, only the youngest one is exceptional. If anything happens to him, I am done." Then he decided not to dispatch his army and told Sun Ch'ien, "When you return, you may tell Hsüan-te the real reason. If he is in trouble, he can come here and join me. I will find some way to help him." T'ien Feng struck the ground with his staff, saying, "When faced with this rare opportunity, not to grab it because of a child's sickness, what a pity! The future is doomed, alas!" With a deep sigh, he stamped his feet and walked out.[50]

This scene is based on Ch'en Shou's history:

> T'ien Feng advised Yuan Shao to attack Ts'ao Ts'ao from behind, but, on the excuse of his son's illness, Shao disallowed the move. Feng struck the ground with his staff, saying, "When faced with this rare opportunity, not to grab it because of a child's sickness, what a pity!" [51]

The expanded passage has retained the basic situation and the angry exclamation of T'ien Feng. But by specifying his son's disease as something of no consequence, it has also permanently fixed the image of an indecisive Yuan Shao plagued by unreasoned paternal love. Furthermore, we have not been told earlier of his great fondness for his youngest son and Lo Kuan-chung has made no attempt to analyze this partiality of his which contributes to his defeat and death and to the subsequent contention among his sons. He respects the given historical data with the result that, in their unromanticized complexity, they retain the makings of a tragic myth.

As Yuan Shao heads toward disaster, his weak character is continually revealed through the comments of friends and foes alike. Among other things, he continues to disregard the advice of T'ien Feng and eventually places him in prison. After his defeat at

Kuan-tu, however, we are told that Yuan Shao speaks with great remorse: "Because I did not heed T'ien Feng's advice, I suffered a great defeat and lost many generals. How could I have the face to see him on my return?"

The next day [the story continues], Yuan Shao mounted his horse for the return journey. As he was about to start, he was met by another counselor, Feng Chi, and his reinforcements. Shao said to Feng Chi, "I suffered this defeat because I didn't listen to T'ien Feng. I am now going back, but I am ashamed to face him." Feng Chi therefore took the opportunity to slander T'ien Feng. "While in prison Feng heard of my lord's defeat and he clapped his hands and laughed, 'Precisely as I have predicted.'" Yuan Shao was highly incensed. "How dare a mere scholar make fun of me? I must kill him." He then gave a messenger his personal sword and ordered him to leave for Chi-chou immediately and kill T'ien Feng in prison.

While T'ien Feng was in prison, one day the jailer came to congratulate him. Feng asked, "What for?" The jailer replied, "General Yuan is returning from a great defeat. He must treat you from now on with redoubled respect." Feng laughed, "Now I am a dead man." The jailer asked, "Why speak of death when everyone is pleased with your change of fortune?" Feng said, "General Yuan appears generous but is actually envious of talent and never thankful for one's loyal and honest service. Elated with victory, he might have pardoned me; now that he has been put to shame over his defeat, I may not hope to live."

The jailer was still incredulous. Before long the messenger with the sword came with Yuan Shao's orders to take T'ien Feng's head and the jailer was dismayed. Feng said, "I knew all along I was to die." The jail attendants all shed tears. Feng said, "Stupid indeed is he who, born into this world with all his talent and ambition, has chosen to serve an unworthy lord. Today I die, but I deserve no pity." He then killed himself in prison.[52]

This episode, also adapted from Ch'en Shou, places Yuan Shao with finality. As for T'ien Feng, he appears as another of those minor characters who could have done greater deeds if he had served a worthier master. If for Yuan Shao and all those enjoying the exercise of leadership their fate is inseparable from their character, then for T'ien Feng, Ch'en Kung, and a host of others whose very survival depends upon the trust and favor of a master, fate is something far more capricious than character. Asking for no pity, T'ien Feng blames only himself for having made a wrong choice, but that choice itself can be seen as an act of fate. Already in Ssu-ma Ch'ien's *Records* we are impressed with the inscrutable workings of heaven in determining the fate of many a man of ambition and talent. Because in *San kuo* history is no longer broken up into a series of individual and collective biographies, the ultimate sense of fate as heaven's design emerges with even greater clarity. Not only the battle at Kuan-tu but scores of other weighty and little fictionalized events contribute to the impression that, while heaven's design is inscrutable, it is at the same time the sum total of men's conscious endeavor. From the meanest general who makes a brief appearance only to forfeit his life in the battlefield to the sagacious Chu-ko Liang whose prolonged attempt to rectify the design of heaven ends in failure, the crowded stage of *San kuo* is enkindled with this sense of earnest endeavor. However small his role in history, each candidate for fame enacts a personal drama which is the impingement of his endeavor upon his fate.

CHAPTER III

THE WATER
MARGIN

Compared with *The Romance of the Three Kingdoms, The Water Margin* has advanced the art of the Chinese novel in at least two major respects: it is by and large recorded in a vernacular that has retained its vitality for today's readers, and it shows a far greater independence of historical sources in its elaboration of character and incident. These indisputable gains, however, are offset by concomitant liabilities stemming from the work's greater indebtedness to professional storytellers: along with the colloquial style we see the wholesale importation of oral conventions, including the numerous poems and descriptive passages in parallel prose interspersed in the prose narrative, and in the absence of authentic history we see a conscious fabrication of pseudo history in the manner of the dynastic romances. While the first drawback is shared by nearly all vernacular novels of the Ming period and can be seen, in fact, as a basic feature of the tradition, the second defect indicates the tardiness of the popular imagination in creating a form other than historical for the Chinese novel. *The Water Margin*, with its several sagas of picaresque heroes depicted in settings of everyday truth, certainly achieves far greater circumstantial realism than *The Romance of the Three Kingdoms*, and it also claims greater psychological interest with its affirmation of the darker aspects of the Chinese mentality. But its form remains synthetic and, popular opinion to the contrary, it must be rated a lesser work of art than the straightforward historical narrative of the earlier novel.

Shui hu chuan tells of Sung Chiang and his band of outlaws who flourished briefly during the reign of Hui-tsung of the Northern Sung dynasty (1101–25).[1] They surrendered in 1121 and, according to some sources, they were enlisted in the government campaign against a rebel of far greater historical significance, Fang La.[2] But legends about the band soon grew, and by the time the Sung court moved south before the invading forces of the Chin they must have attracted the special attention of storytellers at the new capital Hangchow because of their great appeal to a patriotic audience nostalgically attached to the inglorious reigns of Hui-tsung and Ch'in-tsung. The names of thirty-six heroes of that band and a few of their exploits are recorded in a short chronicle in both classical and colloquial language called *Hsüan-ho i-shih*. This chronicle almost certainly dates from the last years of the Southern Sung dynasty, and its account of these heroes shows clearly the influence of the storytellers.[3]

No primitive Yuan version of the novel has been found, but the legend must have continued to grow at a time when the Chinese were under Mongol subjugation and would certainly have delighted in stalwart heroes of an independent and rebellious temper wreaking vengeance on a corrupt and oppressive bureaucracy. The Yuan playwrights frequently raided the legend for their plots. Though many of these plays have been lost, judging from the small number of the surviving plays, we know that their heroes are concerned mainly with the requital of official injustice and the punishment of adulterous women.[4] These plays also agree on certain basic features of the legend. Sung Chiang, for example, killed his slave girl Yen P'o-hsi, and it was this murder that precipitated his flight to the outlaws' hide-out in Shantung called Liang-shan-po, a region composed of Mt. Liang (Liangshan) and its surrounding marshes. Under his leadership the band eventually consists of thirty-six major heroes and seventy-two lesser ones.

Judging from the random notes on fiction left by scholars as well as the title pages of its extant editions, Ming opinion was divided on the authorship of *Shui hu:* it was attributed either solely to Lo Kuan-chung or jointly to Shih Nai-an and Lo Kuan-chung.[5] But in the editions that give credit to Shih Nai-an he is described as author of the primary source from which Lo compiled his novel. It would seem probable, then, that Lo used Shih for *Shui hu* in the same manner as he used Ch'en Shou for *San kuo.* Since we know practically nothing about Shih and since his version of *Shui hu,* if it ever existed, had been long submerged in the Lo version, in all fairness the first version of the novel should be assigned to Lo Kuan-chung if to anyone in particular.[6]

By the Chia-ching period several novels were redacted and published in response to the growing popular and scholarly interest in fiction. (*San-kuo-chih t'ung-su yen-i,* as we have seen, was printed at that time.) About 1550, Kuo Hsün, the marquis of Wu-ting, a noted patron of the arts, commissioned an expanded, 20-volume (*chüan*) edition of *Shui hu* in 100 chapters. Though only a single volume comprising chapters 51–55 has survived, a comparison of these five chapters with corresponding chapters in other extant 100-chapter editions dating from the late Ming period would indicate that the latter editions are all based on the Kuo Hsün edition despite numerous small instances of textual discrepancy.[7] (A K'ang-hsi reprint of the complete text of one such edition, with a preface dated 1589, serves as the basic text for the variorum edition of *Shui-hu ch'üan-chuan,* published in 1954 under the general supervision of Cheng Chen-to.) Scholars are now agreed that the Kuo Hsün edition follows faithfully the Lo Kuan-chung version in recounting the pre-Liangshan careers of several individual heroes, the gathering of the 108 heroes at Liangshan, their repeated routing of government forces under the command of corrupt ministers, their honorable surrender, their expedition against Fang La with the loss of the lives of most of the heroes, and the final betrayal and death of the remaining leaders. But in Kuo Hsün's version there is a new section on the band's expedition against the Liao kingdom, which now precedes the Fang La expedition. The distinctive contribution of this edition, however, is not so much the added material, which is rather dull, as its adoption of a decidedly colloquial style to replace what, judging from *San kuo* and other novels whose authorship is ultimately traceable to Lo Kuan-chung, must have been a style more literary and economical. Whoever he was, this redactor must be honored as the second most important author of *Shui hu*.

During the Wan-li period (1573–1619) a publisher in southern Fukien, Yü Hsiang-tou, put out a shorter version of the novel (only a fragment of a copy has been preserved in the Bibliothèque Nationale of Paris) which includes nevertheless two new sections on the band's expeditions against the rebels T'ien Hu and Wang Ch'ing. This version must have been very popular because it prompted other booksellers to print similar editions of 110, 115, and 124 chapters. During the early seventeenth century, however, a 120-chapter edition was published which, while substantially reprinting the fuller 100-chapter edition, also includes the expeditions against T'ien and Wang, but in a considerably revised form. Yang Ting-chien, who supplied a preface, may have been the reviser. Modern scholars properly regard it as the culminating point in the evolution of the Liangshan saga.

But for its own time this edition did not dominate the market long: during the Ch'ung-chen period (1628–43) Chin Sheng-t'an prepared a 70-chapter edition which retains only its first seventy-one chapters (with chapter 1 serving as a prologue). He provides for his edition a running critical commentary, an arbitrary new ending, and a preface supposedly by Shih Nai-an.[8] Until recent times this has been the only version in wide circulation, and Shih Nai-an is still generally believed to be the sole author of the novel.

Before the 70-chapter edition came along, however, the fuller and shorter versions were competing for public acceptance. It is not therefore a merely academic question to ask whether and to what extent the shorter versions bear any resemblance to the Lo Kuan-chung text. In his major article, "The Evolution of *Shui-hu-chuan*" (1929), Cheng Chen-to supports Lu Hsün's belief that, except for its interpolated sections, the shorter version as represented by the 115-chapter edition substantially copies the Lo text, and he cites parallel passages from this and the 100-chapter version to prove his contention that "the shorter text absolutely could not have been an abridgment of the fuller text." [9] Many years later, however, in his preface to the variorum edition, he has swung around to the majority view of Hu Shih, Sun K'ai-ti, and Richard G. Irwin that the shorter editions were indeed put out by less reputable booksellers for quick profit and bear no relation whatever to the Lo version. These four scholars further uphold the debatable theory that the shorter versions of all novels printed during the late Ming period were abridgments of longer ones. Ho Hsin and Liu Ts'un-yan appear to be the only scholars who have challenged this theory in connection with their respective studies in *Shui hu* and *Hsi yu chi*.[10] Ho Hsin maintains with Lu Hsün that the 115-chapter edition is the nearest in text to the Lo version, though he concedes that it is obviously an abridgment since some episodes present in the 100-chapter version are missing and many passages (he doesn't specify the number) show evidence of being marred by drastic condensation.

Brought up on the standard 70-chapter version since their childhood, Chinese scholars are understandably predisposed to dismiss the so-called abridged texts as of poor quality. Even Lu Hsün deplores the clumsy style of the 115-chapter edition. Irwin agrees and further maintains that its reversion to "classical terseness" reflects the trend for "the conscious imitation of pre-Ch'in works practiced by Ming writers" [11] at the time when such abridged novels were in demand. But the style of the 115-chapter version, except in the added sections and in other places obviously marred by abridgment or deletion, is by no means halting and clumsy, nor does it bear any resemblance to pre-Ch'in prose. It is an efficient style that reminds one of the style of the Chia-ching edition of *San kuo,* even though its dependence on storytellers' promptbooks has given it a stronger colloquial character. The 115-chapter version also contains many passages in verse or parallel prose which may or may not have been in Lo's original.

Scholars have customarily compared the best and most detailed episodes in the fuller version, such as Lu Chih-shen's fatal beating of Butcher Cheng, Lin Ch'ung's narrow escape from a fire at the fodder depot, and Wu Sung's single-handed fight with a tiger, with corresponding passages in the shorter version to demonstrate the latter's stylistic inferiority.[12] But, even if this is so, it would seem that such comparisons only confirm Cheng Chen-to's earlier position that the editor of the 100-chapter novel is elaborating upon the shorter version, providing fuller description and exposition and longer conversations. While such elaborations usually enhance the visual and dramatic appeal, they also contain a good deal of rhetoric that actually detracts from the simple effectiveness of the shorter version. A careful examination of the first three chapters shows that the longer version is at times unjustifiably verbose, cluttered with clichés and storytellers' tags that are not present in the shorter one. Except for the regular substitution of *tao* for *yüeh* (said), the redactor has preserved practically the entire first three chapters of the shorter text as he expands from paragraph to paragraph without, however, always attending to the narrative logic of its context.[13] And indeed, aside from considerations of style, on the sole evidence of a few instances where the two versions of an episode differ in significant detail, the shorter text would seem to be earlier than the longer.[14]

One would have to examine all the rare copies of the Ming editions of the shorter text in order to determine its status in the evolution of the novel. In offering a few tentative remarks on this text based on a cursory reading of a badly printed Ch'ing edition of the 115-chapter version and a detailed examination of only a few of its chapters, it has not been my intention to make high claims for it as a piece of fiction or to challenge with incontrovertible evidence of my own the reigning opinion that it was a late commercial product of little literary value. It is rather my plea that we should give credit where due to the several authors responsible for shaping the Liangshan legend into its present form. If the shorter text were substantially the version that Lo Kuan-chung wrote, then it should be given more serious critical attention than scholars have been willing to give it. For, in approaching a work of multiple authorship like *The Water Margin,* the critical tendency has been simply to regard it as a folk novel that has embodied the inventive genius and noble aspirations of the Chinese people. First of all, however, even the professional storytellers who shaped the Liangshan legend were not quite identical with the people. Like all commercial entertainers, the storytellers had to consult the wishes of their audience, but not to the point of entirely abdicating their creative responsibility. The Liangshan legend certainly would not have arisen except for the fact that the people had shown an initial interest in the events upon which it is based, and its further development certainly reflected the taste and education of the people. But once certain characters and episodes had caught the popular fancy, it would have been the prerogative of the storytellers to delineate them fully, and one may suppose that, as the repertoire was handed down from master storyteller to apprentice, such characters and episodes received further professional elaboration. In *The Water Margin* as we now have it, we can see the curious contrast between the professional polish of several well-developed sagas and the recurrence of certain themes and situations that seem to have resulted from the storytellers' compliance with the public's inveterate demand for the familiar and stereotyped.

In the absence of a primitive version of the novel, of course, we cannot even tell how inventive Lo Kuan-chung was in adapting the promptbooks. It is reasonable to assume that, in compiling the earlier sagas of Lu Chih-shen, Lin Ch'ung, and Wu Sung, he took pains to make them more vivid and memorable but that he soon bogged down in the unpromising material he had to work with and contented himself with a more perfunctory job of adaptation. If the Lo Kuan-chung version is at all identifiable with the 115-chapter edition, then the role of the compiler of the 100-chapter version can be easily ascertained. He has not only recast the novel in a more colloquial language and enlarged its narrative; he has also accentuated the notes of savagery and sadism in scenes of vengeful killing.

By the time the 100-chapter edition was published, the people had ceased to be a decisive influence on the evolution of the novel. Instead, commercial publishers brazenly added to it new episodes designed to exploit the public's appetite for stories of the band. This commercial phase of expansion came to an end when, as already noted, Chin Sheng-t'an put out his 70-chapter edition with subtle changes in the text to improve its style and underscore his personal dislike for the rebel leader Sung Chiang. The public was pleased with his version, and all other editions rapidly disappeared.

Even though in recent years *San kuo* has received serious attention as a major Chinese novel, the prevalent critical opinion would still rank it below *Shui hu*. Yet, precisely because it is a compilation of history, *San kuo* is indubitably a work greater in conception, design, and narrative interest. For the major historical novels like *San kuo* and *Sui T'ang yen-i* (The romance of Sui and T'ang—in its original form, it was also the work of Lo Kuan-chung),[15] history itself has supplied an intriguing variety of characters and episodes. With their little developed sense of fictional realism, the romancers when departing from history tended to borrow stereotyped plots from the professional storytellers and could not be half as successful. As a romance that grew under the dominance of the *yen-i* type of historical chronicle, *Shui hu* was an anomaly. It could have become the first full-bodied nonhistorical novel, a genuine attempt at large-scale mythmaking; yet, after its initial successful sallies in the direction of picaresque fiction, it settles down as a historical novel, necessarily to its disadvantage. Whereas *San kuo* and *Sui T'ang* depict two of the most colorful periods in Chinese history, *Shui hu* suffers from extreme historical undernourishment. With the possible exception of Yang Chih, none of Sung Chiang's followers has been mentioned by name in reliable historical sources, and even the rebel leader himself merits only a few bald entries. In catering to the public interest in the Liangshan legend, the professional storytellers had to devise the kind of incident that could suggest the weightiness of the events of history. And they were unequal to the task.

The storytellers treated the legend, then, as if it had mattered as history, as if Sung Chiang and his band could have offered a real alternative to the corrupt regime of Hui-tsung. For one thing, the band is conspicuous for the number of heroes either patterned after or supposedly descended from illustrious personages in history or legend. Thus Ch'ai Chin is a descendant of Ch'ai Jung, Emperor Shih-tsung of the Later Chou dynasty, under whom the future founder of the Sung dynasty rose in power and popularity; Yang Chih is a scion of the Yang family of generals famed in early Sung history; and Hu-yen Cho carries forward the proud martial tradition of Hu-yen Tsan, another famed Sung general.[16] Two heroes are patterned after Kuan Yü: Kuan Sheng, who resembles his ancestor in features, disposition, and prowess, and another look-alike, the beautiful-bearded Chu T'ung. One could easily imagine how this process of imitation came about. Pressed for interesting and easily identifiable characters to fill out the destined number of heroes, the storytellers, to enhance the popularity of their own cycle of stories, ascribed to many the family names and features of beloved heroes in history and fiction.

The presence of these imitation-generals is but one reason why, as the novel progresses, it becomes increasingly preoccupied with large-scale military campaigns. The reciters of the Liangshan legend were competing in their own game with their rival specialists in the histories of the Three Kingdoms, Sui and T'ang, and the Five Dynasties. But with all their partiality for a particular hero or a particular dynastic house, the latter storytellers could not openly flout history to make either invincible. Even without the transforming genius of Lo Kuan-chung, the story of the Three Kingdoms as popularly retold could not have so idealized the Shu leaders as to make them win every battle. With all his military genius, Chu-ko Liang could not easily prevail when his generals were mediocre, and he had to die of exhaustion after a series of expeditions against Wei had ended in a stalemate. But the nonhistorical heroes of the Liang-shan band were free from this handicap, and, to the delight of a partial public, the storytellers and later the continuators of the legend depicted them as victors in every military encounter. The last third of *The Water Margin,* especially the interpolated material provided by publishers cashing in on the popularity of the 100-chapter edition, is mostly embarrassing pseudo history, but even in the first two thirds this tendency toward pseudo history becomes increasingly pronounced as the story advances.[17] Logically, by chapter 82, at the moment of his surrender to the emperor, it is Sung Chiang, more than any aspirant to the Chinese throne, who is in an uncontested position to take over the empire. He has defeated the finest generals of the nation and forced them to join him at the lair, he has made friends with the few upright ministers remaining at court, and, without any show of effort, he has repeatedly routed and could have easily annihilated the imperial forces under the command of the evil ministers T'ung Kuan and Kao Ch'iu. He does capture Kao Ch'iu, the band's archenemy, but he proceeds to treat him as an honored guest and even sends him off with magnificent gifts in the hope that he may intercede with the emperor for the band's honorable surrender. To talk of surrender when, by all indications, the sympathy of the storytellers has earned for Sung Chiang the mandate of heaven—there could have been no parallel situation in the annals of Chinese history.

The band has to surrender because the storytellers are bound to the fact that, in all matters touching the fate of the dynasty, it really matters little. So in the original Lo version, after their surrender the heroes depart from the capital to lead the expedition against Fang La; in the expanded versions they are first sent on three other expeditions so as to prolong their reign of glory in the battlefield while they remain political ciphers at court. The note of realism returns as a great many heroes die in their expedition against Fang La, and the novel triumphantly ends on an elegiac note as the remaining leaders still in the loyal service of their emperor submit to treachery and death. But one wonders whether it is really worth while to have followed the band through all its interminable campaigns only to be finally rewarded with a touching scene in the last chapter. In its bare episodes concerning Hui-tsung and Ch'in-tsung in captivity, the brief chronicle *Hsüan-ho i-shih* has captured the elegiac note much more successfully with far less fuss and bustle. In the absence of a fully self-conscious tradition of literary realism, the chronicler has every advantage over the fictionist.

I have isolated the deplorable features of the novel—its pseudo-historical design and the military emphasis of its implausible plot —so as to define more sharply the considerable achievement of the "fictional" portion of the work. This consists largely of stories of individual heroes that have no pretension to being "history." Though 108 heroes are identified by name, those that really count as presences in the novel are, in the order of their appearance, Lu Chih-shen, Lin Ch'ung, Yang Chih, Sung Chiang, Wu Sung, Li K'uei, Shih Hsiu, and Yen Ch'ing. And the truly great creations among these are Lu Chih-shen, Wu Sung, Li K'uei, and possibly Lin Ch'ung. With the prominent exception of Sung Chiang and Li K'uei, most of the heroes are memorable only for their pre-Liang-shan career. Once they join the band, they tend to lose their identity and become less distinguishable from one another in their uniform capacity as military commanders. One commander, the "Featherless Arrow" Chang Ch'ing, is indeed accorded a great deal of romantic attention but he remains nevertheless a storybook hero.[18] Before they become merged in the stream of pseudo history, the more memorable heroes inhabit by and large a picaresque world of military officers and yamen officials, merchants and innkeepers, thieves and prostitutes, Buddhist monks and Taoist priests, who constitute a far more diversified and vibrant human landscape than the world of *The Three Kingdoms*. It is this bustling and often savage world that gives *The Water Margin* its distinctive aura of human truth.

In this world of endless adventure, the dominant symbol is the road upon which the heroes are forever traveling, and the symbol next in importance is the inn where they stop to regale themselves on wine and meat. To the beginning reader, the heroes are at times indistinguishable from the villains in their equal proneness to violence. But a hero (*hao han,* good fellow) can always tell his kind from the bad fellows because of the latter's failure to observe the hero's code. According to this code, a hero has to be honorable, though the concept of honor is not defined in the traditional Confucian manner. Filial piety is indeed stressed in the case of several heroes, particularly Sung Chiang, Li K'uei, and Kung-sun Sheng, and loyalty to the emperor is always affirmed even though two or three violent souls are against the idea. But the code departs from Confucian teaching in its observance of the other basic human ties. It pays little attention to the conjugal relationship so long as a wife is presumed faithful (any suspicion of adultery or any threat to her honor, however, would call for heroic action), and it exalts the ideal of friendship to the point of usurping the language of brotherhood. This ideal not only endorses the Confucian saying often invoked in the book, "Within the four seas all men are brothers," but encourages the practice of knight-errantry insofar as it is preferable to execute justice by one's own hand rather than through the official channels.

Though the heroic code endorses every Confucian virtue, it actually abolishes finer ethical distinctions by insisting that one must above all follow the dictates of friendship or *i*. In the novel, therefore, the reader finds few heroes in a state of dilemma over the conflicting goods between which they have to choose. When Ch'ao Kai is about to be arrested for his theft of birthday presents intended for Grand Preceptor Ts'ai Ching, Sung Chiang, a yamen officer assigned the duty of arresting him, warns him instead.[19] Though he thereby incurs the charges of disobedience to his superior and disloyalty to the emperor and also filial impiety (since his father will be implicated in his crime), he doesn't hesitate at all because his duty to his friend comes first. To cite a different case, Yang Hsiung temporarily distrusts his friend Shih Hsiu after his licentious wife, P'an Ch'iao-yün, has maligned him. But when Shih Hsiu disproves P'an's allegation and produces evidence of her adultery with a monk, Yang Hsiung kills her in a most brutal manner not only to punish her wickedness but also to cement his bond with Shih Hsiu in a blood ritual.[20] It is his way of asking his friend's forgiveness for having momentarily questioned his honor. The heroic code enjoins a certain kind of altruistic love but, in its disregard of the laws and bonds of society, in practice it encourages a gang morality which is the reverse of altruism.

Moreover, friendship is not lightly bestowed, despite the injunction that all men are brothers. The existence of an unwritten code implies that members of the heroic community are able to spot one another by unmistakable signs of behavior. A hero, if he doesn't excel in gymnastics or the use of some weapon, is usually fond of these arts, or else he is in possession of some cunning or skill or magic lore which makes him a valuable member of the community. But, since nearly all bad fellows covet these arts, the good fellows must also be distinguished by their generosity, that is, their readiness to befriend and protect all potential members of the heroic community. Chang Ts'ing the "Vegetable Gardener" and his wife run a black inn and make a regular business out of butchering their guests and stealing their property. But they are qualified for the community because they make an exception of the underworld of convicts, monks, prostitutes, and so forth. At the other extreme, Ch'ai Chin, the scion of an emperor, though he is not so proficient in the military arts, regularly hides convicts and entertains all kinds of heroes at his home, and his fame spreads far and wide. Though not a wealthy patrician, Sung Chiang is above all known for his generosity so that, even in the worst of straits at a strange place, just to reveal his identity is to elicit homage from the members of the heroic community around him and to effect his rescue.[21] Members of the underworld who show a miserly temper are disqualified from the community. During his peregrination, Lu Chih-shen, who prides himself on his generosity though he seldom pays for his meals, is displeased with several minor heroes for their miserliness. These eventually join the Liangshan band, but they remain just names to fill the required number of lesser heroes.

Another, and perhaps even more crucial, test for a hero is that he should be above sexual temptation. Most members of the Liangshan band are bachelors, and as for the married heroes the conjugal aspect of their life is rarely mentioned unless they are brought to trouble through their wives. It is said of Yang Hsiung and Lu Chün-i that they practice gymnastics so strenuously that they leave their wives completely in the cold. Out of charity, Sung Chiang has bought a girl named Yen P'o-hsi, but he visits her with the greatest reluctance. Even so, to Li K'uei, the rude hero par excellence, his affair with Yen P'o-hsi is a mark against him, as is his secret trip to the capital to visit the reigning courtesan Li Shih-shih. For the gymnastically minded, sexual abstinence was probably at first regarded as a health measure, but by the time the Liangshan legend was being formed, it had become a cardinal article of the code. Since not too many of the heroes are rich enough to be openhanded and since all of them could commit murder, theft, and arson without incurring any disapprobation from their fellows, sexual abstinence becomes their only test of spiritual strength. The only hero openly censured and ridiculed by his comrades at Liangshan is the thwarted lecher, Wang Ying, who is eventually matched to a female warrior.[22] (Such amazons are "heroes" in their own right and are no longer viewed as objects of male hostility.) To set them apart from the good heroes, the bad rebel leaders T'ien Hu, Wang Ch'ing, and Fang La along with many lesser villains are depicted as men given to debauchery. Wu Sung and Lu Chih-shen are often moved to murderous wrath when seeing disreputable Taoist or Buddhist priests in the compromising company of young women. Li K'uei abhors the very sight of pretty girls. Once, while dining with Sung Chiang in a restaurant, he is so enraged by the officious presence of a singer that with one push he reduces her to a state of total unconsciousness.[23]

In most societies sexual puritanism is usually accompanied by an equally strong injunction against indulgence in food and liquor. In *The Water Margin,* however, the heroes compensate for their sexual abstinence by their gross delight in meat and wine. The strongest heroes, while impervious to female charm, are also the greatest eaters and drinkers: Wu Sung, Lu Chih-shen, and Li K'uei. To Western readers brought up on such comic classics as *Gargantua and Pantagruel* and *Tom Jones,* which oppose sensuality to the hypocrisies of civilization, the depiction of rude humanity heartily indulging its appetite (even if in the context of a sexual puritanism) should perhaps prove the most endearing trait of the Chinese novel. At its best, *Shui hu* does provide the comedy of animal exuberance, in contrast to much of its action which is merely violent without the saving grace of laughter. The best comic scenes involve Lu Chih-shen, once a military officer, now living in hiding as a monk on Mount Wu-t'ai. A man of matchless strength and huge appetite, he is now constrained to live on a vegetarian diet under strict monastic discipline. Inevitably he comes down the mountain for heartier fare. On his second such trip, he stops by a blacksmith's place to order an iron staff made to his specifications and then goes in search of wine. After being refused service at several places, he finally spies a more friendly tavern:

Chih-shen went to the inn and chose a seat close to the window. Then he called out, "Wine seller, a bowl of wine for a passing monk." The innkeeper scanned him, saying, "Priest, where are you from?" Chih-shen replied, "I am a wandering monk just passing through here and I want to order a bowl of wine." The innkeeper said, "Priest, if you are a resident monk at the temple on Mount Wu-t'ai, I won't dare serve you wine." Chih-shen said, "I am not. Get my order quick." Seeing that he certainly didn't look or talk like the monks around here, the innkeeper was reassured and asked, "How much wine would you have me draw?" "Don't ask how much," Chih-shen said, "just get me a big bowl and keep on filling it."

After he had had about ten bowls, Chih-shen asked, "What kinds of meat do you have? Bring me a plateful." The innkeeper replied, "I had some beef, but it was all sold." Suddenly smelling meat, Chih-shen got up and looked the place over and saw by the wall an earthenware pot in which a dog was cooking. "So you have got dogmeat," said Chih-shen, "why didn't you serve me that?" The innkeeper replied, "I was afraid monks like you wouldn't touch dogmeat. So I didn't ask." "I've got silver for you," said Chih-shen as he handed some silver to the innkeeper, "and let me have half of that dog." The innkeeper fetched half of the dog along with a plate of leek sauce and in no time placed them before Chih-shen. Overjoyed, Chih-shen tore the meat with his hands, dipped it in the leek sauce, and started to eat. As he chewed away, he downed another dozen bowls of wine.

The wine tasted so good going down his throat that he kept asking for more. The astounded innkeeper finally protested in a loud voice, "Priest, you've had about enough." Chih-shen popped his eyes and said in anger, "I'm not eating anything without paying for it. It's none of your business how much I should drink." The innkeeper asked, "How much more?" "Bring me another bucket," said Chih-shen. The inn-keeper dared not disobey and brought him another bucketful. In no time at all this bucket was also consumed and there was left on the table only a dog's leg. Chih-shen thrust this in his bosom, and as he was leaving the place, he said, "Keep the change. I'll come back tomorrow to eat another meal on that." The innkeeper was too dumfounded to know how to answer. He saw, however, that the monk was taking the path that would lead to Mount Wu-t'ai.

Chih-shen walked halfway up the mountain and then took a brief rest in a pavilion. As he sat there, however, he felt the wine coming up. He leaped up and said to himself, "For a long while I haven't done any posture boxing. No wonder my body is getting tired. Let me try a few rounds now." He stepped out of the pavilion, held his sleeves in his hands, and thus up and down, right and left, he exercised his limbs. After a while, his strength rose, and as he flung out one arm, it struck a pillar of the pavilion. Hearing a loud crash, he saw that he had felled the pillar and one half of the roof had collapsed.

The gatekeepers at the temple heard this noise from halfway down the mountain. Looking down from above, they saw that Lu Chih-shen was fast ascending the mountain even though his steps were none too steady. The two gatekeepers cried out, "My heavens, this beast is once again dead drunk!" They then closed the gate and drew the bar across it. Through a crack they saw that Chih-shen was rushing up and almost at the gate.

When he found the gate barred, he knocked with his fists as if he were beating a drum. How could the gatekeepers dare open the gate! After knocking for a while, Chih-shen turned around and saw at his left the statue of a temple guardian and shouted at it, "You big idiot, you should be knocking the gate for me—why are you raising your fists instead to scare me? I am not easily scared." He leaped on the platform where the statue stood and pulled up the palings about it as if they were stalks of leek. He took up one of the broken staves and thrashed the legs of the idol until all the clay and paint rattled off. Seeing this, the gatekeepers cried "Woe!" and could only leave their post to report to the abbot.

Chih-shen paused for a while and then turned around and saw the temple guardian at his right. "You rascal with your mouth wide open," he shouted, "how dare you laugh at me!" So he leaped on its platform and thrashed its legs twice. Right away there was a big crash: the idol had fallen from the platform. Chih-shen stood there with the broken staff in his hand and guffawed. . . .

Chih-shen shouted aloud from outside, "You baldpated asses, if you don't let me in, I'll start a fire and burn down this damned temple." Hearing this, the monks could only ask the gatekeepers to draw back the bar and let the beast in. They thought he would really do it if the gate stayed shut. The gatekeepers tiptoed to the gate, and, as soon as they had drawn back the bar, they flew to their room to hide themselves. The rest of the monks also ran and hid.

Lu Chih-shen was pushing his hands against the gate with all his might, and, when the gate opened, he fell flat on his face. He scrambled up, rubbed his head, and dashed straight into the meditation hall. The *ch'an* monks there were all sitting in meditation, and when they saw Chih-shen pull away the curtains and plunge into the hall, they were all frightened and bowed their heads. Chih-shen was now by the edge of the meditation platform, and the wine was rising to his throat. So he leaned over and vomited all over the platform. Unable to stand the stink, the monks muttered "My goodness!" and then covered their mouths and noses with their hands. After vomiting for a while, Chih-shen climbed up the platform and, in his hurry to loosen the belt, tore the sashes on his robe. The dog's leg fell out. Chih-shen said, "Excellent—I'm just getting hungry." So he picked up the leg and began to gnaw it. Seeing this, all the monks covered their faces with their sleeves. And the two monks sitting closest to him even tried to move away from him. Seeing their attempt, Chih-shen tore off a piece of dog meat and stared at the monk on his right, saying, "You also taste some." That monk only hid his face deeper in his sleeves. "You don't want any, eh?" said Chih-shen. Then he turned and stuffed the meat into the mouth of the monk sitting on his left. That monk couldn't dodge; even as he was trying to get down from the platform, Chih-shen pulled him back by the ear and kept stuffing meat into him. Four or five monks sitting opposite him on the platform bounded over and begged him not to torment the other monk so. Chih-shen now dropped the dog's leg and raised his fists and directed his blows on the shining pates of these monks. The rest of the monks in the hall all raised an outcry. Prepared to leave the place, they scampered to their cabinets to get out their cassocks and begging bowls. Among storytellers, this riotous episode is called "Panic in the Hall." [24]

In his hearty enjoyment of wine and dogmeat, in his drunken rage against the plastered idols, and in his torture of the monks with his proffered meat, Lu Chih-shen appears as the embodiment of exuberant energy completely at the service of robust comedy. Placed in the palpable context of overexaggeration, the Friar John of *Gargantua and Pantagruel* never reaches the same pinnacle of elemental glory.

I have so far characterized the heroes by reference to their code: their sense of brotherhood and camaraderie, their love of the gymnastic arts, their generosity, their sexual puritanism, and their hearty appetite for food and wine. Anyone at all familiar with the textbook accounts of *The Water Margin* would also expect some mention of their antigovernment stand and revolutionary ambition. But, even though a few violent souls articulate this feeling, an antigovernment attitude is not required of the hero. After repeatedly routing the government forces, the Liangshan band insists on honorable surrender and goes on to fight the enemies of the state, and in many novels patterned after *Shui hu* the heroes actively work for the government without ever going through the rebellious phase. Though they do not fully live up to the code, many prominent members of the band were initially commanding officers charged with the task of subduing the Liangshan rebels, and their primary ambition, as with the heroes of *San kuo,* was to honor their family name and achieve fame in the service of the state. Some plebeian heroes, prominently the Juan brothers, voice the discontent of the people under government oppression, and their speeches and songs are often arbitrarily cited by critics as expressive of the book's theme.[25] But, generally, though the heroes are against bad officials as they are against all evil and unjust men, they are incapable of the kind of abstract hatred that motivates revolution. The proverbial expression "Forced to climb Liangshan" is usually taken to mean that the heroes, suffering extreme persecution by officials, are compelled to turn to Liang-shan-po as their last refuge. Yet with the prominent exception of Lin Ch'ung, a military coach relentlessly hounded by Kao Ch'iu, few heroes fit that description. The majority of the minor heroes join voluntarily, attracted by Sung Chiang's name and the greater security the lair affords. Most of them are already men of the underworld, if not bandits and robbers; the initial misfortune or injustice which has led them to embrace an underworld career is sometimes briefly mentioned but never emphasized. Far from being the victims of government persecution, the prominent cases of conversion—military commanders, petty officers, and leading citizens —nearly always submit to the band's pressure with the greatest reluctance.

So far as the antigovernment theme is concerned, then, we have to make an all-important distinction between individual heroes and the band as a whole. Whereas the individual heroes are governed by the heroic code, the band follows a gang morality which is only a caricature of that code. The heroes of individual sagas—Lu Chih-shen, Lin Ch'ung, Wu Sung, and even Sung Chiang—are all men of honor. If they are unjustly persecuted, they cope with that injustice with courage and dignity and, in doing so, define their manhood. But, right after the sagas of Wang Chin, Shih Chin, Lu Chih-shen, and Lin Ch'ung, we are introduced to a major episode which glorifies deceit and cunning. In this episode, assisted by a minor hero, seven adventurers, who form the nucleus of the Liangshan band, cleverly intercept a shipment of birthday presents sent by an official to Ts'ai Ching. Granted that the latter is one of the four evil ministers at court and that these valuables represent wealth unjustly exacted from the people, the point nevertheless is that the heroes of the earlier chapters would have scorned to participate in the plot because they would have been ashamed to yield to greed. But Wu Yung, Ch'ao Kai, the Juan brothers, and the other plotters see nothing wrong in turning outlaws so as to possess these presents. Moreover, their scheme does not call for personal valor and strength; it is careful teamwork directed by the "Star of Wisdom" Wu Yung and successfully carried out to the last detail.

Whereas the individual heroes are reckless of personal safety in their pursuit of vengeance and glory, the seven plotters, once they have captured the Liangshan lair, are primarily concerned with group survival. Until the predestined number of heroes is assembled, the growing band attends mainly to the practical problem of conserving and increasing its strength despite its boast that it will carry out the will of heaven by removing evil ministers at court. As a history of the Liangshan band, therefore, the novel in its standard 70-chapter form is mainly concerned with two things: recruitment and aggression.

To recruit its heroes, the band often resorts to the most diabolic tactics. The first victim of such tactics is the military commander Ch'in Ming. Coveting his usefulness as a fierce warrior, Sung Chiang adopts a stratagem whereby Ch'in Ming will be denounced by the government as a traitor and his family punished with death. Now a captive guest in Sung Chiang's power, the explosive-tempered commander listens to his apology and bows before the inevitable:

Having heard him, Ch'in Ming became very angry and wanted to fight to the death with Sung Chiang and his group. But then he thought that the stars were destined to meet in fellowship, that he was now their prisoner though treated with respect, and that he could not overcome them alone. For these reasons he suppressed his anger and said, "It is kind of you brothers to want me to stay with you, but you have treated me most cruelly. You have caused the death of my wife and children." [26]

The passage is of curious interest as a lame attempt by the shapers of the Liangshan legend to reconcile the claims of personal honor and the higher dictates of gang unity. One wonders how Wu Sung or Lu Chih-shen would have reacted under the same circumstances. Rather cynically, Sung Chiang immediately arranges a new match for Ch'in Ming to compensate for the loss of his wife.

Another victim of such shocking tactics is Chu T'ung, Sung Chiang's onetime yamen colleague, who all along has been most friendly with the band. He is now exiled to the city of Ts'ang-chou for the crime of having enabled a prisoner to join the band, but for himself he prefers the humiliation of a convict's exile to the dishonor of joining his outlaw friends. He is doing rather well at Ts'ang-chou; the local magistrate likes him and often entrusts him with the care of his four-year-old son. But the Liangshan leaders will not be satisfied until he becomes one of their own. So Li K'uei and two others are dispatched to Ts'ang-chou with the sole purpose of implicating him in a flagrant crime and thereby ensuring his surrender. Li K'uei kidnaps the magistrate's son while he is in Chu T'ung's charge, splits his skull, and abandons his body in a nearby grove. Notorious for his wanton killings, Li K'uei in the present instance is merely doing the bidding of the leaders, as he later claims when defending himself before the enraged Chu T'ung. The latter shows greater indignation over the murder of the child than Ch'in Ming shows over the slaughter of his family, but he too submits under pressure.[27]

Along with recruiting heroes, the band is concurrently engaged in acts of military aggression. While it is often impelled to attack cities either to rescue trapped comrades or to obtain needed provisions, its systematic annihilation of two villages, Chu-chia-chuang and Tseng-t'ou-shih, can only speak for its sadistic rapacity.[28] These villages are militant homesteads not unlike those from which the band has recruited such heroes as the K'ung brothers. In their independence of spirit and in their cultivation of military arts so as to ensure freedom from government oppression, the inhabitants are not much different from the Liangshan band. Yet the latter hates their hostile independence and turns implacably against them over the most trivial issues. For each village, destruction is sure and complete. When the clan leader of Tseng-t'ou-shih, inconsolable over the death of two of his sons in their foredoomed resistance against the Liangshan troops, begs for peace, the latter, heeding the advice of Wu Yung, avail themselves of the opportunity to trap the whole clan and kill them all. The military coach Shih Wen-kung, who alone has managed to escape, is forthwith caught and then disemboweled for the crime of having fatally shot Ch'ao Kai with an arrow. This ritualistic vengeance is carried out even though Shih had shot him in line of duty rather than out of personal hatred.

When such episodes were first told in the market place, they were meant to be entertainment and the storytellers probably could see little difference between deeds of individual heroism and collective acts of sadistic punishment. The continued popularity of such stories to the present day, however, does speak for a peculiar insensibility to pain and cruelty on the part of the Chinese people in general. But, precisely because its celebration of sadism is largely unselfconscious, a modern reader can read the standard 70-chapter version of the novel (after the heroes have been gathered together, they become merely an efficient instrument of the government and lose their gang character) as a political fable which supports the paradoxical observation that, whereas official injustice is often the condition of individual heroism, the banding together of heroes frustrates that heroism and creates a reign of injustice and terror far more sinister than the regime of corrupt officials. It is the old story of an underground political party which, in fighting for its survival and expansion, becomes the opposite of what it professes to be. Seen in this light, the 70-chapter novel is a record of the triumph of gang morality over individual heroism.

In one basic respect, however, the individual heroes are not sharply distinguishable from the band: they share a common thirst for vengeance. While acts of individual vengeance are far more often dictated by considerations of honor than is the case with acts of collective vengeance, nevertheless the heroes could not have submitted to the will of the band and supported its vindictive campaigns against cities and villages had they not been already obsessed by that passion. According to his code, a hero cannot wait on the delay and caprice of the law and must take justice in his own hands if he feels that he himself or those dear to him are being wronged. Wu Sung is the prominent example of such a hero, and in the ten chapters devoted to his pre-Liangshan career we see many instances of his passionate retaliation against his or his friends' enemies. After his elder brother has been foully murdered by his adulterous wife, P'an Chin-lien, Wu Sung sacrifices her in a gruesome ritual and then slays her lover Hsi-men Ch'ing. He reports himself to the local magistrate and is sentenced to a term of imprisonment in a distant city. He has expected lighter punishment, but he submits to his sentence because he doesn't care what happens to him now that he has done the right thing for his dead brother. Later, as a convict at Meng-chou, he is befriended by an underworld boss named Shih En, and he avenges the latter's humiliation by thrashing his enemy, Chiang the "Gate God," with the utmost bravado. As a result, Wu Sung himself becomes an object of attempted murder by Chiang and his backers, Sheriff Chang and Commander Chang of the local garrison. After slaying four men suborned to kill him, Wu Sung becomes thoroughly infuriated and goes straightway to Commander Chang's house where, he is told, his three enemies are carousing over his presumed death. I must now quote a major portion of the subsequent scene of massacre because, like Lu Chih-shen's riot at the temple, it is one of the justly celebrated and most impressive scenes in the book:

Wu Sung heard all this [the self-congratulatory coversation of his three enemies], and the angry flame in his heart shot up thirty thousand feet, piercing the blue heaven. His dagger in his right hand and the five fingers of his left palm outstretched, he dashed into the hall. He saw that the hall was very bright with three or five lit candles and the moonlight pouring in through one or two windows and that the wine service was still on the table and had not been taken away.

Chiang the Gate God was sitting in an armchair, and when he saw Wu Sung he was so frightened that his heart and liver and his five entrails became, as it were, suspended in the ninth heaven. Words can hardly suggest the speed of what took place next: just as Chiang the Gate God was about to put up some defense, Wu Sung's dagger had already come down; it smote him right in the face and even the armchair met the blade and was overturned. Then Wu Sung turned around and swung his dagger in another direction. Commander Chang had barely time to get on his feet when the dagger fell and it slashed him below the ear and through the neck, and he collapsed on the floor. Both wounded men writhed in pain.

Now Sheriff Chang was after all a military officer; though drunk, he had still some strength left in him. Seeing that Wu Sung had already felled two, he knew he wouldn't be able to get away and he lifted up an armchair and plunged forward. Wu Sung grasped the chair and, taking advantage of its momentum, gave Sheriff Chang a push. Even if he were sober, he could not have withstood Wu Sung's great strength; but he was now drunk and down he fell on his back.

Wu Sung was right at him, and with one stroke of his dagger he cut off his head. Now Chiang the Gate God had gathered his strength and was getting up. But Wu Sung had already lifted his left foot, and he kicked him over and, holding him down with his foot, cut off his head. Then he turned around and cut off the head of Commander Chang also.

After this, seeing that there was still wine and meat on the table, he gulped down one goblet of wine and continued to drink until he had finished three or four more. Then he went to one of the dead bodies and cut a strip off his coat. He dipped it in blood and wrote with it eight big characters on the white plastered wall: "The slayer of these men is Tiger-killer Wu Sung." He then took the silver dishes and vessels from the table and stamped on them until they were all flat and he thrust several of them into his bosom.

He was on the point of going downstairs when he heard the voice of Lady Chang ordering the servants about, "The lords upstairs must all be drunken—let the two of you go up there to support them on their way down." No sooner was this said than two men started upstairs. Hiding himself by the staircase, Wu Sung saw that these two were

Commander Chang's personal attendants who had earlier arrested him. There in the darkness Wu Sung let them pass but blocked their exit. The two went into the hall, and, when they saw three corpses lying in blood, they were so frightened that they could only stare at each other and remain tongue-tied. It was as though the eight plates of their skulls had burst asunder and into each head a half bucket of icy water had been poured. Even as they were starting to leave, Wu Sung was at their backs. He lifted his dagger and straightway cut one down. The other one knelt down and pleaded for his life. But Wu Sung said, "I cannot let you go!" He seized him and also cut off his head. Verily blood splattered the gorgeous hall and corpses lay outstretched under the light of the candles.

Wu Sung now said, "Since I have begun, let me finish. I can only die once even if I kill a hundred." So he held his dagger and went downstairs. The lady was now asking, "What's all this commotion upstairs?" Wu Sung rushed to her room, and the lady, seeing a big tall man coming in, was puzzled as to who it could be. But Wu Sung's dagger was already upon her; it struck her right in the face and she fell in the front part of the room, crying for help. Wu Sung stepped on her and was about to cut off her head, but the blade wouldn't cut. Puzzled, Wu Sung examined the blade in the light of the moon and saw that its edge was turned. Wu Sung said, "No wonder I could not cut her head off."

Then swiftly he turned and went through the backdoor. He got his sword and threw away his broken dagger. And swiftly he was back at the downstairs hall. There was a light shining. The nurse Magnolia, who had once sung before Commander Chang, had two of his children with her, and she was holding her lamp in her hand and gazing at her dead mistress on the floor. She had barely cried out in alarm when Wu Sung thrust his sword into her chest. He stabbed the two children also; a stab to each and they were dead. Then he went out of the central hall and barred the front gates. Again he came in and found two or three women and he thrust the sword into them and killed them all. Wu Sung then said, "Now I am satisfied. It's time to leave." [29]

This orgy of murder is one of the most sharply visualized scenes in the novel. When describing a person or a landscape or even a routine combat between two warriors, Chinese novelists tend to adopt ready-made verse descriptions which, however interesting in themselves, are usually so conventional in character and so studded with clichés that they add little to one's visual knowledge of the scene concerned. Chin Sheng-t'an has actually tightened *Shui hu* by systematically deleting all such poetic passages from his edition. The best descriptions in *Shui hu* as in most other Chinese novels are therefore those of specific actions that cannot be given in conventional and generalized terms. In the present scene we are given an account of Wu Sung's actions interspersed with short turns of dialogue and bare descriptions of setting that for vivid immediacy invite comparison with the combat scenes in *The Iliad* and the Icelandic sagas. We follow the movement of Wu Sung's dagger as it smites someone right in the face and cuts into the armchair in which he is sitting, or as it slashes another below the ear and through the neck. Such graphic reports of detail are in the Homeric epic style rather than the florid romance style. Especially when Wu Sung pauses in the middle of his killings to drink several goblets of wine or finds the edge of his dagger too blunt to cut off a woman's head, we are being shown the art of realistic invention at its best. In terms of strict narrative economy, of getting on with the story, there is no need for the hero to drink the wine or replace the dagger: after slaying his three enemies, he could as well go straightway downstairs and kill the rest of the household with the same weapon. But it is precisely these seemingly superfluous details, long praised by Chinese commentators, that restore for us the actuality of the whole massacre. Never in *The Romance of the Three Kingdoms* and only rarely again in *The Water Margin* do we get comparable luxury of detail in reinforcement of strict realistic economy.

But if I am correct in surmising that the author of the 100-chapter edition has amplified the Lo Kuan-chung text to make it conform more closely to the style of oral storytelling, the present scene also provides instances of redaction that run counter to the art of visual realization. In many places the redactor has applied stock rhetorical phrases that merely encumber the narrative. Thus, when Chiang the Gate God first sees Wu Sung, we are told that he is so frightened that "his heart and liver and his five entrails became, as it were, suspended in the ninth heaven"—a conventional hyperbole that adds nothing to our actual apprehension of his fear. Again, the next sentence, "Words can hardly suggest the speed of what took place next" (literally, in Pearl Buck's rendition, "To tell it is slow but how swift it was in the doing!"),[30] is strictly a storyteller's cliché that could as well be omitted.

There is also evidence that the redactor has not thought out the entire scene clearly. We do not know where the three enemies are seated in relation to the table when Wu Sung first enters the hall: his attention is curiously arrested by the light in the room and the silver service (I have supplied the additional information "on the table"). We are also not too clear about the layout of the ground floor. Furthermore, in conformity with the style of oral storytelling, we are seldom given the exact number of things we are invited to see. In the Mandarin Duck Hall, there are three or five candles and one or two places where moonlight can pour in. Possibly, in his hurry to attack his enemies, Wu Sung cannot catch all these fine details, but he certainly could remember whether he has stabbed to death two or three women after he has finished off the nurse and the two children (how old are the children, and of what sex?). According to the later official tabulation, Wu Sung has killed altogether fifteen people and so he must have killed three rather than two women after he has killed the nurse and children. But a Chinese storyteller would naturally prefer the rhetorical imprecision of the phrase "two or three" to the verbal flatness of a precise numeral.

In the 115-chapter edition, after he has slain his three enemies, Wu Sung eats a big meal of wine and meats off the table. If this version is at all traceable to the Lo Kuan-chung version, then the redactor has improved the story considerably by omitting any reference to eating. Wu Sung would pause to drink, but it is unlikely that he would enjoy a meal at that particular juncture. But the redactor has retained the business of his stamping the silverware flat and putting it in his bosom. It is a stock situation in *Shui hu* that after killing people a hero would steal their valuables or else burn their house down, and for such heroes as Lu Chih-shen, a sly rogue despite his vaunted generosity, this is entirely in character. But from all his preceding adventures we would expect Wu Sung to be above this kind of petty thievery. To make him a thief is to demean his stature as an avenger going berserk under the excitement of killing. Rather thoughtlessly, however, the redactor has allowed this incident to stand and spoil our image of the hero.

Despite these blemishes, it must be said that, in elaborating upon a barer account of less precision, the redactor has taken considerable pains to render the scene more sharp and vivid even though he is not at all times driven by the urge for the perfect expression. The massacre at the Mandarin Duck Hall represents the climax in the career of a hero singled out for the most detailed attention, and it is at such moments that the storyteller or his redactor becomes more than usually conscious of his artistic responsibility. Though the 100-chapter edition of *Shui hu* was composed at a time when the Chinese novel could hardly be said to have attracted authors consciously striving for precision of statement, at his intermittent best the redactor was making progress in this direction.

If Lu Chih-shen appears as the incarnation of animal exuberance during his riot at the monastery, then Wu Sung the indiscriminate killer must be seen as the embodiment of a daemonic possession. But the latter condition, properly understood, should partake of the spirit of tragedy just as the former rightly breathes the air of comedy. In Greek tragedy, excessive heroism is as much deplored as excessive pride and ambition: Ajax among the cattle is a hero under a curse. It is a fundamental criticism of *Shui hu* that, with all his vengeance-sustained fury, Wu Sung is presented as a completely admirable character of simple heroism rather than as a man of some inner complexity whom we can love because our admiration for him is now tinged with pity. In *San kuo* the brave and honorable Kuan Yü is a tragic figure; in *Shui hu* the brave and honorable Wu Sung is denied that further dimension. In his massacre at the Mandarin Duck Hall, as in his dealings with his sister-in-law, we are given all the data from which we could reconstruct the case of an inner compulsion, but these data largely lie unused because the novelist— I use this term primarily as a collective reference to Lo Kuan-chung and the compiler of the 100-chapter edition—prefers to see him as a hero of the code.

Wu Sung remains a simple honorable character in a work pre-occupied with vengeance because the novelist sees no need to provide a moral and philosophical critique of that overruling passion. Granted that Wu Sung's daemonic fury is fully justifiable, the novel also depicts acts of revenge, undertaken in the spirit of cold-blooded hatred, that are less deserving of sympathy. The punishment meted out to Huang Wen-ping, for example, is bloodcurdling in its nonchalant sadism. Huang, an ambitious and zealous official, once informed against Sung Chiang and has earned the latter's undying hatred. Now Huang, stripped naked and bound to a tree, is a captive of the band; when Sung Chiang asks someone to perform the ritual of vengeance in front of all the heroes, Li K'uei volunteers with alacrity:

Then with his pointed knife he carved the flesh from the legs up. He picked out the good meat and, right before Huang Wen-ping's eyes, he broiled it on the coals and ate it with the wine. Thus carving and broiling, he had in no time stripped Huang Wen-ping to the bones. Only then did Li K'uei slit the chest open and take out the heart and liver. With these he made a broth for the chieftains to drink after their wine.[31]

Since the novelist unambiguously sides with the heroes in all their actions, we are supposed to endorse and admire Li K'uei's calculated cannibalism as much as Wu Sung's impetuous massacre.

In Chinese official history and dynastic novels, tortures and murders are of course a commonplace, but there the perpetrators of such sadism are nearly always implicitly condemned for their departure from the Confucian norms of behavior. As recorded by Ssu-ma Ch'ien, Empress Lü's mutilation of Lady Ch'i, her late husband Kao-tsu's favorite, is surely as shocking as Li K'uei's lynching of Huang Wen-ping:

Empress Lü later cut off Lady Ch'i's hands and feet, plucked out her eyes, burned her ears, gave her a potion to drink which made her dumb, and had her thrown into the privy, calling her the "human pig." After a few days, she sent for Emperor Hui and showed him the "human pig." Staring at her, he asked who the person was, and only then did he realize that it was Lady Ch'i. Thereupon he wept so bitterly that he grew ill and for over a year could not leave his bed. He sent a messenger to report to his mother, "No human being could have done such a deed as this! Since I am your son, I will never be fit to rule the empire." From this time on Emperor Hui gave himself up each day to drink and no longer took part in affairs of state, so that his illness grew worse.[32]

His objective description of the mutilation notwithstanding, in his depiction of her son's violent revulsion Ssu-ma Ch'ien has rendered his verdict on Empress Lü for all eternity. The *Records of the Grand Historian* affirms the cause of civilization; in its positive delight in all the savage acts of revenge so long as they are performed by the heroes, *The Water Margin* does not.

With all its affirmation of heroic ideals, its actual endorsement of savagery and sadism makes *The Water Margin* a document of disturbing significance for the cultural historian of China. To gain a better perspective, we may compare it with works of equal stature in another tradition. The Icelandic family sagas share with the Chinese novel a preoccupation with vengeance. Surely, the nearest European counterparts to Lin Ch'ung, Wu Sung, Shih Hsiu, and the like are such heroes of *Njal's Saga* as Gunnar, Skarp-Hedin, and Kari. Yet the traits that distinguish Lin Ch'ung from all his fellows —his forbearance and his refusal to kill until thoroughly aroused —are more commonly seen in the Icelandic heroes. Gunnar, like many Icelanders before him, goes to the high seas to seek adventure; to prove his mettle, he may kill as many Vikings as he wishes. But, once he settles down as a homesteader, he minds the peace and order of his land and does his best to avoid blood feuds. He kills only when grossly insulted or when ambushed by his enemies; for most disputes, he seeks legal settlement at the Althing. What impresses the reader of *Njal's Saga*, the *Laxdæla Saga*, and kindred works is the persistent efforts of men of good will to settle disputes, and the equally persistent efforts of men and women of ingrained malice to break the peace and provoke quarrels. The resultant scenes of combat are as explosively violent as anything in *Shui hu,* but the reader is never for a moment in doubt that the saga-writers stand for peace, order, and justice. Unlike the Chinese novel with its equivocal stand on justice and its childish enjoyment of mere violence, the best sagas depict with tragic irony man's perverse disposition to malice and aggression.

Between the sagas and *Shui hu* there is another fundamental difference—their respective attitudes toward the role of women in a dominantly virile society. Behind the blood feuds of *Njal's Saga* are the frustrated women who make specious appeals to their menfolk's sense of honor and provoke them to acts of murder. They are portrayed as devious schemers, implacable enemies, proud creatures who cannot brook the slightest insult. Njal, the man of peace, is powerless to prevent his wife from inciting his unmanageable sons. Gunnar has the misfortune of falling in love with Hallgerd, a dangerous vixen who has already caused the death of her two previous husbands; in marrying her, Gunnar gets involved in no end of trouble. When finally ambushed at his home, he appeals to her for some help; but she remembers that once he had slapped her face and so she refuses to render any assistance in his hour of mortal peril. Yet the saga-writers accept the treacherous and vengeful spirit of women as an unavoidable part of human life: they actually show a fascinated respect for their spirited willfulness. They give no evidence of being misogynists determined to "get even" with women. In *The Water Margin,* where the mischief of women is actually far more limited in scope, one notices on the contrary a pronounced streak of misogyny. Hallgerd, the cause of so much unnecessary tragic contention, is permitted to live unmolested after Gunnar's death; in the Chinese novel, she could not have long survived her first husband.

The women in *The Water Margin* are punished not merely for their malice and treachery; in the last analysis, they are punished for being women, for being such helpless creatures of lust. A psychological chasm divides them from the self-disciplined heroes. Precisely because of their sexual puritanism, these heroes harbor a subconscious hatred of women as their worst enemy, as a teasing reminder of the unnaturalness of their heroic self-sufficiency. Whatever their additional crimes, the four major examples of female wickedness in the novel—the blackmailer Yen P'o-hsi, the husband-killer P'an Chin-lien, the slanderer P'an Ch'iao-yün, the informer-wife of Lu Chün-i—are all adulteresses discontented with their marital or captive lot. With them, deceit and cruelty are means to sexual fulfillment. And their nemeses, honorable heroes all, hate them for that itching after pleasure, that craving for life; they sacrifice them so that the heroic code may endure. A key scene will demonstrate the kind of misogynic sadism that is as much an expression of irrational vengeance as the earlier instanced torture of Huang Wen-ping. The present victim, P'an Ch'iao-yün, is trapped on top of an unfrequented hill by the two injured heroes, Yang Hsiung and Shih Hsiu:

Yang Hsiung said, "Brother, tear off the harlot's head ornaments and strip off her clothes. I'll then attend to her myself."

Shih Hsiu tore off the woman's head ornaments and stripped her of her clothes. Yang Hsiung then ripped two sashes off her skirt and bound her to a tree with these. . . .

Yang Hsiung then went forward, pulled out her tongue with his knife and with one stroke cut it off, to make sure that the woman couldn't make any noise. Pointing his finger at her, he now reviled her, "You cheap harlot, for a while I was almost deceived by your lies. You could have estranged me from my brother, and given time you would surely have killed me. It's better that I finish you off first. I am curious what kind of heart and liver and what kind of five entrails a woman like you would have. I want to have a look at them." With one stroke he slashed her open from above her heart down to her lower belly. He took out her heart, liver, and five entrails and hung them upon the pine tree. He then chopped the woman into seven parts and tied up her head ornaments and clothes into a bundle.[33]

Communist critics have invariably praised The Water Margin as a great revolutionary novel.[34] They are mistaken insofar as they conceive of the Liangshan band as the vanguard of a class-conscious peasant force striving for enlightened political and economic revolution. Among the major heroes of the novel, perhaps only Li K'uei can be called a peasant, though even he has long deserted his village to join the riffraff of the underworld. But since the novel does express a deep-seated popular discontent with the government and hatred for bad officials and ministers at court, this revolutionary sentiment must be seen as another expression of that dark compulsion for vengeance we have earlier discussed. On one hand, therefore, the novel consciously affirms the ideals of loyalty and justice and depicts the band as faithful servants of the throne whose devotion remains uncontested even in their temporary state of disaffection. On the other, several prominent heroes and the band itself must be seen as instruments of anarchy in their apparent delight in violence and sadism. Theirs is not so much the enlightened force for revolution as the unleashed energy of the unconscious which every civilization must hold in check if it is to survive. Li K'uei is the prime symbol of that dark force, just as his master and friend Sung Chiang is the prime symbol of Confucian service to the throne. In the subtle interactions of this inseparable pair exist the ideological tensions of the novel.

The character of Sung Chiang has always puzzled the Chinese. The great Ming critic Li Chih views him as an incarnation of loyalty and justice, but the even more influential commentator Chin Sheng-t'an sees in him nothing but a hypocrite and he accordingly introduces small changes in the text to make his hypocrisy more obvious.[35] A rebel leader capable of utter ruthlessness but forever mouthing the sentiments of loyalty and benevolence must always remain a somewhat baffling character, but in the total design of the work his role is much less ambiguous if seen in conjunction with that of Li K'uei. These two, in fact, constitute a double character, fully comparable to such famous Western pairs as Don Quixote and Sancho Panza, Prince Myshkin and Rogozhin, Prospero and Caliban. Quite apart from the active individual roles they play in the affairs of the band, the complementary characters of Sung Chiang and Li K'uei provide whatever thematic unity the novel achieves despite its contentment with an episodic and mechanically plotted narrative.

Right at their first meeting in chapter 38, Sung Chiang and Li K'uei take to each other. Li K'uei, who literally worships his new master, can be seen as a Caliban divested of his cunning and concupiscence but retaining in full measure his savagery and natural piety, and Sung Chiang, who appreciates his rude manhood and returns his love, is a less arrogant Prospero who readily acknowledges his kinship with the savage. But, aside from their instinctive friendship, these two are also complementary opposites in the political dimension. If Sung Chiang represents the rhetoric and honor of an enlightened rebel, Li K'uei is an anarchic rebel in the complete freedom of his innocence and savagery. As a shrewd leader conditioned by Confucian ideals, Sung Chiang can never openly avow the fun of being a rebel: the sheer delight in destruction and in taking over an empire. Li K'uei, who acknowledges these joys and presses upon his master the destiny of an emperor, is on the other hand too much of a savage to want the burdens and responsibilities of political ambition. For him, to win an empire is to perpetuate the delights of the Liangshan fellowship and to have fun on an even grander scale. Even before Sung Chiang has assumed the leadership of the band, Li K'uei advocates open rebellion:

With our great strength in troops and horses, we should overturn the government—what's there to be afraid of? Right now let Brother Ch'ao Kai assume the position of the big emperor of the Sung dynasty and Brother Sung Chiang that of the little emperor. Let Mr. Wu Yung be prime minister and Kung-sun Sheng be state counselor, and let the rest of us all become generals. Then we can attack the Eastern Capital and seize the damned throne and enjoy ourselves. Won't that be fun? Won't it be better than staying put in a stinking marsh? [36]

Later, Li K'uei repeatedly speaks out against Sung Chiang's policy of honorable surrender, and every time he infuriates his master. Suave and diplomatic, Sung Chiang is seldom angry, but when he rebukes Li K'uei, it is as if he were rebuking a part of himself whose existence he dares not openly acknowledge. When the policy is initially announced (in chapter 71), Wu Sung and Lu Chih-shen, who share something of Li K'uei's wildness, join him in protest. But it is Li K'uei who reacts most explosively:

Popping wide his queer-looking eyes, the Black Whirlwind yelled, "Amnesty, amnesty, who wants this damned amnesty!" With one kick, he hurled the table into space and it came down to smash into pieces. Sung Chiang also cried out in anger, "This black fellow is getting completely insolent! You guards take him to the execution ground and return with his head." [37]

Yet Sung Chiang immediately relents, and confesses, "He has been my greatest friend." As for Li K'uei, he doesn't mind dying at all: "You people were afraid that I would resist the order. But I won't complain if my brother wants me to die; I won't show any resentment even if he wants to hack me to pieces. Him I obey, though I am not even afraid of heaven." [38]

If Li K'uei speaks for Sung Chiang's suppressed desire to become emperor, there is the further irony that he also speaks for the latter's nostalgia for the simple fellowship at Liang-shan-po, for the Robin Hood type of pastoralism, when, following his course of honorable surrender, he has become increasingly vexed at the intrigues and plots hatched at court and designed to deprive him of his due honors as a loyal servant of the throne. As for Li K'uei, though he glories in the battlefield, he doesn't care at all for emoluments: he could as well enjoy himself carousing with his comrades or seeking new adventure on the road with a chosen companion. When Sung Chiang is once again disappointed in his hopes for imperial recognition following the successful completion of his campaign against Wang Ch'ing, Li K'uei nags him, speaking as his conscience: "Brother, it was really stupid of you. Formerly, when we were at Liang-shan-po, we never had to suffer indignity from anybody. It was you who day in and day out clamored for amnesty, and now that we have got our amnesty, we have got into all kinds of vexation. Since we brothers are all here, why don't we go back to Liang-shan-po and enjoy ourselves?"[39]

Though they are poles apart on the issue of service to the throne, both Sung Chiang and Li K'uei desire the removal from court of the four evil ministers: Ts'ai Ching, T'ung Kuan, Yang Chien, and Kao Ch'iu.[40] These four symbolize corruption and weakness in the national life, and, for the spokesman of loyal service as for the anarchic rebel, sound government cannot be restored without their ouster and punishment. But these four have the ear of the emperor throughout the novel and they foredoom any attempt by the band to become an effective force in the government. In the end, Hui-tsung the titular emperor can only commiserate with Sung Chiang the potential emperor, over their equal impotence before the power of the four. Li K'uei gets angry with both but can do little on his own initiative.

Probably out of consideration for his pitiful end as a captive of the Chin conquerors, the storytellers have always treated Hui-tsung with kindness and sympathy. They do not ignore the weakness of his regime but, by blaming mainly his evil ministers, they have not pressed the issue of his willful irresponsibility. In *Shui hu,* as in *Hsüan-ho i-shih,* he appears as a man of weak character not unin-clined toward good government. He is also the lover of Li Shih-shih. Since, as legend has it, the reigning courtesan, unlike many unprincipled ministers, eventually dies a patriotic martyr,[41] the emperor's liaison with her actually counts in his favor. In the novel, therefore, while Hui-tsung appears always at the mercy of the four ministers when at court, he is not unaware of the suffering of the people and not unsympathetic with the aims of the Liangshan band when he unburdens his soul in the privacy of the courtesan's chamber.

In chapter 72, while visiting the capital at the Lantern Festival season with a select number of his comrades, Sung Chiang seeks an interview with Li Shih-shih in the hope that she may act as his intermediary to negotiate the band's honorable surrender with the emperor. During the interview, Hui-tsung also arrives. But Sung Chiang is denied the opportunity to disclose his heart to either the courtesan or the emperor because, enraged at the proceedings, Li K'uei sets fire to the place and precipitates a riot at the capital. He has the further pleasure of throwing a chair at Yang Chien. But though the scene is all set for a major confrontation, the novelist soon shirks his task to introduce further bustling action.

It is not until the last chapter that Hui-tsung once again meets with Sung Chiang and Li K'uei while resting in the boudoir of Li Shih-shih. But by this time both heroes have been poisoned and they can meet the emperor only in a dream. The latter, who has had no knowledge of Sung Chiang's murder, is transported to Liang-shan-po, where he is startled to see the deceased members of the band all assembled before him. Sung Chiang enlightens him with a long memorial:

"Though we once resisted the imperial troops, fidelity and justice were our constant principles, and we never entertained the slightest thought of rebellion. After we received Your Majesty's command to submit, we first drove off the Liao, then subdued the three brigands, at a cost of eight out of ten of our brotherhood. Your Majesty ordered me to defend Ch'u-chou, and from the time I took up my duties I interfered neither with troops nor civilians, as heaven and earth can testify. When Your Majesty sent me a gift of poisoned wine with instructions to drink it, I went to my death without resentment. But I was afraid Li K'uei might harbor animosity and be led to struggles of revolt, so I sent a man to Jun-chou to summon him; then I brought about his death by giving him poisoned wine. Wu Yung and Hua Jung are also here out of fidelity and rectitude, having hung themselves at the site of my tomb. We four are buried here together at Liao-erh-wa, outside the south gate of Ch'u-chou. To show their sympathy, the people there have erected a temple before our graves. Now, even in death, we have not separated, but are here together making our statement to Your Majesty, one which reveals the thoughts we cherished throughout our lives, loyal from first to last. I pray Your Majesty to give it attention."

Greatly shocked at what he had heard, the emperor replied, "I myself dispatched the messenger and gave him the imperial wine under a yellow seal with my own hands. I wonder who could have exchanged it for the poisoned wine given you?"

"If Your Majesty were to inquire of the envoy you could learn how the treachery came about."

. . . . .

As the emperor left the hall, he turned back to look at the plaque above the door on which were inscribed the words, "Hall of Fidelity and Justice." Then, nodding, he descended the steps.

Suddenly Li K'uei emerged from behind Sung, a broadaxe in each hand. "Emperor, emperor!" he cried in a fierce voice, "Why did you believe the charges of those four rogues and put us to death unjustly? Now that we've met it's a good time to take revenge!"

With these words the "Black Whirlwind" rushed at the emperor brandishing his broadaxes. Startled, the emperor awoke with a jerk, for it was only a dream. But he was in a cold sweat. Glancing around, he found the candles flickering, and Li Shih-shih had not yet retired.[42]

Even as spirits, Sung Chiang and Li K'uei are strictly in character: one affirming his loyalty to the emperor and petitioning for posthumous honors and the other brandishing his axes at him to seek revenge. But whereas ghosts in Chinese nonhistorical fiction are often most effective agents of retribution, the spirits of the two heroes are forestalled by history from advancing their cause. Sung Chiang seeks the powerless Hui-tsung for mutual consolation, and Li K'uei can only threaten the latter with his phantom axes. The four ministers, of course, go unpunished, and with all the posthumous honors accorded the band, the novel ultimately records its pathetic defeat in their hands because it has never properly stood up to their evil.

In the end, therefore, Sung Chiang, Li K'uei, and Hui-tsung can only be considered creations of the popular imagination. In their own realm they have their legendary existence, but they cannot cope with the objective reality of an evil force. It is not just that the storytellers were too circumscribed by the facts of history to accord the Liangshan heroes a triumphant destiny; it is also possible that they were truly baffled by an evil beyond the solution of Confucian dedication and underworld chivalry. Except for Kao Ch'iu in some early episodes, the four ministers remain stock villains in the novel, but their malice and hatred take on a metaphysical reality as the heroes become increasingly frustrated in their design for recognition and achievement. The novel which begins on such a lusty note of virile confidence ends in sad disillusionment not untinged with a note of unworldly resignation. It is hard to imagine that Lu Chih-shen and Wu Sung, who early took on the garb of priesthood for pure convenience, could have ended as true devotees of their faith, but Lu Chih-shen dies an enlightened monk and Wu Sung, crippled by the loss of one arm, lives out his life in a Buddhist temple.[43] Dreams and mystical experiences now recur to compensate for the unfulfillment of the heroes' ambition. Li K'uei, who threatens to kill Hui-tsung in his last dream, has earlier dreamed (in chapter 93) that he has killed all four of the evil ministers. This long dream which projects the hero's lasting obsession in proper terms of fantasy is one of the most remarkable things in the last portion of the novel, and it is especially poignant for the sharp contrast it affords between dream-fulfillment and waking impotence. Even Li K'uei, the prime symbol of the dark energies of the unconscious, achieves his crowning success only in a dream:

Li K'uei hid his broadaxes and looked straight ahead. He saw far in the distance the emperor on the throne flanked on both sides by many officials. Most properly he prostrated himself three times before the throne, and then he thought, "Heavens, I guess I should have prostrated myself a fourth time." The Son of Heaven asked, "Why did you kill so many people just now?" Li K'uei answered on his knees, "These rascals tried to abduct a girl. I was carried away with anger and so killed them." The Son of Heaven said, "Li K'uei, your righteousness and bravery are deserving of commendation because, seeing injustice on the road, you were moved to exterminate a nest of rascals. I pronounce you not guilty and further appoint you a court-attendant general." Much pleased, Li K'uei said to himself, "My, the emperor is really smart and can tell right from wrong." He kowtowed a dozen times and got up to wait in attendance.

Not long after, he saw Ts'ai Ching, T'ung Kuan, Yang Chien, and Kao Ch'iu kneeling down in unison and memorializing the emperor: "Sung Chiang, though in command of an army to quell T'ien Hu, has loitered on his march and spent all his time drinking wine. May Your Majesty mete out to him just punishment." On hearing this, the fire of wrath in Li K'uei's bosom shot up thirty thousand feet and could no longer be contained. He lifted his two axes and dashed forward. With each stroke down went one head, and in no time he killed all four of them. He then shouted out, "Emperor, don't listen to the advice of those traitorous ministers. My brother Sung Chiang has captured in succession three cities. Now he stations his army in Kai-chou and is on the point of starting again. How could they lie so brazenly?" Seeing that he had killed four ministers, the civil and military officers all came forward to seize Li K'uei. Raising his two axes, Li K'uei warned, "Whoever dares to seize me will die like these four." They didn't dare make any move. Li K'uei laughed aloud, "Great, great! These four traitors finally got their due today. I'll go and tell Brother Sung." And with big strides he left the palace.[44]

When Sung Chiang is about to die, as his dream memorial to the emperor has informed us, he summons Li K'uei to his side and poisons him. He does this not simply out of loyalty to the emperor to forestall an act of vengeance which Li K'uei is bound to commit. It is out of his yearning for his dearest friend that he, much in the fashion of a despairing lover in Western and Japanese literature, enjoins upon Li K'uei a suicide pact. But in Chinese terms, this pact only reenacts the ritual at the peach orchard where Liu Pei, Kuan Yü, and Chang Fei pledged their desire to die on the same day even if they were not born in the same year. Though *The Water Margin* delights in cunning, deceit, savagery, and sadism, in the last chapter it, too, rises to a moment of true sublimity as it affirms the highest claims of *i* or selfless friendship. Li K'uei's response to Sung Chiang's request rings with the true eloquence of undying devotion: "Li K'uei, too, wept, as he replied, 'Enough, enough, enough! In life I served you, and in death I'll simply be an attendant-ghost in your command.' "[45]

CHAPTER IV

JOURNEY TO
THE WEST

As a work of comic fantasy, *Hsi yu chi* (Journey to the west) is readily accessible to the Western imagination, as witness the popularity of Arthur Waley's abridged version, *Monkey,* with the general public and especially with the college audience. But Waley has chosen to present only a few of the forty-odd adventures in the latter half of the book; translated in its entirety, the journey of the pilgrims may prove tiresome to the Western reader, as many of its episodes are repetitious in character, though invariably narrated with gusto. However, even if bored at times, he will find it a civilized and humane book and one, moreover, that meets his expectation of what a novel of comic adventure should be. Though, like *San kuo* and *Shui hu, Hsi yu chi* is crowded with characters and episodes, its design of a journey makes it inevitable that only the pilgrims are the objects of continual attention while the assorted gods, monsters, and human characters they meet on the road claim only secondary interest. And its author, Wu Ch'eng-en, though he also builds upon an earlier, simpler version of the story, proves his originality precisely in his subordination of story as such to the larger considerations of theme and character and in his firm comic portrayal of at least the main pilgrims—Tripitaka, Monkey, and Pigsy. The last two, especially, are fully as memorable as another pair of complementary characters famed in world literature—Don Quixote and Sancho Panza. As a satiric fantasy grounded in realistic observation and philosophical wisdom, *Hsi yu chi* does suggest *Don Quixote*—two works of comparable importance in the respective developments of Chinese and European fiction.

Ever since Hu Shih published his pioneer study of the novel in 1923,[1] the authorship of the 100-chapter *Hsi yu chi* has by general scholarly agreement been assigned to Wu Ch'eng-en (*ca.* 1506–82), a native of Shan-yang *hsien,* Huai-an *fu* (in present-day northern Kiangsu), enjoying a good reputation among his friends for wit and literary talent. None of the premodern editions of *Hsi yu chi,* however, bear his name as author or compiler, and Mr. Glen Dudbridge has recently questioned the slim documentary basis for this attribution.[2] But it is highly unlikely that anyone will come up with a stronger candidate, and all circumstantial evidence seems to indicate that Wu Ch'eng-en possessed the necessary leisure, incentive, and talent for the composition of this novel. A volume of classical poetry and prose left by Wu has been recently edited by Miss Liu Hsiu-yeh with a detailed chronological table of his life and valuable bibliographical information.[3]

If we agree with the general opinion that *Hsi yu chi* is the work of an individual author who adapts his sources in the Shakespearean fashion of exuberant invention (later I shall present recent views that challenge this opinion), then the 100-chapter novel as we now have it poses few perplexing problems as to its text and derivation. Its earliest extant edition is the Shih-te-t'ang edition of 1592, published only ten or eleven years after the author's death. It may not have been the earliest printed version, but it has undergone no serious revision except for the incorporation of the legend of Tripitaka's birth and youth in chapter 9, first introduced in an edition prepared during the K'ang-hsi period (1662–1722).[4] Subsequent editions, though they have added commentaries on its religious allegory, have introduced only minor stylistic changes, and the best modern edition of 1954 has restored the Shih-te-t'ang text wherever later emendations seem unjustified.[5] Unlike *Shui hu* with its many competing versions, *Hsi yu chi* has always retained the integrity of Wu Ch'eng-en's original text.

The novel has its historical basis in the epic pilgrimage of Hsüan-tsang to India. Also known by his honorific title Tripitaka or T'ang San-tsang, this saintly monk of great intellectual ability is a major figure in Chinese Buddhism. He traveled abroad for seventeen years (629–45) and brought back from India 657 Buddhist texts. Upon his return, he devoted the remainder of his life to translating these scriptures and establishing the abstruse Mere Ideation school of Chinese Buddhism.[6] His school was never too popular, but even during his lifetime his travels became a matter of public interest. Two accounts were written of them, one by Hsüan-tsang himself as told to his disciple Pien-chi and the other by the disciple Hui-li.[7] According to the latter source, Hsüan-tsang suffered many hardships during the earlier stages of his journey. After he had crossed the Chinese border, he once upset his water container and spilled the supply that was to sustain him until he was safely across the desert:

All around me was a vast expanse: no travelers or birds. At night there were glimmerings of monstrous fires, shining like stars; in the daytime the frightening winds hugged the sand and scattered it like rain. Even though I had met with this disaster, my heart was not afraid. My only worry was the lack of water because in my thirst I could not push on. For four nights and five days I had not a single drop to moisten my throat. My mouth and intestines became so parched that I was on the point of dying. I could not go on, and lay in the sand. But no matter how debilitated I was, I kept repeating the name of Kuan-yin in silence. I also prayed to the Bodhisattva, "This trip of Hsüan-tsang's is not undertaken for profit or fame; it is solely to seek the right law of the incomparable truth. I have always known that your mercy extends to all living things and that your task is to save them from distress. I am now in distress—have you not noticed it?" Thus praying, I kept my heart in a state of unceasing hope.

In the middle of the fifth night, a cool breeze suddenly brushed against me, so crisp and cold that I felt as if I were bathing in icy water. My eyes again could see and my horse could get up. With my body refreshed, I could now enjoy a little sleep. . . . Wakened from my slumber, I traveled on about ten li, and my horse suddenly took another path despite my attempt to change its direction. After a few more li, I saw several *mou* of green pasture, and I let my horse graze to its heart's content. Ten steps from the grass, following another turn, there was a pond whose water was sweet and clear like a mirror. I prostrated myself to drink it, and my life was restored.[8]

Hu Shih is right in believing that it is passages like this which fostered the growth of the Tripitaka legend: ever since the time of the poet Ch'ü Yuan, the Chinese imagination had invested the desert regions outside China proper with monsters and ogres.[9] One further notices in the passage Hsüan-tsang's invocation of the Bodhisattva Kuan-yin, who becomes in the novel the deity most actively concerned with the welfare of the pilgrims, rescuing them from straits in which even the might of Monkey proved to be of no avail.

As his legend grew with his fame, Hsüan-tsang became like the Liangshan heroes a popular subject for storytellers. There is extant a brief promptbook of seventeen chapters (the first chapter missing) dating from the Southern Sung period entitled *Ta-T'ang San-tsang ch'ü-ching shih-hua* (The tale, interspersed with verses, of the quest of scriptures by Tripitaka of the great T'ang dynasty). In it we can already see that Monkey has emerged as Hsüan-tsang's chief guardian on the road and that the adventures they encounter are fantastic in character—involving gods, demons, and bizarre kingdoms. In time the legend supplied material for plays of the Chin and Yuan period; a few of these have survived in fragments. By the turn of the Yuan and Ming dynasties, Yang Ching-hsien wrote a series of six plays in twenty-four acts known under the collective title of *Hsi-yu-chi tsa-chü*.[10] This extensive work indicates that by then the legend of the journey had not only taken a definite shape but had also grown considerably in size—most probably thanks to the work of elaboration carried on by the storytellers of the Yuan period. By the late Yuan period there must have existed a fuller version of the story recorded largely in the vernacular, which served Wu Ch'eng-en as his immediate model. Unfortunately, only two small fragments of this work, one surviving in an adapted form, are believed to be extant. Under the section on dreams in the *Yung-lo ta-tien,* a partially preserved encyclopaedic compilation dating from the Yung-lo period (1403–24), we have an entry of some 1,200 characters presumably taken from that version, telling of the slaying of a dragon king by the T'ang minister Wei Cheng. *Pak t'ongsa ǒnhae (P'u t'ung-shih yen-chieh)*, a Korean reader of colloquial Chinese first printed in 1423, contains an account, in some 1,100 characters, of the adventure in the Cart-Slow Kingdom, which was probably adapted from the same source.[11] These two episodes can be profitably compared with their fuller counterparts in Wu Ch'eng-en's novel. The following passage is translated from the fragment preserved in the Ming encyclopaedia:

The Dragon of the Ching River Slain in a Dream (*Hsi yu chi*)

To the southwest of Ch'ang-an there was a river called the Ching. In the thirteenth year of Chen-kuan two fishermen met by the riverside, one called Chang Shao and the other Li Ting. Chang Shao said to Li Ting, "Inside the West Gate of Ch'ang-an there is a fortuneteller's booth, and the fortuneteller is called the Recluse of Divine Prophecy. Every day I give him a carp, and he then tells me where to cast my nets. I catch fish every day by following his tips." Li Ting said, "Someday I will also consult this fortuneteller." While they were thus talking, who could suspect that a yaksha patrolling the river had overheard them? "I'll report this to the dragon king," he told himself.

This dragon king was called the Dragon of the Ching River, and he was at that time sitting on his throne in the Crystal Palace, facing the south. Suddenly the yaksha arrived and reported to him, "On the bank there were two fishermen. They were saying that inside the West Gate there was a fortuneteller who knew about what went on in the river. If they followed his instructions, they could exterminate all the watery tribes." Upon hearing this, the dragon king was greatly angered. He disguised himself as a scholar-commoner and went into the city.[12]

In adapting this portion of the tale, Wu Ch'eng-en has retained Chang Shao as a fisherman but made Li Ting into a woodcutter. Both are presented as lettered countrymen so that they can carry on a poetic debate about the relative advantages and disadvantages of their callings. A staple in the pastoral literature of the European Renaissance, such debates are not uncommon in Ming fiction. In *Feng-shen yen-i* (The investiture of the gods), a historical fantasy contemporaneous with *Hsi yu chi,* we find a fisherman and a woodcutter pointedly referring to their conversation as *yü-ch'iao wen-ta* (dialogue between fisherman and woodcutter).[13] Wu Ch'eng-en introduces his debate scene mainly to show off his poetic skill since it contains altogether ten *tz'u* poems to the tune of five airs, two seven-syllabic poems in the regular *lü-shih* style, and two long poems in the *p'ai-lü* style. While they are not of enough fictional interest to deserve translation, I must remark that, whereas the verse passages in *The Water Margin* are usually set pieces of conventional description, most of the poems and long poetic passages in *Hsi yu chi* show evidence of being specifically composed for the contexts and they are at once elegantly antithetical and concretely and very often humorously descriptive. On the basis of these numerous poetic pieces, Wu Ch'eng-en must be considered one of the most skilled descriptive poets in all Chinese literature. Certainly, few poets and *fu* writers before him have been so often called upon to celebrate the comic behavior of animals and the awesome grandeur of picturesque as well as grotesque scenery.

Following the friendly debate, the author has to turn to the main topic of conversation which is of fatal consequence for the dragon king. Since Li Ting is not a fellow fisherman, there is no special need for Chang Shao to confide his secret to him, certainly not after a long poetic debate. Notice, therefore, the adroitness with which Wu Ch'eng-en brings about this change of topic in the two friends' conversation:

Having recited their *tz'u* poems and composed matching stanzas of *shih* poetry, these two soon came to a parting of the ways and bowed to each other in token of farewell. Chang Shao said, "Brother Li, be very careful. When on a mountain, be sure to be always on the lookout for tigers. If anything happens, verily 'On the streets of tomorrow there will be a friend missing.' " Hearing this, Li Ting became furious. "You good-for-nothing," said he, "one is supposed to offer his own life when his best friend is in mortal danger. How could you curse me, then? If I got eaten by a tiger, then you would surely meet with a storm and get drowned in the river." Chang Shao said, "I'll never get drowned as long as I live." Li Ting said, "It is said 'The sky unpredictably lowers, and a man unexpectedly meets disaster or good fortune.' How can you be so sure?" Chang Shao replied, "Brother Li, even though you appear so confident, you are never assured of safety in your way of making a living. In my line I am always safe and I'll never meet with anything untoward." Li Ting asked, "You make your living on water, which is full of hazards. Everything is so uncertain. How can you say you are always safe?" Chang Shao said, "You don't know. On the West Gate Street of Ch'ang-an there is a soothsayer who tells fortune by means of the eight trigrams. Every day I present him with a golden carp and he tells me my fortune for the day. I cast my net at whatever location he tells me, and I always get a full load of fish. Today I went to him again, and he told me to cast my net to the east of the big bend of the Ching River and cast my line from the west bank. And I am sure to get a full load of fish and shrimp. Tomorrow I'll go into the city to sell the fish and invite you to have wine with me." The two then said goodbye to each other.[14]

What is apparent here is the author's gift for comedy, his effortless management of the scene so that Li Ting's angry retort follows Chang Shao's malicious banter, and the disclosure of the latter's secret follows his friend's incredulous prompting as a matter of course. The elaboration of the subsequent scene at the crystal palace is less distinguished, but it also has a comic verve lacking in the original:

Highly angered, the dragon king quickly seized his sword, intent on going into Ch'ang-an right away to destroy that soothsayer. But from the side emerged the dragon sons and grandsons, the shrimp courtiers and crab guards, the shad counselor, the perch and carp ministers, who entreated in unison: "Your Majesty, please pacify your anger. It is said, 'What one hears is not always true.' When you rush off like this, you will be trailed by clouds and attended by rain. You will surely frighten the populace of Ch'ang-an and in turn may even incur a reprimand from heaven. Your Majesty possesses the wondrous power of making yourself appear and disappear at will and transforming yourself in numberless ways. Why not transform yourself into a scholar and go into Ch'ang-an to make an investigation? If there is indeed such a soothsayer around, you will have ample time to destroy him; but if the report be untrue, wouldn't it be a pity to kill an innocent man?" The dragon king followed this advice. He did not take the sword along nor did he have the clouds and rain accompany him. When alighting on the riverbank, he shook himself once and was turned into a scholar-commoner.[15]

The evolution of the Tripitaka legend properly culminates in Wu Ch'eng-en's massive creation. But just as the 100-chapter edition of *Shui hu* was followed by many shorter editions, at about the time of the publication of the Shih-te-t'ang edition there appeared two abridged versions of the Tripitaka story. The first was compiled by Chu Ting-ch'en and published by a bookseller of southern Fukien during the reign of Lung-ch'ing (1567–72) or Wan-li. Scholars usually refer to it by the title *T'ang San-tsang hsi-yu shih-o chuan* (The history of T'ang San-tsang's deliverance from calamities during his western journey). Less than one fourth of the Wu version in length, it covers the earlier episodes quite fully but drastically abridges the adventures on the road after Tripitaka has accepted the service of his three disciples. However, it contains the prose narrative of Tripitaka's birth and youth which was eventually incorporated into the Wu text.[16]

The other short text, commonly known as *Hsi-yu chi* or *Hsi-yu-chi chuan,* was compiled by Yang Chih-ho. It forms Part III of an omnibus volume of *Ssu yu-chi* (Four pilgrimages), comprising novelette-length accounts of travels respectively to the east, south, west, north.[17] Though the earliest extant edition of that work dates back to the mid-Ch'ing period, it must have been in print by early Ch'ing or late Ming times. Independent separate editions of *Voyage to the East* (*Tung-yu chi*), *Voyage to the South* (*Nan-yu-chih chuan*), and *Voyage to the North* (*Pei-yu chi*) dating from the late Ming have in fact been found in the Japanese Cabinet Library and the British Museum, though a similar edition of *Journey to the West* is still beyond the search of scholars.[18] According to Cheng Chen-to, who was the first scholar to make a detailed attempt to clarify the relations of the three texts, Yang Chih-ho must have adapted the Wu and the Chu texts.[19] He shows a better sense of proportion than Chu, however, in that he has not unduly emphasized the earlier episodes at the expense of the later. Cheng confirms Sun K'ai-ti's opinion that both texts are abridgments of the 100-chapter novel.[20]

As in the case of *Shui hu,* it is always possible to argue that Wu Ch'eng-en built his novel upon the shorter versions rather than the other way around. In 1963 Professor Liu Ts'un-yan offered new bibliographical and textual evidence to support his thesis that the Chu text, the earliest of the three texts, was the direct model for Wu's version while the Yang text, in the main a condensed adaptation of the Chu version, also served as a prototype. In the following year, however, Glen Dudbridge reaffirmed the position of Sun K'ai-ti and Cheng Chen-to by citing omissions and non sequiturs in the Chu and Yang texts "that clearly point to careless transcription and abridgement." [21] While on the whole agreeing with Liu and Cheng Chen-to that Yang adapted Chu, he also speculated that the Chu text could have derived from the Yang edition.

The papers by both Liu and Dudbridge are very technical and I shall not try to reproduce their arguments here. We may regard the Yang text as of lesser importance since it was clearly an adaptation of the Chu version; for several of his sections not covered by the Chu version, Yang Chih-ho could have consulted the Wu version or the immediate source of the Chu text, which may or may not have been identical with the Wu version. For in its present form, with the highly abbreviated character of its later episodes, the Chu version must have been an abridgment. The crucial question remains therefore whether Chu's immediate model was Wu Ch'eng-en or some anonymous author who had already elaborated upon the primitive Yuan version, fragments of which are preserved in the *Yung-lo ta-tien* and the Korean reader.[22] Without having read Liu Ts'un-yan and Dudbridge, Chao Ts'ung came up with the plausible hypothesis that both the Chu and the Wu version were based on that anonymous author's enlargement (though Chao unjustifiably claimed the same distinction for the Yang version).[23] One consideration favoring this hypothesis is that in all probability the Chu text was published earlier than the Shih-te-t'ang edition. Another fact worthy of serious consideration (duly stressed by Liu) is that, whereas the Yang and Wu versions both begin with a proem ending with a line reading respectively "You ought to read *San-tsang shih-o chuan*" and "You ought to read *Hsi-yu shih-o chuan,*" the Chu edition is indeed titled *T'ang San-tsang hsi-yu shih-o chuan*. There can be little doubt that the original Ming version of the novel must have borne that title, and we know that one such version once existed—the Ta-lüeh-t'ang edition of *Hsi-yu shih-o chuan,* which must have predated the Shih-te-t'ang edition. If Wu Ch'eng-en was indeed the author of the Ta-lüeh-t'ang edition of *Shih-o chuan,* then its text would have to be identical with the Shih-te-t'ang text except for its inclusion of the account of Hsüan-tsang's birth and youth subsequently reintegrated into the novel. If Wu were the enlarger of *Hsi-yu shih-o chuan* (as Liu and Chao believe), then much of the credit I have earlier assigned to the novelist for his skillful expansion of the Yuan version must be given to an anonymous redactor. For the remainder of the chapter I shall assume the position that Wu Ch'eng-en was the creator of the novel, his main source being the primitive Yuan version. If subsequent scholarly opinion should assign *Hsi-yu shih-o chuan* to some other author, then whenever the name Wu Ch'eng-en occurs in a nonbiographical context in the following pages, it should be understood to be a combined reference to Wu and that author.

What must be apparent to every reader of *Hsi yu chi* is that the Tripitaka of the novel, who often appears as a deliberate caricature of a saintly monk, could not have borne any resemblance to his historical counterpart. Though Hsüan-tsang's initial difficulties in the desert had provided clues for the storytellers, few details of his subsequent journey could have interested them. Soon after crossing the desert, the historical Hsüan-tsang meets with the king of Turfan, who sends him off with a splendid retinue, letters of recommendation to rulers of other countries, and an abundant supply of gold, silver, and silk. It is true that the handsomely equipped traveler once meets with robbers and is on another occasion about to be sacrificed by pirates when a miraculous storm rises to avert his fate,[24] but during the years spent at the various courts in India in the company of kings, holy men, and leading scholars, Hsüan-tsang appears primarily as a man of piety, courage, and tact, and one, moreover, endowed with great intellectual curiosity and deeply versed in scholastic Indian logic. We find no trace of this revered foreign intellectual in popular literary representations of Tripitaka.

The Tripitaka of the novel is at least three different persons. First of all, he is the saintly monk of popular legend, a mythical hero suggestive of Moses and Oedipus. Son of a *chuang-yuan* (one who has earned the highest honors at the palace examination) and a prime minister's daughter, soon after his birth he is abandoned by his mother out of fear that someone is going to kill him. He drifts on a river until he is picked up by a Buddhist abbot, who rears him. At eighteen, he is ordained as a priest and goes in search of his lost parents. After he has found them both, his filial piety and evident holiness attract so much attention at court that he is soon entrusted by Emperor T'ai-tsung with a mission to India to procure Mahayana Buddhist scriptures. Modeled upon many earlier legends of Buddhist saints, the youthful Tripitaka is strictly a product of the popular imagination.

Upon this story of a folk hero is engrafted the myth that Hsüan-tsang was originally the Elder Golden Cicada, a disciple of Buddha in the Western Paradise. He was once inattentive to a sermon given by Buddha and as a result was banished to earth. It is widely known among all monsters and demons lusting after his flesh that during his succeeding ten incarnations on earth he had lived a life of strict purity and had never lost even one drop of his semen.[25] After the completion of his final earthly mission to bring scriptures to China, he is again welcomed back to the Western Paradise in his new role as the Buddha of Precocious Merit.

This second aspect of Tripitaka as a potential Buddha is central to the plot of the novel. After all, the monsters and demons are not interested in a monk from China, however saintly he may be, but in a magic host whose flesh can confer upon them everlasting life. But insofar as Tripitaka is aware of himself as an object of supreme temptation, he becomes in the novel a person forever apprehensive of his danger. His initial image as a pious monk endowed with wisdom and determination notwithstanding, Wu Ch'eng-en therefore presents Tripitaka primarily in his third aspect, as an ordinary mortal undertaking a hazardous journey and easily upset by the smallest inconvenience. Peevish and humorless, he also shows little perception as a bad leader partial to the most indolent of his group and little true faith as a strict Pharisee in his ostentatious attempt to keep to his vegetarian diet and avoid compromising female company. Certainly he suggests nothing of the courage of his historic namesake, nor the fortitude of Christian saints willing to undergo temptation in order to reach the higher stages of illumination. He neither withstands nor yields to the cannibalistic and sexual assault of the demons and monsters; he is merely helpless. Whereas in such Western allegories as *Everyman* and *The Pilgrim's Progress* the hero goes through a carefully charted journey to enable him to accept death or enter heaven at the end, Tripitaka shows no sign of spiritual improvement during his journey through the calamities. If anything, he gets more peevish and ill-tempered as his journey progresses. Even while he is being ferried to the Further Shore of

Salvation to face Buddha himself and get the scriptures, he is resentful of the fact that Monkey has pushed him into the bottomless boat and got him soaked, and so "sitting miserably here, he wrung out his clothes, shook out his shoes, and grumbled at Monkey for having got him into this scrape." [26]

As a comic figure in his own right, Tripitaka is indeed Everyman, as critics have often remarked,[27] but the religious implications of that designation can be understood only by reference to the kind of idealistic Buddhist philosophy which the novel exemplifies. If Tripitaka shows no spiritual progress on his journey, it is because in the light of that philosophy he is the embodiment of fearful self-consciousness forever enslaved by phenomena and therefore forever incapable of reaching that peace of mind which alone can rout the terror of the senses. Early on his journey, after he has taken Monkey and Pigsy as disciples but before his meeting with Sandy, he is instructed to seek out the Zen master Crow Nest (Wu-ch'ao) and to receive from him the Heart Sutra, which is duly recorded in the novel in the historical Hsüan-tsang's own standard translation.[28] Tripitaka appears so transported by the truth of that sutra that he immediately composes a poem to indicate his new state of spiritual illumination. What has so far escaped the notice of modern critics is that, like his monster-disciples, the sutra is itself a spiritual companion appointed for Tripitaka's protection on his perilous journey. And in the scheme of the Buddhist allegory, it is a far more important guide than any of his disciples since a Tripitaka in true possession of its teaching would have no need for their service and would realize the illusory character of his calamities.

Because of its brevity, the Heart Sutra is the central wisdom (*prajnaparamita*) text of Mahayana Buddhism.[29] Historically, it was a text dear to Hsüan-tsang; "for when he was crossing the desert in 629," Waley informs us, "the recitation of it had routed the desert-goblins that attacked him far more effectively than appeals to the Bodhisattva Avalokitesvara [Kuan-yin]." [30] In the primitive Sung version of the story, accordingly, we find that the receiving of this sutra constitutes the crowning success of Tripitaka's quest. He has already been to the kingdom of T'ien-chu (traditional Chinese name for India) where he received 5,048 scrolls of Buddhist scriptures; though none of these are identified by name, it is pointedly mentioned that the Heart Sutra is still missing. Now on his return journey, he stops by the Fragrant Grove Market (or Fragrant Grove Temple)[31] of the P'an-lü Kingdom and a god informs him in a dream that he is going to receive the Heart Sutra the next day. And the next day a Buddha who looks like a fifteen-year-old monk descends upon a cloud and hands him the sutra, saying, "I transmit to you this Heart Sutra. When you return to court, you must protect it and cherish it. Its power reaches to heaven and hell. It is compact with the mysterious forces of yin and yang, and therefore do not lightly transmit it to anybody. It will be extremely difficult for the less fortunate multitudes to receive it." [32]

By the time the storytellers' version was recorded in the Yuan period, we may presume that, in view of its climactic importance in the primitive version, the episode of the transmission of the Heart Sutra must have been transposed to a much earlier section of the narrative so that the meaning of that sutra could be further expounded by the pilgrims on their journey. And we may further maintain that, in adapting this source, Wu Ch'eng-en has done nothing less than make his whole novel a philosophical commentary on the sutra. George Steiner has brilliantly observed that the major characters in Tolstoy and Dostoevsky, when confronted with personal problems of crucial moral importance, often recite and discuss passages from the New Testament, which in turn keynote and illuminate the meaning of the novels in which these characters appear.[33] In *Hsi yu chi* the Heart Sutra is a subject of repeated discussion between Tripitaka and Monkey and serves the same novelistic function.

Though Tripitaka seems to have gained immediate illumination upon receiving the sutra and recites it constantly afterwards, its transcendent teaching that "form is emptiness and the very emptiness is form" [34] is so far beyond his mortal understanding that every calamity that befalls him demonstrates anew his actual incomprehension. During pauses between adventures, therefore, it is Monkey with his far superior spiritual understanding that repeatedly asks his master to heed the sutra. Thus, in chapter 43, he makes another attempt, "Reverend master, you have forgotten the verse, 'No eye, ear, nose, tongue, body, mind.' Of all of us who have forsaken the world, our eyes should not see color, our ears should not hear sound, our nose should not smell, our tongue should not taste, our body should not feel cold and heat, and our mind should not harbor vain illusions: this is known as 'routing the six thieves.' Now your mind is constantly occupied with the task of seeking the scriptures, you are afraid of the monsters and unwilling to give up your body, you beg for food and move your tongue, you are fond of sweet smells and titillate your nose, you listen to sounds and excite your ear, you see things around you and strain your pupils. Since you have welcomed these six thieves on your own invitation, how can you hope to see Buddha in the Western Paradise?" [35] Tripitaka is often aware of Monkey's superior understanding. In chapter 93, when Pigsy and Sandy laugh at Monkey's pretensions as a Zen master because he has again reminded their master to heed the Heart Sutra, Tripitaka upbraids the two less discerning disciples, "Sandy and Pigsy, don't talk so foolishly. What Monkey comprehends is the wordless language. This is true comprehension." [36] Measured against the standard of nonattachment upheld by Monkey, therefore, Tripitaka's every manifestation of fear and credulity, of fanatical obsession with correct conduct and peevish concern over his creaturely comforts is as much part of a deliberate comedy as the obviously gross behavior of Pigsy.

But Tripitaka is not only enslaved by his senses; his humanitarian pity—the most endearing trait about him—is itself a form of enslavement. Upon joining Tripitaka, Monkey's first act is to slay the six thieves—Eye, Ear, Nose, Tongue, Mind, Body—an allegorical event indicative of his superior detachment in comparison with the other pilgrims.[37] But Tripitaka is horrified because, among his other frailties, he is still obsessed with love and compassion for phenomenal beings. This episode causes the first temporary rift between master and disciple, and Monkey is later twice punished with dismissal, following his seemingly merciless killing of first a demon in pathetic human disguise and then a number of brigands.[38] From the viewpoint of popular Buddhism, Tripitaka has on all occasions followed the command not to kill, but because the novel inculcates the kind of Buddhist wisdom which excludes even the finest human sentiments as a guide to salvation, he is seen as a victim of perpetual delusion and can never make the same kind of spiritual progress as the hero of a Christian allegory. The novel, however, ultimately demonstrates the paradoxical character of this wisdom in that its nominal hero is granted Buddhahood at the end precisely because he has done nothing to earn it. To consciously strive for Buddhahood would again have placed him under bondage.

Monkey (Sun Wu-k'ung or Sun Aware of Vacuity), who repeatedly warns Tripitaka of his spiritual blindness, is, of course, the real hero of the book. He has already assumed the role of Tripitaka's protector on the road in the Sung shih-hua, and many of his deeds familiar to the reader of the 100-chapter novel must have appeared in the Yuan version, in however sketchy a fashion. But it is Wu Ch'eng-en who has enlarged upon these deeds and consistently defined his hero's character in terms of his spiritual detachment, his prankish humor, his restless energy, and his passionate devotion to his master. In face of this magnificent creation, scholars have been given to wondering which characters in folklore and literature could have served as Monkey's prototypes. Since he bears little resemblance to the few monkey characters to be found in the classical tales of the T'ang period and earlier, Hu Shih suggested Hanuman, the monkey warrior in The Ramayana, as the most likely model.[39] Until recently this hypothesis has been rarely challenged even though Hu Shih actually made no attempt to measure the influence of this Indian epic on Chinese folklore and literature. Accepting this theory on a provisional basis, Cheng Chen-to has examined Chinese stories about monkeys and come up with the interesting speculation that the Chinese must have received the Ramayana story in a garbled form since they often confused Hanuman with Ravana. In two well-known Chinese tales the monkey-villain appears as an abductor of women, and in Yang Ching-hsien's plays Monkey himself kidnaps a princess and takes her to wife. As depicted in the novel, the pre-Buddhist phase of Monkey's career also suggests the defiance of Ravana.[40]

Chinese Communist scholars, however, have vehemently repudiated the theory of Monkey's Indian origin—to them, this is another instance of Hu Shih's deliberate slighting of China's creative self-sufficiency.[41] In an important paper the learned scholar Wu Hsiao-ling has traced all references to *The Ramayana* in Chinese literature. According to him, while Buddhist missionaries from India were of course familiar with the epic, they were extremely chary of referring to stories that did not specifically promote the Buddhist cause. Therefore, though there are actually two sutras which retell portions of the epic in a Buddhist fashion, in addition to other scattered references to its major characters in the Chinese Buddhist canon, Chinese readers could not have made much of these synopses and names in the absence of a Chinese translation of *The Ramayana*. Since neither Wu Ch'eng-en nor the storytellers before him were erudite students of the Buddhist canon, Wu Hsiao-ling concludes, they could not possibly have been exposed to the story of Hanuman.[42]

But, of course, Wu Hsiao-ling makes no explicit denial that the *Ramayana* story could have been introduced to China through oral transmission. Especially during the T'ang, merchants from Central Asia carried on an active trade in China and they brought with them stories of their own regions which stimulated the Chinese literati to compose tales of a romantic and supernatural cast known as *ch'uan-ch'i*. *The Ramayana* may or may not have contributed to the character Sun Wu-k'ung, but there is no doubt that his many tricks and feats along with other supernatural motives in the novel are ultimately traceable to the influence of Indian as well as Persian and Arab literature. Monkey, for example, is an adept at magical transformations. In his celebrated battle with the celestial general Erh-lang Shen in chapter 6, the two combatants pursue each other through a series of disguises. I quote a small excerpt:

Monkey, trembling in every limb, hastily turned his cudgel into an embroidery needle, and hiding it about his person, changed himself into a fish, and slipped into the stream. Rushing down to the bank, Erh-lang could see nothing of him. "This simian," he said, "has certainly changed himself into a fish and hidden under the water. I must change myself too if I am to catch him." So he changed himself into a cormorant and skimmed hither and thither over the stream. Monkey, looking up out of the water, suddenly saw a bird hovering above. It was like a blue kite, but its plumage was not blue. It was like a heron, but had no tuft on its head. It was like a crane, but its feet were not red. "I'll be bound that's Erh-lang looking for me . . ." He released a few bubbles and swam swiftly away. "That fish letting bubbles," said Erh-lang to himself, "is like a carp, but its tail is not red; it is like a tench, but there are no patterns on its scales. It is like a black-fish, but there are no stars on its head; it is like a bream, but there are no bristles on its gills. Why did it make off like that when it saw me? I'll be bound it's Monkey, who has changed himself into a fish." And swooping down, he opened his beak and snapped at him. Monkey whisked out of the water, and changed himself into a freckled bustard, standing all alone on the bank.[43]

In one of the better-known tales from *The Arabian Nights,* "The Porter and the Three Ladies of Bagdad," an afreet and a princess gifted with magical arts are engaged in mortal combat, and they too undergo a series of transformations. When the afreet had turned himself into a scorpion,

the Princess became a huge serpent and set upon the accursed scorpion, and the two fought, coiling and uncoiling, a stiff fight for an hour at least. Then the scorpion changed to a vulture and the serpent became an eagle which set upon the vulture, and hunted him for an hour's time, till he became a black tom-cat, which miauled and grinned and spat. Thereupon the eagle changed into a piebald wolf and these two battled in the palace for a long time. . . .[44]

Though we find even in pre-T'ang literature legendary or ficti-tious characters who are able to transform themselves into bestial shapes,[45] the possessors of such powers could not assume any shape at will and certainly could not put on a performance of magical virtuosity as Monkey and Erh-lang have done in the quoted scene. Their resemblance in this respect to the combatants from *The Arabian Nights* does not mean that the makers of the Monkey legend were specifically indebted to that book, but it certainly indicates their general awareness of the popular literature of the Middle and Near East. *The Ramayana,* too, boasts characters who can transform themselves. And so does *The Mahabharata.* The oral transmission of this vast literature during the T'ang and after forms a fascinating subject still awaiting full-scale exploration by qualified scholars.

Whatever its prototypes, the character of Monkey as finally shaped by Wu Ch'eng-en also suggests such Western mythical heroes as Prometheus and Faust in his defiance of established authority and quest for knowledge and power. In chapter 1, as the leader of monkeys on the Flower and Fruit Mountain, he enjoys an idyllic existence of pure bliss. Provided with an infinite supply of food and unmolested by hunters or predators, the monkey colony behind the Water Curtain Cave is far more carefree than the Peach Fountain colony celebrated by T'ao Ch'ien. Yet Monkey is not content:

"Your Majesty is very hard to please," said the monkeys, laughing. "Every day we have happy meetings on fairy mountains, in blessed spots, in ancient caves, on holy islands. We are not subject to the Unicorn or Phoenix, nor to the restraints of any human king. Such freedom is an immeasurable blessing. What can it be that causes you this sad misgiving?" "It is true," said the Monkey King, "that to-day I am not answerable to the law of any human king, nor need I fear the menace of any beast or bird. But the time will come when I shall grow old and weak. Yama, King of Death, is secretly waiting to destroy me. Is there no way by which, instead of being born again on earth, I might live forever among the people of the sky?" [46]

His ambition, then, is to seek immortality, to perpetuate his enjoyment of life beyond the control of Yama. He presently undertakes a long voyage across the oceans to seek a master able to teach him how to conquer death. Allegorically, it is a quest for spiritual understanding, but in the larger mythical framework of the novel it is also a quest for magical power. Even for the most exalted celestials, their badges of power are invariably instruments of life-sustaining and death-causing magic. Lao Tzu (T'ai-shang Lao-chün), the supreme deity in the Taoist pantheon, cherishes as his chief possession the Crucible of the Eight Trigrams by means of which he manufactures longevity pills and melts down intransigent enemies.[47] And Subodhi, the Zen patriarch whom Monkey has chosen to serve, also respects his desire to prolong life and learn magical arts. Monkey is eventually dismissed because he has become vain of his attainments before the other disciples: the inherent desirability of these arts is not held in question.

Monkey was hatched from a stone egg, under the influence of the sun and moon. Like many other Chinese novels, *Hsi yu chi* begins at the beginning, with the creation myth. In this regard, Monkey's discontent with a pastoral mode of life and his ambition to seek power and knowledge can be seen as signs of a conscious striving upward—from inanimate stone to animal shape with human intelligence to the highest spiritual attainment possible. Until this striving is deflected into the Buddhist path of obedient service following his humiliating defeat in the palm of Buddha, Monkey is but the smartest of all the monsters who share with him this unquenchable desire for evolution. In his brilliant reinterpretation of the novel in Communist terms, Chang T'ien-i, a great short-story writer of the pre-Communist period, boldly allies Monkey with all the eventually captive or destroyed monsters in their aspect of revolt against the powers of heaven jealous of their aspirations. In this light, Monkey's later career can only be viewed as that of an apostate who systematically kills or subdues his former comrades to serve the interests of a heavenly bureaucracy. But Chang T'ien-i's view (first expressed in an article in 1954)[48] has understandably provoked unanimous protest from Communist critics who believe that it not only maligns Monkey but also discredits the whole purpose of the journey: it would be far better to regard the monsters as the "enemies of the people" and Monkey as their friend and savior.[49]

These critics are right insofar as Monkey is too mischievous and spirited an animal to be always contemplating his quest. Even in his rebellious phase, he differs from the other monsters and from Ravana and the Satan of *Paradise Lost* in his ability to view himself in a humorous light and his actual detachment from whatever business he is engaged in. He is never too solemn even when fighting a whole battalion of heavenly troops. Without his sense of humor, Monkey would have become a tragic hero or else shared the fate of the other monsters. With his sense of humor, he can turn from rebel to Buddha's obedient servant without forfeiting our sympathy. This sense of humor, however coarsely and at times cruelly expressed at the expense of his companions and enemies, implies his ultimate transcendence of all human desires to which Pigsy remains a prey and from which Tripitaka barely detaches himself by his vigilant exercise of self-control. It is consonant with the Buddhist insistence on detachment that laughter should be adopted as the ultimate mode of viewing the world. In the novel, therefore, comedy mediates between myth and allegory. Monkey is at once a hero of boundless energy and an eloquent spokesman for the esoteric doctrine of emptiness (quite rightly, traditional commentators have regarded him as the mind or intelligence in the allegoric scheme of the novel).[50] But to the end he retains the comic image of a mischievous monkey whose very zeal and mockery become an expression of gay detachment.

If Monkey is always the spirit of mischief when he is in command of a situation, there are occasions, nevertheless, when he impresses us with his passionate sorrow and anger. If humanitarian pity remains an endearing trait of Tripitaka, then, with all his superior understanding and mocking detachment, Monkey is also the antithesis of Buddhist emptiness in his passionate attachment to the cause of the journey and to his master. At times one gets the feeling that he is the only serious pilgrim, perpetually harassed by the mistrust and indolence of his fellow pilgrims and the indifference and malice of the deities above. Even Kuan-yin, who succors the pilgrims on numerous occasions, appears to Monkey to be at times patently cruel in tormenting them needlessly. In chapter 35, after Monkey has with great difficulty captured two powerfully armed demons, he learns to his consternation that the demons in their original shapes, together with their weapons, are actually the property of Lao Tzu and that it is with the deliberate intention of testing the pilgrims that Kuan-yin has borrowed them from him:

Hearing this, the Great Sage thought to himself, "This Bodhisattva is a double-crosser. Formerly, after she had restored my freedom, she asked me to protect Tripitaka on the western journey to get the scriptures. I told her then that the journey would be very hard, and she promised that during dangers she would personally come to my rescue. Now she has incited demons to harm us and her words are not trustworthy. No wonder she will remain a spinster all her life!" [51]

But it is his master Tripitaka who causes him the greatest anguish. Monkey is completely loyal to him, but the latter, who listens to the envious Pigsy, frequently mistrusts him. Moreover, Tripitaka is so selfish that once, after Monkey has dispatched two brigands, he prays for their peace and explicitly dissociates himself from the supposed crime:

> He is Sun,
> And I am Ch'en—
> Our surnames differ.
> To redress your wrong,
> Seek your murderer—
> Pray do not incriminate me,
> A monk on his way to get the scriptures.[52]

In chapter 27, after Monkey has finally killed a demon who has thrice assumed human shape to deceive the pilgrims, the enraged Tripitaka gives him a note of dismissal, saying, "Monkey-head, take this as proof that I no longer want you as my disciple. If I ever see you again, may I be instantly condemned to the Avici Hell!" [53] Monkey, who has killed the demon to protect his master, takes it extremely hard:

Monkey hurriedly took this instrument of dismissal, saying, "Master, you don't have to swear oaths; old Monkey is going." He folded the document and placed it in his sleeve and then again addressed Tripitaka in a placating manner, "Master, I have followed you for some time and I have done so by the instructions of the Bodhisattva. Today I am dismissed in the middle of this journey and deprived of my chance to win merit in this enterprise. Please be seated and accept my homage so that I may feel better as I leave you." Tripitaka turned around and bowed to Monkey, saying, "I am a good monk and I refuse to accept the homage of an evil person like you." Seeing that he was ignored, Monkey resorted to the trick of stepping out of himself. He plucked three hairs from the back of his head, blew on them and said, "Transform!" and the three hairs turned into three monkeys identical with himself. These four then surrounded the master and prostrated themselves before him. Tripitaka could not avoid him either on the right or on the left and reluctantly accepted his homage. The Great Sage jumped up, gave his body a shake, and reclaimed his three hairs. Then he admonished Sandy, "Dear brother, you are a good man and so be on guard against Pigsy's silly and malicious tongue and be especially careful on the road. If by chance a monster or demon has captured our master, just tell him that Monkey is his eldest disciple. The furry monsters of the west have all heard of my might and won't dare harm our master." Tripitaka said, "I am a good monk and will not mention the name of an evil person like you. Now go home." Seeing that the elder repeatedly showed no signs of relenting, the Great Sage finally had to leave. . . .

Swallowing his resentment, he parted from his master and soon he was borne aloft on the somersault cloud, on his way back to the Water-Curtain Cave of the Flower and Fruit Mountain. Riding all alone, he was extremely miserable. Suddenly his ears caught the sound of waters. Looking down, the Great Sage knew that it was the noise made by the rising tide in the Eastern Ocean. He was again reminded of Tripitaka and could not hold his tears from falling over his cheeks. He stopped the cloud and stood there for a while and then went on . . . saying to himself, "I have not been on this route for five hundred years!" . . . That Monkey then made a big leap over the Eastern Ocean and soon he was at the Flower and Fruit Mountain. He got off his cloud and looked around him. On the mountain were neither flowers nor grass. Mountain hazes had vanished, peaks and cliffs had fallen, and forest trees were all charred. Do you know how this could have happened? At the time when, after his riot in heaven, Monkey had been handed over to the upper realm, the Illustrious God Erh-lang had come with the seven brothers of Mount Mei and burned the mountain. The Great Sage now became twice as despondent as before.[54]

It is this passionate devotion to his home, to Tripitaka and his cause, that sets Monkey apart from the rest of the pilgrims. Above and beyond his mythic and comic roles, he shows himself as an endearing person subject to misunderstanding and jealousy and given to frequent outbursts of genuine emotion. He, too, belies his superior attainment in Buddhist wisdom with his incorrigible humanity.

In the preceding section, I have sketched Tripitaka and Monkey against their historical-literary backgrounds and, in doing so, have indicated the intricate connections between the diverse modes of myth, allegory, and comedy to be observed in the novel. In view of this complexity of structure, it is understandable that critics have tended to emphasize one mode at the expense of the others. Traditional commentators, more attuned to the mystical teaching of the book, have one and all stressed its allegory. Starting with Hu Shih, modern critics have repudiated the allegorical interpretation and stressed its wealth of comedy and satire. "Freed from all kinds of allegorical interpretations by Buddhist, Taoist, and Confucianist commentators," declares Hu Shih in his foreword to Waley's translation, "*Monkey* is simply a book of good humor, profound nonsense, good-natured satire and delightful entertainment." [55] (The phrase "profound nonsense," however, concedes the necessity for philosophical or allegorical interpretation.) Communist critics have further elaborated on the political aspects of the comedy, paying special attention to the revolutionary implications of its satire on traditional bureaucracy. They have cited instances in Ming history of gross official injustice and of the pampered arrogance of Taoist priests at court, a class repeatedly ridiculed in the novel, as sources of Wu Ch'eng-en's satiric inspiration.

The Communist approach, however, presupposes a political novelist deliberately scoring the evils of his time. But, under the autocratic rule of the Ming, it is very unlikely that Wu would have dared to make political remarks or concoct political fables in the Swiftian manner even if he had felt the urge to do so. [56] A repeated failure at the examinations (he finally earned a senior licentiateship in 1544 and many years later served briefly in a minor official capacity), he could have become an embittered satirist of political intent, but, judging by his novel as well as his poetry and prose, he was rather a man of genial humor, not at all obsessed with his lack of worldly success or with the degeneracy of the Ming court at his time. He records in his novel, to be sure, many shrewd observations on Chinese bureaucracy, but they strike us as the quintessence of folk wisdom rather than pointed satire of contemporary events. As a matter of fact, he regularly quotes proverbs for comic effect and makes fun of all traditional butts of satire. If Taoist priests are derided in some of the most hilarious episodes, Buddhists have not fared much better, since Tripitaka himself is seen as the constant source of ridicule. And yet in his didactic moments the novelist is not above adopting the traditional gesture of showing equal reverence for the three teachings: Confucianism, Buddhism, and Taoism.[57]

In extolling the novel as satire, however, modern critics have paid inadequate attention to its mythical strength. They have, of course, praised its author's mythological imagination, but they see it at work mainly in his elaboration of the many fantastic episodes presumably already present in the Yuan version. Yet, as a critical concept in the study of literature, "myth" actually refers to the representation of any reality suggestive of the archetypal situations of primordial humanity.[58] *Ulysses* is structured on myth though it deals with the Dublin of the early twentieth century. In like fashion, the mythical significance of *Hsi yu chi* lies not so much in its use of Indic, Buddhist, and Taoist mythologies as in its rendition of archetypal characters and events. Thus, despite its endless round of fantastic combats between opposing ranks of celestial and human warriors, *Fengshen yen-i* appears mythically significant only when it depicts the early careers of a few such heroes as No-cha, whose enmity with his father is an Oedipal myth traceable to Indic sources.[59] With *Hsi yu chi*, however, even a reader of Waley's abridgment will be struck by the resemblance of its major episodes to classic embodiments of mythical reality in Western and Indic literature. The story of the

Crow-Cock Kingdom, for instance, has the makings of a Hamlet myth—a foully murdered king, a crafty confidant who usurps his throne and his conjugal bed, and an estranged prince enjoined with the task of revenge.[60] In the story of the Cart-Slow Kingdom, the Buddhist inhabitants suffer the same fate as the Israelites in their Egyptian captivity, and Monkey and Pigsy vanquish the king's three Taoist counselors in the same magical fashion as Moses and Aaron triumphed over Pharaoh's priests.[61] As for the monster that rules over the River that Leads to Heaven, his demand for an annual sacrifice of live children makes him kin to such familiar figures of Western and Chinese mythology as the Minotaur and Ho-po.[62]

But in the last three episodes instanced, and numerous other episodes of this type excluded from Waley's version, their possibly coincidental resemblance to earlier myths is a less impressive proof of their mythical status than their striking suggestion of the fertility cults of primitive man. Thus the monster at the River that Leads to Heaven has to be propitiated because failure to observe the annual sacrifice will bring agricultural ruin to the area under his control. Similarly, the three Taoists enjoy the complete trust of their king because, as rain makers of proved competence, they guarantee the fertility of his country. And, upon entering the Cock-Crow Kingdom, the future usurper breaks a long siege of drought and thereby earns the gratitude and love of the king. In this respect, the wizard is even more suggestive of Oedipus than of Claudius in that his clearly manifested mana entitles him to the slaying of the powerless king and the possession of his wife. Yet, on the other hand, the story of the Crow-Cock Kingdom only goes through the motions of primitive ritual and tragic murder. Though the king is pushed into the well, he reposes down there quite unharmed and is eventually revived. The usurper is a castrated lion so that, with all the lewdness implicit in his violation of the queen and the harem, the ladies actually complain of his neglect. And, quite unlike Hamlet, the prince is filial to his mother rather than obsessed with her supposed perfidy; with the aid of the pilgrims, he restores the old order without bloodshed. And after his spree on earth, the lion is reclaimed by his owner, the Bodhisattva Manjusri. With this episode as with numerous other episodes, myth is ultimately placed in a larger comic framework: a primordial reality is represented so that its unreality may be the more effectively exposed.

Two kinds of monsters and demons live on this mythical plane. The first kind, represented by the castrated lion and the three Taoist demons (in reality, a tiger, a deer, and an antelope), live in human disguise and use their evil cunning to subvert a country. Some of these instigate crimes on a diabolic scale. In the Bhikshu Kingdom, for instance, the White Deer marries his supposed daughter to the ruler and ruins his health. He then counsels him to take a rejuvenating tonic to be prepared from hearts ripped from 1,111 boys aged five to seven.[63] The other kind live as monster-chieftains in their chosen territory, whether a mountain, a cave, or a river. (The monster at the River that Leads to Heaven is a golden carp.) They are less directly involved in human affairs, but, since they eat human flesh and usually enjoy an unrestrained sexual life, they invariably pose a menace to the region under their control.

In terms of origins, these monsters and demons can again be divided into two categories: those that belong to the heavenly menagerie and have escaped therefrom to enjoy their spree on earth, and those that have always been earth creatures and scorn to have any traffic with the celestial government even though some of them claim bonds of kinship to deities in heaven. In most cases, the refugees from heaven usurp a kingdom while the earthly monsters prefer their freedom and live a caveman's existence not unlike that of the Cyclopes in *The Odyssey*. But this is not always true: the three Taoist demons in the Cart-Slow Kingdom are creatures of the earth. In terms of their ultimate fate, the refugees from heaven once subdued by Monkey with or without divine aid are claimed by their masters and return to their original servile posts, while the independent monsters are usually destroyed. There are again exceptions: the Red Boy eventually serves Kuan-yin as a page, and, after putting up a ferocious fight against all the heavenly powers, his parents, the

Bull Monster King and Rakshas, also submit themselves and embrace Buddhism.

From the human point of view, these monsters and demons are of course all evil. But, with the exception of those diabolic counselors, the majority could perhaps be better regarded as amoral creatures beyond good and evil in their untrammeled enjoyment of their appetites. The Yellow-robed Monster has lived with a neighboring princess for thirteen years before he is finally subdued and turned into his original shape as the Wolf Star of K'uei-mu. He explains his truancy from heaven to the Jade Emperor:

Your Majesty, please forgive your servant's crime that is deserving of the death sentence. That princess of the Precious Elephant Kingdom was no ordinary mortal. She was a jade maiden in charge of incense-burning in the Pi-hsiang Palace. When she wanted to form a liaison with me, I was afraid that an affair of this kind would pollute the heavenly palaces, but she, still obsessed with love, went down to earth first and was born in the inner court of a palace. Not to break my earlier promise, I, too, later transformed myself into a demon, took possession of a famous mountain, and abducted her to my cave dwelling. We lived for thirteen years as man and wife. It is said, "One swallow of water, one bite of grain—everything is foreordained." Now the Great Sage has arrived and achieved merit.[64]

But if, back in heaven, the Wolf Star is able to give a rational explanation of his mission on earth—to expedite a romance that could not take place in the celestial courts, his actual earthly existence as the Yellow-robed Monster obliterates all memory of his heavenly origin. He indeed abducts the princess, but she lives most unwillingly with him and it is with her instrumental help that the pilgrims are able to relay her news to her parents and subdue the monster. In handsome disguise, he finally presents himself before the king as his son-in-law, but he soon betrays his bestial nature under the influence of liquor:

That evening, after the courtiers had retired from court, that monster entered the Silver Peace Palace and hand-picked eighteen palace girls to serve him wine and entertain him with music and dancing. That monster sat alone in the seat of honor and ranged around him were all these exquisite beauties. Just watch him enjoy the wine! By the second watch, however, he had become intoxicated and could no longer restrain himself from wanton acts. He jumped up and with one loud guffaw turned himself into his original shape. His murderous wrath now fully aroused, he stretched out his hand the size of a dust-bin, grabbed a *p'i-p'a* player, pulled her over, and bit off her head. The seventeen other frightened palace girls now ran in all directions, trying to hide from him. . . . They finally left the hall, but they didn't dare make an outcry nor awaken the king at such a late hour. They just huddled against the short wall under the eaves, in a state of fright. Meanwhile the monster sat by himself and kept on drinking. After finishing one cup, he would pull the corpse over and bite off two more pieces of her flesh, blood dripping from his teeth.[65]

But the monsters are not just bestial. Often they exhibit a remarkable range of human passions that would have delighted Balzac. The Bull Monster King, for example, used to live with Rakshas, the mother of his son the Red Boy, but for two years he has been cohabiting with another female. In the words of a local deity who explains their situation to Monkey:

The Bull Monster King is the husband of Madame Rakshas. For some time he has abandoned Rakshas and now he lives in the Cloud-scraping Cave of the Mountain of Piled-up Thunderbolts. There was a fox king of great longevity who finally died. A single daughter survived him, called the Jade-face Princess. That princess enjoyed an estate worth one million taels of silver which was left unattended. Two years ago she found out that the Bull Monster King commanded great magical powers, and she was willing to give him all her property and take him in as her husband in residence. That Bull King then abandoned Rakshas and never went back.[66]

Notice here how the economic factor has entered into the lives of the monsters. The Bull Monster King is not only tired of Rakshas but is given the additional incentive to live with the Jade-face Princess because of her great wealth. When Monkey appears before the two ladies in the guise of the Bull Monster, he fully explores the comic possibilities of their mutual jealousy.

Most monsters, however, are strongly committed to their clan and are not incapable of strong sexual attachment. If a monster is killed, his kinsmen would risk their lives in the hands of Monkey to avenge his death. The White Deer in the Bhikshu Kingdom is surely one of the most evil animal-spirits in the book. His supposed daughter is really his paramour, a White-faced Fox of bewitching beauty. After she has been killed by Pigsy and he himself has been exposed by his master, the Star of the South Pole, he shows genuine sorrow over his deceased mistress:

Pigsy threw the dead fox before the deer, asking, "Isn't that your daughter?" Nodding his head, the deer bent down his snout to smell her a few times and made whimpering sounds as if he were so much in love that he could not part from her. But the Star of the South Pole slapped him right on the head, scolding, "You cursed beast, it is enough that your own life is saved; what's the point of smelling her?" [67]

One exceptionally gentle group of demons is that of the tree spirits who engage Tripitaka in lofty discourse in chapter 64. While, as usual, Tripitaka is wafted to their haunt on the strength of an evil wind, his abductors this time are the Spirits of the Pine, the Cypress, the Juniper, and the Bamboo, all of otherworldly appearance and reverend longevity. In their company Tripitaka feels quite at home; he discourses on Zen and composes poems with evident pleasure until the beautiful Apricot Fairy arrives on the scene. She is also a talented poet but, as a female spirit, she associates poetry with love and invites Tripitaka to make love to her:

That girl, showing signs of falling in love, cuddled close to him, whispering in his ears, "Handsome guest, let's dally while the night is so beautiful. How short is one's life, and how sad to waste it!" The Pine Spirit said, "Since the Apricot Fairy aspires to your friendship, it would not be right if you, a saintly monk, did not condescend to reciprocate her love. It would be very obtuse of you not to show her some pity." The Cypress Spirit advised, "Our holy monk is a renowned scholar of spiritual discernment. I am sure he would not agree to a hasty arrangement. If we do things rashly, we would be giving unnecessary offense. To sully one's name and compromise one's virtue: this is not the way of the wise and far-sighted. If the Apricot Fairy is truly interested, she may ask the Juniper Spirit and the Pine Spirit to serve as matchmakers and the Bamboo Spirit and myself to be guarantors. Wouldn't it be wonderful if this marriage could be consummated?" [68]

Tripitaka refuses vehemently and further accuses the tree spirits of deliberately trying to win his good graces and then trapping him with this outrageous proposal. But, judging from the text, one cannot tell if the four reverend tree spirits have entered into a scheme with the Apricot Fairy: it could be that she fell in love on the spur of the moment. Rather rashly, Pigsy soon afterwards digs up all the trees in the grove that could assume human speech and form, with their roots "dripping with blood." [69] With the sole exception of the Maple Spirit, these are gentle spirits of the least harmfulness and they die without offering any resistance. In this episode, therefore, is exposed the illusory nature of the idyllic world of love, poetry, and philosophic discourse which Tripitaka, too, must leave behind.

For Tripitaka, of course, the temptation of the trees is but a mild interlude amid the far more ferocious and cunning assaults on his person by the ogres and demons. Whatever their other characteristics —I have described a few earlier—these monsters share a boundless will to live, in defiance of all restraint and authority, and of death itself. They live on human flesh because in accordance with the magical view that food is mana—and the gods in heaven concur in that view—they believe that human flesh confers greater power and intelligence than any other food. Moreover, since the eating of human flesh is taboo in the heavenly court, they regard their cannibalism, if one may apply that word to creatures not strictly human, as a proud badge of their defiant freedom. The Garuda, a giant bird, is a conspicuous example. Like Monkey, he is an especially powerful monster whose subdual requires the personal intervention of Buddha himself, who exposes him to the beam of his golden light and reduces him to impotence:

He opened his beak and talked directly to Buddha, "Tathagata, why did you exercise your great might to keep me in captivity?" Tathagata said, "You have been living here to create bad karma. Go with me so that you may advance in merit." The evil spirit replied, "Over at your place, you keep fasts and stick to a vegetarian diet and lead an extremely miserable life. Over here, I live on human flesh and enjoy myself no end. I will hold you responsible if you try to starve me." Tathagata said, "I am in control of the four continents and receive worship from numberless living things. Whenever there are offerings, I'll let you feed on them first." The Garuda wanted to get away but he couldn't. Under the circumstances, he could but submit.[70]

To the Garuda, energy is eternal delight and is equated with the condition of cannibalism while heaven means only abstinence and slavery. He undergoes no real conversion, and Buddha himself does not seriously expect him to change his nature and can only placate him with offerings of food. For all monsters who reluctantly submit when their only alternative is the annihilation of their life and their ten thousands of years of striving, heaven is a joyless place. Its government is as despotic as any on earth, but with a suggestion of arbitrary cruelty beyond human contrivance. Thus Pigsy, a heavenly general, was banished because he flirted with a moon goddess while in a state of drunkenness. The Jade Emperor gave him two thousand stripes before banishing him.[71] Sandy, a river monster who once also served as a celestial general, tells his liberator Kuan-yin of his unendurable punishment:

Bodhisattva, please forgive my crime and let me tell of my unfair treatment. I am not an evil spirit. I was General Curtain-folding in charge of the imperial chariot at the Ling-hsiao Palace. At a peach party, a glass cup accidentally slipped out of my hand and was broken to pieces. The Jade Emperor gave me eight hundred strokes before banishing me and transformed me to my present shape. Every seven days he would cause a flying sword to stab my chest and ribs over a hundred times before he recalled it. Under such punishment I can't help being in great misery. Cold and hungry, I am compelled to step out of the waves every two or three days to prey upon some traveler as food. I didn't realize that in my ignorance I could have offended the compassionate Bodhisattva.[72]

In Greek mythology the kind of punishment received by Sandy, subsequently a mild-mannered pilgrim, would be reserved for Tityus and Prometheus who, in the eyes of the Olympian gods, have committed heinous crimes. But Sandy is punished for a light misdemeanor which could not, in any scheme of justice, have merited such harsh treatment.

Little wonder that, disgusted with heaven and craving for an eternity of cannibalistc freedom, all monsters and demons would regard Tripitaka as their supreme catch. The word has got around to them that to eat his flesh or to absorb his semen is to acquire the gift of automatic immortality. The novel therefore stages the recurrent comedy of assault, with the male monsters trying to eat Tripitaka and the female ones trying to force him to have sexual relations with them. In this comedy, while Tripitaka is exposed for his fear, the monsters are exposed for their inordinate lust for life. Granted the awesome splendor of many of these monsters and granted also their cruel treatment at the hands of their heavenly masters, nevertheless the constant negation of their struggle through death and surrender must be seen as a comic critique of the life-force itself: the monsters' ferocious aggressiveness only magnifies the hideousness of craving in every one of us, that craving which, in accordance with Buddhist teaching, is the cause of all suffering. Wu Ch'eng-en is undeniably sympathetic with the mythical life of amoral autonomy and critical of mundane bureaucracy as mirrored in the arbitrary despotism of the heavenly government, but ultimately he is far more concerned with the comic absurdity of the mythical life that sanctions the limitless gratification of one's desires.

With his sense of the ridiculous anchored in the Buddhist doctrine of emptiness, therefore, the author mocks all the monsters as he mocks all the pilgrims and celestials in the book. Not only is everything infinitely amusing to his observant eye, but in the ultimate religious sense everything that exists is but maya with which we are infatuated. Even the most serious character and the one nearest to approaching an understanding of emptiness, Monkey himself, is not spared this affectionate ridicule. To readers conditioned to accept the reality of literary fiction, this attempt at constant negation can be at times very unsettling. Writing from the Christian viewpoint which accords reality to every soul be it suffering eternal damnation in hell or rejoicing in eternal bliss in paradise, Dante has created a massive comedy of substantial reality designed to elicit our strongest emotional responses. Wu Ch'eng-en, on the other hand, provides in episode after comic episode the illusion of mythical reality, but then inevitably exposes the falsehood of that reality in furtherance of his Buddhist comedy. Every time he kills off a fascinating monster or arbitrarily returns him to heaven, we are justified in feeling that he is mocking our emotional attachment to that monster. Like Tripitaka himself, we are too much creatures of the senses and of humanitarian sympathy to be able to adjust adequately to the Buddhist reality of emptiness. The reason why, of all the monsters blocking the path of Buddhist enlightenment, nearly every modern critic has betrayed a special affection for the Bull Monster King is that, for once, we are trapped in an emotional situation that seems to defy the Buddhist assumptions of unreality. The Bull Monster remembers Monkey as a sworn brother, but, since the latter is instrumental in bringing about the subjugation of the Red Boy, he has to repudiate his fraternal oath in order to avenge his son. Moreover, living with two wives, he has his domestic problems to attend to. He grips our attention, therefore, as an inhabitant of the epic world of human passions. For the duration of three chapters (chaps. 59–61), the mythical drama of primordial reality almost prevails over the Buddhist comedy of illusion, and we applaud the author for his uncharacteristic lapse.

But to applaud so is to be less than just to the Buddhist design of the book and to the author's genial comic vision stemming from a proper awareness of the delusions of the self. In the story of the Bull Monster, as in the far more sympathetic account of Monkey's defiance of heaven, a careful reader will find a sufficient amount of material in the style of burlesque, mockery, and comic exaggeration to warn him against total emotional involvement. Possibly we are too much in love with the irrational and mythic to fully appreciate the sanity of the Buddhist vision. But when we place Wu Ch'eng-en beside a self-obsessed precursor of modern fiction like Poe, we can immediately see a tremendous difference. Allen Tate has admirably characterized Poe as a writer of the angelic imagination in that he aspires to the condition of an angel, if not of God. The characters in his serious stories are actually vampires.[73] Like the female ogres in *Hsi yu chi* determined to assault Tripitaka in order to enrich their own vitality, these vampires cling desperately to life so as to vindicate Poe's favorite epigram, "Man does not yield himself to the angels, nor unto death utterly, save only through the weakness of his feeble will." [74] Wu Ch'eng-en would have found this arrogance quite laughable, and his monsters are actually far less monstrous than the morbid human beings in Poe's stories, with all their philosophic intensity. Whereas Poe has neither humor nor kindness nor generosity of spirit, it is Wu Ch'eng-en's special comic distinction that he destroys or reclaims his monsters before they turn into introspective philosophers, before they take themselves too seriously in the fashion of the heroes of modern fiction. They remain plain monsters, amenable to a religious interpretation in the dual modes of myth and comedy.

Wu Ch'eng-en's supreme comic creation is Pigsy, who symbolizes the gross sensual life in the absence of religious striving and mythical ambition. He is doubly comic because as a reluctant pilgrim he has no calling whatever for the monastic life and because with all his monstrous size and strength he entertains no ambition beyond a huge meal and a good sleep with a woman in his arms. He is the average sensual man writ large who could have become more serious if he had been provided with the proper incentives for worldly success and domestic contentment. He deteriorates on the road, turning into an envious, mendacious, and cowardly glutton obsessed with the life of sensual ease, precisely because these incentives are lacking. As the son-in-law in the Kao family, he appears as a selfish and hard-working individualist, no different from any conscientious family man who works in the day and comes home in the evening to attend to his family and beautify his home. Though lecherous, he is perfectly happy if he has the nightly consolation of sleeping with his wife. By ordinary standards, therefore, he is something of a model husband. His father-in-law may object to his hideous features but he cannot complain that he does not work extremely hard on the farm. Even his huge appetite is a direct consequence of his hard labor. When, in order to expose Pigsy as a monster, Monkey disguises himself as his wife and refuses his embrace, the injured husband is extremely puzzled. He rightly demands an answer to her show of discontent:

What are you grumbling about? Since I came here, I've cost you something in food and drink, that I own. But I've more than earned what I have got. Haven't I cleaned the ground and drained ditches, carried bricks and tiles, built walls, ploughed fields, planted grain, and improved the farm out of all knowing? Now you wear silk clothes and gold ornaments and enjoy fresh fruit all the four seasons. During the eight festivals of the year, especially, you have all kinds of boiled and fried vegetable dishes to eat. In what thing haven't you got your heart's desire, and what's all this nonsense about your sighing and grumbling that you are unhappy? [75]

Furthermore, though when Monkey declares his identity Pigsy is at first afraid because he doesn't have his weapon with him, once he gets hold of his rake, he fights two battles with the utmost ferocity. The first battle lasts "all night long, from the second watch till dawn began to whiten in the sky," [76] and the descriptive verse passage, omitted from Waley's version, fully accents the heroic note. Later, as a pilgrim, Pigsy becomes much less brave. Unless, in his encounter with lesser monsters, he is sure of victory and wishes to excel himself in the eyes of Tripitaka, he is a regular shirker leaving the main burden of the fighting to Monkey. The reason for his progressive sloth is that there is now no incentive for further exertion except the flattery of praise and the occasional fun of teasing and tormenting an inferior enemy. And he is envious: since Monkey is so much more powerful and resourceful, why bother? When he is sent on an individual assignment unaccompanied by Monkey or Sandy, his natural inclination is to lie down on the grass and take a long nap. He regularly complains of Tripitaka's simple luggage (it could not have placed any perceptible weight on his capacious shoulders) to indicate his unwillingness to participate in an enterprise that is to him completely meaningless.

When finally forced to leave his wife, Pigsy gives Mr. Kao a parting message:

"And father-in-law, I'll trouble you to take good care of my bride. For if we don't bring off this scripture business, I shall turn layman again and live with you as your son-in-law." "Lout!" cried Monkey. "Don't talk rubbish." "It's not rubbish," said Pigsy. "Things may go wrong, and then I shall be in a pretty pass! No salvation, and no wife either." [77]

The exchange is funny precisely because Pigsy is in dead earnest. Repeatedly, when disaster overtakes the group and Tripitaka is believed to be dead, Pigsy harps on the theme of going home to his wife. Unlike Monkey, with his loyal attachment to his master, Pigsy shows on these occasions no signs of distress; he is actually happy to be rid of his fellow pilgrims. Once, after Monkey himself has been swallowed by a monster (chap. 75), he again talks about separation:

"Sandy," yelled Pigsy, "bring the luggage here and let us two divide it up." Sandy asked, "What for?" Pigsy said, "Let's part and each go his own way. You go back to the Flowing Sand River to prey on people and I'll return to the Kao Farm to look up my wife. We'll sell the white horse and with the proceeds buy a coffin for our master against his death." In violent agitation over these words, the elder burst out into a loud wail. [78]

In this, as in similar scenes, the author brings out the sinister aspect of Pigsy's selfishness as well as the unbelievable childishness of the easily despondent Tripitaka. Both being self-centered, Pigsy cares only for his own welfare and Tripitaka thinks only of his personal danger. Both therefore are often seen in league against Monkey: if, with his superior understanding, Monkey exposes Tripitaka's obsession with fear, with his zest for a life of disinterested action he puts to shame Pigsy's sensuality, sloth, and envy. The allegorical meaning of these contrasts is quite obvious, but in their frequent altercations these three are properly travelers undertaking an arduous journey who sooner or later must get on each other's nerves. In this realistic perspective, Tripitaka appears an unobservant, easily flattered father while Monkey and Pigsy are rival brothers in the fashion of Tom Jones and Blifil.

In his lack of incentive for further striving, Pigsy appears primarily as a glutton who looks forward to a huge supper as the sole compensation for a hard day's journey. Thus in the episode of the River that Leads to Heaven, despite the apprehension of his host over the fate of his daughter and nephew about to be sacrificed to a monster, Pigsy eats unconcernedly one of his heartiest meals in the novel, prepared from "a ton of flour, five bushels of rice, and a load or two of vegetables." [79] Food certainly is a dominant motive in the novel: not only are the pilgrims perpetually hungry (it is usually to relieve Tripitaka's hunger that Monkey has to search for food and, in doing so, comes upon new adventures) and the cannibalistic monsters forever intent on eating Tripitaka, but even the gods themselves are obsessed with their magic foods and jealously guard against their theft by brazen outsiders. It is Monkey's prankish eating of the celestial peaches in his charge that prompts the heavenly court to mobilize all its strength against him. And later, in league with Pigsy, his plundering and felling of the mandrake-fruit trees could have caused him equal trouble with their owner, the self-important deity Chen-yuan Tzu, if Kuan-yin had not intervened.[80] Among his other mythical roles, Monkey is also the intruder into the Hesperidian garden.

With all its wild conceits about food, *Hsi yu chi* bears some important resemblance to *Gargantua and Pantagruel*. Rabelais and Wu Ch'eng-en, moreover, were almost exact contemporaries, who bequeathed to their respective national cultures two comic masterpieces unsurpassed for their sheer animal exuberance. In their gross passages, both works can shock the more fastidious modern taste by their disregard of humanitarian feelings. Just as Gargantua, Pantagruel, and Friar John show the greatest contempt for their enemies and slaughter them for a joke, so do Monkey and Pigsy, when the latter has shaken off his usual indolence to share his fellow pilgrim's prankish sense of humor, display the liveliest spirit in teasing and punishing their defenseless enemies. In chapter 67 Pigsy eggs Monkey on to torment a helpless Red-scaled Python. That giant serpent is a dumb creature who has not yet mastered human speech though he could, in Pigsy's estimation, easily swallow five hundred people for one meal. He eventually swallows Monkey, who enjoys nothing more than playing havoc inside a monster:

Pigsy beat his breast and stamped his feet, yelling, "Brother, you are done for!" Inside the monster's stomach Monkey raised his cudgel and said, "Don't worry, Pigsy. I'll make him into a bridge, you just watch." That monster arched his back and looked like a rainbow-shaped bridge. Pigsy said, "Though it looks like a bridge, no one would dare walk on it." Monkey said, "I'll have him changed into a boat. You watch." Monkey pressed the length of his cudgel against the underside of the monster's belly. The whole length of his belly now touched the ground, and, when he raised his head, he looked like a tall-prowed boat. Pigsy said, "Though it looks like a boat, it doesn't have sails and cannot be propelled by the wind." Monkey said, "You make way for me. I'll make him sail under wind." Thus, while still inside the belly, he exerted his utmost strength to push his cudgel through the back and it stood out for fifty or seventy feet and looked like a mast. That creature could hardly endure his pain and he slithered back on his old path in a vain attempt to save his life, faster than if wind-driven. He plunged down the mountain and kept moving for the length of some twenty li and then he collapsed in the dust and could no longer move. He was dead.[81]

While on a voyage with his friends in Book IV of *Gargantua and Pantagruel,* Pantagruel spies a whale and shoots giant-sized arrows at it until it resembles a galleon:

The first of these arrows, of which there was a great store aboard, he drove so deep into the spouter's forehead that he pierced both its jaws and its tongue, so that it could no longer open its mouth, or draw in or spout out water. With his second shot he gouged out its right eye, and with his third its left. Then, to the great delight of everyone, the spouter was seen bearing these three horns on its forehead, slightly tipped forward, in the shape of an equilateral triangle, and veering from one side to another, staggering and swaying, as if stunned, blind, and going to its death. Not content with this, Pantagruel shot another bolt at its tail, which struck obliquely like the rest; then three more perpendicularly along its spine, which they divided exactly into three equal parts between its nose and its tail. Lastly he shot fifty into one of its flanks, and fifty into the other; after which the spouter's body looked like the hull of a three-masted galleon, mortised together by beams of regular dimensions, which might have been the ribs and chain-wales of the keel. It was a jolly sight to see. Then, as it died, the spouter turned over on its back, like all dead fish; and lying on the water, with its beams beneath it, it looked like that scolopendra, or hundred-legged serpent, described by the ancient sage Nicander.[82]

But, despite their comparable sense of humor, the two authors differ in their attitudes toward appetite. Turning away from the ascetic monkish existence to which he himself has been subjected, Rabelais intends his characters of almost limitless capacity for food and drink and limitless sexual prowess to be unqualified positive metaphors for man's emancipation from the life-denying disciplines of the Church. Gargantua, Pantagruel, and their friends are giants rather than monsters, and their giant appetite unambiguously corresponds to their giant intellectual powers. Compared with the Chinese novelist, Rabelais is also far more ribald and scatological because, placing his faith in a nonreligious humanism, he finds the anatomical functions not only infinitely amusing but worthy of the most serious contemplation. With all his comic exuberance, Wu Ch'eng-en is not a Renaissance humanist; in point of moral sensibility, he is far more Chaucerian than Rabelaisian in that he finds man's insatiable appetite ultimately laughable as a negative confirmation of his absurdity. Pigsy, his major symbol of appetite, has no spiritual and intellectual pretensions whatever. Though the author good-humoredly indulges his appetite for food since, in Chinese eyes, gluttony calls for far less moral disapprobation than lechery and is properly a matter for comic attention (we have seen how the heroes of *The Water Margin* shun female company though they are hearty eaters), he never once gives free rein to Pigsy's equally strong desire for sex. Instead, he tortures him for his easily aroused concupiscence. Pigsy was exiled to earth for his flirtation with a moon goddess. In one of the last episodes in the book (chapter 95), he again meets with his old flame, who has appeared in the sky with T'ai-yin Hsing-chün, the presiding god of the moon, to expose a false princess:

> Pigsy was moved to lust. Unable to restrain himself, he leaped into the sky and hugged the moon fairy, saying, "Sister, you and I are old acquaintances. Let's have some fun." Monkey came forward to clutch him, slapping him twice in the face and then scolding him, "You crazy fool, where do you think you are, to dare give rein to your lust!" Pigsy said, "All I want is to play and have some fun." [83]

This is an astonishingly good scene because, for once, comedy almost yields place to drama in Pigsy's agonizing cry of sexual hunger. But usually Pigsy merely undergoes the exquisite comic torture of his unfulfilled lust without tasting even for one second the compensating sweetness of love. Since the dangers of lust are taken for granted by the Chinese and require no full illustration as is the custom with Western allegorists, the comedy of lust in the Chinese mode exposes mainly the initial stage of sexual titillation. In chapter 23, the goddess Li-shan Lao-mu and three Bodhisattvas transform themselves into women to tempt the pilgrims with their beauty and wealth. Pigsy naturally falls for the bait, and Tripitaka is also tempted though any such trial immediately prompts him to assume the posture of frightened silence. When Li-shan Lao-mu, as a widow of fabulous wealth, rehearses the accomplishments of her three nubile daughters, "Tripitaka sat on his seat, like a child frightened by thunder or a toad drenched with rain, idiotically rolling his eyes." [84] He adopts the same attitude when, many episodes later, he is compelled to marry the queen of the Country of Women. Pigsy, therefore, is the main butt of the four deities. I shall now translate a major portion of this episode to give an idea of the novel's allegory at its best and also to show the kind of subtle psychological realism not apparent in Waley's *Monkey*. Tripitaka has now rejected the widow's proposal of marriage:

Hearing this, the woman became very angry, saying, "What insolence from an ill-mannered monk! If I didn't take into consideration the fact that you are pilgrims from the distant East, I would have driven you out of my house. In all sincerity I was inviting you to be my sons-in-law and to enjoy my property, and you even dare to make fun of me by your sarcasm. Even if you have embraced the discipline and taken the vow and won't ever return to lay life, there's nothing wrong if I invite one of your disciples to join my family. Why are you so strict?" Tripitaka could only turn very apologetic under this wrath. He appealed to Monkey, "Wu-k'ung, how about you staying here?" Monkey replied, "This is rather out of my line. Let Pigsy stay." Pigsy said to Monkey, "Elder brother, don't make fun of me. Let's take more time to think this over." Tripitaka then suggested, "Since you two are unwilling, let Sandy stay on." Sandy replied, "Master, what words are these! Your disciple was honored to be converted by Kuan-yin and to embrace the discipline and await your arrival. Since then I have been further privileged to become your disciple and receive instruction from you. It's not even two months and I haven't yet accomplished any meritorious deeds. How dare I seek this wealth and honor? I would rather risk death faring forward to the Western Paradise than do such a dishonorable thing."

Seeing them all making excuses, that woman swiftly turned around and disappeared behind the door screen. She further slammed the side door leading to the parlor as she went in. The master and disciples were left by themselves, without refreshments. No one came out to wait on them.

Highly vexed, Pigsy complained to Tripitaka, "Master, how undiplomatic of you to have refused her so flatly. If you had given her some ground for hope with a vague yes, we would have got a free meal from her and had a jolly evening. Each of us could surely give her a definite answer tomorrow. As it is, she has shut the door on us and won't come out. We are now as short of food as a stove with nothing in it but cold ashes. How can we pass the night?" Sandy suggested, "Second brother, then you stay on as her son-in-law." Pigsy said, "Younger brother, don't tease me—let's take time to deliberate this." Monkey said, "What's there to deliberate? If you are willing, then let our master and that woman sponsor your marriage and let you be her son-in-law and stay with her family. She is so fabulously wealthy she would certainly provide you with a dowry and prepare a wedding banquet for all the relatives. We would certainly enjoy this while you return to lay life here. Won't that be nice for all concerned?" Pigsy replied, "Finely said. Only to return to lay life after you have forsaken it, to marry again after you have severed ties with your first wife—that's kind of difficult."

"So our second brother was once married?" asked Sandy. "You wouldn't have guessed," replied Monkey. "He was originally the son-in-law of old Mr. Kao of the Kao Farm at Wu-ssu-tsang. After I subdued him—he had earlier received the discipline from the Bodhisattva Kuan-yin—he was captured to serve as a monk. So he abandoned his first wife and became a disciple of our master to go westward to pay homage to Buddha. Probably he has been away from home too long and is again itching with desire. Just now he has heard this offer—undoubtedly he is tempted." Then he turned to Pigsy, "Fool, you stay here as a son-in-law. Only don't forget to give proper thanks to old Monkey; so I won't make trouble for you." The fool said, "Nonsense, nonsense. All of us are tempted, don't just single me out for ridicule. The saying goes, 'Monks are sex-starved fiends.' Who isn't like that? If we all act so damned coy, we will only be ruining our evening. No tea, and no lights either! I suppose we can survive the night, but that poor horse has to carry our master tomorrow and has a whole day's journey ahead of it. If it is famished in the night, the only good we can get from it will be to strip its hide. You stay here and I'll put the horse to pasture."

In a great hurry the fool loosened the reins and led the horse out. Monkey said, "Sandy, you stay here and keep Master company. I'll follow him and see where he is grazing the horse." Tripitaka said, "It's all right if you go and watch him. Only don't plan on just teasing him." Monkey replied, "I know."

The Great Sage then left the hall and, giving his body a shake, turned himself into a red dragonfly, darting out of the front gate to catch up with Pigsy. Pulling the horse, the fool didn't stop where there was grass, but shooed it and dragged it toward the back door. That woman was standing there with the three girls, idly enjoying the sight of the chrysanthemums. Seeing Pigsy approach them, the three girls swiftly disappeared behind the door. The woman, however, stood there and asked him, "Little priest, where are you going?" The fool dropped the reins, and came forward with a bow, saying, "Mother, I'm pasturing the horse." The woman said, "Your master is too goody-goody. Won't it be much better to stay on as my son-in-law than to be a mendicant priest trudging westward?" Pigsy smiled, "They are doing this by the order of the T'ang emperor; so they daren't disobey and won't consent to settling down here. Just a moment ago, they were even making fun of me in the hall. But on my part, I am kind of diffident—I'm afraid Mother will object to my long snout and big ears." The woman said, "I don't mind, really. Since there is no man in the house, it won't be a bad idea to take in a son-in-law. But I am afraid my daughters may object to your ugliness." Pigsy replied, "Mother, please tell your honored daughters not to be so picky. The T'ang monk may be good to look at, but he is no good on other accounts. I may be ugly, but there is a poem. . . ." The woman asked, "How does it go?" Pigsy recited:

> "Though I am ugly,
> My industry is commendable:
> A thousand *ch'ing* of land
> Needs no oxen to plow it;
> I rake it once, and
> The seeds will sprout in time.
> No rain and I am a rain maker,
> No breeze and I will summon the wind;
> If the house is too low,
> I will add two or three stories;
> The unswept floor I will sweep;
> The clogged sewers I will unclog.
> Household chores big and small,
> I can manage all."

The woman said, "Since you can manage the chores around the house, why don't you go back to consult your master? If nothing goes wrong, we'll have you." Pigsy said, "No need to consult him. He is not my father or mother. The decision rests entirely with me." The woman said, "All right, I'll talk it over with my daughters." She then darted inside, shutting the back door behind her.

Pigsy didn't even bother to pasture the horse, but pulled it toward the front door. How could he know that Monkey had seen everything? Monkey flew back, changed into his real shape, and told Tripitaka, "Pigsy is leading the horse back." The elder said, "If the horse is not led, he may get excited and wander away." Monkey couldn't help laughing as he told from the beginning about the transactions between Pigsy and that woman. Tripitaka wasn't sure whether he should believe the whole story. Presently the fool pulled the horse in and tied him to a post. "Did you graze the horse?" asked the elder. Pigsy replied, "There's no good grass and I didn't graze it." "If there was no place to graze it," Monkey asked, "wasn't there a place where the horse could be led?" [85] Hearing this, the fool knew for sure that the news had leaked out. He hung his head and pouted, not saying a word.

Then the side door swung open, and in came the woman with her three daughters, who carried with them two pairs of red gauze lanterns and one pair of portable censers. The pendants on these girls tinkled while the censers exhaled a cloud of fragrance. The woman led Truth, Love, and Pity forward and bade them make obeisance to the pilgrims. These girls, standing in a row in the center of the hall, bowed to them. Truly they were beautiful:

> Their moth-brows curved and penciled,
> Their powder-white faces fresh like spring,
> Seductive with beauty that could topple a kingdom,
> Graceful with charm that could pierce one's heart;
> The flowers and adornments on their hair, how gorgeous,
> The embroidered sashes floating about their dresses, how elegant;
> Cherry lips half-open with a smile,
> Feet stepping daintily with odor of orchid and musk,
> Their tall coiffures studded with jewels
> And countless precious hairpins;
> Their bodies exuding rare fragrance
> And decked with flowers made of golden threads;
> The beauties of Ch'u,
> Hsi Shih of the West Lake
> Could not compare with them:
> Truly, they are fairies descending from the ninth heaven
> And moon goddesses emerging from the Kuang-han Palace!

Tripitaka placed his palms together and bowed while Monkey pretended not to notice them and Sandy turned his back toward them. But not so Pigsy: his eyes were glued on the sight and his lustful heart was turbulent with uncontrollable desire. With simpering gallantry, he spoke softly, "It is an honor that you celestial ladies have descended to visit us. Mother, please ask our sisters to retire." The three girls went behind the door screen, leaving behind them a pair of gauze lanterns. The woman then asked, "Have you four elders made up your minds as to which one of you is to be matched to one of my daughters?" Sandy replied, "We have. That one called Pigsy is to be your son-in-law." Pigsy said, "Younger brother, please don't make fun of me—let's deliberate together." Monkey said, "What's there to deliberate? Haven't you concluded everything at the back door, and haven't you even called her Mother? Our master will represent the groom's family, and that woman, the bride's family. Old Monkey will serve as a guarantor, and Sandy as a matchmaker. There will be no need to consult the almanac either, since today is an auspicious day blessed with heaven's favors. First bow before your master and then go in as a groom." Pigsy protested, "This can't be done, can't be done! How could I do such a thing!" Monkey said, "Fool, stop protesting. What can you mean by 'This can't be done' when you have already called her Mother so many times? Quickly get on with the ceremony so that we may attend your wedding banquet. There's a good boy." With one hand he grabbed Pigsy and with the other he pulled the woman, saying, "Dear mother-in-law, take your son-in-law inside." Pigsy was now quite eager to go in and so the woman gave orders to the boys, "Wipe clean the table and chairs, and spread out a vegetarian dinner to entertain my three relatives while I take my son-in-law to his room." She also gave orders to the cooks to prepare a feast next morning in honor of the relatives. The servants took their orders. Soon afterwards, the three pilgrims ate their vegetarian supper and in no time at all they went to sleep where they sat.

In the meantime Pigsy followed his mother-in-law and passed through he didn't know how many suites of rooms. Most of the way he bumped his head against the walls and stumbled over the doorsills. The fool said, "Mother, please go slower. I am new here and you'd better guide me." The woman said, "We are now passing by the granaries, storerooms for money and valuables, and flour mills. We haven't reached the kitchen yet." Pigsy exclaimed, "What a big place!" Again bumping and stumbling, he managed to get through many narrow passages and turns until he finally reached the chambers of the inner court.

The woman said, "Son, your elder brother said that today is an auspicious day blessed with heaven's favors, and so I have made you a son-in-law. But in our hurry we haven't brought along a fortuneteller to guide the rites of worshiping heaven and earth and throwing coins and balls of colored silk against the bed curtains.[86] You'd better kneel eight times before the seat of honor." "Mother is right," replied Pigsy. "Please sit in the seat of honor and let me prostrate myself a few times before you. This would serve the dual purpose of thanking heaven and earth and thanking you. Two things done at once, isn't that simple?" His mother-in-law smiled, "All right, you are really practical, an efficient son-in-law. I'll sit here and you pay your respects to me." In a hall refulgent with the silvery glitter of candles, the fool prostrated himself before her. That done, he asked, "Mother, which one of the sisters will be mine?" His mother-in-law replied, "That's precisely what's bothering me. If I let the eldest marry you, the second might complain. If I marry you to the second, the third might complain. And the eldest might complain if I marry you to the third. So I've not decided yet." Pigsy said, "If you are afraid they might fight over me, then give all three to me. That would prevent bickerings and quarrels and preserve propriety." His mother-in-law said, "How absurd! Do you mean to say that you want to possess all three of my daughters?" Pigsy said, "The way you talk, Mother! Who doesn't have three or four wives? Even if there are a few more, your son-in-law will be happy to receive them. In my early youth I have learned the art of staying firm in battle. I guarantee I can please every one of them." The woman said, "That can't be done. I have with me a handkerchief. Place it on your head and cover your face, and let luck decide your marriage. I'll let my daughters pass before you and you stretch your hands out to grab. Whoever you get hold of will be your bride." The fool agreed, took the handkerchief, and placed it on his head. There is a poem commenting on this:

> The crazy and foolish, ignorant of their essence, cherish
> The sex-sword that injures their health and causes their destruction:

Formerly there were the rites of the Duke of Chou,
Today a bridegroom wears a handkerchief on his head.

Having finished wrapping it around his head, the fool said, "Mother, please ask the sisters to come out." His mother-in-law called, "Truth, Love, and Pity, you all come out to try your luck. See who gets married." Then the tinkling of the jade ornaments announced their arrival, and the fragrance of orchid and musk pervaded the room as if celestial fairies were flitting to and fro. The fool stretched out his hands to grab them. He rushed to the left and right, but to no avail. There seemed to be many, many girls passing by him, but he couldn't get hold of any one of them. He dashed west only to embrace a pillar, and he dashed east only to encounter a wall. With so much running around, he finally got dizzy and began to fall and stumble all the time. Going forward, he would knock himself against the leaf of a door, and turning back, he would bump into a brick wall. He was bumped and knocked so often that his mouth became swollen and his head was covered with black and blue bruises. Finally, sitting on the floor, he panted, "Mother, your daughters are all so slippery I can't get hold of them. What am I supposed to do now?" That woman removed his wrapping, saying, "Son, it is not that my daughters are all so slippery. They are all too modest to want to marry you." Pigsy said, "Mother, since they won't have me, then you marry me." The woman said, "My good son-in-law, how shocking! How could you think of marrying your mother-in-law! My three daughters, they are all very clever. Each has made a brocade shirt embroidered with pearls. Let the one whose shirt fits you marry you, how about that?" Pigsy said, "Good, good. Let me try all three. If they all fit, let me marry them all." The woman went to an inner chamber, brought out only one shirt, and handed it to Pigsy. He stripped off his blue gown, took the shirt, and put it on right away. He had not yet tied the sashes together when, thump! he suffered another fall and down on the floor he went. What happened was that he had become tightly bound by several ropes and the fool was now suffering unendurable agony. But the woman and her three daughters had vanished.

Now the story goes that Tripitaka, Monkey, and Sandy woke up from a sound slumber, not realizing that the east had turned white. They stared hard all around them, and where could they see any large mansion or tall hall, carved beams or storied pillars? They had slept in a grove of pines and cypresses. Frightened, the elder called for Monkey. And Sandy also called, "Elder brother, we are finished. We have met with ghosts." Monkey, who had known it all along, now asked with a smile, "What's the trouble?" The elder said, "Just see where we have been sleeping." Monkey said, "It was fun to be in the pine grove. Wait till you see where the fool has been tortured." The elder asked, "Who's been tortured?" Monkey smiled, "I don't know which Bodhisattvas appeared before us yesterday in the guise of those ladies. Probably they left in the middle of the night after putting poor Pigsy to torture." [87]

The temptation by the four deities is one of the finest episodes in the novel. It is broadly allegorical in intention, but its allegory is fully compatible with the aims of realistic fiction. In *Allegory and Courtesy in Spenser,* one of the few fruitful ventures into comparative studies of Chinese and Western literature and manners, Dr. H. C. Chang has admirably stated that whereas Western allegory as represented by *The Faerie Queene* personifies abstract mental and moral states, Chinese allegory, which is expressive of a more practical ethical impulse, primarily illustrates the fact of temptation.[88] The temptation of Pigsy is therefore far more suggestive of a latter-day Western allegory like Tolstoy's story "How Much Land Does a Man Need?" in its impulse toward concrete fictional realization. Given the simpler conventions of Chinese storytelling, it is as gripping a study of lust as the latter is a study of greed. It is certainly far more psychologically subtle than anything in *The Water Margin* or *The Romance of the Three Kingdoms.*

The characterization of Pigsy in this self-contained allegory, one may further note, is of a piece with his characterization in the rest of the novel. The Pigsy that wants to marry and stay on the widow's estate is the same person who reluctantly bids farewell to the Kao family. As always, he is an object of ridicule to the others, but he himself is serious throughout. He is very much on his best behavior in his negotiations with the widow though time and again his impatience betrays his desperation. He is apologetic about his appearance, but again he brags about his usefulness on the farm. His sexual hunger is given astonishing reality when, faced with the daughters' refusal, he begs the widow to marry him. But this sexual hunger is inseparable from his hunger for purposive activity. Like any other spiritually ungifted average sensual person, Pigsy sees challenge in the ownership and management of a large estate but no challenge at all in a wearisome pilgrimage. In *The Faerie Queene* the voluptuous nymphs in the Bower of Bliss appear primarily in the aspect of naked sensuality, and the men who succumb to their lure immediately lose their self-respect and turn bestial in their oblivion of all duties and responsibilities. With Pigsy, the sight of beautiful women in possession of a fabulous estate only fully arouses his domestic instinct. (In his subsequent temptation by the spider-spirits, who are mere sirens without property, Pigsy behaves far more impudently because he is not serious about them.)[89] If he is starved of sex on his journey, he is at the same time stultified by his lack of opportunity to prove his usefulness as a householder. In Pigsy, with all his unflattering physical and moral features, Wu Ch'eng-en has drawn the portrait of every common man who finds his fulfillment in his pursuit of respectable mundane goals.

CHAPTER V

CHIN P'ING
MEI

Chin P'ing Mei, traditionally ranked with *San kuo, Shui hu,* and *Hsi yu chi* as one of the four great novels of the Ming period, has done extremely well at the hands of Western translators and scholars. Clement Egerton's four-volume translation entitled *The Golden Lotus* (1939) was a difficult undertaking admirably carried out. Granted that the translator has used the Ch'ung-chen edition of the novel rather than the earlier and fuller Wan-li edition and that he has further trimmed or deleted verse passages, it nevertheless remains a labor of love free of serious errors, thanks partly to the "untiring and generously given help" of the Chinese novelist, Lao She, to whom Egerton has dedicated his work.[1] Though we may regret its omission of erotic passages, Franz Kuhn's abridged German version (retranslated into English under the title *Chin P'ing Mei*) has actually enhanced the novel's readability by eliminating many of its tiresome episodes.[2] Lately, Professor Patrick Hanan has published two important papers, "The Text of the *Chin P'ing Mei*" and "Sources of the *Chin P'ing Mei,*" which have added a great deal to the pioneering research by Chinese and Japanese scholars.[3] Further study of the composition and structure of the novel must build upon his solid contributions to scholarship.

In China *Chin P'ing Mei* has long suffered under its notoriety as a work of uninhibited pornography. In modern times, however, scholars have treated it with much greater kindness, regarding it as the first genuine Chinese novel as well as a profound work of naturalism.[4] So far as its subject matter is concerned, *Chin P'ing Mei* certainly is a milestone in the development of Chinese fiction: it has departed from history and legend to treat a world of its own creation, peopled by life-size men and women in their actual bourgeois surroundings divested of heroism and grandeur. Though its pornography had been anticipated, its patient chronicling of the quotidian events of a Chinese household in all their squalor and depravity was something revolutionary, and there has been nothing quite like it in the further development of the Chinese novel. But for all its appropriation of a new territory for fiction, its method of presentation is something else again. Far more than *Shui hu,* it is a work consciously designed to meet the expectations of an audience used to various forms of oral entertainment. Its generous inclusion of songs and jokes, of mundane and Buddhist tales, constantly mars the naturalistic texture of its narrative so that, from the viewpoint of style and structure, it must be rated the most disappointing novel we have thus far considered.

Its reversion to a popular mode of storytelling is especially puzzling since, though the novel starts with an episode from *Shui hu* involving Hsi-men Ch'ing and P'an Chin-lien, the subsequent development of that episode has all the markings of an original story little indebted to history or legend. In its earliest extant editions, dating from the last years of the Wan-li period (1573–1619), the novel bears the title *Chin P'ing Mei tz'u-hua* (A story interspersed with *tz'u* songs of three women named Chin, P'ing, and Mei).[5] Like the earlier novels, it contains numerous verse passages of description, but it also includes a copious number of *tz'u* or *ch'ü* songs and song sequences of a lyrical character. In view of this distinguishing feature, the hypothesis has been seriously proposed by P'an K'ai-p'ei that the novel must have evolved from the repertoire of generations of storytellers whose specialty was to accompany the recital of the tale of Hsi-men Ch'ing with precisely such songs and song sequences. I find this theory quite persuasive even though Communist critics jealous of the reputation and creative integrity of the classical novels have vehemently opposed it and Professor Hanan, who has examined the novel far more carefully than anyone else in the West, sees no reason to countenance it.[6] If this theory is indeed to be ruled out, then the author must have been one completely at home in the various forms of popular entertainment of his time who wrote the novel partly to show off his virtuosity as an adapter of these forms.

Who that person was has remained a mystery. At a time when most novelists preferred to hide their identity, the pornographic character of *Chin P'ing Mei* made it highly unlikely that anyone would want to accept credit for composing it, even though by the late Ming period pornographic stories and woodcuts had become quite popular.[7] In the Wan-li edition of the novel, the author is given the pseudonym of Hsiao-hsiao Sheng of Lan-ling. There are three prefaces, also by pseudonymous authors, which are already defensive about the book's pornographic reputation; thus Lung-chu K'e cautions, "Those who read *Chin P'ing Mei* and feel compassion are Bodhisattvas, those who feel fear are gentlemen, those who feel only agreeably entertained are 'small men,' and those who are incited to imitate the actions described in the work are birds and beasts." [8] Early Ch'ing anecdotists have further reported that the book was written as an act of filial piety. According to this legend, which could have started soon after the publication of the novel and was not discredited until modern times, its author was none other than Wang Shih-chen (1526–90), the leading poet and essayist of his time, who wrote the work to avenge the death of his father for which the evil minister Yen Shih-fan was mainly responsible. Because Yen was addicted to pornography, Wang poisoned the lower corner of every page of his completed manuscript and submitted it to him. As Yen mechanically moistened his fingertip with his own saliva to turn the pages, he eventually swallowed enough poison to cause his death.[9]

In place of this preposterous attribution, Arthur Waley has suggested as the most likely candidate for author the writer and painter Hsü Wei (1521–93), a beloved hero of Chinese folklore well known for his sympathy for vernacular literature.[10] A noted playwright, Hsü Wei would have been familiar with the type of popular songs introduced in *Chin P'ing Mei,* though one may question whether his eccentric genius could have fathered a book of such low culture and ordinary mentality. But quite apart from internal evidence, there is very little likelihood that the author could have been a leading intellectual of his time. During the 1590s at least one manuscript of the novel passed through the hands of Tung Ch'i-ch'ang, the brothers Yuan Hung-tao and Yuan Chung-tao, T'ao Wang-ling, and T'ang Hsien-tsu—all leading intellectuals and writers more or less infected with the individualist and antipuritanical temper of the late Ming period.[11] Their delight over the work was understandable since they could not have encountered elsewhere such graphic descriptions of bourgeois and boudoir life. But the fact that none of these writers knew of its author would indicate his relative obscurity, his not being a member of the national elite. He could have been an obscure tutor, as suggested by Yüan Chung-tao: "Formerly there was a Captain Hsi-men in the capital, who engaged an old scholar from Shaohsing to serve in his household. The scholar had little to occupy his time, and so day by day recorded the erotic and licentious goings-on there. In the figure of Hsi-men Ch'ing he portrayed his master, and in the other figures, his master's various concubines. . . ."[12] Or, to swing to the other extreme of the social ladder, he could have been one of those parasitic imperial descendants scattered among all the cities of China, known for their patronage of the theater and other forms of popular entertainment. He could have lived the life of a licentious autocrat and have had the leisure and incentive to record it.

The signal service rendered by Hanan's article on "Sources of the *Chin P'ing Mei*" has been to drive home the author's extensive borrowing and adaptation of all kinds of material and therefore the patchwork quality of his narrative. Hanan lists eight types of sources: 1) the novel—*Shui-hu chuan*; 2) the venacular short story; 2a) the crime-case story; 3) the erotic short story in literary Chinese; 4) histories of the Sung period; 5) the drama; 6) the popular song; 7) *chantefable* literature, especially the form of Buddhist recitation known as *pao-chüan* (precious scrolls). Of these, the popular song has been used with the greatest regularity and, according to Hanan, the greatest success. This genre comprises individual songs (*hsiao-ling*) and song sequences (*san-t'ao*) which are in form and music identical with those found in plays. Many of these were originally drawn from the plays but have later assumed an independent life as the courtesan-singers appropriated them as part of their repertoire. By late Ming times, such songs and song sequences were very popular and many songbooks were printed to meet the public demand.[13] The author of *Chin P'ing Mei,* a great connoisseur of this literary form, may have quoted all his songs and song sequences from memory since, though many of them are preserved in the songbooks, they sometimes differ in wording from the printed texts.

In the *tz'u-hua* version there are quoted in full as many as 20 song sequences and 120 individual songs. Since the novel has only 100 chapters, it follows that such quotations are present in nearly every chapter. It is, in fact, the regular practice of the author to introduce songs or a song sequence at the end of a chapter. Since, unlike the verse passages in *Hsi yu chi* which are each individually composed for a descriptive occasion, these songs are merely copied into the novel, the author often takes considerable pains to devise situations where the use of such songs is dramatically appropriate.[14] In a sense, the novel is almost a poetic anthology within a narrative framework.

Next to the popular song, the author also goes to great trouble to adapt popular stories. In nearly every case, such importations detract from the strength of the novel. Fortunately, the long central section, comprising chapters 9–79, is relatively less encumbered with such stories, and claims greater interest as serious fiction. But the last 21 chapters (one may legitimately doubt whether they were by the author of the first 79 chapters)[15] appear to be nothing but a crazy quilt of adapted stories, though so far only a small number have been identified.

In view of the author's inveterate passion for quoting songs and adapting stories (I must refer the reader to Hanan for a thorough discussion of other types of indebtedness), he appears to us as a perverse writer who apparently prizes his ingenuity as much as, if not more than, his creativity. Despite his manifest talent for realistic fiction, he tampers with it so as to impress a special audience who will applaud his cleverness in offering other kinds of borrowed attractions. But, even in Ming China, readers of novels were primarily interested in the story: by the Ch'ung-chen period (1628–43), the songs and song sequences that had been incorporated with so much care were already felt to be a mere encumbrance and they were duly deleted or trimmed along with other kinds of poetry in the so-called novel edition, which soon supplanted the *tz'u-hua* version in popular favor to become the standard edition in the Ch'ing dynasty.[16] As far as its prose text is concerned, this abridged edition differs significantly from the earlier edition only in chapter 1 and chapters 53–55. According to Hanan, both editions are traceable to a nonextant first edition of a somewhat earlier date.

Despite its large number of borrowed stories, the main plot of *Chin P'ing Mei* can be easily summarized. The novel still progresses in an episodic fashion, but the episodes are mainly concerned with members of the Hsi-men household. After Golden Lotus (P'an Chin-lien) has committed adultery with Hsi-men Ch'ing and murdered her dwarf husband, she is soon installed in her paramour's house as the fifth wife. Hsi-men is legitimately married to Moon Lady (Yüeh-niang) and has earlier acquired three concubines: the courtesan Li Chiao-erh; the widow of a cloth merchant, Meng Yü-lou; and the maid Hsüeh-o who, despite her promotion, remains in the kitchen as a cook.

Soon after Golden Lotus' arrival, Hsi-men forms a liaison with Vase (Li P'ing-erh), the wife of his neighbor and sworn brother, Hua Tzu-hsü. Vase, who hates her husband, soon contrives his financial ruin and hastens his death as a debauchee. After a brief marriage to a quack doctor whom she also detests for his sexual inadequacy, the repentant Vase returns to Hsi-men a changed person divested of her ruthless and unscrupulous character. As the sixth wife, she is a contrast to Golden Lotus for her generosity and independent wealth, her conjugal devotion and kindness to the servants, and her capacity for self-abnegation. Lotus is quite jealous of her, as she is of every woman to whom Hsi-men pays attention. After Vase has given birth to a frail son, Lotus sees to it that he does not live beyond his first year. The success of her scheme also hurries the grief-stricken Vase to her grave. Hsi-men is for weeks inconsolable.

As a reward for his many services and presents to Grand Preceptor Ts'ai Ching, Hsi-men is summoned to the capital to have an audience with him and receive a promotion. While there, he is warned of his impending doom by Vase, who appears in a dream; nevertheless, he returns home in a more cheerful mood, apparently cured of his grief. By now he is a very active businessman and a local military officer of some importance, with a demanding social schedule. Even though he still goes about seeking new conquests, he has been for some time relying on aphrodisiac pills (given him by a mysterious Indian monk) to sustain his virility, and, to the consternation of his other wives, he has long since become a prey to Lotus' insatiable lust. Moon Lady, especially, suffers in quiet desperation, and turns increasingly to the company of Buddhist nuns for consolation and instruction. But, like Lotus, she relies on magic recipes to make herself pregnant.

One night during the Lantern Festival, Hsi-men returns home to Lotus' bed already exhausted from a long sexual bout with Wang VI, wife of one of his store managers. Forever insatiable, Lotus feeds Hsi-men three of his aphrodisiac pills and mechanically engages him in sexual combat. He soon turns ghastly sick and unconscious. A few days later he dies while Moon Lady gives birth to his son, Hsiao-ko.

In the last 21 chapters, the story becomes much more hurried. Friends begin to drop off after Hsi-men's death, and servants and business agents abscond with money and goods. Li Chiao-erh, the second wife, steals valuables from the house, returns to her old profession, and soon remarries. A magistrate's son falls in love with the third wife, Meng Yü-lou, and gives her a new lease on happy married life. Now asserting power in a simpler household, Moon Lady first sells Plum Blossom (Ch'un-mei), Lotus' personal maid and ally, as a concubine to Chou Hsiu, a military commander of rising importance who eventually dies a general. Next, she expels Hsi-men's son-in-law and Lotus' paramour, Ch'en Ching-chi, and sells Lotus to Wu Sung, who in no time at all kills her to avenge his elder brother's murder.

A former servant named Lai Wang returns to the scene and elopes with Hsüeh-o, Hsi-men's fourth widow. Both are caught and punished, and Hsüeh-o is eventually sold to Plum Blossom, now Chou Hsiu's favorite wife living in splendor and luxury. Because Hsüeh-o was Lotus' enemy, her new mistress treats her with utter harshness and hastens her suicide by forcing upon her the fate of a low-class prostitute. In the meantime, Ching-chi has undergone many adventures and tribulations before he is finally rescued from pauperdom by Plum Blossom. While her husband is on military duty elsewhere, she openly cohabits with her old friend and gives him a new wife (his first wife has died years earlier, a victim of his cruelty). Ching-chi is eventually killed by Chou Hsiu's retainer for his adultery though, incredibly enough, by that time he has earned the undying love of his new wife and another girl who is fanatically devoted to him. Plum Blossom dies of excessive sexual indulgence soon after.

When Hsiao-ko grows to be a boy of fifteen, Moon Lady again meets with an old monk named P'u-ching who once wanted to claim him as his disciple when he was barely one year old.[17] This time

Moon Lady reluctantly gives him up and the novel ends hopefully on a note of Buddhist redemption.

In the preceding summary no mention has been made of Hsi-men's many sponging friends, prominently Ying Po-chüeh, who amuse him at his parties, or of the several prostitutes and paramours (besides Wang VI) with whom he dallies, or of his colleagues and associates in the official and business world. All these assorted minor characters contribute considerably to the liveliness of the novel and thicken its satirical texture. But, for the present, the synopsis should enforce our recognition that, in its simple outline, *Chin P'ing Mei* tells quite a gripping story in spite of its implausible melodramatic lapses at the end. If this gripping chronicle does not ultimately measure up to a great novel, it is because the novelist has not at all times fully realized his opportunities for realistic dramatization. In addition to his inordinate passion for inserting extraneous material into his work, he is also guilty of gross carelessness in telling his story and of adopting a certain air of sardonic jocularity that tends to destroy the illusion of realistic credibility. The latter faults I shall now demonstrate.

Early in the novel (chap. 4), Hsi-men Ch'ing runs his hands over Lotus' naked body and finds her *mons Veneris* hairless. This brief scene, however, is immediately followed by a poem in praise of her private parts with due reference to her pubic hair.[18] It is such discrepancies of detail that make the reader lose confidence in the novelist. What has happened here is that, in quoting a jocular poem to support his prose description, he has not bothered to check if the two accounts tally. Such oversights may appear trivial and they are certainly common in traditional Chinese novels, but even in the present scene the implication is that the author has no visual preconception of what Lotus' body should look like even though it is repeatedly exposed to view in his lengthy descriptions of her sexual encounters.

A more glaring example of inconsistency concerns Hsi-men's rebirth. After Moon Lady has become convinced that P'u-ching is an Ancient Buddha temporarily assuming human guise on earth to save sinning souls in times of trouble, he proceeds to demonstrate to her that Hsiao-ko is really the reincarnation of Hsi-men Ch'ing and that, if she persists in keeping him as her own, he will squander the family fortune and die with his head severed from his body. Compelled by the logic of his demonstration, she relinquishes her son. Yet a few pages earlier in the same chapter (chap. 100), P'u-ching recites Buddhist incantations all night long to intercede for the souls of all those who have died a violent death. As a result, the ghosts of some thirteen characters who have died earlier in the book appear before the monk to announce their impending rebirths at various homes. Tiny Jade, Moon Lady's maid, is privileged to witness this scene, and among the ghosts she sees Hsi-men Ch'ing, who declares he will be reborn as Shen Yüeh, the second son of a wealthy man in the Eastern Capital named Shen T'ung.[19] But if Hsi-men had assumed immediate reincarnation as his own son at the time of his death, how could his ghost still flit around fifteen years later, waiting to be reborn? It affects our basic understanding of the novel to know whether, by the compassionate intercession of an Ancient Buddha, Hsi-men is able to cancel out his sins by assuming the holy life of his own son or whether he is going to work out his salvation through a series of reincarnations while Hsiao-ko merely stores merit in his behalf by living a life of purity and renunciation. But the novelist seems to entertain both possibilities.

For the main portion of his narrative the author tries to maintain the illusion of businesslike realism. He gives almost a daily account of the Hsi-men household, reserving the big events for birthdays and festival days, and he records dates, sums of money, and business transactions matter-of-factly so that a beginning reader cannot help being impressed by his attention to minute detail. But, in reality, such seeming scrupulosity at times disguises gross carelessness. Compare *Chin P'ing Mei* with *Dream of the Red Chamber* and one immediately sees that, while the far more opulent aristocrats in the latter novel are plagued by financial difficulties, Hsi-men gives lavish presents and bribes at all times and seems to have few such worries. He is of course a wealthy man in a fair-sized town (Ch'ing-ho, in present-day Shantung), but, as a merchant, he derives his income at first mainly from his pharmacy and pawnshop, and later additionally from his thread shop and two silk stores. When Golden Lotus is finally to be sold for a hundred taels of silver, her lover Ching-chi tries desperately to raise that sum and it is his delay that enables Wu Sung to buy her. The episode shows, for once at least, that money is not something one easily comes by. Ordinarily, a slave girl sells for five to ten taels of silver. Yet we read in chapter 55 that Hsi-men's birthday present to Ts'ai Ching consists of:

One crimson dragon robe, one green dragon robe, twenty rolls of Han satin, twenty rolls of Szechwan silk, twenty rolls of asbestos, twenty rolls of imported cloth, forty other rolls of plain and figured cloth, a jade belt with a buckle in the shape of a lion's head, another belt made of tagaraka wood inlaid with gold, ten pairs each of jade goblets and goblets made of rhinoceros horn, eight gold wine cups with a floral design, ten fine pearls, and two hundred taels of gold.[20]

It is true that Hsi-men is bribing Ts'ai Ching to secure for him the status of an "adopted son," but since his earlier presents to the grand preceptor, also quite lavish, have bought him only a small military post, one wonders whether Hsi-men would have wanted this dubious honor at such an exorbitant price. Not to question where he could have got hold of some of the treasures listed above, two hundred taels of gold alone is not something that even a substantial merchant could afford to give away in expectation of intangible returns.

But Hsi-men appears a complete prodigal in his determination to curry favor with the great. When the new *chuang-yuan* Ts'ai Yün, a protégé of Ts'ai Ching, passes by his town, Hsi-men gives him "a hundred taels of white gold" along with other valuable presents. When Ts'ai, now a salt commissioner, stops by Ch'ing-ho for the second time in the company of Censor Sung, Hsi-men gives them a most lavish banquet to the improbable tune of "one thousand taels of gold and silver."[21] For a sharp contrast, however, when Commissioner Ts'ai arrives to condole with Hsi-men's widows, he brings in addition to fifty taels of silver (a small sum which, by his own admission, he owed the deceased) the following presents: "Two rolls of Hangchow silk, a pair of woolen socks, four dried fish, and four jars of candied fruit." [22] In making this mean inventory, I suppose it is the author's intention to show how, with the death of Hsi-men, his family can no longer expect the esteem of his fair-weather friends. But it would have been far more in character for the salt commissioner not to show up at all than for him to make a fool of himself by the present of four dried fish. The author is therefore indulging here his fondness for satiric exaggeration. In Western literature, many comic masterpieces are marked by their style of robust exaggeration, and it would have been wonderful if the author of *Chin P'ing Mei* had consistently planned his work as a broad farce. But he appears more often as a methodical and meticulous naturalist, and the reader is always made uncomfortable when he makes a violent shift to the comic mode to introduce his rather tedious jokes.

The death of Hsi-men is the most gruesome scene in the whole novel. But right after his passing, his sponging friends are shown deliberating how much money they should spend to show their respect for the dead. They finally decide that each should contribute one *ch'ien* of silver for the grand total of seven *ch'ien* (roughly, 70 cents in U. S. currency). The author apparently delights in this type of low comedy, but, to indulge in it, he has to suspend the novel of manners and to destroy the illusion of reality so carefully maintained in the death scene. To show further his contempt for Hsi-men, he has these same friends commission a scholar to compose a panegyric which reads like an outrageous burlesque since half of it praises in transparent terms the deceased's male member.[23] The author is here at his flippant best. But if he mocks his hero, he is at the same time mocking himself for the pains he has taken to make a credible human being out of Hsi-men.

If Hsi-men deserves the author's mockery, Vase certainly does not. For the latter half of her story she is presented as a thoroughly likable and kind person, and her death is apparently intended to be the most affecting scene in the novel. But when her grave condition

calls for the consultation of several doctors, the author again appears
at his jolliest. For how could he pass up an opportunity to make fun
of quacks, a traditional butt of Chinese satire? After Vase has become seriously ill, two doctors are summoned but they cannot do
anything for her. Then a gynecologist, Dr. Chao, is invited. Upon
arriving, he first boasts of his qualifications and then breaks into
verse:

> I am Dr. Chao; at my door
> People constantly clamor.
> I can only shake a string of bells
> As I walk my daily rounds,
> And have neither skill nor good drugs to sell.
> When prescribing, I do not use good recipes;
> When feeling the pulse, I just talk nonsense.
>
> . . .
>
> I get paid for wrongly administering medicine;
> I aim at profit, caring nothing for success of cure.
> Those who consult me will usually get worse.
> Wherever I make a house call,
> There will be tears and no laughter.[24]

According to Hanan, this song, as well as other speeches by Dr.
Chao, has been copied almost verbatim from scene 28 of the well-
known Ming play by Li K'ai-hsien, *Pao-chien chi* (The precious
sword).[25] The novelist may have thought it very clever to burlesque
the doctor but, after such a scene of broad comedy, could he seriously
expect the reader to reengage his sympathies with the dying Vase
and her perturbed husband?

The doggerel just quoted, of course, departs wholly in spirit from
the songs and song sequences culled from the repertoire of Ming
courtesans. They are quite refined and represent at their best the
sentimental and erotic *tz'u* poetry of the late T'ang period in its final
stage of significant development. In *Chin P'ing Mei* many such
songs and song sequences are sung professionally by courtesans, and
they serve little novelistic function beyond providing a certain poetic
atmosphere of languor and eroticism. But many of them are sung

by Golden Lotus to define her mood of frustration or desolation, and Hanan has praised this use of the popular song as one of the author's assured successes as a technical innovator.[26] However, in the prose narrative Lotus has been early established as a character of extreme cunning and cruelty, a possessive nymphomaniac who would not stop at anything to gratify her sexual appetite. Since the author has not composed new songs suitable for her character and temperament, on the occasions when she is called upon to convey her feelings in song, she appears therefore a much nicer and more sympathetic person than she actually is. In the prose narrative she is a creature of utter moral repulsiveness and the novelist periodically speaks in the first person to condemn her depravity, but on these poetic occasions she appears all grace and beauty, capable of feelings of feminine delicacy. One wonders if she could have expressed these feelings other than as a professional singer parroting them. It would have been wonderful if the author could have reconciled the discordant images of aggressive repulsiveness and poetic delicacy and made a much more complex character out of Lotus; but again, as in his fondness for satiric jocularity, he appears by design a discontinuous realist who sacrifices the logic of realism to satisfy his desire to introduce songs.

The author's apparent carelessness, his impulse toward satire and burlesque on every conceivable occasion, and his penchant for songs all conspire to mar the realistic surface of his novel. But none of these features is so contrary to the spirit of realism as his impulse to "romance," to rapid recital of melodramatic events in place of patient unfolding of the credible and dramatic. Judging from the quality of the narrative, the novel may be divided into three parts: chapters 1–8, 9–79, 80–100.[27] Part I is heavily in debt to *The Water Margin* since the early episodes involving Hsi-men and Lotus, despite their heightened eroticism and stronger notes of burlesque and didacticism, are copied from that novel. The didactic preamble to chapter 1 is so absurd that even the editor of the Ch'ung-chen edition felt compelled to replace it. On the whole, the first eight chapters give one the impression that the author is still feeling his way toward a mode of narration appropriate for domestic fiction and that he has not yet thought out the whole novel. Lotus is described primarily as a desirable sex object with little developed character of her own.

Part II, which begins with the arrival of Lotus in the Hsi-men household and ends with Hsi-men's death, constitutes a novel within the novel. There are many distracting and dull episodes that could be spared, but on the whole this "novel" has remarkable realistic integrity, with all the reservations already made about the author's habit of tampering with realism. With Part III, however, the narrative mode once again changes: no longer engrossed in minute happenings at one particular place, the novelist now rambles over a much wider geographical area over a longer period of time to account for every character that has appeared earlier. It is an uneconomical and clumsy way to conclude a novel in that improbable episodes, when briefly told, can never excite interest. If, except for his two trips to the capital, Hsi-men stays put in Ch'ing-ho, the new hero Ching-chi is always on the go. His motives for such restlessness are hard to follow. For example, in chapter 92, he goes south solely to blackmail the happily married Meng Yü-lou. While Yü-lou was still Hsi-men's third wife, Ching-chi had once got hold of a comb of hers. Now, armed with that comb (would it serve as any kind of evidence that she once had intimate relations with him?), he threatens to expose her if she does not submit to his lust and extortion. The scheme is completely wild. At another time he has been reduced to a beggar and, on being asked by his companions about his past, he sings a sequence of borrowed songs. As Hanan has aptly observed: "Facts relating specifically to the novel occur in only one of the songs; the others all concern Ching-chi's adventures immediately before this episode. It is not unlikely that in this case, as in others we have noticed, the adventures have been inserted simply in order to allow the use, in an adapted form, of a passage—in this case, a song-sequence—that was already known to the author." [28]

In Part III the widows of Hsi-men have all suddenly acquired glamor. Widows are customarily not sought after in Chinese society as suitable mates. Especially since the first four wives have never proved particularly attractive to Hsi-men whose taste is none too discriminating, and since they are all tainted with his notoriety, one wonders why suddenly every one is after them. It is understandable that Plum Blossom, an attractive young woman, once sold to a middle-aged man with a wife blind in one eye, should monopolize his favor. But why should Li Chiao-erh, a former courtesan no longer in her prime and now resuming her trade, be bought by a rich squire to be his second wife at the price of 300 taels of silver when younger courtesans, including Chiao-erh's attractive niece, could be had at a much cheaper price? [29] Why should the thirty-one-year-old son of a magistrate conceive such a strong passion for the thirty-seven-year-old Meng Yü-lou, who has been twice a widow and whose slightly pockmarked face cannot be too attractive? [30] One also wonders why the former servant Lai Wang, hitherto a sympathetic figure much wronged by Hsi-men, should be so smitten with Hsüeh-o that he wants to elope with her.[31] It is unbelievable, too, that Moon Lady, a pious Buddhist in mourning, should arouse the interest of a local bully and become the victim of a near-rape. In this instance, of course, the author has merely availed himself of her pilgrimage to Mount T'ai to borrow some further episodes from *The Water Margin*.[32]

All these episodes are possible but, seen in the perspective of the earlier narrative where marriage is primarily a monetary transaction, not probable. One gets the impression that, faced with the task of supplying melodramatic endings for all his characters, the author is merely spinning yarn after borrowed yarn to entertain and astound the reader, caring little if each episode fits into the larger narrative pattern. With the exception of those scenes dramatizing the continued animosity between the Golden Lotus faction (Plum Blossom and Ching-chi) and its enemies,[33] the novel has degenerated into an implausible omnibus of flimsily related stories.

One cannot expect a work to possess ideological or philosophical coherence when it manifests such obvious structural anarchy. Yet, before one can properly appreciate the finer aspects of *Chin P'ing Mei,* one must attend to its often mutually contradictory moral and religious assumptions. On the whole, the novelist shares those ambivalent attitudes commonly seen in the colloquial tales of the Ming period: outward conformity with Confucian morality versus a covert sympathy for lovers and seekers after individual autonomy; belief in the Buddhist doctrine of karma and retribution versus an undisguised contempt for monks and nuns; envious disapproval of the rich and powerful versus merciless snobbery toward the lowborn and unfortunate. These remain attitudes rather than components of a consistent world view because, like the professional storytellers, the author seems incapable of resolving the contradictions in his own thinking. His mind is nothing if not common as he by turns appeals to one or another of the popular prejudices.

Chin P'ing Mei has been labeled a naturalistic novel by modern critics. If it is one, then its naturalism owes nothing to the nineteenth-century theories of heredity and environment, but is rather an outgrowth of the Buddhist theory of moral retribution. In a sense, Hsi-men Ch'ing and Lotus are just as helplessly conditioned to an evil existence by their previous karma as the unfortunates in Zola are conditioned by their heredity and environment. In Buddhist terms, the novel is about the redemption of Hsi-men's evil deeds by the willing self-sacrifice of Moon Lady and their son's election of a life of Buddhist dedication. If we take Hsiao-ko to be the reincarnation of Hsi-men, then we may say that the wheel of karma has ceased to turn for the latter because his own individual sins have been canceled through the intervention of a Buddha. But the other characters affected by his evil and perpetrating evil on the strength of their own karma—Lotus, Vase, Plum Blossom, Ch'en Ching-chi, and all the rest—have to undergo a series of rebirths until they have acquired enough merit to get off the wheel of suffering. The announcement of their impending rebirths in the last chapter (though in strict accordance with Buddhist morality, perhaps few of them deserve to be reborn as human beings) indicates that for them the drama of retribution is not confined to one mundane existence. *Hsü*

Chin P'ing Mei (A continuation of *Chin P'ing Mei*), written by Ting Yao-k'ang during the early Ch'ing period, does concern itself with the further adventures of Moon Lady and Hsiao-ko as well as those of the deceased characters in their next round of human and animal existence.[34]

But though the author of *Chin P'ing Mei* anchors his work on the Buddhist idea of karma, he speaks in his own person usually not as a Buddhist, but as a Confucianist regretting the religious necessity for renunciation. As a Buddhist, he would have heralded the birth of Hsiao-ko with joy since he is destined to cancel out his father's sins. Instead, we find in chapter 75 the author's disapproving comment on Moon Lady's engrossment in Buddhist tales when she is already big with child:

> In ancient times, a pregnant woman would never sit or recline in such a manner as to cause injury to the unborn child. She would never listen to erotic music or look at anything suggestive of immodesty. She would frequently occupy herself with the classics of *Poetry* and *History* as well as rare objects of gold and jade. Frequently, too, she would ask a blind minstrel to recite old poetry to her. In this way, when the child was born, he would have proper features and a handsome figure, and when he grew up, he would be intelligent. This is known as King Wen's method of educating the child in the womb. Now that Moon Lady was with child, she should not have allowed those nuns to recite "precious scrolls" to her and expound the doctrines of karma and transmigration. In consequence of this, an ancient Buddha was moved to resume incarnation on earth. And a few years after the child was born, he would be claimed by that Buddha and made to foresake the world. Alas, how sad that the child could not inherit the family property and continue the family line![35]

This sense of regret, later reinforced when the novelist describes Moon Lady's extreme reluctance to part with her son, actually strengthens the pathos of the novel. It is as if the author were appealing to the Chinese reader's instinctive preference for Confucian values so as to make him see the horror and desolation wrought by

Hsi-men's evil deeds. If he had not been so wicked, perhaps Moon Lady would not have been so easily seduced by the nuns, and if she had not been so seduced, her son would have been properly brought up on the Confucian classics and would have in time passed the palace examination and become a distinguished official. The family line would have continued and prospered. The author's Confucian sympathies therefore place the Buddhist scheme of redemption in the perspective of tragedy.

For a Buddhist novel, *Chin P'ing Mei* is surprisingly crowded with Buddhist monks and nuns (and also Taoist priests) of dubious character. Except for one or two mysterious monks of obvious sanctity or magic power,[36] there is hardly one reputable representative of the religious community in the book. All the nuns that ingratiate themselves with Moon Lady are somewhat shady, and the author undoubtedly agrees with Hsi-men in placing them among professional matchmakers and other disreputable females whose avocation is to swindle their patrons and bring about amorous liaisons. This contempt for nuns and to a lesser extent for monks, commonly shared by the Chinese, stems not so much from a disrespect for religion as from a sense of snobbery: the nuns and monks, just like matchmakers, quack doctors, and unsuccessful scholars reduced to making a living as pedagogues or scribes, are automatically suspect because their social status is low. If not villains, they are at least comic types to be laughed at without qualms. With its merciless ridicule of all people of humbler status, *Chin P'ing Mei* may be said to have been a book consciously designed for the middle class. In addition to many comic quacks like Dr. Chao, there is Dr. Chiang, briefly Vase's husband, who suffers cruel abuse from his wife and Hsi-men without any redress.[37] The pederast Wen Pi-ku, a poor scholar serving as Hsi-men's secretary, is an object of pure scorn.[38] (In other Chinese novels we find many a pedagogue resorting to pederasty out of necessity rather than by personal choice. The economic implication of his comedy is that he is too poor to afford a wife or the pleasures of a brothel.) Then, of course, the sponging friends of Hsi-men literally eat the crumbs off his table. The novelist, who has very little sense of refined humor, specializes in the comedy of destitution and has great fun with these shiftless clowns.

In this connection, it is interesting to note that Hsi-men Ch'ing has not always been presented in so unfavorable a light as is generally supposed. He is a man of wealth and position, and for the most part he is spared the author's ridicule. Our final impression of him is that of a likable person, cheerful, generous, and capable of genuine feeling. If he is frequently engaged in nefarious deals, he as often impresses us with his bounty. If he is a notorious seducer of women, the author makes it quite clear that his victims are begging to be seduced. In extenuating Hsi-men's crime, he is appealing to the Chinese prejudice that it is inevitably women who bring men to ruin with their sexual aggression and dangerous cunning. Nearly all Hsi-men's mistresses are shown to have been women of shady background and lewd disposition before they are approached by Hsi-men. Wang VI and Madame Lin are notorious for their promiscuity.[39] Even Hui-lien (Wistaria, in Egerton's translation), the wife of the servant Lai Wang and the most pathetic of Hsi-men's victims, has a shady past. A maid in Judge Ts'ai's house, she is dismissed from service after she has been found sharing a paramour with her mistress behind the judge's back. Then she is married to a cook and finds time to have an affair with Lai Wang. After her husband has been conveniently killed in a brawl, she joins the Hsi-men household as Lai Wang's wife and easily attracts the attention of her new master. Though she is not as bad as the novelist initially depicts her,[40] there is no doubt that she is a foolish and vain woman of loose morals.

In his long career as a profligate, then, though Hsi-men has been privileged to deflower young courtesans as an honored customer at brothels, he has not actually seduced a single virgin or virtuous woman from a good family. An indolent sensualist among easy women, he is almost the exact opposite of the energetic seducer in the Western tradition—Don Giovanni. He is certainly not a Vicomte de Valmont, the deliberate corrupter of innocence in Laclos's novel, *Les Liaisons Dangereuses.* But fortunately for the Chinese novel, if Hsi-men is a mere creature of self-indulgence in contrast to the diabolic French hero, his principal partner in lust—Lotus— does suggest the determination and evil cunning of the Marquise de Merteuil. The Chinese author, of course, lacks the artistry and intellect of Laclos, but if his work does attain moments of moral horror, it is certainly due to his unflinching presentation of Lotus' character. To this aspect of the novel's art we shall return.

But, as has been earlier mentioned, even the portrayal of Lotus has not been entirely unsympathetic, largely because of the author's ambivalent attitude toward the sexual function. Superficially, he is the stern moralist who seizes every opportunity to condemn adultery and debauchery, but the very fact that he takes so many pains to describe the sexual act belies the attitude of moral censure. While a dry, slangy, and at times almost clinical style suffices for most of the shorter passages, in the more elaborate accounts of coition the author relishes its every detail (even when he is not resorting to verse) with a kind of dispassionate lyricism which seems to imply that, while the participants may otherwise disgust us, the act itself, the performing organs, and the human bodies themselves are beautiful sights to contemplate. There are nauseating and even sadistic scenes that nullify that impression, and there is coarse comedy as when, for instance, lascivious-minded onlookers watch a copulating couple. But, on the whole, the sexual act when performed to the mutual pleasure of the partners is never entirely robbed of its human meaning, and for the many frustrated women characters it remains the sole redeeming event in their dull captive existence.

It is a pity that, except for the expensive photolithographic reprints of the *tz'u-hua* version, cheap modern editions of the novel have always appeared in an expurgated form even though the longer erotic passages are invariably well written. While on most occasions the author is content to borrow and adapt cliché-ridden verses and popular songs, he seems to have composed these passages with loving care. For one thing, his vocabulary, ranging from low dialectal terms to euphemisms of extreme poetic refinement, is quite astounding. To be sure, it is not all his own since sex manuals have been composed as early as the Han dynasty[41] and erotic imagery has always been noticeable in certain types of Chinese poetry. Nevertheless, *Chin P'ing Mei,* the first full-length erotic novel in China, has gone far beyond its predecessors in its elaboration of sexual description. Like many Western amatory poets, the author is not without humor in his use of the *double-entendre* and the mock-heroic style. But, even in his playfulness, he seems to savor the reciprocal joy of the performers in every movement of their play. For the duration of their coupling, their moral stance outside the bed is forgotten and they are seen solely as lovers absorbed in the game of amorous combat.

The author also appears quite sensitive to the pain of sexual frustration. While Hsi-men cavorts with his women, his neglected wives appear the more lonely as they occupy their time with silly chatter and ugly squabbles, with birthday parties and conversations with nuns. With all her moral rectitude and reluctance to press her sexual claims as the first wife, Moon Lady appears perhaps the loneliest of them all. Even Golden Lotus, when she is being temporarily neglected by Hsi-men, invites commiseration as she projects herself in the role of the lovelorn woman in the popular songs. Though the author of *Chin P'ing Mei* makes no attempt to reconcile the claims of conventional morality and the instinctive self, there is little doubt that his elaborate descriptions of sexual play and his acute sympathy for sexual deprivation represent a kind of personal commitment to values ostensibly denied by the novel.

When all the points that conspire to make the novel a work of haphazard realism and moral ambiguity are conceded, a strong case can nevertheless be made for its being a work of terrifying moral realism if one is able to concentrate on the major episodes involving the main characters—especially Hsi-men, Lotus, Vase, and Moon Lady—and to refuse to be distracted by all the intervening passages of satire and burlesque, of comic frivolity and didactic solemnity. Fortunately, nearly all the "romance" episodes come pell-mell after chapter 80 so that they hardly affect the "novel" within the novel that we shall be considering in this section.[42]

Golden Lotus is clearly the dominant character in that "novel." Except in her poetic moments, when she appears languid and dispirited, she is the most clear-headed and calculating character of the lot. She is born and reared a slave, and her savagery is the savagery of the slave, abject in her selfishness, cunning in her struggle for security and power, and ruthless toward her rivals and enemies. The plaything of an old roué and the victim of a travesty of marriage to a "seven-inch dwarf," she is definitely among the injured and insulted, and the modern tendency, among playwrights and novelists who have portrayed her career, is to sympathize with her, at least for her early attempt to achieve a kind of normal happiness with her brother-in-law Wu Sung.[43] But in the novel there is little evidence that she feels romantic about him, certainly not after her beauty has caught the eye of Hsi-men Ch'ing. (In the end, of course, Wu Sung returns as her nemesis. But one cannot take Part III seriously: if she were consistent with her earlier character, she would have tried to avoid rather than have entered with apparent alacrity the trap he sets for her.) And there is little in her character that calls for pity. She herself is unpitiful, and Plum Blossom, in defending her against her detractors, once praises her spirit of *cheng-ch'iang,* that is, her fierce determination to excel and beat the competition.[44] She is pitiless in her murder of her first husband, as in her treatment of her stepdaughter, Ying-erh. When Hsi-men deliberately neglects her following their first fling together, she releases her fury by clawing Ying-erh's face until blood flows.[45] This is a recurring situation: whenever she feels mistreated or sexually frustrated, she inflicts sadistic punishment on her own slave, whether she be the stepdaughter or the maid Chrysanthemum (Ch'iu-chü).

Her drama proper begins with her removal to the Hsi-men house. Upon being introduced to the other wives, she knows right away that none is her match in beauty. Nevertheless, to safeguard her position, she ingratiates herself with Moon Lady and assiduously cultivates the favor of her lord not only by eagerly complying with his sexual demands but by making him a present of her pretty maid, Plum Blossom. With his favor more or less assured, she further strengthens her position by forming an alliance with the good-natured Meng Yü-lou, and then she tests her power by picking a fight with the wife enjoying the least favor with their husband, Hsüeh-o. Hsi-men is prevailed upon to kick and beat the latter violently.[46] His eagerness to please her reassures Lotus and emboldens her to adopt a more aggressive policy toward Moon Lady. In the future she will time and again incite her lord to punish her enemies and demand from him proofs of his love.

But Lotus is also a nymphomaniac. Early conditioned to the notion that a woman's duty is to please her man, she has long capitalized on her slavery to make her lot endurable: to regard herself indeed as a sex instrument, but not so much to please her partner as to gratify herself. Soon she finds Hsi-men's sexual attentions inadequate: though spending little time with the other wives, he is a man of vigor with a roving eye, and a habitué of the local brothels. During one of his prolonged absences, therefore, Lotus forms a liaison with a boy servant, Ch'in T'ung, to satisfy her sexual hunger, but in doing so she incautiously affords the other wives a chance to avenge themselves. Hsüeh-o and Li Chiao-erh inform against her, and the enraged Hsi-men immediately orders his servants to give the boy "thirty terrible stripes till his flesh was torn and the blood ran down his legs,"[47] and then dismisses him from service. But Lotus herself receives much lighter punishment: she is stripped of her clothes and commanded to kneel before her master to be cross-examined. Since the boy has already been harshly punished for his undeniable crime, one might logically expect Hsi-men to exact a confession from her: if he so wishes, he could beat her to death without incurring any legal difficulty. During the interrogation he does lash her once, but then he "looked again at the kneeling woman, her flower-like body unclothed. She was uttering piteous sounds and weeping so touchingly. His anger flew to Java, and with it all but a fraction of his determination to punish her."[48] Then he beckons Plum Blossom to come over. As he asks her to confirm Lotus' lying words, he keeps on fondling her. His undignified manner of holding court indicates that Lotus' nudity has aroused him (hence his need to fondle Plum Blossom) and he questions the latter so as to get out of a difficult situation without losing face. In this round of battle with her master, Lotus is exposed to public shame and she will be from then on much more on her guard when having trysts with Ching-chi. But the fact that Hsi-men does not have the heart to give her due punishment shows that she still enjoys the upper hand.

Then, to the further advantage of Lotus, Hsi-men becomes much more mellowed as the novel progresses. He still seeks sexual diversity, but more out of habit than out of an inner compulsion. His outbursts of anger become fewer as he becomes increasingly inured to his social and official routine. As a lover, he is now more intent on impressing women with his sexual prowess and giving them pleasure than on receiving pleasure himself. An occasional sadist, he is almost masochistically resigned to punishing himself with strenuous dissipation. In time he shows a more accommodating disposition which finds satisfaction in doing favors for others. His cruel treatment of Vase for her marriage to Dr. Chiang may be said to represent his last imperious act of domestic despotism. Upon installing her as his sixth wife, he absents himself from her chamber for the first three nights. Highly humiliated, she attempts suicide on the third night but, still in a punishing mood the next evening, he whips her and orders her to kneel before him in her nakedness.[49] From then on, however, he finds so much contentment in her love and devotion that he cannot help being humanized under her influence. Vase's great love for Hsi-men is not something easily reconcilable with her cruelty to her first two husbands: this change in her character is primarily dictated by plot requirements so that she may serve as a complete foil to the aggressive and selfish Lotus. But, psychologically speaking, it is not entirely implausible that she should undergo this transformation because, as she repeatedly tells

Hsi-men, with him she has finally found sexual fulfillment.[50] He is able to satisfy her as no one else has been, and out of her supreme gratitude she becomes a concerned and affectionate wife.

For Lotus, Vase constitutes the greatest threat to her continuing enjoyment of her privileged position. Quite unlike Vase, she uses her sex primarily as a weapon in the battle for domination and measures her security by the frequency of her husband's visits. She tolerates his desire for sexual diversity only so long as the objects of his attention pose no threat to that security. In chapters 11–50, she has two rivals besides Vase, neither quite so serious. The first is the courtesan Cassia (Li Kuei-chieh), Li Chiao-erh's niece, who takes herself seriously because Hsi-men is her first, deflowering patron. She engages Lotus in a minor feud but, with so many other minor characters to attend to, the novelist soon loses interest in her and she drops out of the competition after chapter 12. The other rival is the pathetic and simple-minded Hui-lien, whom Lotus regards as more dangerous because there is the possibility of her becoming the seventh wife and therefore sharing Hsi-men's favors with her on a legal basis. And she cannot stand her bragging about her improved status as a mistress. When Hui-lien's husband grumbles about his cuckoldom, therefore, it is Lotus who incites Hsi-men to take harsh measures against him. He is first maltreated in prison and then banished to his home town, and the heartbroken Hui-lien commits suicide as a result.[51] Lotus gloats over this triumph.

But Vase is much harder to dispose of. She is a rich lady well liked by everybody whereas Lotus herself is a lowborn slave generally detested in the household. Moreover, the fair-skinned Vase is a beauty in her own right, and once Lotus whitens her own body in an attempt to lure Hsi-men from his new love.[52] But not only is he genuinely fond of Vase and grateful for her money; she soon becomes pregnant whereas, despite her practice of black magic, Lotus remains childless after her two miscarriages. Powerless to score any advantage over her rival, she is reduced to making jeering remarks about her pregnant condition in front of their husband. Hsi-men, however, immediately puts a stop to her impudence by inflicting upon her a mild form of sadism (in chapter 27, generally regarded by Chinese readers as the most obscene chapter in the whole book). The form of her punishment, however, still expresses his fondness for her in that it merely serves him as an excuse for further sexual experimentation. But insofar as Lotus is denied equal partnership in the game, she is being punished. She suffers a temporary setback.

After Vase has given birth to a boy, Lotus feels keenly her total eclipse. In her desperation, she tries to win her man back with proofs of sexual solicitude or to persuade the other wives to turn against her rival. When nothing comes of these efforts, she punishes her own slave, the maid Chrysanthemum, often without the slightest provocation, to give vent to her frustration. The most shocking instance occurs in chapter 58 where her torture of Chrysanthemum serves at once to spite Vase and to aggravate the condition of her sickly baby, Kuan-ko. That evening Lotus has stepped on dog dung and her new shoes are soiled. With a heavy stick she first beats the guilty dog, whose howling wakes up the child in the adjacent suite of rooms. But she continues beating it for a while even after Vase has sent her maid Welcome Spring over to ask her to desist. Next, Lotus berates Chrysanthemum for having kept the dog in her compound at this late hour and orders her to come forward to examine the shoes:

Tricked, she bent her head to look at them. Golden Lotus struck her face several times with one of the shoes until her lips were cut. Chrysanthemum drew back and tried to stop the blood with her hand.

"You slave, so you want to get away from me, eh?" Golden Lotus cursed her. Then to Plum Blossom: "Drag her here and have her kneel down before me. Then get the whip and strip all her clothes off her. I will give her thirty stripes if she takes them nicely. If she tries to dodge, I'll whip her all over."

Plum Blossom pulled off Chrysanthemum's clothes. Golden Lotus bade her hold the girl's hands, and the blows fell upon her like raindrops. That slave girl shrieked like a pig being killed.

Kuan-ko had only just closed his eyes and now he was startled by the noise. This time Vase bade Embroidered Spring come to Golden Lotus, saying, "My mistress asks the Fifth Lady please to forgive Chrysanthemum. She is afraid the noise will frighten the baby."

A little earlier, old woman P'an [Lotus' mother, who was paying a visit] was lying on the brick-bed in the inner room when she first heard the screams of Chrysanthemum. She hurriedly got up and asked her daughter to stop, but Golden Lotus would not listen to her. Now that Vase had sent Embroidered Spring over, she again came forward and tried to snatch the whip from her daughter's hand, saying, "*Chieh-chieh*, please don't beat her any more and give the lady over there cause to complain that you are trying to frighten her baby. I don't mind your breaking a stick over a donkey, but we must not harm that precious sapling."

Golden Lotus was already wild enough, but when she heard her mother's words she was so inflamed with anger that her face turned purple. She pushed her mother away and the old woman all but fell down. "Old fool," she said, "you go over there and sit. This doesn't concern you and why do you want to interfere? What's all this crap about a precious sapling and breaking a stick over a donkey? You are in league with everyone else to injure me."

"You thief, you will surely die an untimely death," retorted the old woman. "When did I behave like a spy? I came here only to beg a little cold food. How could you push me around like that!"

"If you put in a word for her again, see if I don't fix that old bitch over there," Golden Lotus warned. "And I can tell you this: nobody is going to stew me in a pot and eat me up."

Hearing her daughter scolding her so, old woman P'an went to her room and whimpered. Golden Lotus lashed Chrysanthemum twenty or thirty more times. Then she beat her with a stick until her skin and flesh were torn. Before she let the girl go, she drove her sharp nails into her cheeks and scratched them all over.

All this time Vase could only cover the baby's ears with her hands. Tears coursed down her cheeks. She was furious but there was nothing she could do.[53]

By this scene Lotus has already decided on her course of revenge: to kill Vase's son and deprive her of her major source of advantage. Since the child is especially susceptible to fright, she now trains a cat to pounce on him. Long plagued by illness, he succumbs to the traumatic experience.

Confronted with Lotus' second major act of treachery (her first being her adultery with Ch'in T'ung), Hsi-men acts with surprising timidity. Though both Vase and Moon Lady have no reason to doubt that Lotus has deliberately trained the cat to scare the boy, Hsi-men makes no attempt to find out the truth when informed of his critical condition:

Hsi-men Ch'ing flew into a furious rage. He went straight to Golden Lotus' room and, without a word, took the cat by the legs and dashed out its brains on the stone flags underneath the eaves. There was a thud. The cat's brain was scattered like ten thousand peach blossoms, and its teeth like broken jade. Verily,

> No longer would it catch mice in the world of men,
> As it returned to the world of shades as a feline fairy.

When Golden Lotus saw her cat destroyed, she just sat on her bed and did not stir once. But no sooner had he crossed her doorsill than she muttered a curse, "Thief, someday you will die a robber's death. If you dragged me out of here and killed me, you would indeed be a hero. But what had the cat done to you that you should rush in like one gone crazy and hurl him to his death? When he goes to the court in hell and demands his life from you, I hope you will then be prepared. You thief and fickle scoundrel, you will come to no good end." [54]

Recall how, in dealing with her earlier adultery, Hsi-men has at least gone through the motions of an interrogation; at this more dangerous manifestation of her malignity, he merely vents his wrath on the cat without even bothering to ask her any question. Though at the moment he may be too upset to punish her, still, he never returns to this task following the death of his son. We may blame the novelist for his failure to provide a major scene of confrontation, but his quiet handling of the present scene may imply that Hsi-men is now too much aware of Lotus' power over him to want to challenge it. She remains thoroughly insolent, acting the part of an injured woman whose beloved pet has been unaccountably destroyed. Hsi-men appears to beat a hasty retreat as Lotus' muttered curses trail after him.

The death of her son has also completely broken Vase's spirit. She no longer cares to keep up her struggle against Lotus and resigns herself to ill-health and death, leaving Hsi-men disconsolate and Lotus in a position to regain her dominance. But, in the short run, the removal of her rival has the effect of further alienating Hsi-men from Lotus not because he bears her any grudge but because, in the clutches of grief, he wants to keep vigil in Vase's bedchamber and does not feel the usual sexual stimulation. Then, one night, out of his gratitude to the nurse-maid Ju-i (Heart's Delight, in Egerton's translation), who has remained doggedly loyal to her dead mistress, he takes her to bed with him and lets nature reassert itself. Lotus is amused but not alarmed: she cannot dominate him unless he takes an active interest in women. While still grieving for Vase, Hsi-men now spends his nights with Ju-i; the affectionate courtesan Moon-beam (Cheng Ai-yüeh-erh), certainly the most charming girl in the whole book; and, of course, Lotus. Then he takes his trip to the capital.[55]

Lotus' specialty as a sex partner takes the form of fellatio or, in Chinese euphemism, p'in-hsiao (tasting or playing the flute). The night before Hsi-men takes off for the capital, he and Lotus play that game, indicating his increasingly passive role even in bed. Upon his return, he spends his first night with Lotus, but he cannot fall asleep even after he has made love to her. Since Lotus also remains unsatisfied, she again suggests the game of p'in-hsiao to prove her utter devotion to him. At the risk of offending the reader, I must quote the ensuing important passage which happens to be one of the most disgusting scenes in the novel:

The woman made that suggestion for no other reason than to tie Hsi-men's heart to her. Moreover, he had been away from her for half a month; during all that time she had been so starved of sex that she was aflame with lust. Now that he was again with her, she wished she could enter his belly and stay there for good. So for the whole night she relished the flute without once letting it leave her mouth. When finally Hsi-men wanted to get off the bed to urinate, the woman still would not release the flute, saying, "My dearest, please pass all the urine you have stored up right in my mouth and let me swallow it. It is not worth the trouble to get up and expose your warm body to the cold." Hearing this, Hsi-men was filled with boundless delight. He said, "Baby, I don't believe anyone could love me as much as you do." Then he really passed water in her mouth and she let it go down her throat and slowly she swallowed it all. Hsi-men asked, "Does it taste good?" Golden Lotus answered, "It tastes a little alkaline. I would like to have fragrant tea leaves to take the taste away." Hsi-men said, "There are some fragrant tea leaves in my white silk jacket. Get them for yourself." Golden Lotus pulled the jacket from the headboard toward her, took a few leaves, and put them in her mouth.[56]

For emphasis, the author concludes the scene with a didactic comment:

Readers, concubines are always ready to lead their husbands on and bewitch them. To this end, they will go to any length of shamelessness and endure anything no matter how revolting. Such practices would be abhorrent to a real wife properly married to her husband.[57]

This episode, which could have been thought up only by a perverted genius, marks a new stage of Hsi-men's dotage. Apparently under the impression that Lotus really cares for him, from then on he spends most of his nights with her, to the consternation of his other wives, and she in turn becomes far more demanding and censorious of his behavior. A tired debauchee now occasionally complaining of aches in the groin and limbs, he almost has to get Lotus' permission to stay with other women. One evening he tells her that he is going to stay with Ju-i:

"Why don't you undress?" she asked.

He hugged her and smiled apologetically. "I came especially to tell you I am going over there tonight. Please give me that bundle of love-instruments."

"You convict," the woman scolded him. "So you think you can hoodwink me and get by with a nice excuse. If I had not been waiting at the side door, you would have gone there already. You think you would then have asked for my permission? This morning you promised that slut that you would sleep with her tonight and tell stories about me. That's why you didn't send a maid here, but asked her to bring the fur coat herself and kowtow to me. That slut, what does she take me for, trying to play tricks on me that way! When Vase was alive, you treated me like dirt. You think I won't get mad just because you are going to her old nest with some other birdie?"

"Who said I promised her anything?" Hsi-men Ch'ing said, again putting on a smile. "If she hadn't come and kowtowed to you, you would have had just as much cause to curse her."

The woman deliberated for a long while and then said, "I will let you go, but you shall not take along that bundle. The things will all be filthy after you are through with that slut. Since you are going to sleep with me tomorrow anyway, let them stay clean."

"But I am so accustomed to them I don't know what to do without them."

Hsi-men Ch'ing badgered her for a long time, and she finally threw the silver clasp at him. "Take this thing if you must have it," she said. Hsi-men Ch'ing put it into his sleeve as he said, "This is better than nothing." Then he eagerly stepped out.

The woman called him back. "Come here. I am talking to you. I suppose you are going to sleep with her in the same bed the whole night through? If you do so, even the two maids there will feel ashamed. You'd better stay a little while and then let her sleep elsewhere."

"Who said I shall sleep with her long?" Hsi-men said. He was leaving again.

Again the woman called him back. "Come here," she said, "I order you. Why are you in such a hurry?"

"What do you want now?" Hsi-men Ch'ing said.

"You can sleep with her only because I let you, but I forbid you to talk a lot of nonsense about me. If you do, you'll encourage her to be brazen in front of us. If I find out you have done anything of the sort, I will bite off your thing the next time you come to my room."

"Oh, you funny little whore," Hsi-men Ch'ing said, "how can I put up with so many of your instructions?" Then he went straight to that other place.[58]

One perceives a changed tone in their relationship: Hsi-men is now the furtive and apologetic husband and Lotus the righteous, commanding wife who has him at her beck and call with such rude commands as "I am talking to you" and "I order you."

The next evening Lotus counts on Hsi-men's presence in her bedroom. According to the calendar, it is an auspicious night for getting pregnant, and she has prepared a special medicine for that purpose. But Hsi-men, after a busy day with his colleagues, is being detained in Moon Lady's room where other ladies of the house and women guests are gathered for a party. Impatient, Lotus goes straight to Moon Lady's suite to call him:

Seeing that Hsi-men Ch'ing showed no sign of leaving, she stepped forward and pulled aside the curtain, saying, "If you are not coming, I shall go. I haven't patience to wait for you any longer."

Hsi-men Ch'ing said, "My child, you go first. I will come when I've finished my wine." Golden Lotus went away.[59]

Even for Lotus, this is unheard-of impudence: to charge into Moon Lady's room uninvited and try to drag their common husband away from her in front of all her guests. Little wonder the hitherto uncomplaining Moon Lady is provoked to pour forth in a magnificent tirade the accumulated resentments of the other wives against Lotus:

Then Moon Lady said, "I don't want you to go to her. And I have something more to tell you. It looks as if you two were wearing only one pair of pants. What kind of manners are these to barge in like that and force you to leave! That shameless slut! She thinks that she alone is your wife and the rest of us nobodies, and you are contemptible enough to go along with her. No wonder people are criticizing you behind your back. We are all your wives and you ought to treat us decently. You needn't advertise the fact that that one in the front court has got you body and soul. Since you came back from the Eastern Capital, you haven't spent a single night in the inner courts. Naturally people are annoyed. You should put fire into the cold stove before you begin on the hot one, and you have no right to allow one woman to monopolize you. So far as I am concerned, it doesn't matter because I don't care for games of this sort. But the others can't stand it. They don't say anything but, however good-natured they are, they must feel resentful. Third Sister Meng didn't eat a thing all the time we were at Brother Ying's place. She probably caught a chill in the stomach and has been feeling nauseated ever since. Mistress Ying gave her two cups of wine, but she couldn't keep it down. You should really go and see her." [60]

Hsi-men stays that night with Meng Yü-lou. But, even though her plans for the night remain unfulfilled, Lotus has affronted Moon Lady not thoughtlessly but deliberately, to advertise her improved position that can stand the combined assault of the other wives. Chapter 75, from which the preceding three excerpts have been taken, details their belated desperate attempts to curb her power. But their efforts come to little: Lotus is brought to give perfunctory apologies to Moon Lady but she retains her absolute dominion over their common husband.

By now Lotus is openly carrying on with Ching-chi whenever Hsi-men is not around to watch her. Precisely because Hsi-men himself is approaching his end (he dies in chapter 79), he seems to have partially recovered his zest for sexual conquest. His new mistress is Madame Lin, a lewd woman of the higher class, but for the first time in his life he is itching after something virtuous and unobtainable: the young and attractive wife of his newly arrived colleague, Captain Ho.[61] The night during the Lantern Festival when he is keeping his tryst with Wang VI, remembrance of the beautiful image of Mrs. Ho gives him a semblance of passion and he is literally exhausted. He falls into a dead sleep as soon as he returns to Lotus' bed in the small hours of the night. Lotus, wide awake with lust, finds him completely limp and incapable of sexual combat. In deep frustration, she finally wakes him up to ask where the aphrodisiac pills are, empties out the last four pills in the box, and takes one herself. Though well aware that the normal dosage per night is one pill (and Hsi-men has already taken that pill in readiness for his bout with Wang VI), Lotus has him swallow all three with a cup of strong white liquor so as to restore his virility even in his state of extreme fatigue. Soon the pills take effect. She then sits astride his inert body, applies some aphrodisiac ointment to harden the erection, and hungrily seeks deep penetration. She reaches orgasm twice, wetting in all five towels. But the somnolent Hsi-men cannot release himself even though his thoroughly congested glans is now assuming the color of raw liver. Scared, Lotus sucks it with her mouth until a large quantity of semen finally squirts out.

At first it was semen, and then it turned into a fluid composed mainly of blood, and there was no more hope for him. Hsi-men had fainted away, with his stiff limbs outstretched. Frightened, the woman hurriedly placed a few red dates in his mouth. But blood had followed semen and, now that the blood supply had been exhausted, his penis kept on squirting nothing but cold air until the ejaculatory motion stopped.[62]

The author immediately adds to this grim passage a didactic summary of Hsi-men's career as follows:

Gentle reader, a man's supply of vitality is limited even though there are no bounds to his desire for sexual pleasure. It is also said that the addict to sexual pleasure has shallow spiritual capacities. Hsi-men Ch'ing had abandoned himself to lust, not realizing that when the oil in a lamp is exhausted its light will fail and that when the marrow in his bones goes dry a man will die.[63]

But even a short-lived rake doesn't necessarily have to die a horrible death. The ghastly account of Hsi-men's collapse, while supporting the didactic passage, actually gives the impression of his murder by an unfeeling and insatiable nymphomaniac. In the next few days, while the best doctors are being summoned to succor him, Lotus still takes advantage of his peculiar condition ("His swollen scrotum was large and shiny like an eggplant")[64] to get sexual satisfaction: "His penis was firm as iron and day and night it stayed erect. At night, Lotus, who should have known better, would still sit astride him and have intercourse with him. And during a single night he would faint away and then regain consciousness several times over."[65]

The cumulative use of explicit pornography has finally yielded an unmistakable moral interest—in her triumphant posture over a moribund body to extract the last few pleasurable moments out of it and in her total contempt for the person of Hsi-men Ch'ing, Lotus is herself exposed as a loathsome creature of utter depravity. But, ultimately, Lotus' triumph proves her undoing. If Hsi-men is her instrument of pleasure, he is more importantly her source of power and security. Without his protection, she will be again a slave girl defenseless against the world. But in her insane pursuit of momentary pleasure, she becomes quite reckless of her future, and the ultimate pathos of her life is that all her cunning and cruel schemes for assuring herself a favored position in the Hsi-men household have been designed to secure a steady supply of sexual pleasure. She sees nothing beyond sex.

In reviewing the highlights of this self-contained novel about Lotus and Hsi-men, we have seen that their relationship is informed neither by the sentiment of love nor by what we would normally call sexual passion. As Westerners understand it, passion demands exclusiveness: though for obvious reasons Lotus wants to monopolize Hsi-men, she does not seriously expect from him complete loyalty, nor is she loyal to him though, confined to the house under the jealous surveillance of all the womenfolk, she has far less opportunity for promiscuity than her husband. She takes a passing fancy to a boy servant and later forms a liaison with a son-in-law, practically the only man in the household besides her master who is not of the servant class. For both sensualists, their bond is mainly physical: with all his variety of erotic adventures, Hsi-men still regards Lotus as the most satisfactory bedfellow, and Lotus, with her limited association with men, cannot expect a sexual partner of greater virility. On the elementary level, therefore, theirs is the biological drama of animal copulation. While man appears initially more aggressive and domineering than woman, he is her biological inferior and is inevitably beaten in the unequal combat. On that level Lotus appears as the queen bee or black widow spider except that, in her conscious contrivance for pleasure, her rapacity has ceased to be procreative.[66]

Their relationship further shows the degeneracy of love in a polygamous and promiscuous society. When a man can buy as many concubines and slave girls and enjoy as many mistresses and prostitutes as his money and strength incline him to, he tends to regard each of his acquisitions as a thing rather than as a person. (It is of interest to note that in China pornographic stories began as reports of life in a royal or imperial harem.)[67] A concubine can, of course, secure the love of her husband with her infinite solicitude, as Vase does in the novel, but normally when a woman is regarded by her master as a thing, she, too, loses sight of her humanity. The apparent irony that the slave girl Lotus should turn out to be far more evil than the slave master Hsi-men is therefore understandable. As a man of wealth and position, he receives so much flattering attention from his wives and mistresses, his friends and hangers-on, that he can afford to be pleased with himself and to appear good-natured and generous. Though obsessed with sex, he has so many business interests and official duties to attend to that he turns to his women in the evenings as an agreeable break in his routine. Moreover, as a social conformist, he has to be pleasant and polite to the outside world and maintain a façade of good manners. Lotus, on the other hand, enjoys none of these social advantages. Isolated from the outside world and living in a household of constant squabbles, she doesn't have to be pleasant and watch her manners (in contrast, the courtesans, because it is their job to entertain their customers, appear much more vivacious and courteous than the wives of Hsi-men). She pursues no cultural interests (except her occasional singing) and has no visitors of her own (except her mother). All her thoughts are therefore directed to the one object that redeems her dull and mean existence—her enjoyment of sex—and her life is further brutalized as a consequence.

Katherine Anne Porter once wrote that *Lady Chatterley's Lover* describes a life that is nothing "but a long, dull grey, monotonous chain of days, lightened now and then by a sexual bout." [68] If this description is somewhat unfair to Lawrence's novel, it could be applied to *Chin P'ing Mei* with far greater justice except that the chain of days in the Hsi-men household is not lightened but rendered more ponderous by the high frequency of sexual combat. Lotus is so dead earnest about sex that its enjoyment leaves no room for spontaneous and carefree fun. She is at nearly all times so grimly occupied that one is almost startled to find her in a rare moment of thoughtless merriment. In chapter 15, while on a visit to Vase's house during the Lantern Festival, Lotus stays upstairs to watch the street sights below:

Golden Lotus, Meng Yü-lou, and two singing-girls continued to look out the window at the fair.

Golden Lotus rolled up the sleeves of her white-silk outer jacket to show off the sleeves of her inner jacket which were embroidered all over with gold thread. She further displayed her ten fingers, all lustrous and daintily shaped like stalks of scallion. On them were six gold rings in the form of stirrups. Leaning half out of the window, she cracked melon seeds with her teeth and threw the shells at the people in the street. She laughed with Yü-lou all the time. Now and again she would point to something in the street and say excitedly, "Big sister, come and look at the pair of hydrangea-lanterns under the eaves of that house. They whirl back and forth and up and down so prettily." Then: "Second sister, come and look at the big fish-lantern hanging from the lantern-frame by the gate opposite our house. Dangling from that big fish are so many little fish, turtles, shrimps, and crabs. They move about in unison so gaily." Then she called Yü-lou, "Third sister, look over there at the grandma-lantern and grandpa-lantern."

Suddenly a gust of wind made a large hole in the lower part of the grandma-lantern, and Golden Lotus laughed unceasingly.[69]

In this scene Lotus is still new in the Hsi-men household and she flaunts her beauty without guile and retains the natural grace of a child in her gleeful enjoyment of the sights. The child in her rarely emerges after that. For Lotus as for most other members of that household, it is their willing forfeiture of innocence through their preoccupation with pleasure, security, or salvation that spells the boredom and horror of their existence.

CHAPTER VI

THE SCHOLARS

Chin P'ing Mei was first published in 1610 or 1611 [1] and *The Scholars* (*Ju-lin wai-shih* or The unofficial history of the literati) was completed about 1750. Between these two dates a great many Chinese novels were produced. While the majority of these were modeled upon the four great works that had preceded them, not all of them are without originality in their further exploration of the worlds of history and legend, of fantasy and sexual passion. Though none of these has as yet received extensive critical attention, among the titles available in Western-language translations we may take notice of two that appear especially interesting: *Hao-ch'iu chuan,* a short novel of eighteen chapters about the pursuit of a virtuous girl by a determined playboy, and *Jou p'u-t'uan* (The prayer mat of flesh), a twenty-chapter novel perhaps even more notorious than *Chin P'ing Mei* for its pornography. The former is the first Chinese novel ever to have been translated into English; [2] edited with a preface by Bishop Thomas Percy at a time (the second edition bears the date 1761) when Richardson and Fielding were the reigning novelists, it must have attracted immediate notice for its thematic similarity to their works. The latter was first translated into German in 1959 and soon retranslated into French and English to capitalize on the current Western craze for erotica.[3] Despite its grotesque obscenity, it is a work of greater artistic and intellectual coherence than *Chin P'ing Mei* and far more lively. A short novel still awaiting translation is Tung Yüeh's *Hsi-yu pu* (A supplement to *Journey to the West*). Though a religious allegory, it studies the bafflement of its hero Monkey in terms of dream psychology that are subtle and modern.[4] Among the full-length novels produced during these 140 years, the one most deserving of notice is surely *Hsing-shih yin-yuan* (A romance to awaken the world), about a henpecked man suffering cruelly at the hands of his wife and concubine to atone for his crimes in a previous existence. Though in this respect a conventional Buddhist tale of moral retribution, the novel is distinguished for its grotesque humor and coarse vitality.[5]

But, whatever their individual merits, none of these works and others of the same period can compare with *The Scholars* for its revolutionary importance in stylistic and technical innovation and for the enormous influence it has exerted on the development of the Chinese novel. *Hao-ch'iu chuan, Jou p'u-t'uan, Hsi-yu pu,* and *Hsing-shih yin-yuan* are all works of pure invention, but, out of habit, their authors still felt obliged to adopt the rhetorical conventions of professional storytellers. *The Scholars,* on the contrary, is far less dependent on these conventions. Its author, Wu Ching-tzu, to be sure, still observes the minimal formal requirements: each of his fifty-five chapters employs an antithetical couplet for its heading and nearly every one begins with the phrase *hua-shuo* (It is now told) and ends with four lines of verse followed by the formula, "To know what followed, you must listen to the next round of recital." But songs and verse descriptions are conspicuously absent. For the first time in a major vernacular novel, descriptive passages are completely integrated with the narrative text because they are now recorded in colloquial prose. In his avoidance of the standard poetic vocabulary, the author has actually relied on his own observations of persons and places. Nanking, Hangchow, Soochow, Chiahsing, and other cities of the Chiang-nan region are vividly recalled with their teeming life and their famous scenic attractions still recognizable today. In addition, dialectal and slang terms are rare and classical phrases usually occur only in the speeches of scholars. Because of all these virtues, one must agree with Ch'ien Hsüan-t'ung that *The Scholars* is a landmark of Chinese literature for its conscious use of *kuo-yü* or a national vernacular.[6] Certainly, the prose of no other classic novel, *Dream of the Red Chamber* not excepted, is as pure and functional. Much imitated by late Ch'ing and early Republican novelists, the style of *The Scholars* remains an active influence among present-day prose writers.

Ideologically, *The Scholars* was the first work of satiric realism to achieve an almost complete dissociation from the religious beliefs of the people. Although popular Buddhism, with its insistence on moral retribution, can interpret reality only in a naïve fashion, to please their audience, the storytellers had to adopt the Buddhist viewpoint, with the result that even among the finest colloquial tales a happy ending for the virtuous along with corresponding punishment for the wicked had always been observed. (Popular Confucianism and Taoism also abetted this didactic tendency.) In *Chin P'ing Mei, Hsing-shih yin-yuan,* and other novels of satiric intent, the presence of this vulgar religious world view is always a nuisance, if not a main cause of their failure to achieve realistic integrity. During the Ch'ing dynasty, novels were being increasingly written by well-educated scholars, and there was little reason for them to keep up the pretense of being simple preachers. Though several prominent Ch'ing authors and scholars—notably, P'u Sung-ling (1640–1716), Yuan Mei (1716–97), and Chi Yün (1724–1805)—are known for their collections of supernatural stories and anecdotes which countenance the popular world view,[7] Wu Ching-tzu probably represents the majority of Confucian intellectuals of his time in his distaste for popular superstitions and Buddhist morality. Still, it bespeaks his great artistic courage that he attempted to liberate the novel from the fetters of popular religion: in *The Scholars* we have finally come to a novel which upholds a personal view of life and makes significant use of autobiographical experience. No longer circumscribed by the didactic necessity to reward virtue and punish wickedness, the author draws upon his wide acquaintance with all classes of people to etch characters of shrewd realism and intelligent satire.

Wu Ching-tzu (1701–54) came from a scholarly family of Ch'üan-chiao, Anhwei Province, which had distinguished itself in government service in late Ming and early Ch'ing times. But Wu himself seems to have inherited from his short-lived grandfather and unambitious father a weak strain which ill prepared him for a competitive official life. His eldest son, Wu Lang, however, early distinguished himself as an official and scholar, especially in the field of mathematics. Measured against his more illustrious ancestors and his own brilliant son, Wu appeared in the eyes of the local townspeople something of a wastrel who squandered his patrimony by his reckless generosity, his careless management of his affairs and, if we may cite his own poetry as evidence, his patronage of high-class brothels in Nanking.[8] He acquired the preliminary degree of *hsiu-ts'ai* at the age of twenty-two but had apparently no further luck in examinations.[9] When, at thirty-two, he decided to move his family to Nanking, he was already quite poor. Three years later (1736), he was recommended by an official to participate in a special examination in Peking designed for scholars of note without advanced degrees. But whether because he fell ill at that time, as Hu Shih believed, or because, according to the less likely theory of some Communist scholars, he was in principle opposed to an official career, he declined the honor.[10] He lived the rest of his life as a *ming-shih,* that is, a scholar of some literary note, shunning the responsibilities and indignities of official life and composing poetry and prose to amuse himself and his friends. He left twelve *chüan* of such writings, of which four *chüan* now remain. His *Shih shuo* (Discourse on the *Book of Poetry*) is no longer extant.[11]

But, unlike other idle scholars, Wu Ching-tzu in his later years was also writing a novel to vindicate his apparent failure in life and formulate his own impressions of the society around him. In his postface to the 1869 edition of *The Scholars,* the poet Chin Ho (1819–85), a native of Ch'üan-chiao related to the Wu family, has informed us that many of its characters are modeled upon the author's friends and other known historical characters of his time and that one hero at least—Tu Shao-ch'ing—is a self-portrait. Taking up this clue, Hu Shih has provided further information concerning these prototypes in his biography of Wu Ching-tzu. In 1957 Ho Tse-han gathered an impressive amount of data concerning thirty such persons in his important study, *Ju-lin wai-shih jen-wu pen-shih k'ao-lüeh* (The characters and stories in *The Scholars*: a source study). Many of these show a striking resemblance to their fictional counterparts in career and personality, and all of them bear names similar in sound, meaning, or written shape to those of their parallels.[12]

Wu Ching-tzu, of course, could not have achieved fame as a novelist if he had merely transcribed the biographies of his contemporaries. To cite a modern parallel, many of the characters in *Point Counter Point* are modeled upon Aldous Huxley's literary friends and acquaintances, but the kind of life they enjoy in the satiric novel has little to do with the fidelity of these portraits to their originals. Similarly, Wu Ching-tzu may have applied to a character the features, idiosyncrasies, and biographical circumstances of a particular friend, but to give that character its fictional reality and its satiric relevance in the scheme of the novel, he would still have had to exercise his powers of invention. Indeed, an ultimate criticism of the author would be that he has not tried hard enough to exercise these powers. While, in a novel of relatively small size, he has given us a surprisingly large number of memorable vignettes, one nevertheless has the suspicion that he has supplemented his comic insight into character with material borrowed from his reading, especially in the second half of his book. If Wu Ching-tzu has asserted a greater independence of the tradition of the popular novel than earlier authors, he is nevertheless still indebted to the classical and colloquial genres of the short story and to the voluminous literature of anecdotes and jokes compiled by scholars. Ho Tse-han, among others, has already ventured into this type of background study for *The Scholars*,[13] and there is little doubt that a full-scale investigation will yield results as illuminating as those obtained in Hanan's study of the sources of *Chin P'ing Mei*. At his best Wu Ching-tzu has adapted these jokes and anecdotal stories to define character, but sometimes he has merely inserted them for their independent comic value regardless of their satiric relevance to the story context. The novel suffers in consequence.

Before embarking on his novel, Wu Ching-tzu had accomplished something else of which he was very proud. Despite his poverty he had once devoted a great deal of money and time to the renovation of a temple. According to the gazetteer of his native city, *Ch'üan-chiao-hsien chih:*

On the Yü-hua Terrace of Nanking there was the Temple of Former Sages whose function it was to give sacrifices to some five hundred worthies from T'ai-po down. The temple had long been in disrepair, and Ching-tzu advocated its renovation and raised money for that purpose. When these funds were used up, he sold his old house north of the river to complete the job.[14]

This must have been Wu's singular achievement in public service since it was considered important enough to deserve mention in the gazetteer (it is also mentioned in Chin Ho's postface). Accordingly, we read in the novel about the good scholars' collaborative effort to build a new temple dedicated to the sage of the Wu region, T'ai-po. The initial sacrifice at that temple, described in chapter 37, constitutes the climax of the novel.

Hu Shih dates the renovation of the Temple of Former Sages at around 1740, when Wu Ching-tzu was thirty-nine years old. A year earlier he had completed a volume of poems and had probably had it printed. Hu Shih cannot be far wrong in assuming that in that year he also began his novel. He had accomplished one symbolic Confucian deed and sacrificed what remained of his fortune in doing so, and he had finally renounced all ambition to pursue an official career. He could now afford to examine the scholars around him with considerable detachment and some personal amusement. The novel was probably completed in 1750.

Wu Ching-tzu died in 1754, at the age of fifty-three, without having arranged for his novel's publication. It was first published between 1768 and 1779, though neither the manuscript nor this earliest edition is now extant. The standard edition as prepared by Chin Ho has 55 chapters. Hu Shih believed, however, that the novel as the author wrote it should have only 50 chapters since both *Ch'üan-chiao-hsien chih* and an early biography of Wu by his good friend Ch'eng Chin-fang describe it as a work of 50 *chüan*. Though some of the later episodes in the novel are clearly inferior, Hu Shih did not specify the five spurious chapters, contenting himself with the broad guess that they are among the 55 chapters we now have. Liu Ts'un-yan has recently challenged Hu Shih's view, believing that *The Scholars* was originally a novel of 55 chapters and that the two early sources might have erred.[15]

The Scholars was the first satiric novel consciously written from the Confucian point of view. But, unlike the kind of Confucian heroism endorsed in historical novels, its Confucianism is tinged with melancholy over the futility of government action or social reform. A few military commanders in the novel achieve conspicuous success in quelling rebellions among aborigines and launching a program of farming and education in the newly colonized areas, but they are reproved at court and financially penalized for their supposedly overzealous and spendthrift efforts.[16] The implication is that even by military officers, to say nothing of scholars, no lasting achievement could be attempted under a stupid rule. The author endorses the Confucian maxim that in times of peace and good government it is a scholar's honor and obligation to seek official appointment while in times of decay and disorder it is no dishonor but actually a sign of personal integrity to withdraw from government service. But for the finicky, no times will be good enough.

Wu Ching-tzu wrote during the height of Manchu prosperity, under the Ch'ien-lung Emperor. Since his novel takes place in the preceding Ming dynasty, his affirmation of personal integrity through withdrawal from government service has often been taken as a form of patriotic protest, an indirect criticism of the Manchu rule.[17] But there is nothing in his extant writings to indicate a case of deliberate noncooperation. Wu Ching-tzu has not placed his novel in the Ming period merely as a matter of convenience; he shows an active interest in Ming history and comments on it shrewdly. Thus, though the founder of the Ming dynasty is generally spoken of in favorable terms, he is deplored for his adoption of the simplified examination system, which prizes mainly a degree candidate's skill in expounding brief quotations from the Four Books and the Five Classics in a stereotyped type of discourse in eight sections known as *pa-ku wen* (the "eight-legged" essay). He is further indirectly criticized for his cruel execution of the poet Kao Ch'i, apparently one of the author's great heroes. One scholar gains recognition by printing a manuscript of Kao's, and another is arrested for owning his works.[18] For an author who espouses withdrawal from government service, Wu Ching-tzu shows curiously strong admiration for men of action. Through his mouthpieces, he praises Emperor Ch'eng-tsu, the shrewd usurper, in consideration that, but for him, the Ming empire would have far sooner embarked on its course of luxury and decadence.[19] The rebel Ch'en-hao, the prince of Ning, is also defended by one of the characters: his rebellion took place at a time when the dynasty had already gone soft and his success would have revitalized it.[20] In all these comments, the author seems to be seriously offering his own views of Ming history rather than making veiled criticisms of the Ch'ing government.

In form *The Scholars* is a series of tenuously linked stories. Because each episode takes place later than the preceding one, the novel spans a long period of time, from 1487 to 1595. But the introductory chapter goes even further back, to the last years of the Yuan dynasty, to tell the story of a famous artist-recluse, Wang Mien. He serves as an exemplary hero against whom are measured the vices and stupidities of the scholars of later times. For a novel which has no plot, this prologue serves admirably to state its theme.

Two famous writers have preceded Wu Ching-tzu as biographers of Wang Mien: the great essayist of the early Ming period Sung Lien (1310–81), and the Ch'ing poet Chu I-tsun (1629–1709). As

Sung Lien sees him, Wang Mien was not a hermit by choice. In his youth he had repeatedly tried to pass the examinations under the Yuan. Even after he had given up hope of academic success, he went to Peking to serve as retainer of a prominent Mongol official, who was later killed by the Chinese rebels. Wang Mien, moreover, is portrayed as an eccentric genius far more suggestive of the knights-errant of antiquity and the unconventional intellectuals of the Wei-Chin period than of a sedentary recluse. In Chu I-tsun's biography he remains a proud and eccentric scholar and poet though his unworldliness has been to some extent idealized.

In Wu Ching-tzu's account, however, Wang Mien has become an artist-recluse without a trace of worldly ambition and too mild-mannered and retiring to be called an eccentric. Early bereaved of his father, he lives with his mother in a village near Chu-chi, Chekiang, and tends a water buffalo for his neighbor, Old Ch'in. He studies on his own, however, and develops a passion for painting, especially flowers. He soon gains a local reputation and attracts the notice of Magistrate Shih of Chu-chi, who buys from him an album of water colors and presents it to his patron Wei Su, an eminent author and historian then visiting his home town. Highly impressed, he says to the magistrate, "I left home so long ago that, though my native place has produced so great a man, I did not know it. I am ashamed. He shows not only remarkable skill but exceptional insight, and in future his fame and rank will at least equal ours. I wonder if you would invite him to pay me a visit?" [21] When Magistrate Shih sends one of his men to invite Wang Mien, he declines the honor and cites two ancient recluses to justify his behavior before the incredulous Old Ch'in. Magistrate Shih now visits him in person, but Wang Mien stays in hiding and refuses to see him. When Old Ch'in wonders why he has acted so rudely, he answers, "Please sit down, uncle, . . . and I will explain. This magistrate relies on Mr. Wei's authority to tyrannize over the common people here, and do all kinds of bad things. Why should I have anything to do with such a man? But now that he has gone back, he will certainly tell Mr. Wei; and if Mr. Wei becomes angry he may want to make trouble for me. So now I shall pack up my things, leave my mother, and go into hiding for a time. The only thing that worries me is leaving my mother here by herself." [22] He leaves for the distant province Shantung.

Wei Su, who served under both Yuan and Ming, has not left an unblemished name for posterity. But in the present instance, he appears primarily as a discoverer of talent and a potential patron. As for the magistrate, despite Wang Mien's allegation that he is evil, there is little indication in the narrative that this is so. His very willingness to see a humble villager would certainly indicate openness of mind though, like his patron, he is quite conscious of the fame he would receive as a magistrate able to discover talent in his own district. (Throughout the novel the reader will face the problem of narrative authority. Whose words can he trust when contradictory reports of a character's behavior are given?) Wang Mien has already been selling his pictures to villagers and townspeople to eke out a living so that acceptance of his art in the higher circles would not mean any breach of principle. But he shrinks from contact with the official world that would bring him recognition and fame. For him, the official world, especially when under the suspicion of corruption and injustice, is vulgar company to be avoided at all cost.

As Wu Ching-tzu portrays him, Wang Mien is a man constitutionally averse to an active life. He recoils from vulgarity and, since life cannot but be contaminated by vulgarity (earning a living by whatever means is a vulgar form of occupation), there is something sad about him. Unlike Po-i and Shu-ch'i,[23] he is not engaged in political protest. (Some critics still see him as the author's symbol of patriotic integrity for his refusal to serve under a foreign dynasty. But, as depicted in the novel, he doesn't serve under the Ming either, and, historically, he did serve under the Mongols.) And unlike T'ao Ch'ien, he has not earned his right to retire since he does not know what official servitude is like. He is, therefore, more like Yen Tzu-ling, a schoolmate of Emperor Kuang-wu of the Later Han dynasty, who hides himself and declines the emperor's invitation to serve though once he comes to court and sleeps in the same bed with his old friend.[24] Wang Mien is not an intimate of any emperor but, after he has returned from his exile in Shantung, Chu Yuan-chang, the future founder of the Ming dynasty, pays him a visit:

One day at noon, just as Wang Mien was returning from his mother's grave, he saw a dozen horsemen entering the village. The leader of the band wore a military cap and flowered silk costume. He had a clear complexion, his beard was fine, and he looked every inch a king. When this man reached Wang Mien's door, he alighted from his horse, saluted and said, "May I ask where Mr. Wang Mien lives?"

"I am he," replied Wang Mien, "and this is my humble house."

"I am in luck then," said the stranger, "for I have come specially to pay my respects." [25]

After Wang Mien has invited him in, Chu reveals his identity and seeks advice about how to win the love of the people of his region:

"Your Highness is far-sighted," said Wang Mien. "There is no need for a humble person like myself to say much. If you use goodness and justice to win the people, you will win them all—not only those in Chekiang. But if you try to conquer by force, weak as the people of Chekiang are, I am afraid they will not submit. Look at the case of Fang Kuo-chen whom you defeated."

The prince nodded and expressed approval; and sitting face to face they talked till evening. The prince's followers had brought rations, and Wang Mien went to the kitchen to make bread and fry leeks for the prince, sharing the meal with him. The prince then thanked him for his advice, mounted his horse and rode away.[26]

The particular glory of a recluse is that, while he is sincerely sought after by a virtuous prince, he maintains his integrity by refusing to serve. His ability is actually untested, but his advice, however platitudinous, is always treasured. He is more honored than the high ministers because, while the latter are merely the emperor's servants, the recluse, so long as he refuses to serve, remains his friend and mentor. Appropriately, Wu Ching-tzu concludes his biography with this comment, "Curiously enough, writers and scholars nowadays refer to Wang Mien as the Commissioner of Records, though actually he never served as an official for a single day, as I have tried to make clear."[27]

In view of Wu Ching-tzu's failure to reach success through the examinations, it is plausible to see Wang Mien as an idealized self-portrait—a recluse distinguished for his art and filial piety, undistracted by wine and women, and unperturbed by ambition and honor. Though it is rather odd for a filial son not to marry, Wang Mien remains a bachelor all his life and seems to find perfect contentment in the company of Old Ch'in, who briefly survives him. Nevertheless, it marks Wu Ching-tzu's serious limitation as a satirist that he should have chosen such an unapproachable paragon as his ideal. The individualistic intellectuals of the late Ming period, who also scorned officialdom, behaved differently. They sought a life of unbridled freedom amid the pleasures of wine, women, nature, and unorthodox ideas. By the time of Wu Ching-tzu, however, this tide of individualistic thought had retreated and a more methodical and puritanical Confucianism was in fashion.[28] When the late Ming intellectuals protested against vulgarity and officialdom, we know that they were at the same time affirming an exuberant life for the senses and the intellect. Wu's protest, however, may stem from a sour-grapes mentality symptomatic of his own obsession with his failure. As a determined recluse, even his ideal Wang Mien could be taken as one who seeks fame through the way of negation.

Wang Mien also serves as the author's mouthpiece on one prominent subject of his satiric attack: the simplified examination system introduced by the first Ming emperor and persisting unchanged till the end of the Ch'ing dynasty. When informed of the new regulations for the examinations, Wang Mien confides to Old Ch'in, "These rules are not good. Future candidates, knowing that there is an easy way to high position, will look down on real scholarship and correct behavior."[29] The author develops this theme with great brilliance in the chapters immediately following. But his overinsistent ridicule of the system and its victims is perhaps as autobiographically revealing as his exaltation of a pure and unworldly recluse.

In the very first chapter Wu Ching-tzu shows himself to be a chaste writer who records his observations with economy and precision. Take the following pastoral scene, which inspires Wang Mien to become a painter:

One sultry day in early summer, tired after leading the buffalo to graze, he sat down on the grass. Suddenly dense clouds gathered, and there was a heavy shower of rain. Then the black storm clouds fringed with fleecy white drifted apart, and the sun shone through, bathing the whole lake in crimson light. The hills by the lake were blue, violet and emerald. The trees, freshly washed by the rain, were a lovelier green than ever. Crystal drops were dripping from a dozen lotus buds in the lake, while beads of water rolled about the leaves.[30]

In a modern Chinese novel this passage would be unexceptional; it might even appear a little hackneyed because so many authors of the May Fourth period were fond of this type of scenic description. But it is a marvel that Wu Ching-tzu, writing in the traditional mode, should have rendered the scene so accurately without resorting to stock poetic phrases. In style, this passage represents a colloquial adaptation of the classical mode of landscape description to be seen in such T'ang and Sung essayists as Liu Tsung-yuan and Su Shih, with their preference for sharp concrete detail over imprecise, allusive imagery. Wu Ch'eng-en, the best descriptive poet among the earlier novelists, explored the resources of *fu* poetry and parallel prose; Wu Ching-tzu has now appropriated the classical *ku-wen* essay for the novel.

If the introductory chapter has shown the author as a master of prose, the second chapter is even more astounding for its use of a revolutionary technique in character portrayal. An earlier novelist usually assumes the role of a puppet-master who introduces his marionettes one by one and tells us who they are and what they are about. Wu Ching-tzu, however, no longer bluntly guides the reader but places him in a dramatized scene. As the actors in that scene go about their business and talk about sundry matters, they gradually reveal themselves. Here are the opening paragraphs:

In Hsueh [Hsüeh] Market, a village of Wenshang County, Shantung, there lived over a hundred families, all of whom worked on the land. At the entrance to the village was a Kuanyin Temple with three halls and a dozen empty rooms. Its back door overlooked the river. Peasants from all around contributed to the upkeep of this temple, and only one monk lived there. Here the villagers would come to discuss public business.

It was the last year of the Cheng Hua [Ch'eng-hua] period . . . , when the country was prosperous. . . . On the eighth of the first month, just after New Year, some of the villagers met in the temple to discuss the dragon lantern dance which is held on the fifteenth. At breakfast time the man who usually took the lead, Shen Hsiang-fu, walked in, followed by seven or eight others. In the main hall they bowed to Buddha, and the monk came to wish them a happy New Year. As soon as they had returned his greeting, Shen reproved him.

"Monk! At New Year you should burn more incense before Buddha! Gracious Heaven! You've been pocketing money from all sides, and you ought to spend a little of it. Come here, all of you, and take a look at this lamp: it's only half filled with oil." Then, pointing to an old man who was better dressed than most: "Not to mention others, Mr. Hsun [Hsün] alone sent you fifty catties of oil on New Year's Eve. But you are using it all for your cooking, instead of for the glory of Buddha."

The monk apologized profusely when Shen had finished. Then he fetched a pewter kettle, put in a handful of tea leaves, filled the kettle with water, boiled it over the fire and poured out tea for them. Old Mr. Hsun was the first to speak.

"How much do we each have to pay for the lantern dance in the temple this year?" he asked.

"Wait till my relative [his son's father-in-law] comes," said Shen. "We'll discuss it together."

As they were speaking, a man walked in. He had red-rimmed eyes, a swarthy face, and sparse, dingy whiskers. His cap was cocked to one side, his blue cloth gown was greasy as an oil-vat, and he carried a donkey switch in one hand. Making a casual gesture of greeting to the company, he plumped himself down in the seat of honour. This was Hsia, the new village head for Hsueh Market.

Sitting there in the seat of honour, he shouted: "Monk! Take my donkey to the manger in the backyard, unsaddle it and give it plenty of hay. After my business here I have to go to a feast with Bailiff Huang of the county yamen." Having given these orders, he hoisted one foot on to the bench, and started massaging the small of his back with his fists, saying, "I envy you farmers these days. This New Year I've got invitations from everybody in the magistrate's yamen, literally everybody! And I have to go to wish them all the season's greetings. I trot about on this donkey to the county-seat and back until my head reels. And this damned beast stumbled on the road and threw me, so that my backside is still sore."

"On the third I prepared a small dinner for you," said Shen. "I suppose it was because you were so busy that you didn't come."

"You don't have to remind me," said Village Head Hsia. "Since New Year, for the last seven or eight days, what free time have I had? Even if I had two mouths, I couldn't get through all the eating. Take Bailiff Huang, who's invited me today. He's a man who can talk face to face with the magistrate. And since he honours me like this, wouldn't he be offended if I didn't go?"

"I heard that Bailiff Huang had been sent out on some business for the magistrate since the beginning of the year," said Shen. "He has no brothers or sons, so who will act as host?"

"You don't understand," said Hsia. "Today's feast is given by Constable Li. His own rooms are small, so he is using Bailiff Huang's house." [31]

No other classic Chinese novel begins with such immediate assurance of realism. We are first given, with the minimum of preliminary exposition, the place and the time. The Kuan-yin temple is singled out for special mention not only because it is the most important building in the village but because it serves to introduce without delay the villagers gathered there to discuss a specific problem. The author does not then proceed to tell us that of these villagers Shen Hsiang-fu commands the greatest respect: rather, his position is indicated by the way he dominates the group and by the peremptory tone he adopts to scold the monk. Also, from his flattering citation of Old Mr. Hsün's generosity, we infer that the latter is his senior in years, most probably wealthier and having

better claims to gentility, though no longer as active in village affairs. Since Shen won't start discussing the business on hand until
his son's father-in-law arrives, we are further made aware that Hsia,
the new village head, is the real power in Hsüeh Market and that
Shen's self-importance reflects to some degree his borrowed glory.
For a novelist today, the advantages of indirect dramatic presentation are of course taken for granted, but Wu Ching-tzu was certainly the first Chinese to make regular, deliberate use of this
method.

Hsia is presented with even greater dramatic verve: his self-as-
sumed importance is contrasted quite effectively with his lowborn
features, his greasy clothes, and his boorish manners. But, as a new
village head, he is not too sure of himself and he brags about his new
connections and his busy social schedule. We don't know what to
make of his bragging until with evident malice Shen politely exposes him in the lie. He is not flustered by the challenge and he is
too important to be exposed to further ridicule. Nevertheless, the
author has subtly led us to doubt all his statements: whether he is
so busy after all, whether he has been thrown by the donkey, and
whether he is to go to a feast after the meeting at the temple. The
village head Hsia is the first of the many characters in the book who
expose themselves through bragging. With sure instinct, the novelist
apprehends the fact that in the comedy of social manners nearly
every one is a snob.

After they have made provisions for the dragon lantern dance,
the villagers turn to another item of business—the hiring of a tutor
to teach the local children. In this manner we are introduced to
Chou Chin, a poor student over sixty who has never had any luck
at the examinations and is therefore looked down upon by all who
are financially and academically better off than he. However, he
eventually enjoys an extraordinary run of luck, passes all the examinations, and is appointed a provincial commissioner of education.
In the latter capacity, he discovers another impoverished old student,
Fan Chin, who in time also earns his *chin-shih* degree and becomes
an examiner. These two characters set a brisk comic pace for the

novel and give it its reputation as a satiric exposé of the examination system. But even in these two accounts of assured comic success, the reader has to discriminate between scenes of comedy rooted in a realistic knowledge of manners and those of exaggerated satire that turn away from the realistic to the intentionally absurd. Wu Ching-tzu shuttles back and forth between these two modes of comedy, and he manages his task so well that scholars have usually taken the scenes of satiric absurdity as if they were meant to be realistic. But in such scenes, as has been earlier mentioned, the author is not infrequently adapting jokes and tall tales garnered from his reading, and they tend to lead a life of their own, providing a note of burlesque and buffoonery that ill suits the serious comic portrayal of manners to be seen in the bulk of the novel.

Take Chou Chin for instance. One day a new provincial graduate, Wang Hui, stops by the temple at Hsüeh Market, and Chou Chin is asked to keep him company. The graduate tells all sorts of tales to impress the humble tutor of village children and show off his boundless conceit. Then dinner is introduced:

As they were chatting, lights were brought in, and the servants spread the desk with wine, rice, chicken, fish, duck and pork. Wang Hui fell to, without inviting Chou Chin to join him; and when Wang Hui had finished, the monk sent up the teacher's rice with one dish of cabbage and a jug of hot water. When Chou Chin had eaten, they both went to bed. The next day the weather cleared. Wang Hui got up, washed and dressed, bade Chou a casual goodbye and went away in his boat, leaving the schoolroom floor so littered with chicken, duck and fish bones, and melon-seed shells, that it took Chou Chin a whole morning to clear them all away, and the sweeping made him dizzy.[32]

This is a comic scene in keeping with the realistic mode: the contrast of the two kinds of fare is delicious with its slight air of exaggeration. The itemizing of the debris of Wang's dinner amounts to a stroke of genius.

We are soon introduced to a comic scene of greater exaggeration but no less brilliance. After having been dismissed as a tutor, Chou Chin serves as an accountant for his brother-in-law, Chin Yu-yü, and his business associates. It is a great humiliation for an old man with academic ambitions to make his living among merchants. But he is not completely resigned, and once, upon reaching the provincial capital, he asks his associates to take him to see the examination hall. Arriving there, he knocks his head against a desk in one of the cubicles in the hall and falls unconscious. He is soon revived and helped to his feet:

But when Chou Chin saw the desk he beat his head against it again. Only, instead of falling unconscious, this time he burst out into loud sobbing. Not all their entreaties could stop him.

"Are you out of your mind?" demanded Chin. "We came to the examination school to enjoy a bit of sightseeing. Nobody has died in your family. Why take on like this?" But Chou Chin paid no attention. He just leaned his head against the desk and went on crying. After crying in the first room, he rushed over to cry in the second and then the third, rolling over and over on the floor till all his friends felt sorry for him. Seeing the state he was in, Chin and the guild head tried to lift him up, one on each side; but he refused to budge. He cried and cried, until he spat blood. Then all the others lent a hand to carry him out and set him down in a tea-house in front of the examination school. They urged him to drink a bowl of tea. But he just went on sniffling and blinking away his tears, looking quite broken-hearted.[33]

This episode may have been Wu Ching-tzu's invention, but again it may have been an adaptation of a popular story since jokes about frustrated old pupils were quite popular in Ming and Ch'ing times. But even if it is an adapted story, it is entirely appropriate in the comic context of Chou Chin's career. Its tone of exaggeration only enhances the grief of a frustrated scholar reduced to contemplating the privilege of sitting in the examination hall which, as an accountant, he could no longer enjoy. A meek mouse deferential to all his tormentors, Chou Chin finally enjoys an outburst of crying, which is entirely in character.

But as the author rambles on from episode to comic episode, forever introducing new characters to supplant the old ones, he gradually shows signs of losing sight of his satiric perspective so that sometimes a joke is introduced which does almost nothing to advance our understanding of a particular character. Take the celebrated scene of the rich man Yen Chih-ho's death in chapters 5 and 6:

But after the Mid-Autumn Festival the doctors stopped prescribing medicine, and all the stewards and servants were summoned back from the estates.

For three days Mr. Yen hovered between life and death, too weak to speak. On the evening of the third day an oil lamp was lit on his table, and the room was crowded with relatives. They could hear the beginning of the death-rattle in his throat; but he refused to die. He took his hand from beneath the quilt and stretched out two fingers.

The eldest nephew stepped up to the bed and asked, "Do you mean that there are two relatives who haven't come, uncle?"

Yen shook his head.

The second nephew stepped forward and asked, "Do you mean there are still two lots of silver you haven't told us about, uncle?"

Yen stared hard at him, shook his head even more vehemently, and held out his fingers more earnestly than ever.

The wet-nurse, who was carrying his son, put in, "The master must be thinking of the two uncles who aren't here."

But when he heard this, he closed his eyes and shook his head. Only his fingers did not move.

Then the new wife hastily stepped forward, dabbing at her eyes. "They're all wide of the mark," she said. "I'm the only one who knows what you mean. . . . You're worried because there are two wicks in the lamp—that's a waste of oil. If I take out one wick, it will be all right."

Suiting her actions to her words, she removed one wick. All eyes were fixed on Mr. Yen, who nodded his head, let fall his hand, and breathed his last.[34]

Isolated from the context, the story is an extremely effective caricature of a miser. But for the novelist, his first consideration for including this gem should be: is it appropriate? When Yen Chih-ho first appears on the scene, we are told that he is a wealthy but frugal man of timid disposition. We soon see him, however, settling his brother's lawsuits to the tune of some dozen taels of silver. Upon the death of his first wife, nee Wang, her two brothers back Concubine Chao's claim to succeed her as the legitimate wife. To thank them for their support, Yen Chih-ho repeatedly gives the Wang brothers large sums of money, and for his wife's funeral and other expenses incurred during the period of mourning he uses up four or five thousand taels of silver. A true miser would not have squandered so much money on his deceased wife, nor would he have become so careless upon her death as to permit the brazen theft of gold, clothes, and jewelry by his sisters-in-law. In reading this diverting tale of Yen Chih-ho, one gets the impression that the author had meant to cast him in the role of a wealthy miser so as to contrast him effectively with his rascally brother, who remains penniless despite his cunning schemes for making money. But he soon saw greater comic possibilities in Yen as a dupe of the rapacious Wang brothers and depicted him accordingly as a weak, gullible, and morose sort of person given to gestures of extravagance. However, Wu Ching-tzu had been saving the story of the two wicks (which he had thought up or read in a joke book) for Yen Chih-ho. It was too good to throw away, and so Yen had to die an extreme miser even though earlier episodes contradict that impression.

To cite another example, in chapter 7 the author borrows an anecdote to prove Fan Chin's shocking ignorance. The story of Fan's dramatic rise from pauperdom (chap. 3) is one of the great comedies in the book, but in his subsequent intermittent appearances his character becomes rather vague and colorless and in the present instance he merely serves to expose the illiteracy of the bureaucratic world as a whole. At a dinner he worries over his failure to locate a student named Hsün Mei, who should have taken the recent prefectural examination:

"Sir," said a young secretary called Chu Chin-yu [Ch'ü Ching-yü], "this reminds me of a story. Several years ago, an old scholar was appointed commissioner for Szechuan. One day he was feasting with Mr. Ho Ching-ming,[35] when Mr. Ho got drunk and shouted, 'In Szechuan, essays like Su Shih's only deserve the sixth rank!' The old gentleman made a mental note of this; and three years later, when he left Szechuan and met Mr. Ho again, he told him, 'I have been in Szechuan for three years, and checked the papers extremely carefully, but I did not find one by Su Shih. He can't have entered.' " Laughing up his sleeve, the young man continued, "In what connection did the vice-president [Chou Chin] bring up Hsun Mei's name, sir?"

Commissioner Fan was too simple to realize that he was being made a fool of. With a worried frown, he said, "Since Su Shih's essays were no good, it did not matter if he was not found. But Vice-President Chou wants me to help this Hsun Mei; and if I can't find him it will be rather embarrassing." [36]

The story told by the young secretary must have been a popular joke by Wu Ching-tzu's time: it had earlier appeared in *Yin-shu-wu shu-ying,* a book of miscellaneous notes by Chou Liang-kung (1612–72), and in the biography of a poet prepared by Ch'ien Ch'ien-i (1582–1664) for his massive anthology of Ming poetry, *Lieh-ch'ao shih-chi.*[37] In applying this joke to a *chin-shih* who has devoted himself to study since his early youth, however, there is again the problem of propriety. If the name of Su Shih is familiar to American college students who have been at all exposed to Chinese culture and history, it would be utterly unlikely that Fan Chin should not have become acquainted with it, however narrow his course of studies. Wu Ching-tzu, however, is quite fond of this type of over-disdainful ridicule. Another scholar, Ma Ch'un-shang, is exposed for his failure to recognize the names of women poets like Li Ch'ing-chao.[38] As a renowned anthologist of examination essays, Ma practically lives in bookstores; he may not have read Li Ch'ing-chao, but he would certainly have heard her name. Jokes like these, usually praised by critics for their withering exposure of the scholarly class, actually carry very little satiric weight because they strain one's credulity.[39] It is as if, in attacking the dunces of his time, Pope should single out for mention their unfamiliarity with the names of Milton and Dryden.

Wu Ching-tzu is also fond of another type of joke which, so far as I can see, makes no point whatever. It is broad farce which may be enjoyed for its own sake but is satirically irrelevant. Ch'ü Kung-sun, a young scholar of the *ming-shih* type, strikes the fancy of a retired minister, who affiances him to his only daughter. Brought up on an exclusive intellectual diet of Confucian classics and examination essays, she is incompatible with her dilettantish husband. The subsequent comedy of this discordant couple is quite delightful, but for the present we are at the wedding feast and watch the farcical accidents of a rat slipping down from the ceiling and plunging right into the bridegroom's bowl of hot soup and of a waiter kicking two dogs with such fury that one of his hobnailed shoes flies into the air and lands on the table where the matchmaker sits: "He was just raising his chopsticks to his mouth when something black hurtled from behind the table to smash the two plates of sweetmeats. And as Chen [Ch'en] Ho-fu jumped up in a fright, he caught the bowl of soup with his sleeve and overturned it, so that it slopped all over the table." [40] According to Ho Tse-han, this incident is suggested by a brief episode in the T'ang historian Li Yen-shou's *Nan shih* (History of the southern dynasties), [41] and we may presume that the story of the rat, too, is derived from some written source. Ostensibly, these absurd happenings augur an unhappy marriage. But they are too hilarious to be ominous, and the author may have included them just for their independent farcical value.

Though a series of tenuously related stories, *The Scholars* has a discernible structure of three parts flanked by a prologue and an epilogue (chap. 55). Part I (chaps. 2–30) contains all the beloved stories about different types of individuals in search of rank, fame, and wealth. Part II (chaps. 31–37) constitutes the moral backbone of the book and tells of the hero Tu Shao-ch'ing and his friends, the good scholars of Nanking. They eventually gather to perform the ritual of worship at the T'ai-po Temple. Part III (chaps. 37–54) comprises a miscellaneous group of stories without apparent design. While several of these revert to the satiric and didactic modes of Parts I and II, several others are conventional "romances" in praise of military commanders and of men and women of extraordinary

Confucian conduct. On the whole, this part leaves the impression of great unevenness.

It is unfortunate that the critical fashion has been to regard *The Scholars* mainly as a satire on the examination system. Even in Part I, where the author is mainly concerned with satire, the objects of ridicule comprise many other types besides scholars and pseudo scholars obsessed with examinations. The latter groups are first given prominent attention because in traditional China to pass the provincial and metropolitan examinations is the quickest way to attain fame, rank, and wealth. But the novel soon concerns itself with the scholars' equal obsession with fame in a social and literary context rather than in a bureaucratic context. A scholar can become famous as a *ming-shih* if he disdains official rank and cultivates a reputation for elegance or unconventionality. He can get his own poems published or bring out a limited edition of some rare manuscript, he can sponsor a poetry contest or organize an excursion to a scenic spot, he can judge the merits of opera singers or show hospitality to impoverished men of unusual virtue and talent. Ch'ü Kung-sun, the Lou brothers, and Tu Shen-ch'ing attract attention in this manner.[42] With their self-conscious unconventionality (*ya*), these scholars usually look down upon their examination-obsessed brethren for their narrow-minded vulgarity (*su*). But it is a satiric strength of the novel that the author does not play favorites between these two types of scholars. If the kind of education that goes with academic-bureaucratic success is too narrow, the type of aesthetic dilettantism cultivated by the elegant scholars is reprehensible in its own fashion. Viewed against the exemplary life of Wang Mien, to seek after *ya* is perhaps only a more insidious form of vulgarity than to seek after bureaucratic success.

The idea of culture plays an important part in Wu Ching-tzu's satire against the scholars. Sooner or later, as we have seen in the cases of Fan Chin and Ma Ch'un-shang, they are exposed for their ignorance. But to be ignorant is far less blameworthy than to be immoral, and ultimately the idea of morality determines the author's attitude toward his characters. A scholar may retain his moral integrity even if his culture is seriously warped by his program of studies. Ma Ch'un-shang, modeled after a dear friend of the author's, exhibits in his conversations a very narrow culture indeed, maintaining, for example, that if Confucius were living in the present age, even he would buckle down to prepare for the examinations.[43] He is also insensitive to nature and boorish in his table manners. But his heart is as big as his appetite for food and his humanity shines through his provinciality so that he must be placed among the most endearing characters in the book, far more interesting than the good Confucian scholars of Part II. Once Ma exhausts his savings to help a friend who is being blackmailed for treason.[44] Another time, he gives money to a studious youth working as a fortuneteller in Hangchow to enable him to go home to serve his parents and prepare for the examinations. With all his open mockery of Ma's provincial culture, the author nevertheless prizes his sterling qualities as a person. Chou Chin and Fan Chin, too, may have been scholars who deserve their long obscurity rather than their later eminence (since Chou Chin is the sole judge of Fan Chin's ability as an essayist at the examinations, we are not even sure whether Fan writes good eight-legged essays or not), but they have imbibed enough of the dull, orthodox Confucian culture to stray too far from rectitude in their subsequent roles as officials. They are not opportunists, even though their initial entry into the official world requires an enormous amount of luck.

A number of the satiric targets, however, are young opportunists and their signal contrast with the exemplary hero Wang Mien appears in their readiness to compromise their moral integrity when opportunity knocks on the door. The youth given the most ironic attention is K'uang Ch'ao-jen, the fortuneteller befriended by Ma Ch'un-shang. He is introduced as a filial son, hard-working and studious: upon returning to his native village, he tends his bed-ridden father, sells cooked pork and bean curd, and devotes the remainder of his time to study. His piety and industry attract the attention of the village head P'an and later of Magistrate Li of his county:

One night he had read till nearly midnight, and was declaiming an essay with great gusto when he heard gongs sound outside the window and saw a sedan-chair pass, surrounded by torches and followed by out-riders. He knew this must be the county magistrate, but he went on reading aloud while the party passed.

Now the magistrate decided to spend the night in the village office, for he marvelled to himself: "How remarkable to find a man studying so hard late at night in a little country place like this! I wonder whether he is a successful candidate or a student? Why not send for the headman to find out?" [45]

The magistrate is even more impressed when P'an tells him of the youth's extraordinary filial piety. He befriends K'uang, who soon passes the prefectural examination and becomes a *hsiu-ts'ai*.

When Wang Mien is approached by a magistrate, he refuses to see him. K'uang accepts Magistrate Li's patronage and attains a fair degree of success. One cannot blame K'uang for wanting to be discovered; indeed, at this stage of his story, one can only be pleased that things have worked out so well for this good lad, even though the author may have intended to show by his eagerness to accept help a certain sign of moral weakness. In time K'uang's father dies and his patron is dismissed from office. The young man now goes back to Hangchow and meets with dandies and merchants who af-fect the style of poets. He passes as one of them and, further, achieves some reputation as an anthologist of eight-legged essays. Bailiff P'an, a cousin of the village headman, befriends him and asks him to forge official documents and substitute for someone at an examina-tion. All these misdeeds K'uang commits without hesitation, even though one would not have expected a filial son to be so interested in dishonorable gain. Also at the bailiff's suggestion, he marries into the family of an honest yamen runner, Old Cheng. After passing another examination, he becomes a *kung-sheng* or senior licentiate.

Bailiff P'an is soon imprisoned for his nefarious deeds. Afraid to get involved, K'uang sends his wife to his village home and goes to Peking at the invitation of Censor Li, the former magistrate, who has been now restored to favor. He is delighted to see his former protégé, and, on being told that he is not yet married (K'uang thinks Censor Li would look down upon him for being married to a plebeian's daughter), affiances him to his own niece, a beautiful girl with a big dowry. Soon they are happily married.

A few months later, K'uang goes back to Hangchow to get a testimonial from local authorities in connection with his appointment to the Imperial College as a tutor. Luckily for him, he learns that his first wife has died and no one will now know of his bigamy. But his friend and benefactor, Bailiff P'an, who is still in prison, requests an interview. K'uang, however, tells the intermediary, the yamen clerk Chiang:

"It's a pity he's in this fix! I would have gone to the gaol to see him, but my position has changed. As a servant of the throne I have to abide by the law; and to call on him in such a place would show no respect for the law."

"You are not a local official," countered Chiang, "and you would only be visiting a friend. What harm can there be in that?"

"Gentlemen," said Kuang [K'uang], "I shouldn't say this, but to friends it doesn't matter. In view of what our friend Pan [P'an] has done, if I had been in office here I would have had to arrest him. If I were to go to the prison to call on him, it would look as if I disapproved of the sentence. That is not the way of a loyal subject. Besides, all the yamens here know I have come back for my testimonial. If I were to go to the gaol and the story reached my superiors, my official reputation would be ruined. How can I do such a thing? I will trouble you, Mr. Chiang, to send my regards to Pan Number Three and tell him that I shall remember him. If I am lucky enough to be appointed to some profitable post on my return to the capital, I shall be glad to send him a few hundred taels in a year or so to help him." [46]

Except for one additional paragraph in which the author rather tediously shows him to be a braggart unable to decipher a simple phrase, the story of K'uang Ch'ao-jen ends with his self-righteous repudiation of a benefactor. Though a crook, Bailiff P'an had been in his fashion a genuine friend to K'uang at a time when he was a stranger in Hangchow and in need of financial assistance. His refusal to see P'an in prison when he could be in a position to help him is in the author's eyes a far more unforgivable crime than his ready consent to a bigamous marriage. But Wu Ching-tzu does not mete out to him any punishment as earlier storytellers surely would have done. Instead, he sends him on his road to further and greater success: the innuendo of moral disapproval is enough.

The story of K'uang Ch'ao-jen is extremely interesting, but it is told in such a way that we are never allowed a glimpse of his mental condition as things happen to him. For many readers it will remain puzzling that a filial son of apparent moral integrity could have degenerated so fast. But for the author the answer is quite clear: it is the very taste of success that generates corruption. In his last instructions to K'uang, his father specifically warns him against the temptation of success:

Now, Ch'ao-jen, you have been lucky enough to pass the examination, and may go farther later. But rank and fame are external things after all; virtuous conduct is all that really counts. You have tried your hardest to be a good son and a loyal brother, and such dutifulness is rare nowadays. However, now that things are going more smoothly for you, it is my earnest wish that you do not change your ways and start to act important by looking down on the poor and seeking exclusively the company of the rich and powerful. After I'm dead and you've observed the mourning period, you must lose no time in finding a wife. But choose a girl from a humble family, and don't ever entertain the thought of improving your fortune and position by marrying into a family that is rich and noble. Your elder brother is no good; but you must go on showing him the same respect that you would me." [47]

K'uang's subsequent career confirms his father's worst fears.

It is Wu Ching-tzu's regular practice to juxtapose stories whose heroes offer obvious points for comparison and contrast (as we have seen in the case of Chou Chin and Fan Chin and of the Yen brothers), while at the same time they recall or anticipate other characters in the book. Following the exit of K'uang, therefore, another poor but ambitious youth takes over the stage—Niu P'u-lang. An orphan whose grandfather runs a chandler's shop, Niu is apparently very bright and industrious, but he studies mainly poetry for pleasure and self-improvement because he has no intention of preparing for the examinations. He is befriended by a kind old monk and studies at his temple every evening till midnight. A well-known middle-aged poet, Niu Pu-yi, who died at the temple, had left in the monk's care two manuscript volumes of his poems. Out of curiosity, the orphan examines these volumes in the monk's absence:

He was in raptures. He also noticed such titles as "To Prime Minister So-and-So," "Thinking of Examiner Chou," "A Visit to the Lake with Mr. Lou, Also Dedicated to the Commissioner," "Saying Goodbye to Censor Lu," "To Intendant Wang." The remaining poems were dedicated to prefects, district magistrates, county magistrates or other high officials.

"These are all titles of present-day officials," thought Niu Pu-lang. "Apparently a man who can write poems doesn't have to pass the examinations in order to make friends with great officials. This is wonderful!"

Then it occurred to him: "This man's name is Niu and so is mine; and he has only written a pen-name Niu Pu-yi on these volumes without putting down his real name. Why shouldn't I add my name to his? I will have two seals made and stamp these books with them: then these poems will become mine and from now on I shall call myself Niu Pu-yi." [48]

If K'uang's downfall has been gradual, Niu's, then, is sudden, over the immediate prospect of poetic fame and material betterment. There is something absurd about a youth in his late teens posturing as a well-known poet, and in the course of time Niu undergoes several hilarious misadventures. However, when the deceased poet's widow finally drags him to court on the charge that he has murdered her husband and assumed his name, Niu's credit has been too well established with the local magistrate for him to receive any punishment. By that time, like K'uang at the comparable stage of his career, Niu has committed bigamy and earned the good will and protection of several influential men.

In reading the stories of these two opportunists, one is especially struck by the fact that so many good-hearted and gullible men are ready to serve as their guardian angels. Both K'uang and Niu began as innocents, and they could not have exploited their advantages successfully if everyone around them had been mistrustful, self-seeking, and unscrupulous. With all his peevish superciliousness toward ignoramuses and vulgar upstarts, Wu Ching-tzu treats the world on the whole kindly, with benign humor. If he ends the story of K'uang on a sharp satiric note, his treatment of Niu is farcical throughout, at once less sympathetic and less severe. Both stories carry the same moral lesson, but the author's greater severity toward K'uang implies also a greater sense of personal regret because, if he had not been early corrupted by success, he would have been such a nice young man of virtue and talent.

As a sharp contrast to the young opportunists, Wu Ching-tzu introduces upon the exit of Niu an old actor named Pao Wen-ch'ing who, despite his mean profession (actors are looked down upon in traditional Chinese society), upholds the highest ideals of loyalty and benevolence. His story is very touching, but several Communist critics, while praising it, have also expressed their regret that the author's high regard for this old man implies an endorsement of the slave morality of the exploited classes.[49] But when we remember the attitude of jocular contempt or stern disapproval held by professional storytellers (and by the author of *Chin P'ing Mei*) toward such lowly people as actors, prostitutes, and concubines, Wu Ching-tzu, with his generous sympathy for them and his predilection to choose from among them examples of unspoiled humanity and Confucian conduct, stands out in shining contrast. With all his penchant for satire and ridicule, he was the first true humanitarian among Chinese novelists.

Ultimately, of course, both K'uang and Niu are contrasted with Wang Mien, who lives as a recluse primarily to maintain his moral integrity and artistic sensibility. By his standard, it would seem that to entertain the very thought of worldly success dooms one to his fall. The novelist would approve of K'uang's father's saying that "virtuous conduct (*te-hsing*) is all that really counts," and for ordinary folk, it is enough that they maintain their simple competence and live in virtue. If the old actor Pao Wen-ch'ing is an outstanding example of virtuous conduct, minor characters of lesser heroism who nevertheless maintain their rectitude and honesty in their humble environment occur repeatedly in the novel. Wang Mien himself lives under the beneficent influence of two simple souls, his mother and Old Ch'in. K'uang's father and Niu's grandfather and the fathers of their first wives are of the same type, and, if the young heroes had imbibed their influence, they would not have strayed from the true path. Through all these characters, the novelist seems to express his yearning for a simple Taoist world instinctively governed by Confucian morality.

But for scholars the problem is more complex. Their roles as civil servants and as inheritors of the humane tradition of letters expose them to the temptations of fame and wealth and make their practice of virtue far more difficult. Since it is the ultimate aim of Confucian learning and Confucian government to manifest a moral culture, it would actually be far better for all concerned, the novelist keeps on saying, if most would-be scholars could stay content as simple farmers, tradesmen, and artisans rather than expose themselves to the forces of corruption in their very struggle for worldly success. Wu Ching-tzu shows therefore an unmistakable aristocratic temper not unmixed with peevishness in his scorn for all pretenders to learning and seekers after office. With his illustrious family background, he apparently thought that fame, rank, and wealth are things that one just takes for granted and that it is extremely low to covet them. His subsequent impoverishment seems to have further confirmed his prejudice against all upstarts who had lately come into possession of fame and fortune. In this context, even Wang Mien can be seen as a man of extreme pride who refuses to accept the patronage of a mere magistrate. This pride is expressed most clearly by the autobiographical hero, Tu Shao-ch'ing, also the scion of a distinguished family now living in reduced circumstances. When the local magistrate wishes to see him, he ignores his invitation and reasons as follows:

Why, in my father's time—to say nothing of my grandfather's and great-grandfather's—heaven knows how many magistrates came here! If he really respects me, why doesn't he call on me first? Why should I call on him? I'm sorry I passed the district examination, since it means I have to address the local magistrate as my patron! As for this Magistrate Wang, who crawled out of some dust-heap to pass the metropolitan examination—I wouldn't even want him as my student! Why should I meet him? [50]

Unlike Wang Mien, a recluse never contaminated by rank and wealth, Tu Shao-ch'ing is born with a proud family name and a family fortune. Since he cannot get rid of his name, which actually becomes more illustrious following his acts of extravagant liberality, it gives him a certain perverse satisfaction to get rid of his fortune so as to regain his freedom—freedom from sycophants, certainly; freedom to travel and do what he likes; and, subconsciously, freedom from the burden of family tradition. He is certainly proud of his distinguished ancestors but, unless he should be called upon to serve the emperor in an important advisory or ministerial capacity, he sees no point in going through the infuriating routine of examinations to reach the top level of government service. He passed the *hsiu-ts'ai* degree so as to gain a scholar's social equality with officials, but he has not attempted the higher degrees. Moreover, so long as he remains on his family estate, he will always be subjected to an invidious comparison with his ancestors by his friends, neighbors, and even servants, and stuck with the tedious responsibility of managing that estate. It would be so much better to pull up his roots and move with his family to a metropolis like Nanking to enjoy its scenic spots and the company of more congenial friends.

I have analyzed Tu Shao-ch'ing's decision to squander his fortune and move to Nanking as if he made it deliberately to cover up for his inferiority complex. As the author presents him, he is of course a far more appealing person—a proud scholar of forthright honesty and reckless generosity. Yet his story up to his departure for Nanking (chaps. 31–32) remains a most curious one: a number of people beg for financial assistance and, in granting them all their wishes, he reduces himself to poverty. Most of these petitioners have no claims whatever on his generosity and they plainly impose upon him to advance their own selfish schemes. Yet Tu helps them with as much alacrity as he would people for whom he feels genuine sympathy: the destitute family of his father's faithful retainer, Old Lou, and a tailor who has no money to bury his mother. Tu, of course, is not blind: he knows that his steward Wang is a crook and that many of his guests are contemptible sycophants. He is touched to tears when the dying Mr. Lou cautions him on his indiscriminate generosity and advises him to pattern himself after his father's virtuous conduct (*te-hsing*) and bring up his precocious son in the proper Confucian manner. (Lou's long speech enjoys the same dramatic function in Tu's story as his dying father's speech in K'uang's story.) Yet he continues to squander money on unworthy recipients until he finally has to sell what remains of his property and move to Nanking.

With all his innate kindness, therefore, Tu's militant generosity appears far more a gesture of aristocratic pride. His cousin, Tu Shen-ch'ing, has early defined his character with facetious precision when he said that "he just loves to act the 'big shot.'"[51] The last phrase, *ta-lao-kuan*, is a colloquial expression meaning one who loves to play the patron or host, insists on paying for everything, and can't say no when people beseech him for help. Just as it is beneath Tu's dignity to call on a magistrate, it is against his grain to turn down a request however impudent. The petitioner has counted on his munificence, and he cannot therefore disappoint that expectation even though he has nothing but the greatest contempt for him. For the same reason, he disdains to look into the accounts of his steward, who regularly cheats him. It is all a matter of style, and prudential considerations for self-protection are just not Tu's style.

As a new arrival in Nanking, Tu Shao-ch'ing sustains his reputation among his friends with his independent views and nonconformist behavior. Unlike most scholars, he treats his wife as his equal and frequently takes her out on excursions. Once they have a particularly good time at the Yao Garden:

Then, revelling in the spring warmth and balmy breeze, he carried the goblet to the balustrade and started to do some heavy drinking. Very drunk at last, he took his wife's hand and walked out of the garden, holding the golden goblet and roaring with laughter. So they strolled several hundred yards down the hillside while the other women followed them, laughing merrily. All who saw were shocked and amazed.[52]

It was then a quite unheard-of thing for a scholar to hold his wife's hand in public and stroll in such merriment. Yet with all his non-conformity, there is not much that Tu can do, and his career peters out amid intellectual conversations and mild hedonistic enjoyment of wine and nature. Once, he is given the chance to make himself more useful. Like Wu Ching-tzu himself, he is recommended for a special examination open to eminent scholars without advanced degrees. Tu, however, pleads illness:

"When you are invited to court to become an official, why refuse on the pretext of illness?" asked Mrs. Tu with a smile.

"Don't be absurd! What! leave an amusing place like Nanking? Don't you enjoy having me at home, to go out with you in the spring and autumn to look at the flowers and drink wine? Why do you want to pack me off to Peking? Suppose I take you along too? It's a cold place, the capital, and you're so delicate that one gust of wind there would freeze you to death! That would never do. No, no, I'd better not go." [53]

Tu's affection for his wife is touching, but the excuse given here is quite beside the point and amounts to a preference for idleness. One can understand Tu's unwillingness to compete with ignoramuses in the regular examinations and seek an office on his own initiative, but on the present occasion he is being invited to court as a distinguished scholar and finally given the opportunity to compete with his ancestors on equal terms. Living in Nanking, however, he has exorcised their spirits as he has long since squandered their patrimony. His decision to preserve his integrity ultimately in the cause of an elegant hedonism leaves the reader with the impression of futility. In the end, it is a moot question whether one doesn't prefer a vulgar official doing his best according to his lights to an intelligent and proud scholar voluntarily withdrawing himself from service to take strolls with his wife. For if all good scholars abdicate their traditional responsibility to serve, won't they be leaving the world forever in the hands of the vulgar and self-seeking?

Wu Ching-tzu is quite aware of this problem and, soon after Tu's refusal to serve, he honors another of the good scholars of Nanking with an invitation to serve the emperor. Far more of a Confucian than Tu, Chuang Shao-kuang is willing to go to the capital, though his parting speech to his wife betrays an attitude of perfunctory compliance: "We are not hermits. . . . Since a decree has been issued summoning me to court, it is my duty as a subject to go. Don't worry, though. I shall come straight back. Lao Lai-tzu's wife will have no excuse to despise me." [54] He seems to grow more interested when granted an interview with the emperor. But just as he is about to answer His Majesty's questions, rather incredibly, a scorpion that has been hiding in his cap stings his crown and incapacitates him from giving an answer forthwith. On discovering the cause of his pain, Chuang exclaims, "It does not seem as if our Confucian ways will avail in this age!" [55] Furthermore, though he eventually submits to the emperor a brilliant memorial, an evil minister has in the meantime turned against him and dissuades His Majesty from giving him an official post. It seems that, even if he is willing to serve, a good Confucian scholar will be prevented from doing so by fate and circumstance: the time is simply not right.

In Part II Tu Shao-ch'ing, Chuang Shao-kuang, and the other good scholars of Nanking donate money and time to the construction of a temple in honor of T'ai-po, the eldest son of a progenitor of the House of Chou who fled to the then barbarous region of Wu so as to yield his right to the throne to a younger brother. It is quite characteristic of these scholars that they propose to honor a worthy better known for his filial piety and self-abnegation than for a career of active service. But T'ai-po did change the barbarian ways of the people around him, and his temple may serve the same civilizing function. In the words of the scholar who proposes this scheme: "I want to persuade some friends to contribute enough to build a temple to Tai Po. Then in mid-spring and mid-autumn we can sacrifice with the ancient ceremonies and music. In this way people will practise ceremony and music, and that should help to produce some genuine scholars who will be able to serve the government well." [56] Since the author had undertaken the restoration of a temple of this sort, it appears that he seriously believed in the efficacy of ancient ritual and music as an educative influence on the people. Probably all serious satirists in world literature are conservatives by temperament. But if it is of crucial satiric relevance to stress the importance of sound Confucian learning and morality in a book about counterfeit scholars, it is indicative of the author's bookish and antiquarian temper that he advocates the revival of ancient ritual and music which had already been in a condition of decay in the time of Confucius.

As a satirist, Wu Ching-tzu should also realize that it is extremely difficult to give a vivid and interesting account of a ritualistic occasion and that, furthermore, when that occasion is designed to body forth all the values negated in the comic episodes, the risks he faces are almost insurmountable. To succeed in his task, ideally the author should bring out all the emotional significance of that event as seen through the eyes of a deeply moved participant or observer. Wu Ching-tzu, of course, could not have hit upon this technique since until modern times all Chinese fiction was written from the point of view of an omniscient third-person narrator. Still, when describing the scholars' worship at the newly erected temple, he is unduly disappointing in merely giving us a bald summary of the proceedings in a solemn fashion:

Then the drum sounded three times for the sacrifice. Chin Tz'u-fu and Pao T'ing-hsi led in the players of the jade chime, lyre, zither, pipe, drum, sonorous wood, bronze tiger, *sheng,* big bell, flute, small bells, and stone chimes, as well as the thirty-six dancing boys. They took their places at both ends of the hall and the courtyard.

Then Chin Tung-yai, followed by Lu Hua-shih, entered the hall. Coming to a halt, he announced, "Let all taking part attend to their duties!"

The musicians picked up their instruments.

"Take your places!" cried Chin.

Wu Shu with his banner led the men bearing wine, jade, and silk to their respective seats to the east of the courtyard. Those bearing wine were Chi Wan, Hsin Tung-chih, Yü K'uei; those bearing jade were Ch'ü Lai-hsün, Lu Te, Yü Kan-ch'i; and those bearing silk were Chu-ko Yu, Ching Pen-hui, Kuo T'ieh-pi. Then Wu Shu led Tsang T'u, who was to read the prayers, to his place before the prayer tablet on the dais. Next he led the men bearing grain and sacrificial viands to the west of the courtyard. The former were Hsiao Ting, Ch'u Hsin, I Chao, and the latter, Chi T'ien-i, Chin Yü-liu, Tsung Chi. Then Wu Shu with his banner took his seat below them.[57]

This is but the beginning of the ceremonies. Upon their completion, the departing celebrants see their path "lined with people who had brought their old folk and children to throng the temple and watch. They pealed cries of joy."[58] But it would take an extremely partial reader to share their sense of jubilation.

By chapter 37, when the sacrifice at the temple takes place, the novel has been getting duller. One would probably expect the good scholars to lead less interesting lives than the bad ones, but there is no reason why they should not be accorded full comic understanding. Ma Ch'un-shang, a good but provincial scholar, has been earlier described with remarkable gusto. The good friends of Tu Shao-ch'ing, however, are treated with much less objectivity either because Wu Ching-tzu is afraid to offend his friends who have served as their models or because (the more likely conjecture) he admires them so much that he really cannot perceive their faults. Thus Dr. Yü Yü-te, the scholar chosen to preside over the sacrifice at the temple, suffers from an insipid portrayal precisely because the author is known to have held his real-life counterpart, Professor Wu Meng-ch'üan, in the highest esteem.[59]

Part III of the novel is only discontinuously satirical. Its many epi-sodes about filial sons, chaste wives, righteous knights-errant, and statesmanlike military commanders share the "romance" spirit of comparable stories in the *San-yen* tradition. In its satiric episodes, moreover, the author now appears intrusively personal in his com-ments on scholars and provincials. The stories about Wu-ho, Anhwei (chaps. 44–47) especially suffer in this respect, for the un-derstandable reason that Wu-ho stands for the author's home town. Whereas in earlier stories about scholars Wu Ching-tzu has aimed at a satire of general application, in these stories he repeatedly tells us that the vices uncovered in Wu-ho are peculiar to that region and not applicable elsewhere. He has obviously lost his satiric poise. In-stead of insinuating himself into our confidence with his customary style of urbane impersonality, he pours scorn upon the citizens of Ch'üan-chiao who had not appreciated his worth and spells out their philistine and mercenary ways in no uncertain terms:

It was the custom at Wu-ho that if a man was praised for his moral character, the people would simply scoff; that if the prominent scholarly families of several decades ago were mentioned, they would just snort; and that if someone was commended for his ability to write in the classical styles of poetry and prose, the citizens' very eyebrows would twitch with laughter. If you asked what there was of note in the scenery of Wu-ho, they would tell you, "Mr. P'eng." If you asked what men commanded the greatest respect, they would answer, "Mr. P'eng." And if you asked who were best known for moral conduct or literary talent, the reply would still be "Mr. P'eng." [60]

This specimen of virulent rhetoric betrays the author's deep-seated hatred of all the vulgar parvenu families of his home town here represented by Mr. P'eng. Yet at the same time his obsession with his past resentments, if one may continue in this speculative vein, has got such an upper hand over his satiric judgment that against these philistine adversaries he sends forth to battle three rather inef-fectual Confucian scholars of no particular brilliance: the Yü broth-ers and Yü Hua-hsüan. The elder brother, Yü Yu-ta, is not even very virtuous since he doesn't mind accepting a large bribe with which to bury his parents: only a Confucian fanatic prizing filial piety to the exclusion of all other virtues could approve of his act. But if the author cannot demonstrate the sage qualities of the brothers by fictional means, he can always assert them. So he writes in chapter 44, "As regards both character and learning, the Yü brothers had never been equaled since antiquity" [61]—surely the most incredible overstatement in the whole book. These two brothers are modeled after the Chin brothers of Ch'üan-chiao, who were the author's first cousins.[62] We know that the Wu and Chin families had for generations intermarried and that the cousins were very close, but still we cannot presume to know what personal causes led Wu Ching-tzu to use such extreme language in his praise of the Yü brothers as well as in his attack on Mr. P'eng. We are only embarrassed that in these stories of Wu-ho his satiric art has become too personal for comfort.

In the epilogue (chap. 55) the author returns to Nanking and introduces four plebeian heroes: a homeless calligrapher who lodges in a temple, a *go* player who sells spills for a living, a painter who runs a small teahouse, and a lute player who plies his trade as a tailor. By that time the good scholars that once gathered in Nanking have either died or grown old, and the proud monument of their Confucian endeavor, the T'ai-po temple, has long been dilapidated. One day one of the new heroes, the painter Kai K'uan, pays a visit to the temple with an older neighbor:

Having climbed the left side of Rain Flower Mount [Yü-hua Terrace] they saw the main hall of Tai Po's Temple with the front half of the roof caving in. Five or six children were playing football beside the double gate, one half of which had fallen to the ground. Going in, they came upon three or four old women, who were picking shepherd's purse in the temple courtyard. All the lattice-work in the hall had disappeared, and the five buildings at the back were completely stripped—not even a floor plank was left. After walking around, Kai sighed.

"To think that so famous a place should have fallen into such ruins!" he said. "And no one will repair an ancient sage's temple!" [63]

The elegiac note is unmistakable.

But the last chapter also contains a note of defiant hope that, however decayed the scholarly class may have become, obscure men in humbler circumstances will carry forward the cause of culture and morality. The four new heroes are all modeled after Wang Mien, and Kai K'uan is also suggestive of Tu Shao-ch'ing in his sheer contempt for money and his indiscriminate generosity. Once a landowner and pawnbroker, he is progressively impoverished until he moves with his son and daughter to a two-room cottage, which also serves as his teahouse:

He would get up early to light the fire, and when he had fanned it into a blaze would put on a kettle to heat, then sit behind his counter to read or paint. In a vase on the counter he kept a few blooms of whichever flowers were in season, and next to this was a pile of old books. He had sold all his other possessions, but could not bear to part with these precious volumes. When customers came in, he would put down his book to bring them a teapot and cups. There was not much money in this. He made one copper on each pot of tea, and since he sold no more than fifty or sixty a day, he made no more than fifty or sixty coppers, which barely sufficed to keep them in fuel and rice! [64]

Few characters in Chinese fiction have been accorded as much human dignity in so few words as the keeper of this teahouse.

Lute playing, *go,* calligraphy, and painting (*ch'in ch'i shu hua*) have been traditionally the four noble recreations of a Chinese scholar. But to the four new heroes, each of these arts is not so much recreation as a form of self-expression, and Wu Ching-tzu would seem to agree with traditional Chinese literary and art critics that no one can arrive at true self-expression without revealing at the same time a pure moral sensibility that delights in virtue and detests evil.[65] As true artists, therefore, the plebeian heroes appear to us also as symbols of moral incorruptibility in a world too easily impressed by official rank and material success.

Wu Ching-tzu may be called the first Chinese novelist to exhibit an introspective turn of mind since his proud scholar-recluse is no less an artist alienated from society than many a hero of modern psychological fiction. And yet, with all his technical contributions to the Chinese novel, Wu shows curiously little ambition to explore that last frontier of fiction, the interior world of consciousness. At a time when his younger contemporary, Ts'ao Hsüeh-ch'in, was venturing into that world, he remained content to depict the external, visible world even though his sensitive recluses could have become far more interesting if their mental conditions had been fully described. With all its importance as an intellectual novel, therefore, *The Scholars* appears strongest as a comedy of manners in its amazing representation of the bustling world of the author's time. In that world we encounter not only scholars and would-be scholars, but rich salt merchants and small storekeepers, bailiffs and yamen runners, actors and prostitutes, matchmakers and pimps, and impostors and confidence men of every description. Whereas the author tends to be schematic and therefore predictable in his portrayal of scholars and would-be scholars, he sketches the latter types with greater comic zest precisely because he is less preoccupied with moral problems. The satire of scholars and officials would have been much thinner fare without the surrounding comedy of social life.

In this social comedy women figure quite importantly. Even though they are far fewer in number than the male characters, this select group of heroines constitutes a diversified gallery of Chinese womanhood and attests especially to the author's command of social and psychological reality. I have earlier mentioned the wife and concubine of Yen Chih-ho and the wife of Ch'ü Kung-sun—each a distinct type remarkably true to life. I might also mention the tragic exception among these women, the daughter of Wang Yü-hui, a chaste widow who commits suicide by starvation following the death of her husband,[66] and a pair of vivacious prostitutes who entertain two playboys and sundry other customers in chapter 42—certainly none of the courtesans in *Chin P'ing Mei* have been as well rendered in the actuality of their milieu. But to illustrate the author's skill in depicting the kind of social reality farthest removed from the world of scholars and officials, we should dwell for a moment upon the case of Mrs. Wang (chaps. 26–27), a woman of some notoriety used to a pampered life but nevertheless serious in her quest for happiness. Once a cast-off concubine and now a widow of independent means, she is finally persuaded to marry Pao T'ing-hsi, a poor actor, without having been informed of his real identity. For mercenary reasons, his adopted mother and the matchmaker conspire to bring this marriage about even though it is quite apparent that it will be a totally incompatible union.

Mrs. Wang is immediately disillusioned by the modest circumstances of her new home. On the third day of her married life, however, she is required by custom to cook a fish to bring luck:

Then Ting-hsi's wife sulkily took off her brocade gown, put on an apron, and went to the kitchen. She scraped the fish three or four times with a knife, picked it up by the tail, and flung it into the boiling pan. Pock-marked Chien's [Ch'ien's] wife who was standing by the stove watching, had her face spattered with hot water and her gold-embroidered brocade jacket soaked.

"Look out!" she called angrily, jumping with fright, then hastily mopped her face with a handkerchief.

Ting-hsi's wife threw down her knife, and flounced scowling back to her room. And that evening, when the guests took their places for the feast, she refused to join them.[67]

Two nights later, she finally discovers her husband's profession:

He was not back till dawn.

"Why did you have to stay all night in your shop?" she asked.

"What shop?" demanded T'ing-hsi. "I'm in charge of a theater company. We've just come back after giving an all-night performance."

This was the last straw. His wife nearly choked with rage. Falling backward with a scream, she clenched her teeth and lost consciousness. T'ing-hsi ordered the maids to revive her with ginger water; but when she came to she sobbed and screamed, rolled on the ground, and tore her hair. Then, wailing loudly, she tried to climb on the wooden roof of the bed, and began to sing snatches of opera. Rage and disappointment had made her mad! When Mrs. Pao [her mother-in-law] and her daughter ran fearfully in, they did not know whether to laugh or to cry.

Just then the matchmaker Big Feet Shen came into the room, bringing with her two packages of pastries as a congratulatory offering. As soon as the wife saw her entering the room, she grabbed her and pulled her to the stool. She opened its lid, grabbed a handful of muck, and smeared it all over Big Feet Shen's face and mouth. Even her nostrils were filled with foul matter.[68]

In view of the raw vitality of the scenes just cited, one could wish that Wu Ching-tzu had focused more of his attention on scenes of ordinary domestic life in all their unpredictable truth. Insofar as his satire of scholars eventually runs out of surprises, we may even regard his choice of theme as a self-imposed limitation that has deprived him of the chance to unfold to the full the panorama of traditional Chinese life, especially that of the middle and lower classes. But no author can be expected to have full self-knowledge; except for his strong animus against the counterfeit scholars and venal officials and his equally strong urge to vindicate himself as a proud recluse of Confucian rectitude, most probably he would not have felt the urge to become a novelist. We would then have been denied his vivid transcript of the social life around him, a record that has preserved for all time the vanished manners of eighteenth-century China.

CHAPTER VII

DREAM
OF THE RED
CHAMBER

Dream of the Red Chamber (*Hung-lou meng*), first published in 1792, is the greatest of all Chinese novels. From Li Ju-chen's *Ching-hua yuan*[1] (Romance of the flowers in the mirror) to Liu Ê's *Lao-ts'an yu-chi* (The travels of Lao Ts'an), many remarkable novels were indeed produced during the remainder of the Ch'ing dynasty, and in the Republican period Chinese fiction has absorbed the Western influence and developed in new directions. But even the finest of the modern novels cannot compare with *Dream of the Red Chamber* in depth and scope: for, with all the new techniques at his disposal, the modern Chinese novelist is, with a few exceptions, too often traditionalist in his lack of philosophical ambition and his failure to probe the deeper psychological truth. To show his scorn for contemporary Chinese writing, a scholar versed in traditional literature would often ask, "What has been produced in the last fifty years that could equal *Dream of the Red Chamber*?"[2] But one could turn the tables on him and ask with equal expectation of a negative answer: "What work previous to *Dream* could equal it?" Some sixty years ago the great scholar Wang Kuo-wei, among the first Chinese to apply Western ideas to a study of Chinese literature, declared unequivocally that *Dream* is the only Chinese work of magnitude fully informed with the spirit of tragedy.[3] Wang, however, is primarily impressed by its author's relentless quest for the meaning of human existence in a world of suffering. But, in a novel, philosophy cannot be divorced from psychology—*Dream* which embodies the supreme tragic experience in Chinese literature is also its supreme work of psychological realism.

Ts'ao Hsüeh-ch'in, the author of *Dream of the Red Chamber*, was a younger contemporary of Wu Ching-tzu. Although they moved in completely different circles and never met each other, at that particular juncture in the development of the Chinese novel they both felt the urge toward greater realism and toward making greater use of their personal experience. A satirist in command of a purer realism and a more economical style, Wu Ching-tzu, however, still adapts existing stories and jokes to embellish his plot and supplement his vision. Ts'ao Hsüeh-ch'in, while his novel is allied to the modes of poetry and allegory and his style is at once more colloquial and elaborate, at the same time resolutely shuns the use of secondary material and mines deeper layers of private experience. With Wu, autobiography is methodized in the interests of affirming the ideal of a scholar-recluse and castigating the vices of a philistine society. Tu Shao-ch'ing is seen in a series of poses, and even his stroll with his wife in the Yao Garden is a pose. It is enough for the reader to know that Tu is affectionate toward his wife and unconventional in behavior: to describe his marital life at closer range would have blurred his image as a proud scholar. We know that Wu squandered his fortune partly through his patronage of the gay quarters in Nanking, but to incorporate this aspect of his personal experience in his portrait of Tu would have again tarnished his image. What is missing in Wu's self-portrait, therefore, is the confessional element, and it is precisely this autobiographical compulsion to tell the private truth, to recapture a more intimate reality that makes Ts'ao Hsüeh-ch'in so much more of a revolutionary against the impersonal tradition of Chinese fiction. Though personal essays and memoirs had become quite popular by the late Ming period, *Dream of the Red Chamber* was nevertheless the first Chinese novel to utilize autobiographical experience on a large scale. Quite appropriately, part of a commentary prefixed to chapter 1 has been incorporated in the main text ever since its first publication: "The author further says that, though he is now a confessed failure, when he suddenly recalled the many girls he had known in the past, he realized that their conduct and understanding were far superior to his. To be a man and yet to be inferior to these girls: this is a thought he could not get over—there is so much he should feel ashamed of, and yet what is the point of futile regret?" [4] The confessional note is quite striking.

The autobiographical approach to *Dream of the Red Chamber,* first adopted by Hu Shih over forty-five years ago, has prompted an intensive search for all records with possible bearing on the author. But even today we know fewer biographical facts about Ts'ao Hsüeh-ch'in than about Shakespeare, and of the many girls in his life, whose importance in the novel had prompted the commentator to provide the headnote, we know practically nothing beyond what we may infer from the commentary. But because the novelist came from a branch of the Ts'ao clan (of Chinese ancestry) which had been for generations bondservants to the Manchu emperors, enough records have survived to enable us to reconstruct his family background.[5] His great-grandfather, grandfather, elder uncle, and father all held the highly lucrative post of commissioner of the Imperial Textile Mills, first in Soochow and then in Nanking. The grandfather, Ts'ao Yin (1658–1712), was a patron of letters and a poet in his own right, and on four successive occasions he played host in Nanking to the K'ang-hsi Emperor on his southern excursions, which greatly taxed his wealth. He was, however, given other lucrative posts to compensate for his expenditures.

When Ts'ao Hsüeh-ch'in (his given name is Ts'ao Chan) was born remains a matter of conjecture. Two suggested dates—1715 and 1724—have carried most weight with recent scholars, but I am more inclined to the belief that his birth took place sometime between 1716 and 1718.[6] The Yung-cheng Emperor, who succeeded K'ang-hsi in 1723, was far less friendly to the Ts'ao house. In 1728 he dismissed Ts'ao Fu, the author's father, from his post as textile commissioner of Nanking, raided his house, and confiscated much of his property. Then about eleven to thirteen years (*sui*) old, Hsüeh-ch'in moved to Peking with his parents, who, while living in reduced circumstances, still kept up their connections with the Manchu aristocracy. Most scholars believe that the Ts'ao clan temporarily regained favor after the Ch'ien-lung Emperor ascended the throne in 1736. But by 1744, when Ts'ao Hsüeh-ch'in started composing his novel, he had moved to the western suburbs of Peking, living in straitened circumstances: the Ts'ao family must have earlier suffered another disaster from which it never recovered. For a time the author lived in dire poverty. Some of his friends, notably the Manchu brothers Tun-ch'eng and Tun-min, have left us poems and jottings about the author as a poet and painter very fond of wine and conversation. According to another Manchu, Yü-jui, Hsüeh-ch'in was swarthy and corpulent, not at all like the handsome hero of his book. Most probably he died on February 12, 1763; according to an elegy by Tun-ch'eng, he had a few months earlier suffered the loss of a young son (most certainly by his first wife) and was survived by a second wife, of whom we know nothing further.[7]

If modern research has not uncovered many incontrovertible facts about Ts'ao Hsüeh-ch'in's life, important manuscript copies of his novel have turned up in recent years and these have enabled us to reconstruct the history of its composition with some degree of objectivity.[8] Many important puzzles, however, still await solution, and earlier theories based on a more subjective reading of fewer documents have prevailed for so long that a more sensible new theory is not yet likely to win immediate universal endorsement. But, for a proper understanding of the novel, the story of its authorship and early texts must be rehearsed even though much of it remains conjectural.

Dream of the Red Chamber, in its standard 120-chapter form, was not published until almost thirty years after Ts'ao Hsüeh-ch'in's death, under the auspices of complete strangers to the Ts'ao clan. The first 80 of these chapters, under the title of *Shih-t'ou chi* or *The Story of a Stone,* had circulated among his friends even when Ts'ao was still alive, and they were usually transcribed in a form which included a commentary by a close relative of the author's, known by the pen name of Chih-yen Chai (Red inkslab studio). The latter had apparently been privileged to read each batch of chapters as soon as they were written, and he had commented on these chapters on different occasions over a long period of time, before and after the author's death. Judging from his comments, and the few other comments by the author's relatives and friends, there can be no doubt as to the authenticity of the first 80 chapters.

The last 40 chapters, however, have remained a problem. Though the commentator Chih-yen Chai had seen drafts of episodes that take place after chapter 80, such completed chapters had apparently never been circulated during the author's lifetime, and even after his death most manuscript copies transcribed and sold contained only 80 chapters. For the public at large, therefore, the complete version became available only with the 1791 printed edition (actually published in 1792) prepared by Ch'eng Wei-yuan and Kao Ê. These two were quite concerned lest readers question the authenticity of the last 40 chapters and so, in their prefaces to that edition and to the revised edition published two months later, they told the reader how Ch'eng had over the years acquired the missing manuscripts and how he had asked Kao to help edit them and make them into these 40 chapters. If, in the fashion of modern editors, they had provided detailed information as to when and from whom each separate lot of manuscripts had been purchased, which manuscripts were in the author's handwriting and which were not, and precisely how much editing had been undertaken, all the subsequent controversies concerning the reliability of the last 40 chapters would have been unnecessary. But since the information they provide is brief and cryptic and since until recently most other kinds of evidence seemed to indicate that Ts'ao Hsüeh-ch'in had completed only the first 80 chapters, it has been the modern fashion to credit Kao Ê with the authorship of the last third of the novel as we now have it.[9] According to this view, Kao wrote a continuation mainly by developing clues contained in the 80 chapters. He had of course incorporated the recovered manuscripts into his narrative, but most scholars tended to minimize the number of such manuscripts actually owned by Ch'eng.

But thanks to the newly discovered source materials, today we know that Ch'eng and Kao were not lying when they maintained that the novel in its complete form should have 120 chapters. While the Chih-yen Chai-annotated manuscripts under the title of *Shih-t'ou chi* were more accessible, manuscripts of the 120-chapter version entitled *Hung-lou meng* were also extant even before Ch'eng and Kao had published their edition. We have found several pre-1791 references to that effect, though it was only in 1959 that one such manuscript was discovered. It has now been reprinted in a sumptuous collotype edition of 12 volumes under the title of *Ch'ien-lung ch'ao-pen pai-nien-hui Hung-lou-meng kao* (A draft copy of the 120-chapter *Dream of the Red Chamber* transcribed in the Ch'ien-lung period).[10] The superimposed title page is actually dated 1855, and the manuscript in its original form did not contain chapters 41–50, which have been copied in by a later owner to make the novel complete. On one of its leaves there is an inscription most probably in the handwriting of Kao Ê, indicating that he had seen it. But, even if this inscription is spurious, the manuscript has been of inestimable value in providing a link between the Chih-yen Chai-annotated, 80-chapter versions and the Ch'eng-Kao editions. Whereas the text of the first 80 chapters (except for the superadded 10 chapters) as originally transcribed in the manuscript is mainly identical with the Chih-yen Chai text, deletions and alterations have been inserted so that the resultant text is on the whole identical with the Ch'eng-Kao edition, though puzzlingly the 1792 version rather than the 1791 version. Similarly, the last 40 chapters as finally revised are almost identical with those in the Ch'eng-Kao edition, though there are no other manuscripts with which to compare the version as originally set down in the manuscript. Moreover, while several hands took part in the transcription of the original manuscript, it was the same hand that made all the revisions in these 110 chapters. Revision in some chapters is heavy, in some light, but many chapters are barely touched by revision. On the basis of these findings, Fan Ning maintains in his postface to the collotype edition that the manuscript was one of the copies made by Ch'eng and Kao in preparation for their edition. It was not the final clean copy since it is only 99 percent identical with the standard edition of 1792.

It is unlikely that Fan Ning's hypothesis will win scholarly concurrence. Yü P'ing-po, whose early book *Hung-lou meng pien* (retitled *Hung-lou meng yen-chiu* [Studies in *Dream of the Red Chamber*] in its revised edition of 1952) had been most influential in urging public acceptance of Kao Ê as a forger, has expressed grave doubts in a recent article as to whether this manuscript copy was indeed prepared under the direction of Ch'eng and Kao.[11] However, in his detailed textual examination of this copy, he has confined himself to the first 80 chapters and refrained from expressing any view about the last 40. He favors the conclusion that the marginal revisions in the manuscript were probably copied from the 1792 edition, but he is equivocal about whether, in its unrevised form, the manuscript came into being before or after Ch'eng and Kao had started work on their edition. One would think that the primary problem raised by this manuscript is to account for the origin of the last 40 chapters in their unrevised state. If they were not the handiwork of Ch'eng and Kao, who could have composed them? Ts'ao Hsüeh-ch'in himself, or some unidentified editor?

The existence of this manuscript has confirmed Yü P'ing-po in his view, however, that Kao Ê did not fabricate the last 40 chapters, a view which he had expressed more tentatively in his preface to

Hung-lou-meng pa-shih-hui chiao-pen (The variorum edition of the eighty-chapter *Hung-lou Meng*, 1958).[12] In his new article he reiterates this view, which amounts to a total repudiation of his earlier position:

We may indeed go further and say that, far from being the independent creation of Ch'eng and Kao, the 1791 and 1792 versions are merely the product of the editorial labor they had expended on various existing versions. This hypothesis, of course, merely confirms their prefatory statements. Unfortunately, people in the past had no faith in these statements and, citing Chang Wen-t'ao's poem as authority,[13] insisted on assigning the authorship of the last 40 chapters to Kao Ê while giving no credit whatever to Ch'eng Wei-yuan. Today, all this looks very absurd. Of course, we have been long aware that in their 1791 and 1792 editions Ch'eng and Kao seemed at times not to know what was going on even in the last 40 chapters: it would be very odd indeed if an author could not follow the threads of the plot in his own composition.[14]

If the discovery of the 120-chapter manuscript had brought about no other result than the final rejection of the theory of Kao Ê's forgery, it would have accomplished a great deal: for over 40 years the study of *Dream of the Red Chamber* has been vitiated by this unchallenged supposition. For scholars on the mainland, however, to absolve Kao Ê of his crime has only meant the renewal of a search for the author of the last 40 chapters. This search has been dictated largely by ideological reasons. Ts'ao Hsüeh-ch'in has long been hailed by the Communist critics as an anti-feudalist writer of revolutionary faith,[15] and this myth makes sense only if his authorship is confined to the first 80 chapters when the ultimate fate of his main characters cannot yet be ascertained with any degree of confidence. Even during the May Fourth period many scholars, and Yü P'ing-po prominently among them, could not stomach the last third of the novel because of its supposed compromises with feudal morality and its pronounced note of Taoist-Buddhist escapism; the Communists have continued to denounce it for the same reasons. Now that Kao Ê can no longer serve as a scapegoat, still it seems far better to preserve Ts'ao's fair name as the author of a hypothetical masterpiece than to identify it with a work that proves incompatible with Communist ideology.

More seriously, scholars hesitate to assign the last third of the novel to Ts'ao because its faulty text fails to meet the expectations of the preceding narrative on several points of plot development and character interpretation. To blunt the force of this argument, however, one can say that the first 80 chapters are by no means a coherent narrative of seamless unity.[16] If these early chapters are full of minor discrepancies and inconsistencies, then it should be hardly too surprising that the later chapters should further disagree with them on minor points. While the editors Ch'eng and Kao had introduced many errors into the first two thirds of the novel, a comparison of their text with the Chih-yen Chai texts would indicate that far more were inadvertently introduced by the author. From Chih-yen Chai's commentary we gather the impression that Ts'ao was addicted to incessant revision. There is every reason to believe that he could have had ample time to complete his novel since, according to a note in the so-called Keng-ch'en (1760) manuscript, the commentator had gone over chapter 75 by June, 1756. It would have been highly unlikely that Ts'ao could not have finished the work in the seven years remaining to him.[17] But, according to Chih-yen Chai, Ts'ao was tinkering with his novel till the very end so that chapter 22 was left in an unfinished state.[18] The first 22 chapters actually abound in minor inconsistencies, many of these assuredly the result of piecemeal revision.

It is now generally agreed that the hero of the novel, Chia Pao-yü, represents a composite portrait of the author and the commentator.[19] Judging from his more personal comments, Chih-yen Chai must have witnessed or taken part in many scenes in the life of the Ts'ao family which are recorded in fictional form. According to two recent theories which have attracted much notice, the commentator was either an uncle of the author's, born in 1697 or earlier, or a female cousin who appears in Dream as the vivacious heroine Shih Hsiang-yün.[20] Chao Kang, the most astute of the younger specialists in the novel, however, has exploded both theories with finality, and come up with a new candidate who should in time win universal scholarly acceptance as the real Chih-yen Chai. He was Ts'ao T'ien-yu, Ts'ao Yin's grandson and a slightly older cousin of Ts'ao Hsüeh-ch'in. The two were brought up together in Nanking and could have shared many kinds of intimate experience referred to in the commentary. Moreover, this cousin owned a red inkslab of rare quality, which would explain his pen name, Red Inkslab Studio.[21]

Because he provides us with unique information about the author and the background of his novel, Chih-yen Chai has received almost as much attention from modern scholars as Ts'ao Hsüeh-ch'in himself. It used to be the critical fashion to accuse Kao Ê of forgery whenever his supposed "supplement" contradicts or excludes episodes that, according to the commentator, should have been included in the last part of the novel. But, apart from his role as a provider of information, Chih-yen Chai could be considered a nuisance to the author. If Ts'ao Hsüeh-ch'in continually revised his work to satisfy his artistic conscience, to some extent he was doing so to satisfy his commentator. In one place the latter states that he had ordered the author to cut out an important episode so as to preserve the fair name of a mutual relative known in the novel as Ch'in K'o-ch'ing.[22] Ts'ao accordingly deleted that episode without, however, undertaking an over-all revision of the context. If Ts'ao indeed left his novel in an unfinished state, Chih-yen Chai must be held partly responsible.

Both author and commentator are engaged in an act of reliving the past. But a basic distinction must be maintained between one who has the courage and passion to commit his past to writing and one who rather sentimentally comments on the result. Though Chih-yen Chai shows occasional astuteness as a literary critic, he habitually harks back to people and events that have inspired certain episodes in the novel and seems to get a deep vicarious thrill in doing so. But, if at heart Chih-yen Chai wants a faithful record of past events rather than a novel, Ts'ao Hsüeh-ch'in must have been under the compulsion to render his own vision of the world. For any great novelist, this impulse toward fidelity to his vision claims priority over, and is not necessarily identical with, the confessional impulse. He transmutes as much personal experience as serves his purpose: he is under no obligation to recount the factual truth about himself and his family. If there had been no Chih-yen Chai, Ts'ao Hsüeh-ch'in would have been a lonelier person but he would not have been as often tempted to tamper with his vision.

Chih-yen Chai notwithstanding, *Dream of the Red Chamber* remains in all essentials a most unified work of imagination. In the last 40 chapters, all the major female characters meet with the fate foretold for them.[23] If minor discrepancies exist in a novel of such a vast and complex design, it is as often due to the author's oversight as to the fact that departures from the preconceived plot were introduced in the heat of actual composition. When the last third of the novel appears to have ignored some of the hints given in the commentary, it could well be that the author had finally made changes in the novel without consulting his commentator. But since Chih-yen Chai presumably had seen all the manuscripts, there must have been an earlier draft of the novel in which both Chia Pao-yü and the Chia clan ended in extreme destitution following the imperial confiscation of the clan's property. Many scholars are therefore persuaded that, since the novel in its present form does not end on a note of unrelieved misery, some unknown hand may have indeed revised it before it was allowed to circulate.

Chao Kang finds it significant that, though Ts'ao had completed more than 80 chapters seven or eight years before his death, only the first 80 chapters were commented on and circulated, while the last part of the novel seems to have been deliberately withheld from circulation. Since the stark account of the Chia family's mal-treatment could have offended the government, this restriction may well have been voluntarily imposed to protect the author and his family from the danger of literary inquisition, which was at times severely enforced during the reign of Ch'ien-lung. When, some years after the death of the author, the Ch'ien-lung Emperor accidentally got hold of a manuscript of the novel in a Manchu family and showed interest in it, some one who had been very close to the author felt duty-bound to provide a politically harmless version so as to free the novel from any suspicion of being a subversive book. If there had indeed been any large-scale revision undertaken after the author's death, it could have happened in the manner suggested by Chao Kang.[24] In support of this hypothesis, we find an explicit disclaimer of political interest in the preface to the Chia-hsü manuscript of the novel: "This book does not presume to concern itself with the government and the court. Whenever government affairs have to be mentioned, they are presented obliquely, with minimal emphasis, because the pen that could only delineate women could not hope to venture rashly into the realm of government."[25]

In presenting the basic facts and the more sensible hypotheses about the authorship and texts of the novel, I have made no attempt to review all the controversies and conjectures of modern scholarship that would offer little help to the general reader. For all its invaluable findings, this scholarship has been notable for its idolatry of Ts'ao Hsüeh-ch'in. Apparently Ts'ao is worthy of our highest regard because his novel is the most considerable work of imagination in Chinese literature. For generations the novel in its 120-chapter form has won the highest praise from scholars who would ordinarily pay little serious attention to vernacular fiction. (Even today the most popular edition remains the Ch'eng-Kao edition of 1792, though as far as the first 80 chapters are concerned scholars now generally prefer the Chih-yen Chai texts. The best critical edition is the aforementioned four-volume Variorum Edition, which also includes the last 40 chapters.) Since we cannot begin to form an idea of the greatness of the novel without these 40 chapters, to attack them and then to praise the author solely on the strength of the first 80 chapters seems to me an act of critical dishonesty. If Ts'ao indeed did not live to complete his novel or if we are unhappy about the last third of the work even though it was substantially his, then our estimate of his genius and accomplishment should be revised accordingly. But any fair-minded reader who reads the novel without preconceptions about its authorship will find no reason to disparage the last 40 chapters, for they give the most impressive proof of the work's tragic and philosophic depth, not plumbed by any other Chinese novel.

Since *Dream of the Red Chamber* is a very complex novel, our critical discussion may properly begin by introducing its more important characters and reviewing the highlights of its plot. The novel is about the aristocratic Chia clan which, like the Ts'ao family, has enjoyed imperial favor for generations. Its two main branches dwell in adjoining compounds in the capital, styled Ningkuofu and Jungkuofu. The nominal head of the Ningkuofu is a selfish student of Taoist alchemy who eventually dies its victim;[26] his son Chia Chen and grandson Chia Yung are both sensualists. A dowager simply called the Matriarch in Chi-chen Wang's English version presides over the Jungkuofu. She has two sons, Chia She and Chia Cheng. Chia Lien, Chia She's pleasure-seeking son, is married to an extremely capable woman, Phoenix (Wang Hsi-feng). Despite her early triumphs in managing the household finances and driving her love rivals to suicide, this handsome and vivacious lady eventually languishes in ill health and dies. Her nefarious dealings are in large part responsible for the raiding of the Chia compounds by imperial guards and the confiscation of their property.

The Matriarch's other son, Chia Cheng, is the only conscientious Confucian member of the family in active government service. A lonely man of narrow vision but undeniable rectitude, he has lost a promising son before the novel opens.[27] Naturally, he expects his younger son by his legitimate wife, Madame Wang, to study hard and prepare for the examinations. But Pao-yü, the hero of the novel, early spoiled by his grandmother, mother, and other female relatives, detests conventional learning and prefers the company of his girl cousins and the maidservants. Since late childhood, he has had as playmate a cousin of delicate beauty beloved by the Matriarch, Black Jade (Lin Tai-yü). Some years later, another beautiful cousin, Precious Clasp (Hsüeh Pao-ch'ai), also moves into the Jungkuofu. In spite of Pao-yü's repeated assurances of his love, Black Jade regards

Precious Clasp as her rival and feels very insecure. As she progressively ruins her health by wallowing in self-pity, Precious Clasp replaces her as the preferred candidate for Pao-yü's wife. But the marriage when it does take place brings no joy to Precious Clasp since by that time Pao-yü has turned into an idiot. Broken-hearted and full of unforgiveness, Black Jade dies on their wedding night.

Pao-yü eventually recovers and obtains the degree of *chü-jen*. But instead of returning home after taking the examination, he renounces the world and becomes a monk. The desolate Precious Clasp takes comfort in her pregnancy. A faithful maid, Pervading Fragrance (Hsi-jen), also heart-broken, is eventually happily married to an actor friend of Pao-yü's. Another maid, Bright Cloud (Ch'ing-wen), to whom Pao-yü was also much attached, had died of calumny and sickness long before his marriage.

The inevitable emphasis placed on the triangular love story in the preceding summary may have given the misleading impression that *Dream of the Red Chamber* is but a conventional romance with a sad or tragic ending. Actually, *Dream* is to be distinguished from all other classic Chinese novels for its fascination with character: even characters of minor consequence are presented as real individuals and not as stereotypes. Though Pao-yü and his two girl cousins are physically attractive and enormously talented, they are far from being the heroes and heroines of the conventional romantic novels that had become very popular by the early Ch'ing period. With all their good looks and talent, the latter lovers possess little individuality and they usually achieve marital happiness at the end. In a sense, *Dream* may be seen as a work written in conscious reaction to these novels. In chapter 54, when some female storytellers try to entertain the Matriarch with a new story, she dismisses the idea with a laugh:

These stories are all alike; invariably they tell about a virtuous beauty and a talented scholar in an insipid manner. They malign the daughters of good families and still have the impudence to call them "virtuous beauties." There is no trace of virtue about them. The story will first of all tell something about a distinguished family of the gentry. The father is either the president of a board or the prime minister. He loves his daughter like a jewel. And this daughter invariably knows all about literature and etiquette, a veritable paragon of virtue and beauty. But once she sees a handsome youth, be he a relative or a friend, she will be obsessed with her future destiny, oblivious alike of parents and books.[28]

The ethical bias against romantic young ladies may be the Matriarch's own, but the author has voiced through her mouth his distaste for the stereotyped love romances.

Though my synopsis suggests no resemblance, *Dream of the Red Chamber* is far more indebted to *Chin P'ing Mei,* the only previous novel devoted to tracing the fortunes of a discordant large family. Ts'ao Hsüeh-ch'in must have known the work well, since on four occasions his commentator refers the reader to *Chin P'ing Mei* for specific comparison.[29] What the author has learned from the latter is, essentially, the art of diurnal realism, the technique of advancing the novel with seemingly inconsequential accounts of day-to-day events and of lingering over days of family significance, such as birthdays and festival days, when something important is usually going on. But whereas *Chin P'ing Mei* is coarse and dull, *Dream* is subtle and lively. In the former, relatives or friends gathered for a party often have nothing better to do than to listen to popular songs or recitals of Buddhist stories, or else they are engaged in banter and horseplay. In the latter, at least the younger set exhibits a high degree of culture. Whenever they have a party, they converse intelligently with poetic wit and genuine humor. This difference does not serve merely to register the social disparity of the two households; it also shows that Ts'ao Hsüeh-ch'in is far more alive to the perennial intellectual and aesthetic concerns of the Chinese tradition than is the author of *Chin P'ing Mei.*

Ts'ao Hsüeh-ch'in, therefore, is not merely content to tell a story of autobiographical significance; he has the further compulsion to test that story against all the existing ideals of Chinese culture. Especially in regard to sexual and romantic love a variety of contradictory attitudes is possible. Confucian teaching values the familial aspects of married love but deplores sexual indulgence and romantic obsession since it regards as a man's primary duty the use of his talents in the service of his country and family. Buddhist and Taoist philosophy emphasizes the need to liberate oneself from all attachments, including sexual love. (The novelist has not finely distinguished Buddhism from Taoism but regards the mystical Buddhism of the Zen school and the original Taoist teaching of Lao Tzu and Chuang Tzu as essentially one in their insistence on individual detachment from craving. Like Wu Ching-tzu, he has little use for popular Buddhism and Taoism.) In the belletristic tradition, however, love between man and woman has been given sympathetic attention ever since *The Book of Poetry,* and in popular fiction and drama even extreme forms of sensual and romantic abandon have been accorded covert sympathy.[30] In *Dream,* therefore, if the hero's ultimate decision to turn monk reinforces the Buddhist-Taoist teaching of individual liberation, the romantic and Confucian ideals are by no means unemphasized. The author's syncretic hospitality to diverse strands of Chinese thought may have created some ambiguity and confusion in his novel, but it is also a necessary condition for its rich complexity and greatness.

There is no doubt that Ts'ao Hsüeh-ch'in consciously places his hero in the romantic tradition of unconventional individualism. In chapter 2, two friends, Leng Tzu-hsing and Chia Yü-ts'un, are discussing the Chia family, thereby introducing to the reader its more important members before their actual appearance. Upon being informed of the personality of Pao-yü, Chia Yü-ts'un immediately places him among those unusual men and women in Chinese history imbued with a peculiar vitality compounded of both good and evil:

Whether men or women, they can become neither sagelike in virtue and wisdom nor utterly wicked and evil. Their uncommon intelligence and vitality place them above ten thousands of men, but their eccentric, heretical unconventionality places them below these ten thousands. If born to high rank and wealth, they become romantics obsessed with love, and if born to bookish families of modest means, they become hermits and proud scholars. Even if born to poverty and lowliness, they would rather achieve distinction as actors and courtesans than submit to the fate of being menials and servants, to be ordered about by the vulgar.[31]

Chia then lists as examples such famous names in Chinese history and legend as the recluse Hsü Yu, the poets T'ao Ch'ien, Juan Chi, and Liu Yung, the emperors T'ang Hsüan-tsung and Sung Hui-tsung, the artists Ni Yün-lin and T'ang Yin, the beauties Cho Wen-chün, Hung-fu, and Hsüeh T'ao. In their detestation of vulgarity and officialdom, several of these could serve as models for the heroes of *The Scholars* but, in the aggregate, they suggest a literary type far more romantic in temper than the recluse-ideal. After Pao-yü has left the world, his Confucian father independently arrives at the' same estimate of his son.[32]

His vast sympathy for suffering young lovers, especially, places the author with such outstanding exponents of the romantic tradition as Wang Shih-fu and T'ang Hsien-tsu (1550–1616). In a few scenes he quotes famous lines from their respective masterpieces, *The Romance of the Western Chamber* and *The Peony Pavilion,* and these lines reverberate through the novel with the aching promise of romantic fulfillment.[33] Neither Pao-yü nor his cousins, it is true, dare imitate the bolder lovers of these plays, and Precious Clasp, docile to Confucian morality, consciously disapproves of them. But she herself has been exposed to the plays since childhood, and her outward compliance with conventional morality only underscores the more poignantly her deliberate suppression of her poetic precocity and romantic longings. Insofar as both plays provide a happy ending for the lovers, Ts'ao Hsüeh-ch'in, by placing his hero and heroines of comparable social status and romantic articulateness in a tragic impasse, may be said to have aimed at a truth at once more socially complex and philosophically meaningful than his predecessors. In *The Peony Pavilion,* love defies death itself and dreams anticipate the lovers' union. In the novel the lovers also dream a great deal, but their dreams often turn out to be nightmares.

To accommodate his complex response to the Chinese tradition, Ts'ao Hsüeh-ch'in uses a great deal of allegory and symbolism. Like

Monkey, Pao-yü is placed in a creation myth in the very first chapter. When the goddess Nü-kua is repairing the Dome of Heaven, she rejects as unfit for use a huge rock of considerable intelligence, which consequently bemoans its fate and develops a longing for the pleasures of the mundane world. It can now turn itself into the size of a stone and, with the help of a Buddhist monk and a Taoist priest, it is eventually born into the Chia family as our hero.[34] Before his birth, however, the Stone has stayed in the court of the Goddess of Disillusionment and shown great kindness to a celestial plant by daily sprinkling it with dew. The plant blossoms into a fairy who vows to repay his love with tears if she may join him on earth. She, then, is Black Jade. Throughout the novel, the mangy Buddhist monk and the lame Taoist priest make periodic appearances to mock or enlighten mundane creatures in their moments of spiritual crisis. Especially, they have much to do with the piece of jade Pao-yü is born with, a miniature stone that symbolizes his spiritual essence.

In chapter 5 the author resumes his allegory by placing the hero in the most celebrated dream sequence in the novel. While on a visit to the Ningkuofu, Pao-yü, then barely a teenager, insists on taking a nap in the bedroom of Ch'in K'o-ch'ing, the young wife of Chia Yung, and presently dreams of a celestial maiden also named K'o-ch'ing. As has already been mentioned, Ch'in is a victim of hasty revision so that, though she dies of a prolonged illness, there are telltale signs that in an earlier version she hangs herself after being exposed in an adulterous affair with her father-in-law, Chia Chen. But she remains otherwise a virtuous girl most concerned with the welfare of the Chia house: even as a ghost, she frequently appears in dreams to warn her best friend Phoenix of its impending doom. The author, therefore, appears to have modeled her after Vase, likewise the victim of a lingering illness, whose spirit counsels Hsi-men Ch'ing in dreams. In the present allegorical context, however, Ch'in K'o-ch'ing is the incarnation of all beauty. Her dream counterpart is also known by the name Chien-mei (Combined Beauty), and upon seeing her, Pao-yü is instantly struck by the fact that she unites in her person the charms and graces of both Black Jade and Precious Clasp. (As an actual presence in the novel, Ch'in K'o-ch'ing does suggest both. Like the former, she is an orphan of delicate constitution and fragile beauty; like the latter, she is a dutiful and kind person beloved by young and old.) The author seems to be saying that the dream image of Ch'in should ideally serve to disillusion Pao-yü about love before he gets too much involved in the fate of the major heroines.

To make Ch'in's bedchamber worthy of the occasion, the novelist furnishes it with objects once in the possession of great beauties and notorious wantons of the past, such as Hsi Shih, Empress Wu, and Yang Kuei-fei. In this suggestive setting, Pao-yü soon falls asleep and enters the Great Void Illusion Land presided over by the Goddess of Disillusionment. While there, he is first shown the fate of some fifteen young ladies and maidservants of the Chia house in verses and emblems whose import he cannot yet guess. Then, at the behest of his worried ancestors, the goddess assumes the role of a Confucian spokesman and berates him for being the most lustful of all men. The goddess, who does allow a distinction between lust (*yin*) and love (*ch'ing*), is of course aware of Pao-yü's sexual innocence, but to her his fate appears the more perilous precisely because of his potential commitment to the kind of crazy love (*ch'ih ch'ing*) that afflicts the unconventional heroes of the romantic tradition. After the lecture she introduces him to her sister K'o-ch'ing for sexual initiation so that "after you have seen for yourself that the pleasures of fairyland are but thus and so, you may perhaps realize their vanity and turn your mind to the teachings of Confucius and Mencius and devote your efforts to the welfare of mankind." [35]

Pao-yü and K'o-ch'ing have a blissful union. But soon he is chased by demons and wild beasts to the brink of an impassable river. Frightened, Pao-yü screams, "K'o-ch'ing, save me!" and wakes up. Ch'in K'o-ch'ing, who is outside her bedchamber, wonders how anyone could know of her childhood name.

The denouement of the dream suggests another alternative not given explicit emphasis by the goddess, which becomes more important as the novel progresses. It is to view love and, for that matter, any human attachment as a source of delusion incompatible with the true peace of mind which comes with one's renunciation of the world. The river is named the Ford of Error, a Buddhist term, and the beasts and demons are of course the passions driving one into delusion. In the novel, the chief spokesman for Confucian duty is Chia Cheng, to whom Pao-yü pays little heed but, as he becomes increasingly involved in the world of pain through his love and sympathy for the many unfortunates around him, he is steadily drawn to the Buddhist-Taoist ideal of renunciation so that for him the ultimate tragic conflict lies in a tug of war between the opposing claims of compassion and detachment.

Ts'ao Hsüeh-ch'in, however, is too good a psychologist to be a thoroughgoing allegorist. The didactic dream is immediately followed by a scene of realism which places the allegory in an ironic perspective. The same evening the supposedly forewarned hero coaxes Pervading Fragrance to have sexual relations with him: the blissful memory of his union with K'o-ch'ing has completely superseded his fear of the demons and beasts. A few chapters later, the author returns to the allegorical mode in describing a case of infatuation, but the implied irony is again the incorrigibility of man once he is exposed to the delights of sex. Chia Jui, a poor tutor's son, has fallen hopelessly in love with Phoenix. He has already become critically ill after being repeatedly punished by the disdainful lady for his impudence in aspiring to her love. Now the mysterious lame Taoist priest offers the dying boy a magic mirror to effect his cure. One side of the mirror shows a skeleton, the consequence of lust; the other side, however, shows a compliant Phoenix beckoning him to make love to her. Naturally Chia Jui dies after repeatedly walking into the enticing side of the mirror.[36]

Many young lovers die in the course of the novel. But their death expresses not so much the author's moral condemnation as his sense of regret that youthful passion is so often a symptom of frail health and extreme moral delicacy. Even Chia Jui is far more a pathetic victim of a double hoax than a dire warning to all lovelorn youth.

The reader who prefers the sympathy of realism to the obvious didacticism of allegory must be forced to conclude that, on the evidence of the realistic narrative alone, it is not so much love that is depicted in hideous colors as is whatever obstructs the course of love: greed, hate, sensuality and, as we may agree with the Communist critics, the callous brutality of the social system. In that narrative, of course, "love" and "lust" are kept quite distinct. The lustful person, be he Chia Chen, Chia Lien, or Precious Clasp's brother, Hsüeh P'an, seeks only the satisfaction of his lust, and stays physically fit in spite of his indulgence. More often than not his sensuality is symptomatic of his being a prey to other evil passions. Unswayed by shame or regard for others, he is apparently happy because he is incapable of moral introspection. The sensitive person whose love is not merely a matter of lust, on the other hand, invariably suffers a great deal. Not only is he a helpless victim of the machinations of the gross characters but, unlike the hardened sensualist, he is physically and morally delicate so that often love exhausts his vitality (as with Ch'in K'o-ch'ing's younger brother, Ch'in Chung) and shame decrees his suicide (as with the maid Chess and the proud daughter of a much abused family, Yu San-chieh).[37] In reading the minor love stories, one feels not so much that the author fails to respect true love as that he regards true love as something inherently fragile, easily shattered under the impact of the slings of a far from outrageous fortune. Yu San-chieh, who shows sustained moral courage in defying the voluptuaries around her, characteristically cannot bear for a minute the understandable mistrust of a person who has only heard of her reputation and knows nothing of the selfless love she is ready to offer him. She impulsively kills herself and, completely disillusioned, Liu Hsiang-lien forsakes the world to wander off with the lame Taoist priest. Logically, Liu cannot have been disillusioned with love since he has barely begun to feel its illusory warmth: his action is more indicative of a profound disgust with the world which has systematically destroyed the possibilities of love.

The schematic presentation of love and lust in the novel, therefore, runs to this formula: those sunk in the mire of gross passions (with the exception of Chia Yü-ts'un, the vulgar and unscrupulous official whose importance in the allegorical scheme entitles him to a final encounter with Taoist wisdom)[38] make no attempt to extricate themselves, while those whose love, given the chance to blossom, could have seriously challenged the ideal of renunciation and represented another kind of fulfillment (and the author's sympathy fully entitles us to this expectation) are systematically destroyed so as to leave room for the Buddhist-Taoist moral. In spite of their comparable scope and ostensible similarity in theme, *Dream* is therefore a different kind of novel from *The Tale of Genji* and *Remembrance of Things Past*. In the latter, love is allowed to run its full course, from initial fascination to eventual satiety or disgust: Genji, Swann, and Marcel love hard and long only to find in the end the disconsolate knowledge of the vanity of passion. The lovers in *Dream* are denied that mature vision: they either remain at the adolescent stage of agonized longing or plunge into the sexual act without having lingered over a period of delicious assurance of returned love. The tragic knowledge which the hero eventually reaches has almost nothing to do with physical passion.

Contrary to popular belief, Pao-yü is not a great lover, nor does he function principally as a lover in the novel. Though he is early forewarned by the Goddess of Disillusionment of the peril of sex, his subsequent behavior, however unorthodox, is remarkably free of the taint of concupiscence. It is true that, since his early teens, he has enjoyed sexual intimacy with Pervading Fragrance, but this fact is referred to explicitly only once and rarely emphasized again. The author's reticence only underscores the point that for the hero sex as such is not the important consideration: his enjoyment of her body alters not a whit his high regard for her as a person and as a friend. In Shakespeare's famous sonnet, "The expense of spirit in a waste of shame," love is primarily seen in its possessive and destructive aspect, and it is Pao-yü's total freedom from this murderous rage that makes him so good a friend to all the girls around him. Whereas the sensualists use their mistresses solely for their own pleasure, Pao-yü offers to all the girls around him the same kind of disinterested friendship and solicitude. When the news of Ch'in K'o-ch'ing's death reaches him, he is so overwhelmed with grief that he spits blood. For cynical readers this means the existence of a special relationship between the two, but Pao-yü reacts with characteristic intensity of grief to the untimely death of every lovely girl in the book—the maid Golden Bracelet, Yu San-chieh, and Bright Cloud.[39] Knowing the ways of men in the Chia compounds, Pao-yü has early made the famous remark that women are made of water and men of mud.[40] Men are muddy with passion, instinct with coarse desire, whereas women, at least in their enchanting youth, look so deceptively ethereal and guileless. But, this epigram notwithstanding, nearly all older women and most married women appear to him as gross in their selfish cunning as the average sensual men. When facing a girl, therefore, Pao-yü is filled with admiration and compassion—admiration for her embodiment of celestial beauty and understanding, and compassion for the fact that all too soon her celestial essence will be obscured in her forced conformity to a marital state and her inevitable enjoyment, if she survives, of the mean pleasures of greed, envy, and malice. Lust is rarely in his thoughts. His secret wish is not unlike that of a much-admired adolescent hero in recent American fiction: to be a catcher in the rye and rescue all lovely maidens from the brink of custom and sensuality (the comparison is made pointedly in view of Holden Caulfield's disgust with all forms of cant and falsity, his youth and extreme sensitivity, and his capacity for compassion).

Pao-yü enjoys the trust and friendship of all the girls around him, therefore, not because they look upon him as a lover but because, almost alone among their menfolk, he sympathizes with their condition and shares their thoughts. With all his foolish effeminacy, his lack of worldly ambition, and his fitful black moods, they know that he will never be coarse and cruel. They can even laugh at him because, ultimately, he is distinguished for his "stupidity" and "idiocy," that is, his capacity for identifying himself with other persons and things to the point of appearing abstracted from his usual self. Many of the girls are heroic and noble-minded, but they lack the hero's supreme gift for self-transcendence.

To borrow Jane Austen's terms, the girl characters in the novel are distinguished for either their sense or their sensibility. Of the four heroines closest to Pao-yü, Precious Clasp and Pervading Fragrance are the sensible ones while their respective counterparts, Black Jade and Bright Cloud, are sensitive, neurotic, and impractical. They also die young while their rivals live on to enjoy their man, and, since readers naturally sympathize with losers, traditional Chinese criticism has invariably contrasted the nobility of Black Jade and Bright Cloud with the supposed sly, calculating shrewdness of Precious Clasp and Pervading Fragrance.[41] Black Jade, especially, is showered with sympathy and praise. Even among Communist critics, who see the novel primarily as a revolutionary protest against the evils of feudalism, one is rather surprised to find the persistence of the traditional attitude of disapproval or hatred toward Precious Clasp and Pervading Fragrance.[42] They are now called the lackeys of feudalism, though their real crime remains that of robbing Black Jade of her life and due marital happiness.

Such partisan criticism reflects the inveterate Chinese habit of regarding *Dream of the Red Chamber* as primarily a love story, and one, moreover, that could have ended happily. Under this sentimental reading, it seems such a pity that Pao-yü and Black Jade, who are so ideally suited to each other, should have loved in vain. Yet, if one examines the novel carefully, long before Black Jade is in danger of being rejected by her elders, she seethes with discontent. Even in their carefree days, her every meeting with Pao-yü ends in a misunderstanding or quarrel, and these frequent quarrels are not, as has been suggested, the high comedy of Beatrice and Benedick, Millamant and Mirabell [43]—they are, for her, fraught with bitter and lacerated feelings. This is so because the two are diametrically opposed in temperament despite the similarity of their tastes. Pao-yü is a person of active sympathy capable of ultimate self-transcendence; Black Jade is a self-centered neurotic who courts self-destruction.

Her attraction for Pao-yü lies not merely in her fragile beauty and poetic sensibility but in her very contrariness—a jealous self-obsession so unlike his expansive gaiety that his love for her is always tinged with infinite sadness. Even if they marry, they cannot be happy in the romantic sense of the term: if Pao-yü continues to love her, it will be largely out of pity—the kind of pity that Prince Myshkin showers upon Nastasya in *The Idiot*.

There can be no doubt that Black Jade exemplifies a type of beauty to which the author is personally drawn. Besides her, there are at least four girls of comparable features and sensibility: Ch'in K'och'ing, Hsiang-ling, Bright Cloud, and the fastidious nun Miao-yü. These five are either orphans or early torn from their parents: two or three are of the same age and actually have the same birthday. Each, of course, is sharply individualized and reaches her distinctive fate. Black Jade can be profitably compared with every one of her sister-beauties but, with reference to her neurotic self-obsession, Hsiang-ling offers the most pointed contrast.

In the first chapter allegorical significance is lavished on Hsiang-ling, then known as Ying-lien, though she is soon relegated to the position of a minor heroine. She is abducted by ruffians when a mere child and lives thereafter a life of unmitigated suffering, first as Hsüeh P'an's slave girl and then as his concubine. She is harshly treated by his wife, Cassia, and eventually dies in childbirth. By contrast, Black Jade's circumstances are far better. Her father is still alive at the time she moves to the Jungkuofu, and, though she has lost her mother, her relatives there surround her with love. Yet she feels insecure even under this affluence of love while the maltreated Hsiang-ling appears a gay and carefree person whenever she is privileged to visit Black Jade and her cousins. A barely literate person, she once studies poetry under Black Jade and shows remarkable progress because she is capable of losing herself in her task. She borders on ecstasy when contemplating some famous lines of T'ang poetry or composing her own verse. Black Jade is the acknowledged poetic genius among the girl cousins, and yet everything she writes is stamped with self-pity. In her best-known poem, "Burying Flowers," she sees herself as the fallen blossoms. With the sentimentality of a narcissist who cannot see nature beyond herself, she sings, "Today people laugh at my craziness because I am burying the flowers, but when the time comes, I wonder who would bury me." [44]

Black Jade is seized with anxiety right upon the arrival of Precious Clasp in the Chia house: the latter wears a golden locket inscribed with characters that match those on Pao-yü's jade piece. Moreover, its origin is almost equally mysterious: it was sent her by the mangy Buddhist during her infancy. The locket and the jade augur a happy union and, though Black Jade knows that Pao-yü prefers her to all her girl cousins, she feels the want of a tangible proof symbolizing her future union with him. On one hand, therefore, she becomes very aggressive toward her rival, sparing no occasion to make sarcastic references to her lucky ownership of the locket, and, on the other, very demanding toward Pao-yü, challenging him under every pretext to avow the kind of love for her that would shatter the symbolic bond of locket and jade. A teenager with a boy's high spirits, Pao-yü is forced into adulthood by her constant craving for reassurance. Yet no verbal protestation can provide the kind of security Black Jade wants and, a most proper girl, she shrinks from the more physical kind of proof and upbraids Pao-yü for even the most innocuous display of affection. So in the end all she can claim as her own are two old handkerchiefs which he once sent her and upon which she has written three poems. Before her death, she burns these handkerchiefs—proofs that have been shown to be completely useless. [45]

Yet, with all her desperate anxiety, Black Jade maintains a fierce pride in her studied indifference to her fate. Chinese girls of good families, of course, are not supposed to evince any interest in their marital future, but most of them would confide in their personal maids, and the heroines of *The Romance of the Western Chamber* and *The Peony Pavilion* take unconventionally bold steps to secure their men. But to Black Jade the very word "marriage" is taboo, and she will not discuss her future even with her maid and best friend, Purple Cuckoo, who frequently pleads with her to take care of her health and take active steps toward fulfilling her life's desire. Black Jade knows quite well that she does not have a powerful advocate actively looking after her interests, but she would rather suffer alone than ingratiate herself with her elders. If she is at all a tragic character, then her tragedy lies in her stubborn impracticality, in the perverse contradiction between her very natural desire to get married to the man of her choice and her fear of compromising herself in the eyes of the world by doing anything to bring about that result. For her, to admit that she is indeed sexually and romantically vulnerable is to consign herself to the greatest shame possible. She vents her emotions through negative acts of aggression, and in time her temper gets worse, her tongue more raspish, and her manners more offensive. A tubercular invalid with few friends, she then falls back on self-pity, thinking that she is indeed a pitiable orphan with no one to plead her cause.

Black Jade's obsession with her orphaned state and her fear for her marital future are magnificently revealed in a dream recorded in chapter 82. According to the textual purists, this dream belongs with the "supplement" and its authorship cannot be positively ascribed to Ts'ao Hsüeh-ch'in; yet it is of such devastating psychological truth that, outside *Dream of the Red Chamber,* only the haunting dreams in the novels of Dostoevsky are strictly comparable. The dream takes place during the period when Pao-yü has temporarily returned to his studies and the Takuanyuan, once the delightful residential quarters of Pao-yü and the female relatives of his age group, has been saddened by the tragedies that have overtaken several of its former inhabitants. One afternoon Pervading Fragrance and an amah from Precious Clasp's quarters come in turn to chat with Black Jade. All but assured of her future status as the second wife of Pao-yü, Pervading Fragrance is not too happy over the prospect of serving under Black Jade as his first wife. She therefore deliberately tests her by reciting the woes of such unfortunate concubines as Yu Erh-chieh and Hsiang-ling. The amah sent by Precious Clasp also enviously teases Black Jade with the compliment that she and Pao-yü will make an ideal couple. As evening approaches, Black Jade is therefore more than usually concerned with her future:

In the quietness of the dusk, a multitude of worries and vexations assailed her heart. Her health was getting worse, she thought, and she was not getting any younger. From the look of things, though Pao-yü did not care for any one else, his grandmother and mother apparently were making no move to bring about her union with him. How wonderful it would have been if, when they were still alive, her parents had arranged the marriage for her! But, on the other hand, she thought, her parents could have very well matched her with someone else, and that person could not possibly have stood up to Pao-yü for talent, character, and tenderness. As things stood now, she could still plan for her happiness. Preoccupied with these thoughts, her heart went up and down like a pulley. For a while she sighed, and then she dropped a few tears. Listlessly she lay down in bed without bothering to take her clothes off.

She didn't know how it happened, but she saw a young maid coming in to tell her that Mr. Chia Yü-ts'un was now waiting outside to see her. Black Jade thought, "Though I once studied under him, I was not a boy pupil studying for the examinations, and so why does he want to see me? Besides, in his dealings with Uncle, he has never mentioned our former relationship. I don't have to receive him." So she asked the maid to tell him that she was indisposed and unfit for company and to give him her best regards. The young maid said, "I am afraid his visit has to do with your marriage. They have sent men from Nanking to escort you back." As the maid was still talking, Black Jade saw Phoenix, Madame Hsing [Chia She's wife], Madame Wang, and Precious Clasp coming in and greeting her with smiles. "We have come to congratulate you and to see you off." Perplexed, Black Jade asked, "What are you talking about?" Phoenix answered, "Now, now, don't pretend ignorance. Could it be possible that you didn't know that your father has been promoted to superintendent of grain transportation in the Hupeh region and has happily remarried? Now he thinks it's quite improper for you to continue staying here, and so he has asked Chia Yü-ts'un to be a matchmaker and has promised you to a relative of your stepmother. We are further told that he is a widower and you will be his second wife. So he has sent people to escort you back. Probably, once you arrive home, you will be married off right away. Your stepmother has got all this planned. Afraid that you will not be properly taken care of on the road, she has asked your second brother [Chia] Lien to accompany you."

Black Jade was shocked by this news, and a cold sweat broke out all over her body. But then she vaguely saw her father attending to his official duties in Hupeh. She was getting really scared though she persisted in disbelieving the story. "This is all nonsense," she said. "It is something made up by Sister Phoenix." "She still doesn't believe us," said Madame Hsing as she threw a significant glance at Madame Wang. With tears, Black Jade begged her two aunts to stay a while longer. But none heeded her appeal, and they all left with chill smiles on their faces.

Black Jade was now in a state of sheer desperation. She could not articulate her thoughts, but, while weeping to herself, she seemed to be transported to the Matriarch's presence. "Surely, only Grandmother can get me out of this," she thought to herself. "I'll beg her for help." She got down on her knees, and, clasping the Matriarch's upper legs, she implored, "Grandmother, please save me. I would rather die than be sent to the South. Moreover, that stepmother is not my real mother, and I wish to stay by Grandmother's side." With a vacant smile, the Matriarch replied, "This doesn't concern me." Black Jade sobbed, "Grandmother, why?" The Matriarch said, "It's after all not a bad idea to be married to a widower. You will inherit an additional dowry." Black Jade continued to sob, "If I stay by Grandmother's side, I'll not spend a penny that's not my due. I only implore you to save me from that marriage." The Matriarch said, "It's no use. You seem not to be aware that every girl has to get married someday. You cannot always live here." Black Jade begged, "I would rather live here and earn my keep as a bond servant. I only pray that you will intercede for me." Seeing that the Matriarch didn't respond to her appeal, Black Jade hugged her knees and made another tearful imploration, "Grandmother, you are the most kind-hearted person here and you have always loved me best. How come you are not helping me now that I am in such straits? It may be that I am only your granddaughter through my mother, but my mother was your own daughter. Please help me for her sake." So saying, she threw herself in the Matriarch's lap and cried most bitterly. Then she heard the Matriarch ordering her maid, "Mandarin Duck, escort *ku-niang* out of here to compose herself. She has tired me out with her outcry."

Black Jade knew that there was no use imploring her further since she was adamant. She thought it would be better to commit suicide and so she got up and walked outside, bitterly regretting the loss of her mother. The grandmother, aunts, and cousins were no help at all even though ordinarily they appeared so friendly. Then another thought struck her, "I haven't seen Pao-yü all day. Maybe, if I see him, he can think of a way of helping me." In front of her now stood Pao-yü, all in giggles. "Hearty congratulations, *mei-mei*," he said. This disconcerted Black Jade more than ever. She couldn't afford to observe good manners and drew him close to her, saying, "Good, Pao-yü. Now I finally know you are a heartless person." "I a heartless person?" said Pao-yü. "You are now promised to another family; so let's go our separate ways." Black Jade was getting more furious than ever and didn't know what to think. So she clutched at Pao-yü and cried, "My dear brother, you tell me whom I am supposed to marry." Pao-yü replied, "If you are not willing to leave, then stay here. You were originally promised to me; that's why you have been living with us. Recall how I have treated you all these years."

Black Jade seemed to remember vaguely that she was indeed promised to Pao-yü. Her grief was now changed to joy, and she said to him, "Dead or alive, I have made up my mind. Just one more word from you: do you want me to stay or leave?" Pao-yü answered, "I have already told you that I want you to stay. If you don't believe me, then look at my heart." So saying, he took a knife and slashed it across his chest. Blood gushed out. Frightened out of her wits, she hurriedly pressed her hand against the gash, crying plaintively, "How could you do such a thing! It would be better if you killed me first." Pao-yü said, "Don't get frightened. I'll take my heart out to show it to you." He then slid his hand inside the cut and fumbled for his heart. Black Jade was now crying convulsively, but at the same time she was afraid that someone might discover them in this condition. She could only hug Pao-yü and continue to wail. Then Pao-yü said, "Alas, I have lost my heart. Now I must die." So saying, he rolled his eyes upward and slumped to the ground with a thud. Black Jade wailed without restraint. Then she heard Purple Cuckoo yelling beside her, "*Ku-niang, ku-niang,* how come you are having a nightmare? Wake up! Undress and go to bed properly." Black Jade turned in her bed and realized that she had been having a bad dream. Her throat was still parched from her crying. Her heart was beating wildly, her pillow was drenched with tears, and her body was clammy with cold sweat.[46]

In view of the traditional Chinese indifference to the subconscious mind, it is most remarkable that in this dream as in other crucial dreams in the book Ts'ao Hsüeh-ch'in should have anticipated the findings of modern psychology. Black Jade is seen in her dream without her social graces, and without her poetic talent and sarcastic wit. She is the desperate girl getting no help at all from those who have meant most to her. Removed to the Jungkuofu upon the death of her mother, she has never seen much of her father. A few years later, Chia Lien accompanies her on her journey south to attend her dying father (this event is briefly referred to in chapters 12 and 14), but she is back soon after his burial. Yet, as a dependent among relatives, she must have often thought that, if her father were still alive and became a high official like Pao-yü's father, she could have regained her pride and sense of security. The dream projects that wish, but so unerring is the author's understanding of feminine psychology that his heroine automatically equates her father's affluence with the implacable enmity of a stepmother, arbitrarily disposing of her future in a most callous manner. (Black Jade could not possibly see herself as a concubine, but Pervading Fragrance's recital of the woes of Yu Erh-chieh and Hsiang-ling has had such a telling effect on her subconscious mind that she imagines for herself the fate of a widower's wife.) She turns to her normally kind protectresses for help and, with the flash of understanding that occurs only in dreams, she exposes them in their true indifference. Her intuitions are later confirmed as the Matriarch, Madame Wang, and Phoenix decide against her as Pao-yü's wife.

Next she turns to Pao-yü for help. He appears to her in his usual role of an extravagant protestant of love. Only this time she drives him to the act of suicide: if she can see his heart, she will surely be satisfied. But Pao-yü gropes for his heart, and it is missing. The last twist of the dream situation is pregnant with meaningful ambiguity. With all his commiseration and protestations of love, does Pao-yü find in her the same kind of sexual attraction that he finds in Bright Cloud? Could he meet her demand for proof only at the cost of his life? Pao-yü dies when he discovers the loss of his heart, but would he have lived if he had ripped out his heart and handed it to Black Jade? What inner compulsions have led her to dream of this gory scene?

Chinese readers have traditionally prized Black Jade as a creature of ethereal enchantment, a delicate beauty and gifted poet too fragile for the world and too good even for the often thoughtless lover Pao-yü. They want to see her purely as the incarnation of a celestial plant, beyond the contamination of ugly emotions. Yet this image is a gross simplification of a complex character. Ts'ao Hsüeh-ch'in, though he also intends her to be an image of unearthly beauty, never flinches from physiological details as he traces her growing emotional sickness in terms of her bodily deterioration. By the time Black Jade dreams that dream, all signs of bloom have long deserted her. She enjoys a good sleep, by her own confession, only ten nights a year; yet at the same time she is so languid she always remains in bed until noon. She cries so often that her eyelids are constantly swollen. The dream marks a further milestone in her progress toward death: that night she coughs up blood with her phlegm. By dawn she asks Purple Cuckoo to replace her spittoon:

As she opened the main door to empty the spittoon, she saw it was filled with sputum, but there were also spots and specks of blood in it. Frightened, Purple Cuckoo couldn't help exclaiming, "Oh, heavens, how terrible!" From inside the house came Black Jade's query, "What's that?" Regretting that she had alarmed her mistress, Purple Cuckoo changed the tone of her voice, saying, "The spittoon almost slipped from my hand." Black Jade asked, "Did you find anything unusual in my phlegm?" Purple Cuckoo answered, "There's nothing." But, even as she spoke, she was so pained at heart that her tears coursed down her cheeks and her voice again lost its composure. Black Jade had suspected something because she felt the sickly sweet taste in her throat; now Purple Cuckoo's cry of astonishment and the sad tone of her voice when she replied to her last question left Black Jade little room for doubt that her maid had found blood in her phlegm. So she called her, "Come in now; it's cold outside." Purple Cuckoo said "yes," but in a tone much more plaintive than the last time, a nasal tone fraught with tears. Hearing this, Black Jade was half numbed with fear.

When Purple Cuckoo came in, Black Jade saw that she was still applying her handkerchief to her eyes. She asked, "Why are you crying so early in the morning?" Purple Cuckoo replied, "Who's crying? As I got up this morning, I felt some irritation in my eyes. *Ku-niang,* you woke up this morning earlier than usual. I heard you coughing half the night through." Black Jade said, "Isn't this so, though! The more one wants to sleep, the more one stays awake." Purple Cuckoo said, "*Ku-niang* is not feeling well. I wish you would listen to me and take things less seriously. The important thing is to take care of your health. It is said, 'While the woods stay green on the hill, there will always be fuel.' And moreover, from your grandmother and aunt down, who doesn't love and care for you?" This last remark brought Black Jade back to her dream state. Suddenly a glob of phlegm was choking her: everything grew black before her eyes and her face changed color for the worse. Purple Cuckoo hurriedly placed the spittoon before her and Snow Goose tapped her back until, after a while, she spat out a mouthful of phlegm. In the phlegm was a coil of purplish blood throbbing with a life of its own. Purple Cuckoo and Snow Goose, their faces ashy with fright, gently eased the semiconscious Black Jade into a reclining position.[47]

In the allegorical scheme, Black Jade is supposedly repaying a debt of tears, but the tears actually taste only of self-commiseration, not of gratitude. In a fully tragic character one demands a certain nobility—a touch of kindness or generosity and a quest for self-knowledge that, however belatedly arrived at, finally enables him to see himself for what he is—and this nobility Black Jade conspicuously lacks. Intellectually she is capable of such knowledge, as I shall have occasion to show later, but she is too much obsessed with her insecurity to see herself in an objective or ironic light. Her role in the novel, therefore, is to be inexorably pathetic, to exhibit to the full the physical and emotional devastation of a self-centered consciousness, however poetically alive. In the scene just quoted, as in the far more nerve-shattering death scene in chapter 98, the author apparently showers her with sympathy, but at the same time he is unsparing in his precise detailing of her physiological condition. In the original, "a coil of purplish blood throbbing with a life of its own" is not a phrase that one can easily forget.

Later that morning Pao-yü's cousin, Compassion Spring, a religious girl who later turns nun, comments on Black Jade's worsening case: "Black Jade is such a clever girl, yet it seems to me she doesn't know how to take things easily. The most trivial thing she will take to be of real consequence. Yet how many things in this world can be taken for real?" [48] Throughout the novel, of course, the author plays on the contrast between *chia* (false, unreal) and *chen* (real): the hero's Confucian counterpart is a youth named Chen Pao-yü who paradoxically belies his name by being far more career-minded and therefore unreal than the "Precious Jade" of the Chia family. Primarily a heroine in the realistic scheme, Black Jade, too, is firmly placed in a religious dimension by her almost total blindness to the real.

If Black Jade is obsessed with her marital future, Pao-yü's wish, as has been stated, is to liberate all girls from the necessity of marriage. He is continually tormented by the question, "Why should girls marry?" Before the novel darkens, therefore, he enjoys nothing more than being with his girl cousins at a poetic party. He comforts himself with the illusion that the demon of marriage can be exorcised so long as he and his beloved relatives can enjoy their parties— art cannot transform the world but one may live for art in the relative serenity of Takuanyuan.

As a matter of fact, parties constitute a stable feature of the novel: not only the nubile maidens, but the elder ladies as well appear visibly merrier at a social gathering. When the latter are by themselves, they tend to be engrossed in their personal problems, and it is only on festival occasions that they seem almost obliged to cheer up. Throughout the novel the Matriarch is never seen except surrounded by company, and she is usually merry until toward the end when, with the family in financial straits, she magnanimously produces her savings to relieve its destitution. [49] Judging from her heroism on that occasion, one wonders whether she has all along been deliberately cultivating an impression of happy contentment for the benefit of others. Likewise, Phoenix always puts on the sparkle of thoughtless gaiety at a party, even though in the small circle of her immediate family she appears a completely different person. For nearly all the ladies of the Chia household, their compulsive gaiety at a family gathering takes the childish forms of riddles, jokes, wine games, and silly prattle. Apparently, it is only through such games that they can momentarily escape from the burdens of adulthood and the mean emotions accompanying it.

(Critics have always praised the comic churlishness of Liu Lao-lao, a country woman, in the splendors of the Jungkuofu. What one should notice, on the contrary, is the Chia ladies' eager acceptance of her company as a way out of tedium and routine: it is not so much that Liu Lao-lao needs their financial assistance and protection as that they need the spiritual refreshment which her presence imparts. It is completely in line with this argument that, when the degenerate members of the Chia clan attempt to sell Phoenix's daughter Ch'iao-chieh as a concubine, she seeks refuge in the rural environment of Liu Lao-lao's humble home and is affianced to the unspoiled son of a substantial farmer.[50] One branch of the Chia family at least is saved for spiritual renewal in a pastoral setting.)

But overtones of sadness are never entirely absent from the festival gatherings. The poetic parties of Pao-yü and his girl cousins may be an exception, but their poignancy becomes readily apparent when one looks at them as the youths' futile attempt to stave off the burdens of adulthood during the brief years they are privileged to live sequestered lives in the garden of Takuanyuan. The garden was built in honor of Pao-yü's elder sister and the emperor's concubine, Cardinal Spring, and it became their retreat at the express command of Her Highness, who wanted them to enjoy fully the kind of friendship and warmth denied her as a lonely woman in the imperial harem. Symbolically, therefore, Takuanyuan may be seen as a paradise for frightened adolescents, designed to lull their awareness of the misery of approaching adulthood. The nubile young ladies live there maintaining their virginal purity and enjoying idyllic peace and poetic conversation while in actuality they are being reared for the marriage market. Whereas in other cultures adolescents rush into adulthood to embrace the challenges of marriage and work, these maidens, while also preoccupied with love and anxious for their future, want at the same time to prolong indefinitely their age of innocence, fearful to step into the realm of experience. With all the examples of unhappy women around them, experience means for them primarily the sexual assault upon their childhood placidity, with all its implied consequences of corruption and unhappiness.

Sex remains the main component of their dreams and aspirations, however: even the nun Miao-yü, also a resident of Takuanyuan, has a sexual dream which foretells her eventual abduction by ruffians to endure an unknown fate.[51] For the rest of the young ladies, it is finally the discovery of a purse embroidered with an obscene picture that precipitates their descent from the garden. To the maid Chess and her cousin-lover P'an Yu-an, this picture is nothing but a memento of their several trysts in the woods of Takuanyuan, but to the elder Chia ladies it means the shocking revelation that the Serpent has entered the garden, endangering the sheltered virtue of the young ladies. So a search party has to be organized and hidden animosities in the family have to be unmasked, all in the supposed interests of punishing vice and protecting innocence.

Chapters 73–74, which contain the episodes of the purse and the search, mark the tragic turning point in the novel: from then on, the Chia family becomes increasingly plagued by unfortunate happenings and can no longer make a pretense of gaiety or merriment. These and the immediately following chapters are also among the finest in the book: nowhere else has Ts'ao Hsüeh-ch'in shown himself to be more dramatic in staging scenes of quarreling or less sentimental in depicting sorrow and death. Particularly, he has presented in these chapters two most memorable heroines of explosive temper and uncompromising integrity: Bright Cloud and Pao-yü's half sister, Quest Spring. Already there has been too much patient suffering in the Chia house while none of its younger members dared raise a finger in protest. Now these two girls, each in her fashion, hurl defiance at unjust authority in the person of Wang Shan-pao's wife, Madame Hsing's most trusted servant charged with the task of seeking out all questionable articles in the possession of the residents of the garden. To ingratiate herself with Madame Wang, this malicious busybody has instigated the idea of a search and has, in addition, accused Bright Cloud of being a dangerous vixen who could cause trouble for Pao-yü. Though she has been ill lately, the innocent maid is peremptorily brought before Madame Wang and given a severe scolding. That evening Bright Cloud can no longer contain her anger as Wang Shan-pao's wife systematically examines the personal belongings of all the maids in Pao-yü's quarters:

One by one the trunks were searched; when she came upon Bright Cloud's trunk, she asked, "Whose is it? Why hasn't it been opened for inspection?" Pervading Fragrance was about to open the trunk for her when Bright Cloud, her hair hurriedly done up in a bun, dashed in and brusquely opened the lid. She lifted the trunk by the handles and then dumped out all its contents onto the floor. Wang Shan-pao's wife was somewhat taken aback, her face flushed purple. She said, "*Ku-niang,* you needn't get angry. We are not here on our own but on the orders of *T'ai-t'ai* [Madame Wang] to search the place. If you are willing to be searched, then we will do a little searching; if you are not, then we won't and we will simply report the case to *T'ai-t'ai.* You don't have to behave like this." Her words only added fuel to Bright Cloud's anger. Pointing her finger at the woman's face, she said, "So you are here by *T'ai-t'ai's* orders. What of it? I am here by *Lao-t'ai-t'ai's* [the Matriarch's] orders. I know all *T'ai-t'ai's* servants, but I don't think I have ever met the likes of you, so cheeky and so high and mighty." [52]

Later, Wang Shan-pao's wife treats Quest Spring with deliberate impudence (as a concubine's child, she is not so wellborn as Pao-yü) and receives a resounding slap in the face. But the servant's ultimate humiliation is that the culprit she is so determined to uncover turns out to be her own niece, Chess. And since Chess serves Welcome

Spring, the daughter of Madame Hsing, Wang Shan-pao's wife has also managed to put her own mistress in a bad light. But these ironies notwithstanding, soon following the search, the blind authority of Madame Wang and Madame Hsing prevails in the swift punishment of all actual and potential troublemakers in the garden. Chess is dismissed and commits suicide. Welcome Spring herself is married off to a libertine of unspeakable cruelty. Bright Cloud, with whose fate Pao-yü is immediately concerned, is expelled from his quarters in her state of grave illness.

Bright Cloud stays with her brother and sister-in-law, also servants of the Chia house, and, as an unattended patient, soon becomes worse. One afternoon Pao-yü steals a visit:

Pao-yü asked the amah to be his sentinel, and then, lifting the cloth curtain, he peered in and saw Bright Cloud sleeping on a bed of rush matting. Though the blankets and coverlets had been brought over from her old quarters, still he was very much pained by the sight. With tears in his eyes, he placed his hand on her and shook her gently, calling her name twice. Bright Cloud had caught a chill and, after enduring insults from her brother and sister-in-law, she had worsened and had coughed most of the day. Now she was just dozing off. Hearing somebody calling her, she opened her eyes with effort, and, when she saw it was Pao-yü, she ached with surprise and joy and clutched his hand tightly. After sobbing for a long while, she finally managed to say, "I thought I would never see you again." Then she choked, coughing. Pao-yü, too, could only weep. "Amitabha," Bright Cloud continued, "you came just when I needed you. Please hand me half a cup of tea. I have been dying of thirst, but not a soul has answered my call for tea." "Where is the tea?" asked Pao-yü, hurriedly wiping his eyes. "There on the stove," answered Bright Cloud. Pao-yü looked and saw a pot whose spout was soot-black with tea-stain; it didn't look like a teapot at all. From the table he took a bowl; even before he picked it up, its rank greasy smell had assaulted his nose. He fetched some water, washed it twice, and wiped it dry with his own silk handkerchief. He then put it to his nose, and it still smelled somewhat. Resignedly, he lifted the pot and filled the bowl half full with tea. Its color was dark red, hardly the right color for tea. Leaning up against the pillow, Bright Cloud said, "Let

me have it. This is tea. You can't expect to find our kind of tea here."
Hearing this, Pao-yü took a sip of it; it was salty and astringent, hardly
the taste of tea. He handed the bowl to Bright Cloud and saw her
gulping it down as if it were sweet dew. In no time it was all gone.
Tears again coursed down his cheeks; he was beside himself with dis-
belief and sorrow.

Then he asked, "If you have anything to tell me, please say it now
while there is no one around." Bright Cloud sobbed, "What is there to
say except to endure the days and hours the best I can? I know I
can't live for more than three or four days and then I shall be gone. But
there is one thing that keeps me from dying content. Though I am a
little better looking than the others, I have never used my good looks
to entice you. How could they keep on saying that I am a she-fox? Now
that I have to bear this stigma and have not long to live, it would not
be improper for me to feel that, had I known things would come to this
pass, formerly I should have . . ." She was choking and could not continue, and her hands were turning cold. Pao-yü was pained by the sight,
and also frightened. Sitting on the bed and leaning toward her, he held
one of her hands and with his free hand tapped her back. He wanted
to cry out loud but didn't dare raise his voice: verily ten thousand arrows were piercing his heart.

After a brief while, however, Bright Cloud got her breath back and
cried audibly. Pao-yü was still holding one of her hands, and he saw
that, though she was still wearing four silver wrist bands, her emaciated
arm was like a dry stick of firewood. He begged tearfully, "You'd better
remove these, and wear them again when you are better." And again,
"When you are all better, you won't be so thin." Bright Cloud then
wiped her tears and forcibly pulled her hand from his grasp and raised
it to her mouth. Then, with all her strength, she bit off the nails of her
two last fingers, which were long and lustrous like stalks of scallion.
She pulled Pao-yü's hand toward her and placed the nails in his palm.
Then she retracted her hand and with both hands she fumbled under
cover of the blanket to strip off the red silk chemise she wore next to
her flesh so that she might give it to Pao-yü. In her thoroughly weak-
ened condition, how could she stand this kind of strenuous activity?
She was panting very hard. Pao-yü knew what was expected of him: hurriedly he took off his outer garment and then removed his inner jacket
and placed it on her as a cover. He put her chemise on without, how-

ever, taking the time to button it up. Next he put on his outer garment and, when he was about to tie the sashes around the waist, Bright Cloud, her eyes wide open, said, "Support me and let me sit up." Pao-yü supported her but, with all his help, she could only sit halfway up. She stretched out her hands to pull his jacket toward her, and Pao-yü helped her put it on. One after the other he pulled the sleeves up her arms, and then gently he eased her into a lying position. After that, he put her nails in his handbag. Bright Cloud sobbed, "Now go! This place is filthy and you can't stand it. Your health will suffer. Now that you have paid me a visit, it at least means that I will not have borne my reputation in vain even though death claims me."

She had not yet finished when her sister-in-law pushed aside the curtain and walked in with a knowing smile on her face, saying, "Well, well. I have heard everything you two have said." Then turning to Pao-yü: "Now, what has brought you, a young master no less, into a servant's quarters? Could it be that, seeing how young and sexy I am, you want to seduce me?" Hearing this, Pao-yü quickly assumed an apologetic smile and pleaded, "Not so loud, my good sister! She has served me for many years, and so I have paid her a visit in private." Nodding with approval, the woman smiled, "No wonder people all say you are so nice to girls." Then she took him by the hand and pulled him into the inner room, saying with a smirk, "I'll easily oblige you by not yelling if you agree to do me one favor." So saying, she herself sat down on the edge of the bed and drew him close to her, tightly encircling him with her thighs.

Pao-yü had never before seen such boldness. His heart beat faster, and his face flushed a hot crimson. He was trembling with shame and embarrassment, with fright and vexation. He could only plead, "My good sister, please stop." With a leer, she smiled, "Pshaw! I have always heard that you would go any length to please a girl. How come you are so panicky now?" Pao-yü answered with an embarrassed smile, "*Chieh-chieh*, please stop. This is hardly the time for anything. How would it look if the old amah out there should hear us?" That woman wouldn't let him go, however, saying with an impudent smile, "I've been back for some time. I have asked that old woman to wait outside the garden gate. I've been dying to meet you and today I've finally got hold of you. If you don't do what I want, then I'll raise a row. If *T'ai-t'ai* hears of this, I wonder what'll become of you. I am surprised you are so timid. I was waiting outside for a long while, eavesdropping under the window. Since there were only the two of you in here, I thought you would surely be making out. Now it seems you two hardly touched each other. But I won't be foolish like her." So saying, she became more aggressive, and Pao-yü struggled desperately to extricate himself. But while this was going on, a voice was heard outside the window asking, "Does Sister Bright Cloud live here?" That woman started up in alarm and quickly released Pao-yü. Pao-yü had been scared stiff and couldn't tell whose voice it was. In the outer room, Bright Cloud had heard her sister-in-law molesting Pao-yü. She was so infuriated and ashamed that she fainted away.[53]

This long quotation is deservedly one of the most celebrated passages in the 120-chapter novel. Part of the credit must go to the editor Kao Ê, for he has significantly enhanced the pathos of Pao-yü's farewell with Bright Cloud and the grim irony of his immediate subjection to a gross sexual assault by her sister-in-law. (In the Chih-yen Chai versions, Bright Cloud clips off her nails with a pair of scissors instead of biting them off, and her sister-in-law is a more sympathetic character who praises Pao-yü for his chaste behavior.)[54] The two contrasting scenes pointedly remove any lingering illusion the reader may have entertained about Pao-yü as a ladies' man, if not a great lover. For he is not only completely helpless before the aggressive woman but appears rather passive by the bedside of Bright Cloud. He is immobilized by suffering, and it is the dying girl herself who repeatedly takes the initiative to demonstrate her need for him and her affection—her request for tea, her half-uttered regret over the wasted years of her undeclared love, her spirited action of biting off the nails, and her struggle to take off a chemise so as to give it to her lover in lieu of the body which she has all along been too guileless and too proud to give. It is these precisely recorded words and movements that make her farewell so hauntingly memorable. Bright Cloud is given far less space than either Black Jade, Precious Clasp, or Pervading Fragrance, but in all her scenes she is so individualized that she must be accounted the most astonishing success among the author's diverse female characters.

The immediate purpose in quoting this long excerpt, of course, is to illustrate the impact upon the hero of the several tragedies that follow in the wake of the search. Deeply moved by Bright Cloud's farewell, he is properly disconsolate over the news of her death. He composes a long memorial ode to her spirit, half believing that, as one of the clever maids has reassured him, she has turned into a fairy guardian of flowers. Like a child, he seizes upon this fiction so that he may obtain partial relief from the pressure of sorrow. The Western reader, and the modern Chinese reader for that matter, will find him too effeminate and too submissive to parental authority: he laments the fate of Bright Cloud and, earlier, that of Golden Bracelet, but does not once remonstrate with his mother, the principal agent of their death. One could well imagine that a Western hero in Pao-yü's position would have been obsessed with hatred for his mother. Yet, in the philosophical scheme of the novel, Pao-yü's feminine sensitivity and passive suffering are necessary conditions for his spiritual awakening: a more assertive hero would have been too much involved in the passions to reach his kind of tragic discernment.

Stunned by the tragic events precipitated by the search, Pao-yü soon falls ill and for a hundred days he is confined to his own quarters. In a summary description, the author says that, during the second half of these hundred days, "he indulged in all sorts of sports with his maids without any restraint or decorum; whatever was unheard of was practiced." [55] Unfortunately, there are no specific accounts of this kind of dissipation: since Pao-yü emerges from his hundred-day confinement practically unchanged in his commiseration with unhappy girls and in his continuing preoccupation with Black Jade's fate, it is most likely that the author has not implied any sexual orgies by his strong words, although it would have been the right psychological moment for them if, like Stavrogin in *The Possessed,* Pao-yü is to undergo his spiritual death by first exhibiting symptoms of wild sensuality.

Pao-yü appears much less spirited after his confinement. He resumes his Confucian studies under pressure while the elder ladies are now seriously discussing his marriage. But he soon reaches his spiritual nadir, symbolized by the mysterious loss of his jade, so that as an idiot nearing death he is merely acted upon when the climactic events—the death of Black Jade and his own marriage to Precious Clasp—take place.

Before birth Pao-yü is a celestial stone longing for the wonders of the red dust. As stone incarnate, he is nevertheless the most sensitive human being in the book, despite his supposed propensity for sensual pleasures and the consequent beclouding of his spiritual understanding. In the absence of his stone, he goes through a travesty of marriage in a state of torpor. Yet, upon its recovery some months later, the awakened hero fights desperately to have it returned to its mysterious sender, the mangy Buddhist monk, to the great horror of his loving household. Interpreted in Taoist-Buddhist terms, this act of course symbolizes the deliverance of the self following the attainment of enlightenment. But what Pao-yü is determined to give up is not only his sensual self but his active sympathy and compassion so that he may be released from his long obsession with suffering. The tragic dilemma posed in the drama of Pao-yü's spiritual awakening is surely this: Is insensibility the price of one's liberation? Is it better to suffer and sympathize, knowing one's complete impotence to redeem the human order, or is it better to seek personal salvation, knowing that, in achieving this, one becomes a mere stone, impervious to the cries of distress around one?

Immediately upon the recovery of his stone, Pao-yü is transported, for the second time, to the Land of Illusion. In a far more dramatic and meaningful dream sequence (the didactic tone of the first dream sequence has been earlier commented upon), he sees again, now strangely indifferent if not actively hostile, the many lovely girls who have departed from the world, and he reponders their fate and the fate of those girls still alive in the light of the verses and emblems which he had found merely puzzling on his first visit to the region. Armed with foreknowledge and resigned to the remorseless operations of fate, he awakens from the dream a changed and cold person, determined to sever all human ties. The solicitude and distress of Precious Clasp and Pervading Fragrance pain him greatly but cannot change his will. With desolate determination he now pursues the path of holy indifference, even while perfunctorily discharging his worldly duties.

Precious Clasp and Pervading Fragrance, who have selflessly served him during his period of insensibility, now face the horror of incomprehension. In the old days, these two had no difficulty in understanding his psychology: they appreciated his kindness and made allowance for his wayward affections and unconventional ideas; they thought that, with love and devotion, they could eventually return him to the path of Confucian responsibility. Even after his recovery, they cling to the hope that his sorrow over the dead will only strengthen his sense of commiseration for those still living. The tragic events are now beyond recall, but it is surely within his power to cherish the suffering women of his own household.

With the exception of a discerning few, traditional and modern commentators alike have compared Precious Clasp unfavorably with Black Jade. In recent Communist criticism, with the important exception of one critic,[56] Precious Clasp has been even more grossly vilified: in marked contrast to the "revolutionary martyr" Black Jade, she is made out to be a cunning and hypocritical schemer thriving under feudalism. This curiously subjective reaction, as has been earlier suggested, is partly due to an instinctive preference for sensibility over sense. Precious Clasp is a virtuous and obedient girl and, especially since she nominally gets her man, it is understandable that her goodness should be counted against her. But when one examines all the passages adduced to prove her cunning and hypocrisy, one finds that every single one of them is based on deliberate misreading. Precious Clasp, of course, is not a rebel: she accepts the role of woman in a Confucian society and believes that it is a scholar's duty to prove his usefulness through the examinations and in the official world. In that sense, Black Jade, who shares Pao-yü's scorn for the eight-legged essay and for officialdom, is much less "vulgar" and certainly to be preferred. But, whereas Black Jade's detestation of vulgarity only hardens her egocentricism, Precious Clasp's acceptance of Confucian morality implies a deliberate suppression of her poetic sensibility. Strictly comparable in talent, both girls are fatherless children living more or less as dependents among relatives. If Precious Clasp can turn to her mother for love and solace, one must remember that she lives in a house of discord dominated by her moronic and wildly irresponsible brother. With her precocity and complicated life at home, she must have embraced the patience and humility of a saint to mold herself into the accepted pattern of virtue. A poet and encyclopedic scholar busying herself with needlework, a peacemaker and loyal friend enduring enmity at home and envy abroad, she is finally the perfect wife sacrificed at the will of the Matriarch to serve a dying idiot.

Although it has been the critical fashion to overemphasize the rivalry between Precious Clasp and Black Jade, it should also be remembered that their open competition ends in chapter 45 when Precious Clasp, concerned with Black Jade's deteriorating health, proffers her unfeigned friendship. And Black Jade, who has been hitherto quite aggressive toward her rival, accepts this friendship gratefully and openly acknowledges her fault in having harbored suspicions about her good intentions. From then on, they become the best of friends: two helpless pawns in the hands of their elders with no control over their marital future. If the elders prefer Precious Clasp as Pao-yü's bride, at the same time they show little regard for her welfare. Though Pao-yü was once a desirable match, by the time the wedding is proposed he is a very sick person with no immediate prospect of recovery. Even more than Black Jade, Precious Clasp is the victim of a cruel hoax, since there can be no doubt that the hastily arranged wedding is regarded by the elder Chia ladies solely as medicine for Pao-yü's health. Madame Hsüeh cannot well refuse the match, but she feels profoundly sorry for her daughter. Precious Clasp herself, to whom her mother's word is law, "bowed her head and didn't say anything in reply; later on, she let her tears fall." [57] With due allowance for all the evil perpetrated by the Matriarch, Madame Wang, and Phoenix, Black Jade has finally only herself to blame for ruining her health and alienating their affections in the first place: for Precious Clasp's martyrdom the brutal and desperate self-interest of her elders is alone responsible.

Once married to Pao-yü, Precious Clasp of course does her level best to change her intolerable situation: to restore her husband to health and to the world of human sentiments. Given his strange indifference in his reawakened state, however, she is willing to forgo comfort, wealth, and rank, to renounce conjugal love. What she wants (and what Pervading Fragrance wants) from Pao-yü is consideration and kindness. Her final shock is that the person whose oversensitiveness to suffering has always been his most endearing trait now doesn't care. In reacquiring his spiritual essence, Pao-yü has turned into a stone.

At this point in the narrative we are introduced to a crucial philosophical debate which presents explicitly the irreconcilable claims of compassion and personal salvation. Earlier in chapter 118, Pao-yü's calm admiration for the decision of Compassion Spring and Purple Cuckoo to turn nuns has already deeply tormented Precious Clasp and Pervading Fragrance, who would normally expect him to make a tearful commotion over their renunciation of the world:

After seeing Madame Wang off, Pao-yü began to study "Autumn Floods" [a chapter in *Chuang Tzu*] with minute attention. Emerging from the inner chamber, Precious Clasp noticed his exultant absentmindedness; she walked toward him to see what he was reading, and then her heart became very heavy. She thought, "He persists in regarding 'escape from the world and detachment from humanity' as his only concern; this is not good." Knowing it would be impossible to dissuade him in his present rapt state, she sat down beside him, watching him intently. Finally noticing her presence, Pao-yü asked, "What are you staring for?" Precious Clasp replied, "It just occurred to me that since we are man and wife you are my lifelong support, even though I agree this relationship is not necessarily built upon our selfish feelings and desires. As for glory and wealth, they are but like fleeting smoke and cloud. But I am thinking that since the time of the ancient sages it has always been stressed that one should cultivate his 'moral character.'" Pao-yü didn't have the patience to listen to the end; he put aside his book and said with a smile, "Just now you mentioned 'moral character' and 'ancient sages,' not knowing that what the ancient sages have stressed is the importance of "not losing the heart of a newborn baby.' What's so precious about the newborn baby except that he has no perception, no knowledge, no greed, and no envy? Once we are born, we all sink deeper and deeper in the mire of greed, hate, and passion; how can we ever escape from the net of red dust? I have just now realized that the ancient saying, 'Whether we are together or apart, what we enjoy is but a floating life,' has awakened few. As for one's moral character, who has ever reached the condition of living in the state of primordial antiquity?"

Precious Clasp answered, "Since you mentioned 'the heart of a newborn baby,' you must know that the ancient sages regard loyalty and filial piety as characteristic of the heart of the newborn baby and not escape from the world and detachment from humanity. Yao, Shun, Yü, T'ang, the Duke of Chou, and Confucius all ceaselessly set their hearts on helping the people and benefiting the world, and the so-called newborn baby's heart finally amounts to 'not being able to bear the pain or suffering about one.' Just now you spoke of being able to bear the pain of forsaking the basic human relationships—what kind of absurdity is this?" Pao-yü nodded his head and smiled. "Yao and Shun did not force their way of life upon Ch'ao Fu and Hsü Yu, nor did King Wen and the Duke of Chou force theirs upon Po-i and Shu-ch'i . . ." Not waiting for him to finish, Precious Clasp retorted, "Your words are getting more and more absurd. If the ancients were all like Ch'ao Fu, Hsü Yu, Po-i, and Shu-ch'i, how come people today still revere Yao, Shun, the Duke of Chou, and Confucius as sages? Moreover, it's even more ridiculous to compare yourself to Po-i and Shu-ch'i. Victims of the declining fortunes of the Shang, they faced many difficulties and so they thought up some excuse for leaving the world. Now, under the present beneficent reign, our family has for generations enjoyed imperial favor, living in splendid style and luxury. Not to say that all your life your late grandmother, your father and mother have all cherished you like a precious jewel.

Just think, is it right for you to maintain all that you just said?" Pao-yü took all this in but made no reply; he only tilted his head and smiled.[58]

The debate given above is the perennial debate in Chinese thought. Both Mencius and Lao Tzu invoke the newborn baby as the norm of human excellence. But whereas for Lao Tzu the baby is desireless and witless, for Mencius the baby is precious because he contains within himself all the virtues of Yao and Shun. To Mencius, love and sympathy are the basic facts of human life; so they are to Precious Clasp, and so they are to Pao-yü until his awakening. If not being able to bear the sight of pain (*pu-jen* is a Mencian phrase) is not the test of one's humanity, what is? How can one remain human by denying the most instinctive promptings of his heart? Precious Clasp cannot figure this out, and Pao-yü cannot answer her on the rational level of human discourse. It is only by placing human life in the cosmological scheme of craving and suffering that one can see the need to liberate oneself. It would be too cruel even for the enlightened Pao-yü to tell Precious Clasp that to cling to love and compassion is to persist in delusion: in the primordial antiquity of Taoism there was no need to love or commiserate.

As a tragedy, *Dream of the Red Chamber* has therefore the overtones of a bitter and sardonic comedy. Its very accumulation of painful and tragic incidents concedes and builds upon the reader's vulnerability to human emotions, and yet in crucial moments of birth, sickness, and death there appear from nowhere the mangy Buddhist and lame Taoist to mock his attachment to these emotions. The death of Black Jade, it is true, occurs in their absence and is described in sheer agonizing human terms, but this scene of unrelieved suffering may have been intended to place the heroine philosophically as a victim of passion who remains to the end untouched by Taoist grace. Her last words, "Pao-yü, Pao-yü, how could you . . ." (*Pao-yü Pao-yü ni-hao*),[59] betray a spirit of total unforgiveness, though her equally helpless lover should be the last person in the world to deserve her hatred. Intellectually, of course, even Black Jade is capable of Buddhist-Taoist understanding. In chapter

91, she engages Pao-yü in a Zen type of discourse at which she shows her superior grasp of the Buddhist doctrine of emptiness. But, typically, she approaches Zen as an intellectual exercise without responding to its mystical call to disengage herself from her all too human passions, though in one powerful scene (in chaps. 96-97) even she appears momentarily detached from her unbearable misery. She has just overheard from an idiotic maid the news of Pao-yü's impending marriage. She wants to return to her own quarters, but "her body felt a thousand pounds heavy, and her feet trod, as it were, upon cotton since they had turned numb." [60] After wandering vacantly for a while, she decides to go to the Matriarch's quarters to have a last interview with Pao-yü. He, however, then in his idiotic condition, only giggles at her:

Suddenly Black Jade was heard to ask, "Pao-yü, why are you sick?" Pao-yü answered with a smile, "I am sick because of you." Pervading Fragrance and Purple Cuckoo changed color with fright and hastened to interrupt their conversation. But the two didn't heed them and continued to grin idiotically at each other. Seeing this, Pervading Fragrance knew that at this minute Black Jade was as beclouded in her understanding as was Pao-yü, and so she said softly to Purple Cuckoo, "Your mistress is just getting better. She should be home taking a rest. I'll ask Ch'iu-wen to assist you in giving support to her on her way back." She then turned around to Ch'iu-wen, "You and Sister Purple Cuckoo escort Lin *ku-niang* home, but don't talk nonsense on the way." Ch'iu-wen gave an answering smile and went with Purple Cuckoo to give support to Black Jade. Of her own accord Black Jade got straight up, beamed at Pao-yü with her silly smile, and kept on nodding to him. Purple Cuckoo pressed, *"Ku-niang,* it's about time to return home and rest." Black Jade said, "You are quite right. It's time for me to return!" Saying this, she turned around and left the place unassisted and, what was most unusual, she walked with flying speed. Purple Cuckoo and Ch'iu-wen followed behind and tried to catch up with her. Black Jade had walked straight ahead after leaving the Matriarch's compound. Purple Cuckoo finally got hold of her and cried, *"Ku-niang,* you should go this way." Black Jade, still laughing, followed her to the Bamboo Lodge. When nearing the front door, Purple Cuckoo said with relief, "Thank Buddha, we are finally home." But no sooner had she uttered this than Black Jade tumbled forward and with a loud cry she spat a mouthful of blood. [61]

With her normal human understanding, Pervading Fragrance has completely misjudged Black Jade's situation: for the dying heroine, her beclouded state is actually a rare interlude of mental lucidity. Under the extreme shock of the news, she is momentarily able to detach herself from her suffering and reconcile herself to failure. She talks the Zen language of double meaning ("It's time for me to return!") and echoes the inhuman laughter of the crazy Buddhist and Taoist. But it is only by a tremendous act of the will that she can replace her habitual self-pity with sardonic self-mockery. Her body cracks under the strain: she spits blood and almost faints away. She never regains her health after that.

When Pao-yü has finally to leave home, he, too, explodes with the crazy laughter of the twin agents of the other world. He is ostensibly taking a short trip for the examinations, but he bids a lingering farewell to all members of the family present and makes a special point of remembering Compassion Spring and Purple Cuckoo, who have earlier withdrawn into a life of meditation:

Taking the conversation in, Precious Clasp was stunned; all those words—not only Pao-yü's but also Madame Wang's and Li Huan's [the widow of Chia Cheng's eldest son]—were ominous. She didn't dare take it seriously and she restrained her tears, not saying anything. But Pao-yü walked up to her and made a deep bow. All those present found this very odd, but, since they didn't know what he was driving at, they didn't dare laugh at him. When they saw tears streaming down Precious Clasp's cheeks, they became even more bewildered. They heard Pao-yü telling her, "*Chieh-chieh,* I am leaving now. You be good to my mother and wait for my good news." Precious Clasp said, "It's time to go; don't waste any more words." Pao-yü said, "It's odd that you are hurrying me to go. I know I ought to leave now."

He scanned the company and, when he saw that Compassion Spring and Purple Cuckoo were the only two absent, he said, "Please relay this message to my fourth sister and Sister Purple Cuckoo: that after all we'll be seeing each other again." All those present thought that all his words seemed crazy though at the same time they seemed to make some kind of sense. They concluded that, because he had never left home for an extended trip, he had been upset by Madame Wang's earlier parting words: it would be better for him to leave right away without further ado. So they said, "People are waiting outside. If you continue to make a fuss, you will cause delay." Tilting his head high, Pao-yü roared with laughter. "I'm leaving, leaving! This will be the end of the fuss: all is finished!" The others also laughed. "Then better hurry!" Only Madame Wang and Precious Clasp felt as if they were facing the final departure of death. Tears gathered from no one knows where flowed straight down, and they almost broke out into loud lamentation. But, laughing like crazy, Pao-yü forthwith left the house for good.[62]

Like the earlier scene, this scene explores the ambiguity of certain key words ("leaving," "good news," "fuss," "finished") to enhance the drama of the hero's double farewell: his seemingly overacted leave-taking for a short trip and his actual departure from the world of human ties. Madame Wang and Precious Clasp, the two closest to him, sense some foreboding though they cannot yet guess his actual plan. Pao-yü, who has made up his mind, lingers over this farewell scene because he, too, cannot bear the cruelty of actually severing all ties. But at the very end he summons enough courage to laugh the crazy laugh of the visitants of the other world, mocking human sorrow in pursuance of his determined plan. Like Black Jade's earlier laughter, it contains an unmistakable note of bitterness.

In his excellent review of the two English versions of the novel, Mr. Anthony West has compared Pao-yü to Dmitri Karamazov.[63] But it seems to me that, while both are deeply tormented souls, Pao-yü lacks Dmitri's earthy passion and vitality and does not exhibit his kind of perpetual vacillation between love and hate, between extreme humility and extreme rebellion. In his candor, in his apparent naïveté and effeminacy, in his capacity for understanding and compassion, Pao-yü bears far more resemblance to another Dostoevskian hero, Prince Myshkin. Both are situated in a depraved world where to love compassionately is to be convicted or suspected of idiocy. Both find the pains of the world insupportable and consequently undergo prolonged spells of delirium and insensibility. Each is painfully involved with two women, and each fails their expectations miserably. Prince Myshkin ends up as an idiot because, with the death of Nastasya, he realizes the complete inefficacy of Christian love in a world of greed and lust; when Pao-yü finally emerges from his idiocy, he, too, realizes the bankruptcy of love, but characteristically he forsakes the world to assume the insensibility of a recluse.

Had Ts'ao Hsüeh-ch'in moved in a Christian culture, he would probably have ended his tale differently: like Myshkin, Pao-yü could have remained in a state of spiritual death; or like Father Zossima and Alyosha Karamazov, he could have regained his sense of humanity to make the remainder of his life a shining example of charity. In the latter case, he would have cherished Precious Clasp and Pervading Fragrance the more, the more he pitied their unredeemed state. But, of course, Ts'ao Hsüeh-ch'in could not have fashioned a Christian fable; ostensibly, therefore, he has written a Taoist or Zen Buddhist comedy, showing mankind's hopeless involvement in desire and pain and the liberation of at least a few select individuals besides the hero.[64] But only ostensibly, because the reader cannot but feel that the reality of suffering as depicted in the novel stirs far deeper layers of his being than the reality of Taoist wisdom; he cannot but respond to the author's vast sympathy for young and old, innocent and scheming, self-denying and self-indulgent. Without this full commitment to sympathy, one could not have gauged the amount of suffering involved in the hero's final decision; without this implicit repudiation of the world, one could not have comprehended human events in all their transitory beauty and ugliness. Although the hero has for a while comforted himself with the illusion of maintaining an oasis of beauty in the deserts of greed and hate, in the end his unavoidable tragedy resides solely in the clash between the opposing claims of love and personal liberation. So overpowering, indeed, is the sense of tragedy implicit in his ordeal that, in choosing to renounce the world, Pao-yü may be said to have embraced an illusion of far less substantial weave than the human cloth of love and compassion, though his final bitterness and coldness should convince us of the inexorable logic of his decision. But, of course, the autobiographical hero is never completely the author. In achieving enlightenment, one cares nothing for his past history: nostalgia is a habit of mind as totally alien to the Buddhist recluse as to the Christian saint. In devoting his creative career to tracing the history of Pao-yü and the Chia clan, Ts'ao Hsüeh-ch'in is therefore the tragic artist caught between nostalgia for, and tormented determination to seek liberation from, the world of red dust.

SOCIETY AND SELF IN THE CHINESE SHORT STORY

Among the many legends which arose during the declining years of the Northern Sung may be listed the minor story of Han Yü-ch'iao, an unhappy beauty in the harem of Hui-tsung. In its final form as Tale 13 [1] of the Ming anthology *Hsing-shih heng-yen* (Tales to rouse the world), we are told that Lady Han, because of the emperor's infatuation with his concubine An Fei, languishes under neglect and falls seriously ill. By imperial command she is sent back to her sponsor Yang Chien (one of the four evil ministers in *The Water Margin*) for a rest cure. Though as lonely as ever in her strictly guarded quarters at the minister's residence, she eventually becomes better and will have to return to the palace. Yang

Chien and his wife,[2] however, accede to her request not to report her recovery, and two months later Lady Han invites them to a dinner to repay their kindness. At the dinner a storyteller recites the tale of a T'ang beauty who, thanks to the rare generosity of her imperial lord, was given permission to marry a scholar who had furtively sympathized with her languishment in the harem.[3] Lady Han cannot help thinking, "If I could be that lucky, I should not have lived in vain."[4] But she immediately suffers a complete relapse upon realizing the futility of her wish, and, soon beyond medical cure, she is advised to pray to two Taoist gods whose temples at the capital are particular favorites with worshipers. About a month later, with her health improving, she sets out for the temples with Lady Yang and a small retinue to give thanks to the gods. While at the temple consecrated to the worship of Erh-lang Shen, a celestial general best known for his fantastic combats with Monkey in *Journey to the West,* Lady Han gently lifts the curtains of the altar only to be stunned by the virile beauty of the godly image. Involuntarily she whispers a prayer: "If I am indeed destined for a bright future, my only wish would be to marry someone cast in your divine mold and then my lifelong desire would be satisfied."[5]

That night, as she is praying in the solitude of her garden, suddenly the god stands before her, exactly like the statue. Overwhelmed with surprise and gratitude, she invites him to her room and reiterates her wish to "marry a good man in your divine image."[6] The god asks her to be of resolute heart and disappears through the window. The next evening he appears again just as she is repeating her prayer and gratifies her with a night of love. After that he comes almost every night, and the lady blooms. Though she still pretends to be ill in order to postpone her return to the palace, her changed condition and the nocturnal whispers in her room arouse suspicion. Lord Yang hires a Taoist priest to unmask her mysterious visitor. Those efforts proving of no avail, a Taoist with greater magical powers is eventually summoned. After due caution has been taken to disarm the lover, the Taoist is able to surprise him and capture one of his black leather shoes. An interesting example

of Chinese detective fiction, the remainder of the story is mainly
taken up with the business of tracing the shoe to its owner. He
proves to be none other than the keeper of the Erh-lang Shen
temple, who had overheard the lady's prayer. As a sorcerer and
impudent scoundrel, he is punished with lingering death. Because
of her disgrace, Lady Han is dismissed from the palace and soon
afterwards marries a merchant at the capital who, though not cast
in the divine mold, presumably gives her a normal and happy life.
Thus it could be said the god did heed her prayer at the cost of
his ministrant's life.

Like a great many love stories that first saw print during the
Ming dynasty, this tale strikes us as divided in its attitude toward
love and morality. At first we are in sympathy with the lady's
plight, and believe that her eventual sexual fulfillment in the arms
of her god could be written only from the point of view that regards
love as a supreme good—a point of view, accordingly, that scorns
conventional morality insofar as morality is identifiable with the
suppression of one's deep-seated instincts for the maintenance of
social decorum. But presently we are on another track—to discover
the identity of the scoundrel bold enough to trespass upon imperial
property in the guise of a god. Our feelings are enlisted on the
side of society; his previous image of divine virility notwithstanding,
the impostor is now exhibited as a sorcerer, a thief, and a cowardly
philanderer (he never once visits the lady after his near capture,
but goes back to his plebeian mistress). Lady Han is all but ignored:
we do not know how she feels when her god is surprised and betrays his mortality, how she reacts to her subsequent desertion, how
she reconciles her imagined state of divine bliss with the ugly reality
of being exploited by a blackguard more mercenary than passionate.
And, just as earlier we have been invited to share the lady's rapture
at her prayer's fulfillment, at the end of the story we are supposed
to applaud justice done in the cruel execution of the impostor.

It is characteristic of the Western imagination to side with a character if what he attempts to do is in accord with one's own ideals: if
Lady Han truly deserves one's sympathy, then her rescuer, however

disreputable he may be in other respects, is for that reason entitled to admiration. In European literature, therefore, the type of impostor-seducer that the Chinese sorcerer here represents usually inhabits the comic world of the crafty and foolish, about whose destinies we are not particularly concerned. Place the Chinese impostor beside a comparable rogue in the *Decameron*—Brother Alberto, say (fourth day, second story),[7] and we are immediately struck by the comic purity of Boccaccio in contrast to the mixed narrative style of the Chinese storyteller, who treats his material at first with the potential gravity of a tragedy. In the Italian story, Brother Alberto, in the guise of the angel Gabriel, seduces the vain and foolish Lisetta. When finally surprised by the woman's brothers-in-law, after many nights of cohabitation, he jumps out of the window into a canal, leaving his wings behind just as the Chinese seducer, when finally cornered, drops his shoe. The merry tone of this tale, however, does not mean that Boccaccio always treats sexual love in a lighthearted manner; on the contrary, it is his conscious upholding of the doctrine of love and nature, of the supreme importance of sexual pleasure in the human scheme that makes Boccaccio, despite the superficial resemblance of many of his tales to Chinese stories in the colloquial tradition, so much more a coherent storyteller and unequivocal moralist.[8] In the cited story, of course, he is merely laughing at the woman's boundless conceit and venting his habitual disgust with the dissembling clergy; moreover, in keeping with the comic mode, love is not presented as a desperate need: neither Lisetta nor Alberto is sexually starved. In contrast, the Chinese storyteller has too much respect for the heroine's instinctive needs to treat love lightly, and too much respect for the established institutions—even the inexcusably cruel institution of the imperial harem—to regard her rescuer as other than a blackguard. This ambivalence is finally indicative of the storyteller's uncertainty as to how far to push the claims of love and nature: in story after erotic story, he inevitably pulls himself and his audience from the brink of sexual license to assert the importance of law and order. The god is the impostor, the savior is the seducer. But, while the fun lasts, one is oblivious to the impending punishment and feels that the pleasure of love's fulfillment, however cunningly brought about and at however low a level of mere physical gratification, is infinitely preferable to the condition of frustration in which so many heroines are initially placed.

An altogether different type of story, one which sings the praises of marital constancy rather than of adulterous love, is Tale 9 of *Hsing-shih heng-yen*. It has been appropriately translated into English under the title "The Everlasting Couple." [9] Again, though, what interests us are its inherent contradictions.

As the story begins (after the inevitable didactic preamble), two neighbors, Ch'en and Chu, are playing a game of chess in the presence of their good friend, the old Mr. Wang. In a particularly good mood that day, Mr. Wang suggests that it is high time that Ch'en's son To-shou and Chu's daughter To-fu, both nine years old, should be engaged. The betrothal is no sooner proposed than agreed upon, since the two families have been always very close. But at the age of fifteen the boy To-shou is attacked by leprosy. A year later "the disease got worse, till his whole appearance was shockingly deformed. The flesh became parched and withered and the skin incrusted with scales. Gradually the poison in his body blossomed into a mass of curious ulcers. Night and day he writhed in torment from the worms corroding him." [10] When three years pass without the faintest sign of recovery, Mrs. Chu, alarmed over the future of her daughter, quarrels with her husband constantly until the boy's parents, of their own good will, propose the annulment of the engagement. But To-fu refuses to listen. Two years later, when the leper himself pleads to be released from the contract, the girl attempts suicide to convince both families of her unshakable will. The wedding finally takes place, and the daughter-in-law is all selfless devotion. "She would gently anoint his itches and sores, and would wash the fetid pus and blood from his garments. Except that she did not suckle him, her tenderness was that of a wet-nurse. . . . Though deprived of all nuptial pleasures she drudged for him like a patient beast of burden, a wife in name alone." [11] But, far from giving him any comfort, her martyrdom only makes him more miserable. Three years slowly go by. Finally, after the prognosis of his future by a blind fortuneteller has particularly depressed him, To-shou seeks release from his suffering by taking arsenic with wine. Upon discovering this act, To-fu drains the wine in order to die with him. Both are of course saved in time, and miraculously the arsenic has neutralized the poison of leprosy in To-shou's system and soon brings about his complete recovery. The couple live happily ever after.

In his pioneer study of Chinese fiction, Lu Hsün cites two passages from this tale to indicate the high level of realism achieved in the colloquial short-story tradition. [12] But this realism, which by contrast only heightens the hagiographical design of the story, again indicates the storyteller's uncertain control over his material: on one hand, the unbearable suffering of the couple leading logically to their act of self-destruction; on the other, the accidental—though in Chinese stories of this type every accident is at the same time an act of Providence—character of their emergence from the nightmare of death. Granted miracles are inevitable in a Chinese exemplary tale as in a Christian legend, the question still remains: in what sense does the suffering of the couple lead to their salvation?

In the European tradition the leper is, of course, regarded as an outcast from humanity. Only his complete submission to the authority of divine love as embodied in the person of Jesus can bring him back into the human fold. Conversely, as in Flaubert's retelling of the memorable legend of St. Julian, the surest proof of a saint is his compassionate regard for the leper, his entire willingness to kiss him on the mouth and embrace his naked body if need be. The Chinese leper and his wife neither kiss nor embrace (for noble reasons they ignore the wish of To-shou's mother that they consummate their marriage and produce a son), and the leper's eventual recovery is not a Christian miracle. With the understandable pride of a deformed person determined to preserve the last shreds of his identity, To-shou from the very first is averse to the idea of subjecting himself to To-fu's ministrations. In sticking to her contract, on the other hand, To-fu is not surrendering herself to the impulse of compassion; neither is she conscious of a mission to bring about his cure. She acts primarily in pursuance of her duty and out of fear of compromising her reputation, since it is traditionally deemed dishonorable for a girl to break her promise to marry even though the promise is invariably imposed upon her by her parents. It would have been far more charitable for her to let the leper alone: his consciousness of being indebted to her unsolicited devotion can only reduce him to despair over the travesty of his marriage. The story therefore cannot be read as an allegory of love's triumph over self-imposed alienation. To-fu is a most conscientious and tireless nurse, but, in the absence of charity, she cannot change her husband's attitude of self-reproachful disgust. The greater her self-sacrifice, the more imperious his need to struggle free of her dominion: his attempt at suicide can be construed only as an eloquent repudiation of her unwelcome martyrdom.

The eventual recovery of the leper, like the eventual denigration of the god in the other tale, is therefore something of a fraud: it disappoints the emotional expectations of the reader. In both stories the conclusion points to the storyteller's determined endorsement of conventional morality in spite of, on one hand, his candid relish of the joy of illicit love and, on the other, his pained recital of the torments of a needless constancy. But of course even To-fu, an apparent victim of this morality, is seen as far more admirable than pathetic in her stubbornness. She is not patient Griselda, a woman completely submissive to her outrageous fortune. She actively seeks her martyrdom against the advice of her parents, her prospective husband, and her father-in-law. If the latter represent society, then her unshakable resolution to embrace her ordeal is actually carried out in the same spirit of defiance as Lady Han's determined quest for happiness.

Both To-fu's monomaniacal obsession with virtue and Lady Han's search for love's fulfillment can be viewed as positive ideals of the self in the Chinese short story. Against them are ranged the conventional moral attitudes—and, paradoxically, the storyteller divides his allegiance between the two sides.

My two examples were among the 120 tales collected between 1621 and 1627, toward the end of the Ming dynasty, in three anthologies containing forty pieces each: *Ku-chin hsiao-shuo* (Stories old and new), *Ching-shih t'ung-yen* (Tales to warn the world), and *Hsing-shih heng-yen*.[13] The first collection was also known as *Yü-shih ming-yen* (Tales to illuminate the world) with the result that the three (*san*) sets, each title ending with the character *yen,* soon came to be known under the abbreviated term *San-yen*.[14] The compiler and publisher of this uniform series, Feng Meng-lung,[15] was a remarkable man of letters passionately devoted to the cause of preserving popular fiction and drama: without his labors, most of the *San-yen* stories would probably have been lost, and the twenty-odd colloquial tales preserved in the extant fragments of an earlier collection, *Ch'ing-p'ing-shan-t'ang hua-pen*,[16] would have given us a very incomplete idea of the diversity and vitality of the tradition of professional storytelling since the Sung period.

The publication of Feng's volumes immediately aroused great interest: during the late Ming and early Ch'ing periods scores of titles, comprising hundreds of stories written by literary men in imitation of the *San-yen* style, saw print. But the genre, which had earlier incurred opprobrium because of its preoccupation with the salacious, eventually died in the Ch'ien-lung period when its obligatory reaffirmation of a sterile didacticism had killed its potential for further growth. For the remainder of the Ch'ing dynasty only one anthology of 40 more or less unobjectionable tales—*Chin-ku ch'i-kuan* (Wonders new and old)[17]—enjoyed a wide circulation. Modern Chinese specialists in vernacular literature had to go to Japan to locate authentic early editions of the *San-yen* and similar collections. In their own country they had been long out of print.

The *San-yen* stories have all retained the oral conventions of storytelling, though a small number may not have been based on promptbooks actually used by storytellers of the Sung, Yuan, and Ming dynasties.[18] Feng Meng-lung must have chosen the 120 stories from a larger number in his personal collection, most of these presumably in manuscript form; judging from available evidence, it would seem that he did not subject any of the chosen stories to extensive editing.[19] Though the majority of these were first written down during the Ming period, a sizable number could be confidently dated back to Sung and Yuan times. The three collections, therefore, provide a historical perspective to the art of storytelling, which must have imperceptibly changed through the centuries—though not always for the better. While a more circumstantial realism is apparent in the later Ming tales, a number of them appear sentimental and contrived beside the more stark Sung tales of murder and scandal. But whether dating from the Sung or the Ming, nearly all the *San-yen* tales are marked by the obtrusive presence of the storyteller as didactic commentator. The earliest storytellers in China were the Buddhist priests, and their secular competitors apparently saw themselves as lay preachers, affirming public morality with the aid of Confucian, Taoist, and Buddhist platitudes, and justifying the apparent inequities of the social order with the consolatory doctrine of karma or moral retribution. The Ming storytellers were no different.

At the same time, however, the development of the storyteller's art in the direction of a convincing realism had increasingly drawn his sympathy to the needs and demands of the individual, with their latent anarchic opposition to the social order. The consequent dichotomy of feeling to be discerned in a great many *San-yen* tales stems therefore from the storyteller's dual allegiance to self and society, his equal commitment to the covert ideals of self-fulfillment and the explicitly endorsed ideals of virtuous conduct and worldly happiness, interpreted with particular reference to the theory of karma. Superficially, society is always given the last word so that the clash within the mind of the storyteller is rarely translated into the dialectic coherence of achieved art. But the punishment of her seducer does not seriously contradict the storyteller's manifest sympathy for Lady Han, nor does To-fu's obedience to the dictates of conventional morality disguise the actual misery of her marriage or change our view of her heroic act as something undertaken in actual disregard of social opinion. Given the preponderant authority of traditional morality in Sung or Ming China, it was most remarkable that the storyteller should have exhibited in his work the conflicting presentation of his private and public loyalties, should have given so much sympathetic attention to the self, in however surreptitious or ingenious a fashion. It would be easy to belittle the *San-yen* stories for their moral compromises, but to do so would be to ignore the vital presence of an alternative moral principle in direct competition with the often fulsomely acclaimed traditional morality. Thus, on the evidence of the apparent discrepancies between an avowed didacticism and the erotic content of many love tales in the *San-yen* collections, one is perfectly justified in dismissing them as mere entertainment, or worse, as pornography disguised in the form of a homily.[20] At the same time, however, one should not forget that the so-called pornography may represent a commitment to life far more serious than the moral view that condemns it.

In referring to the storyteller's private and public loyalties, I may have given the misleading impression that all colloquial tales are ostensibly on the side of society and that the critical task is merely to uncover their secret commitment to the self. But in the great variety of tales in the *San-yen* collections, there are inevitably a few types which, in their exploration of the supernatural or their embellishment of religious folklore, are far removed from the world of manners. In their very unconcern with prudential morality and mundane happiness, however, the idealized beings in such tales provide clues to the character of heroes steeped in the world of duty and passion.

One conspicuous type of tale celebrates the Taoist celestials, legendary characters whose supposed attainment of personal immortality has always exercised the popular Chinese imagination. Ethically speaking, of course, this conquest of death is due to complete transcendence of the temptations of power, wealth, and sex, but in these anecdotal and often playful tales what is stressed is not the fact of moral struggle but the condition of Taoist grace which renders a few select individuals automatically invulnerable to temptation. The candidates for immortality may have to perform a staggering number of good deeds—healing the sick, preventing droughts and floods, and killing dragons, but once translated into heaven the typical immortal, like Lü Tung-pin and Chang Kuo-lao, is shown in his frolicsome liberty and wayward good humor. Allied with the Taoist tales are stories about poetic geniuses: Li Po, Su Shih, Liu Yung, and a few others. They are frankly admired because of their contempt for social manners and Confucian morality, and even their drunkenness and bohemianism are described with relish. Their declared enemy is the philistine official, and at least one such would-be genius comes to extreme grief in his enforced contact with the bureaucratic world.[21] Nearly all the tales about poets and Taoist celestials describe a condition of spontaneity and freedom which is beyond the contamination of official vulgarity and domestic passion.

In its subtler forms, the Taoist tale amounts to an admiration for childlike folly. There is, for example, the memorable story of an old man passionately devoted to the cultivation of flowering plants who eventually attains Taoist immortality in spite of his complete helplessness before worldly power (in the person of a bully).[22] And this praise of unworldly folly and guileless innocence also underlies the dominant group of exemplary tales in which heroes of extraordinary courage and endurance, embodying the various Confucian ideals of loyalty, filial piety, chastity, and selfless friendship, and Buddhist ideals of philanthropy and good works, are pitted against the forces of greed and lust. In this contest, the hero will eventually emerge triumphant, blessed with wealth, longevity, and a distinguished official career; if worldly fortune doesn't smile on him, then his progeny will surely be so rewarded. This concern with mundane success should not blind us to the fact that the hero is admired primarily for his reckless generosity, his determined adherence to a course of action which is foolish in worldly eyes. Even in his submission to the dictates of duty, he shows an inordinate streak of individualism which compels our admiration. The leper's wife, for instance, despite her apparent poverty of spirit, cannot disguise her stubborn pride, her fierce determination to embrace her martyrdom. In one respect the victim of feudal morality, she is in another the upholder of existentialist dignity in her election to live for an absurd cause. Like nearly all heroes and heroines in the exemplary tales, she takes the Blakean road of excess, and, if she doesn't achieve the palace of wisdom, at least she endows her life with a purpose much more intrinsically satisfying than the pursuit of worldly happiness. Nearly all the villains in the exemplary tales are extremely selfish— the grasping official, the rapacious highwayman, the envious brother or sister, the jealous stepmother; the heroes are recklessly unselfish in pursuit of one chosen ideal. That this ideal is initially seen as mere compliance with some traditional moral command is almost immaterial in our admiration for their absurd dignity.

But, like the hagiographical romance of medieval Europe, the fairy tale, the later plays of Shakespeare, or even the *Arabian Nights,* the exemplary tale is more concerned with human possibility than with the actual human scene. While its incidental realism is sometimes of a very high quality, its predominant tone is optimism, an unquestioned acceptance of the value of human endeavor in an almost completely intelligible world, a world in which virtue is always rewarded and wickedness punished. Much of our irritation with the exemplary tale is due to its naïve readiness to explain everything in terms of a rigid providential scheme, whereas we feel it is equally the business of the storyteller to depict human action in all its delightful contingency. Where miracles are commonplace, human life itself is divested of mystery.

The storyteller embellishes the traditional ideals of Confucian heroism and Taoist detachment with a good deal of lively fancy, but it is possible to say that he is not making any new discoveries in his report of Chinese experience. While the absurd hero is an admirable improvement deriving from traditional ideals, the exemplary tale is nevertheless a form of fantasy. Its melodramatic dichotomy of good and evil, virtue and vice actually leaves a large area of reality unexplored. If we use Freudian terms, we may say that the exemplary tale is largely concerned with the ego and superego, while the Taoist tale etherealizes the id in the direction of playful unreality. The futility of the Taoist immortal in his barren freedom, and at times the banality of the Confucian hero as a mere instrument of divine justice, can be traced ultimately to their distortion or suppression of the instinctive self, their failure to enlist the aid of libidinous energy. For a fuller report of social and psychological reality, we have to turn to the love tales.

In celebrating Confucian heroism and Taoist detachment, the storyteller shows the tameness of Chinese imagination. There is nothing in Chinese thought quite like the Western form of moral dualism that sympathetically opposes the instinctive and passionate self to reason: the Apollonian and Dionysian ideals as defined by Nietzsche, the Heaven and Hell of Blake, and similar formulations by modern psychologists.[23] The ethical bent of the Chinese civilization has been toward the suppression of the Dionysian instinct. What remains of the rebellious temper, of the passional instinct for carefree nonconformity and absurd self-assertion has been channeled into the Taoist and Confucianist forms of individualism, with their implied transcendence of the libido. In the realm of practical conduct, this failure to harness the dark sexual energy for the enrichment of life has made possible the orthodoxy of a prudential morality, with its implicit tolerance of a regulated hedonism; in the realm of letters, a similar failure to affirm this energy has resulted in the domestication of the tragic instinct, the refusal to contemplate irrational humanity in all its dire glory. As a theme of polite literature, sexual love tends to be stabilized in sentimental poses, and its savage aspects are little explored.

With the rise of a popular vernacular literature, of course, the stirrings of the instinctive self were gradually given more prominent attention. If we compare the love tales in *San-yen* collections with the more idealistic and self-consciously romantic love tales of the T'ang period, we notice in the former a franker appreciation of sensuality, a more forthright affirmation of the sanctity of impulse, of unreflective, all-consuming passion. Though illicit love is still deplored, and though compulsive lust and excessive debauchery are actually viewed with horror, the young lovers at least, insulated in a world of mutual delight to which the claims of honor and religion are for the moment completely irrelevant, are described with gusto and treated with generous sympathy. In these young lovers we could almost say that the storyteller has fashioned a new self, a self relishing to the hilt its own sensations and feelings, and discovering in its urgent quest for love all the values it needs to sustain life.

But, traditional and eclectic moralists that they were, the storytellers could not proceed from this concept to the creation of a fiction in conscious defiance of society. While the emergence of the new, romantic self in eighteenth-century Europe was heralded by philosophers in full support of its demands, the new self in China was without such intellectual support and its inner needs were often described conventionally in terms of a carnal hedonism.[24] In all probability, the storyteller, though in full sympathy with the lover's seeking after autonomy and delight, couldn't or didn't dare formulate this sympathy in terms of an intellectual and moral approval. Characteristically, therefore, while he did his best to bestow happiness upon young lovers, blameless except for their sexual impetuosity, he often affected the attitude of severity toward adulterous lovers, or toward nuns and monks chafing under their vows of chastity. After all, he could not depart from the mores of a society which had always condemned adultery and looked askance even upon free courtship among the unmarried. It was therefore only in stories about courtesans, whose slavery gave them a certain immunity from social disapproval and the freedom to choose and indulge their lovers, that the storyteller could develop a type of romance in the manner of a Western courtship and fully state his partiality for a passionate, reciprocal love relationship.

The storyteller's greater attentiveness to manners and morals indicates precisely the closer social and psychological texture of the love tale. First of all, unlike the Confucian hero who can afford to scorn the world in proportion as his deed excites the world's admiration, the lover is always aware of social disapproval, whether he is attempting to have a tryst with a neighbor's daughter or to form a liaison with a friend's wife. Even when frequenting brothels, he inevitably courts the disapprobation of his parents. Second, in committing himself to his risky venture, he is pursuing, instead of some recognized ideal, solely a vision of delight which his mind has conjured up for him: the storyteller cannot avoid paying some attention to the interior world of his consciousness. In the love tales, therefore, though the element of fantasy persists in the storyteller's occasional invocation of the principle of karma and his frequent reliance on ghosts, gods, and clever magistrates to tip the scales of justice in favor of the innocent and righteous, a mundane atmosphere has largely replaced the fairy-tale atmosphere of the exemplary tales.

In relation to the lover, of course, society does not always appear in the guise of a censor: it also means a host of prudential considerations whose appeal becomes irresistible the moment his passion cools.[25] In stories about betrayed maidens, their perfidious lovers eventually prefer the calmer joys of an official career and a respectable marriage. Even the romantic courtesan, placing all hope in her chosen lover, is sooner or later brought to face social and economic reality: the rapacity of the bawd, the deliberate brutality of her slighted customers, the lover's financial decline which makes his continued patronage unwelcome, or his sudden recoil from his course of dissipation. In one of the great stories in the Ming collections, "The Courtesan's Jewel Box," [26] the once-spendthrift lover of Tu Shih-niang dreads the prospect of returning home to justify his prolonged stay in a brothel before his angry father and, an even harder task, to make him accept an ex-courtesan as a daughter-in-law. When a rich merchant's son offers to buy Shih-niang for a thousand taels of silver, therefore, he readily agrees. He does not know, however, that she is worth ten thousand taels of silver in jewelry, which represents her accumulated savings during her years as a celebrated courtesan. Though a romantic idealist, Shih-niang is not without a sense of economic prudence herself. Rightly, she wants her husband to exert himself further in her behalf (earlier, she has asked him to borrow money to ransom her) and prove his love and devotion before she shares her wealth with him, though, according to her farewell speech, she has all along intended to equip him handsomely for his trip home to effect an easy reconciliation with his parents. When her husband tells her the shocking news, she wants to die, but at the same time she wants to rekindle his interest in her and thereby prolong his remorse by belatedly presenting herself as an owner of unsuspected wealth. Before a crowd of awed but sympathetic onlookers (she is in a moored boat with her husband, and her prospective buyer is in an adjacent boat), therefore, she displays the contents of her jewel box, throws three trayfuls of jewels overboard, and then jumps into the river hugging the box. Her final act of teasing her husband with her economic worth says as much as his casual way of selling her that her beauty and love are now of no avail. But for her jewel box, she could not have avenged his treachery and vindicated her high-minded love.

Love, of course, is not merely pitted against society; it is eventually seen in the hideous shape of its antithesis—lust. In the imprecise amatory vocabulary of the Chinese tale, the distinction between love and lust is at times hard to maintain. But, just as the romantic tales of young love assure us of the delights of sexual fulfillment, the melodramatic tales of darker passion invite us to examine the horror of sexual indulgence. Though the storyteller charts the rake's progress with skill, he seems particularly fascinated by the uncontrollable sexual frenzy of women once they are led to tear off their masks of decorum. There is a story about two young nuns and their female attendants whose collective sexual rapacity exhausts a rake in a few months.[27] The story, I suppose, is usually read as pornography, but what it reveals is the horror of long suppressed libido finally coming into the open, the completely destructive energy of appetite.

A story which, strangely, has never received any critical acclaim—its title is "While Traveling, Prefect K'uang Judges the Case of a Dead Infant"[28]—provides a tragic look at man's bewilderment over his humiliating surrender to lust. A childless young widow, determined to gain honor for herself, refuses to remarry, to the great disappointment of her parents. Ten years later, through the subtle

stratagem of a rake lusting after her, she yields herself to the em-
braces of a young manservant in her employ. About a year later, she
gives birth to a boy who is immediately drowned so as to preserve
her reputation. But the rake gets hold of the corpse and uses it to
blackmail her into submission. The final horror of the woman upon
discovering his diabolic design—something not unlike the horror of
Beatrice, the heroine of the great tragedy *The Changeling,* upon
finding herself under the sinister spell of De Flores—leads her to
kill the manservant and hang herself. In ably dramatizing the contrast between presumed honor and actual helplessness before temptation, the story has registered a moral truth of universal application.

My preceding remarks on the consequences of lust should place
the love tale in a better perspective. The storyteller's divided alle-
giances to society and self are responsible for its obvious confusions
and also its more fruitful tensions, but its ultimate moral purpose
cannot be called ambiguous. Having examined, with a thorough-
ness not to be found in the traditional Chinese moralists and philosophers, all the beautiful and ugly aspects of passion, the storyteller
comes out with a plea for health and sanity: he is for the individual
insofar as he respects the instinctive integrity of passion and deplores the condition of sexual deprivation, but he is for society insofar as he points out the dangers of compulsive lust and excessive
dissipation. Returning for a moment to my initial example of a love
story, it is possible now to account for the storyteller's divided feelings toward Lady Han and her seducer, though this is not to con-
done the clumsy deception. It would seem that he naturally sympathizes with the lady in her state of languishment, but condemns the
impostor as an unprincipled libertine. Not only is he a threat to
society, but he is the mockery of the very integrity of love for which
the lady longs. The implied moral is that, given their continued indulgence, even she will be transformed into a hideous creature of
lust.

It seems, therefore, that the storyteller's exploration of the world
of passion has only confirmed his traditional regard for prudence
and moderation. He cannot belie his Chinese mentality, with its

customary preference for regulated hedonism over untrammeled passion, with its instinctive recoil from any strong display of Blakean energy and Dionysian savagery. His wholehearted support of the Confucian hero and the Taoist immortal is in marked contrast with his ambivalent attitudes toward the lover as both seeker of self-fulfillment and victim of sensuality. But, of course, this very ambivalence has saved many love tales from the fate of most exemplary tales, from being mere fantasies with little correspondence to reality. And, in the context of Chinese literature as a whole, the human achievement of the colloquial short story lies ultimately in its bold image of the instinctive self, its unsentimental study of the beneficent and destructive aspects of passion. In the best love tales we have an honest realism of generous sympathy which resolves the clashes of society and self in the emotional dialectic of actual human conflict.

Such a tale is "The Pearl-sewn Shirt," [29] to me the greatest story in the Ming collections. Superficially a didactic tale within the framework of a providential comedy, it is nevertheless a human drama of almost complete moral and psychological coherence. Its central plot recalls the seduction of P'an Chin-lien in *The Water Margin* and *Chin P'ing Mei:* a man's accidental, fleeting encounter with a married woman, his dependence on a professional go-between to win her favors, his success and eventual death. But whereas, in the novels mentioned, the man is a notorious rake and bully, the woman a creature of inordinate licentiousness, and her husband a hideous and weak-minded dwarf—characters magnified in all their lust, cunning, and idiocy—the love triangle of "The Pearl-sewn Shirt" consists of three young people of the merchant class, ordinary, decent, capable of love and loyalty. Even the go-between is not as evil as Professor Cyril Birch has maintained in the prefatory remarks to his excellent translation of the story: she can be seen as a female Pandarus ministering to the needs of a Chinese Troilus. And the story does suggest Chaucer's *Troilus and Criseyde* in its wonderful evocation of the joy and agony of love.

Chiang Hsing-ko and Fortune (San-ch'iao-erh) are so happily devoted to each other that for the first three years of their married life in Tsao-yang (in present-day Hupeh) he repeatedly postpones his journey to Kwangtung where he will start on his own as a merchant. In the early spring of the fourth year he finally has to go, but promises to return within a year. Pointing to a cedar in front of their house, Fortune says that she will expect him when the cedar comes into bud next spring. She stays virtuous for the remainder of the year, but with the arrival of the New Year she becomes restless— especially following her consultation with a fortuneteller who predicts her husband's early return. With the kind of epigrammatical understanding of the human heart characteristic of the classical French novelists, the storyteller summarizes her altered condition as follows:

People generally find that if they don't entertain expectations, things don't bother them; once start expecting, and all kinds of silly idle dreams come crowding in and make the time pass with painful slowness. Just because she put faith in what the soothsayer had said, Fortune now found her every thought directed towards her husband's return, and from this time onwards she spent much of her time in the front porch of the house, gazing out from behind the curtain.[30]

One day, after the cedar has already come into bud, she sees a young merchant of handsome appearance passing by, whom at first she mistakes for her husband. She can barely cover her confusion as she retreats from the window. But the merchant, Ch'en Ta-lang, has fallen violently in love and hurries to the jewel-vendor, Dame Hsüeh, for help. Handsomely bribed, the latter proceeds to accomplish the delicate task of weakening Fortune's defenses during her husband's prolonged absence (he has been ill for most of his first year away). On the seventh night of the seventh month Fortune finally accepts Ch'en as a lover. After a few months of uninterrupted bliss, Ch'en has to leave and then by chance meets in a distant city Fortune's husband, who travels under a different name. They become the best of friends, but Hsing-ko knows the truth when one day he sees on Ch'en the pearl-sewn shirt, an heirloom of his family which Fortune has given her lover as a parting present.

Hsing-ko hurries home to divorce his wife; some months later, as Ch'en makes another journey to meet Fortune, he falls ill and dies unattended on the outskirts of Tsao-yang. The subsequent adventures of Hsing-ko and Fortune need not concern us here, but they are eventually reconciled after he has already taken Ch'en's widow to wife.

In view of the credible humanity of all the characters in the story —a rare feat for the Chinese storyteller—I will restrict my comments to a critique of the heroine. I believe that, as a loving and adulterous woman, she is almost in a class by herself in Chinese fiction. Like Criseyde, she is, in the words of C. S. Lewis, "a woman by nature both virtuous and amorous, but above all affectionate." [31] It is her need for affection that causes her to make the initial mistake of confusing Ch'en with her husband. And the same need later on causes her to accept the friendship of Dame Hsüeh, who not only assuages her loneliness with vulgar and pleasant company but most cunningly offers her a complete education in the philosophy of love. Fortune evidently accepts the theory of her husband's possible infidelity and becomes psychologically conditioned to take a lover. Her final awakening implies a grappling with the problem confronting Criseyde as she, under Pandarus' influence, begins seriously to entertain the idea of reciprocating Troilus' love: "To what fyn lyve I thus?" [32] To what end am I living like this? What is life for, what is the body for, if one is denied love? Yet it is a condition of our sympathy for Fortune that she does not give this rebellious attitude a conscious, explicit formulation. In accepting her lover on that memorable festival night, she is only doing what cannot be helped following her complete sexual arousal by Dame Hsüeh's bawdy talk and impudent confessions. But if Dame Hsüeh exhibits the cunning of Mephistopheles in attempting to ruin her guileless victim, nevertheless Fortune rises the next morning an unrepentant Gretchen grateful to her master for a night of love. The storyteller has so compelled our belief in her virtuous and wholesome womanhood that we feel her frank acceptance of a lover has completely dispelled the lewd atmosphere of the previous evening.

Fortune accepts her lover wholeheartedly because she loves and misses her husband so much. And love in the dual sense of affection and sensuality has so refined her conscience that, in comparison with Western heroines in a similar condition, her complete freedom from worry or anxiety is morally refreshing. She isn't the Princesse de Clèves with her nervous diffidence, or Hester Prynne with her obsession with guilt, or Anna Karenina with her restless search after permanent security when Vronsky's passion begins to cool. Nor is she like Madame Bovary, an incurable romantic who feeds her imagination on dreams. I have called upon these famous Western heroines not only to bear witness to Fortune's comparable status as a character in Chinese fiction but to emphasize her natural and inviolable womanhood. She is able to reconcile the claims of virtue and passion precisely because she strives to be neither inordinately virtuous nor inordinately passionate. Had her husband returned at the promised time, she would never have strayed from her marital bonds. But, during her cohabitation with Ch'en, he assumes in her eyes so much the aspect of a husband that it is she who urges him to take her with him when the time comes for them to part. She is unlike Criseyde, who eventually refuses to "stele awey" with Troilus to some other place when ordered to join her father in the Greek camp.

When Hsing-ko comes home to repudiate her, Fortune is greatly ashamed, but she does not blame her misconduct on his protracted absence or on Dame Hsüeh's and Ch'en's cunning exploitation of her vulnerable condition. Rather, she sympathizes with her husband's sense of outrage and forgives him; their eventual reunion is not so much a perfunctory happy ending as the logical outcome of their deep attachment to each other. A memorable episode will illustrate this. Before embarking for home, Hsing-ko is asked by Ch'en to give Fortune a letter, a jade hairpin, and a pink silk sash. In his anger, he tears up the letter and breaks the pin into two pieces. On second thought, however, he preserves the sash and the broken hairpin as evidence of his wife's adultery and later sends them to her parents along with the bill of divorcement. Fortune gives way to a long spell of convulsive crying upon being informed of her unexpected humiliation. Then, somewhat calmed, she ponders over the meaning of her husband's farewell presents:

At last, after long deliberation, she said to herself, "I understand! The broken hairpin means 'the mirror is in pieces, the pair of ornaments sundered'—it is a symbol of our broken marriage. As for the sash, it is obvious that he intends me to hang myself. Remembering the love which was ours he is unwilling to make the truth public. His whole thought is to preserve my fair name. Alas, that four years of love should be destroyed in an instant. And it is all my doing, it was I who turned my back on my husband's love! To live on in society, never knowing a day of tranquillity—no, better to hang myself and have done!" [33]

These are memorable words, not least because she ironically imputes to her husband the highest motive of generosity and decides to repay his kindness with her life. But more important, her deliberations are an ironical comment on the dilemma of love: that loyalty to one's body and spirit is not always incompatible with love for one's husband, that adultery does not necessarily mean marital unfaithfulness. Rarely has a Chinese story shown such generosity of understanding.

In "The Pearl-sewn Shirt" it is no longer necessary to speak of the irreconcilable claims of self and society: ideals as such are dramatized in the conflicts within the individual self and among the all too human characters. Fiction of such depth has already achieved the miracle of understanding: the pseudo miracles of the god and the leper will assuredly be out of place here. But an ultimate criticism of Chinese fiction is that, though there are several other outstanding tales in the colloquial tradition, there is only one "Pearl-sewn Shirt." And, as far as I know, it had no successor in the developing tradition of the novel. The realms of carnality and sentiment are admirably explored in the two distinguished novels *Chin P'ing Mei* and *Dream of the Red Chamber,* but neither strikes the warm, passionate note of normal humanity that distinguishes the shorter tale. And, in structure, nearly all traditional Chinese novels suffer from a plethora of characters and incidents which do not always advance the central theme. By contrast, though it is an unusually long story by Chinese standards (the English translation runs to 50 pages), "The Pearl-sewn Shirt" is a study in discipline and economy. If the Chinese novelists had taken this story as their model, they would, by focusing attention on the main characters and important scenes, by aiming at psychological portrayal and moral comprehension rather than sheer abundance and diversity of incident have arrived at a kind of novel comparable to the European novel of love and adultery which begins with *La Princesse de Clèves* and probably reaches its summit in *Anna Karenina*. Though miracles abound in the colloquial tales, "The Pearl-sewn Shirt" remains the isolated miracle of a mutant species which, had it prospered, would have changed for the better the tradition of Chinese fiction.

Upon their first appearance in the notes bibliographical information is given for all titles except 1) well-known Chinese and Western classics of literature and history; 2) works of traditional fiction whose Chinese titles are transcribed in the Glossary; and 3) all books and articles included in the Bibliography. Of the third category, the following frequently cited titles have been abbreviated as follows:

CPM   *Chin P'ing Mei tz'u-hua.* 21 vols. Peking, Ku-i hsiao-shuo k'an-hsing-hui, 1933.

CWY   Cheng Chen-to. *Chung-kuo wen-hsüeh yen-chiu.* 3 vols. Peking, Tso-chia ch'u-pan-she, 1957.

HLM   *Tsu-pen Hung-lou-meng.* 2 vols. 17th ptg.: Taipei, Shih-chieh shu-chü, 1957.

HLMC   I Su, comp. *Hung-lou-meng chüan.* 2 vols. Peking, Chung-hua shu-chü, 1963.

HSWT   Hu Shih. *Hu Shih wen-ts'un.* 4 vols. Taipei, Yuan-tung t'u-shu-kung-ssu, 1953.

HYC   *Hsi-yu chi.* 2 vols. Peking, Tso-chia ch'u-pan-she, 1954.

JLWS   *Tsu-pen Ju-lin wai-shih.* 2 vols. 4th ptg.: Taipei, Shih-chieh shu-chü, 1957.

SH   *I-pai-erh-shih-hui ti Shui-hu.* 20 vols. Shanghai, Commercial Press, 1929.

SK   *Tsu-pen San-kuo yen-i.* 2 vols. 19th ptg.: Taipei, Shih-chieh shu-chü, 1958.

SKTSYI   *San-kuo-chih t'ung-su yen-i.* 24 vols. Shanghai, Commercial Press, 1929.

"Sources" P. D. Hanan. "Sources of the *Chin P'ing Mei,*" *Asia Major* (new series), X, Pt. 1 (July, 1963).

"Text"   P. D. Hanan. "The Text of the *Chin P'ing Mei,*" *Asia Major* (new series), IX, Pt. 1 (April, 1962).

TS   *The Scholars,* tr. by Yang Hsien-yi and Gladys Yang. Peking, Foreign Languages Press, 1957.

NOTES TO CHAPTER I: INTRODUCTION

1. Among Western sinologists, Richard G. Irwin and P. D. Hanan are best known for their works respectively on *Shui-hu chuan* and *Chin P'ing Mei*. Liu Ts'un-yan, Professor of Chinese at the Australian National University, has in recent years turned his attention to *Hsi-yu chi* and its author Wu Ch'eng-en. Robert Ruhlmann has for years been preparing a study on *San-kuo-chih yen-i*. Before leaving Oxford University for mainland China, Wu Shih-ch'ang wrote *On The Red Chamber Dream: A Critical Study of Two Annotated Manuscripts of the XVIIIth Century*. No Western sinologist has yet made his mark as a specialist in *Ju-lin wai-shih*, though Oldrich Král has published a valuable article on the novel. Cf. Bibliography, Parts II–VII.

2. Cf. *Chung-kuo wen-hsüeh shih* (1959), III, 293–301; and *Chung-kuo wen-hsüeh shih* (1962), III, 942–53.

3. For information on late Ch'ing fiction and its social and political background, see A Ying, "Wan-Ch'ing hsiao-shuo ti fan-jung" (The prosperity of late Ch'ing fiction), in Chang Ching-lu, ed., *Chung-kuo chin-tai ch'u-pan-shih-liao* (Source materials concerning Chinese publications of the recent past), I (Shanghai, Shang-tsa ch'u-pan-she, 1953), 184–203. This is excerpted from the first edition of A Ying, *Wan-Ch'ing hsiao-shuo shih;* the corresponding chapter in the 1955 edition is much abridged. Among late Ch'ing scholars and journalists concerned with the social influence of fiction were Yen Fu and Liang Ch'i-ch'ao. In 1897 Yen Fu wrote with Hsia Sui-ch'ing the first Chinese essay to affirm the social uses of fiction in modern terms. Liang Ch'i-ch'ao wrote in the following year "I-yin cheng-chih hsiao-shuo hsü" (Announcement of the publication of political novels in translation); in 1902 he wrote a much longer and more influential essay "Lun hsiao-shuo yü ch'ün-chih chih kuan-hsi" (Fiction and society). All three pieces are reprinted in Chang Ching-lu, ed., *Chung-kuo ch'u-pan-shih-liao pu-pien* (Addenda to source materials concerning Chinese publications) (Peking, Chung-hua shu-chü, 1957).

4. Liang Ch'i-ch'ao founded in 1902 *Hsin Hsiao-shuo* (The new novel), the first Chinese magazine devoted to fiction. Other magazines followed suit: *Hsiu-hsiang Hsiao-shuo* (Illustrated fiction), 1903; *Yüeh-yüeh Hsiao-shuo* (Monthly fiction), 1906; *Hsiao-shuo Lin* (The grove of fiction), 1907. These magazines serialized the best-known novels of their time, including those by Li Pao-chia and Wu Wo-yao, and Liu Ê's *Lao-ts'an yu-chi* (*The Travels of Lao Ts'an*, tr. Harold Shadick). Liang Ch'i-ch'ao, who wrote for his own magazine only the first four chapters of the novel "Hsin Chung-kuo wei-lai chi" (The new China of the

future), is better known for his biographies of Western patriots and statesmen. *I-ta-li chien-kuo san-chieh chuan,* a collective biography of Cavour, Mazzini, and Garibaldi, was especially influential. For the manifestoes of *Yüeh-yüeh Hsiao-shuo* and *Hsiao-shuo Lin* see Chang, *Chung-kuo ch'u-pan-shih-liao pu-pien.*

5. See "Chien-she-ti wen-hsüeh ke-ming lun" (For a constructive literary revolution), *HSWT,* I, 55–73.

6. Hu Shih wrote on *San-kuo, Shui-hu, Hsi-yu chi, Hsing-shih yin-yuan, Ju-lin wai-shih, Hung-lou meng, San-hsia wu-i, Hai-shang-hua lieh-chuan, Lao-ts'an yu-chi,* and other novels. These prefaces and studies all appear in *HSWT.*

7. Cf. the articles and letters by Hu Shih, Ch'en Tu-hsiu, Ch'ien Hsüan-t'ung, Liu Fu, and others gathered in Hu Shih, ed., *Chien-she li-lun chi,* Pt. II. This title constitutes Vol. 1 of Chao Chia-pi, ed., *Chung-kuo hsin-wen-hsüeh ta-hsi* (A comprehensive anthology of modern Chinese literature), Shanghai, Liang-yu t'u-shu-kung-ssu, 1936.

8. *Ibid.,* Pt. III. See also C. T. Hsia, *A History of Modern Chinese Fiction, 1917–1957* (New Haven, Yale University Press, 1961), pp. 19–21.

9. Hu Shih regards *Shui-hu, Hsi-yu chi, Ju-lin wai-shih,* and *Hung-lou meng* as the four outstanding Chinese novels and is partial to late Ch'ing fiction (cf. *HSWT,* I, 37–40). Of Chinese fiction in general he complains repeatedly of its stale Confucian thought, its pedestrian narrative style, and its technical shoddiness. Even when praising the exceptional qualities of certain novels, he implies a condemnation of the tradition as a whole for its lack of these qualities. Thus in praising humor (*hui-hsieh*) in *San-hsia wu-i,* he notices its absence in most traditional fiction. Likewise, the descriptive prose of *Lao-ts'an yu-chi* is praised because, with the partial exception of the author of *Ju-lin wai-shih,* no earlier novelists have observed people or scenery with their own eyes. Cf. *HSWT,* III, 470–72, 546–48.

10. Hu Shih is the object of virulent attack in a series of compilations entitled *Hu Shih ssu-hsiang p'i-p'an.* Many articles in these compilations denounce Hu Shih's contributions as a literary scholar and critic. Any dicta of his in the least unfavorable to Chinese works or writers are seized upon as evidence of his malicious intention to denigrate traditional literature.

11. *CWY,* I, 478.

12. Thus in *Chung-kuo hsiao-shuo shih-lüeh* (A brief history of Chinese fiction) Lu Hsün dismisses most minor novels with an impatience bordering on scorn.

13. Mao Tun, *Hua-ho-tzu* (Chatterbox) (Shanghai, Liang-yu t'u-shu-kung-ssu, 1934), pp. 177–84.

14. Cf. C. T. Hsia, *Modern Chinese Fiction*, pp. 301–5.

15. Cf. D. W. Fokkema, *Literary Doctrine in China and Soviet Influence, 1956–1960* (The Hague, Mouton & Co., 1965).

16. Waley translated his *Ballads and Stories from Tun-huang* from Wang Chung-min *et al.*, eds., *Tun-huang pien-wen chi* (A collection of *pien-wen* from Tun-huang). This annotated two-volume edition of *pien-wen* is an outstanding achievement of sinological scholarship.

17. Cf. John L. Bishop, *The Colloquial Short Story in China;* Richard G. Irwin, *The Evolution of a Chinese Novel: Shui-hu-chuan;* and the articles by Jaroslav Průšek listed in Bibliography, I.

18. In *T'ang-tai hsiao-shuo yen-chiu* (Studies in T'ang fiction) Liu K'ai-jung emphasizes the influence of Buddhist storytellers upon *ch'uan-ch'i* fiction. The influence of lay storytellers upon that fiction, however, has not yet received sufficient recognition by literary historians partly because these storytellers are treated as a literary phenomenon of the Sung period. But T'ang poets and *ch'uan-ch'i* writers, Yuan Chen for one, have occasionally testified to their interest in popular storytelling. I believe Wang Chi-ssu is right in claiming to see the influence of lay storytellers upon the *ch'uan-ch'i* writers of the mid-T'ang period. See Wang, *Ts'ung Ying-ying-chuan tao Hsi-hsiang-chi* (From "The Story of Ying-ying" to "The Romance of the Western Chamber") (Shanghai, Ku-tien-wen-hsüeh ch'u-pan-she, 1955), pp. 10–11.

19. Cf. Liu K'ai-jung, *T'ang-tai hsiao-shuo yen-chiu;* Ch'en Yin-k'o, *Yuan Po shih chien-cheng kao* (A commentary on the poems of Po Chü-i and Yuan Chen) (Canton, Lingnan University, 1950); and Ch'en, "Han Yü and the T'ang Novel," *Harvard Journal of Asiatic Studies,* I (1936).

20. Bishop, *The Colloquial Short Story*, pp. 7–10. The original sources from which Bishop has culled his information are gathered in Meng Yuan-lao *et al.*, *Tung-ching meng-hua lu (wai ssu-chung)* ("Reminiscences of Pien-liang" and four accounts of Hangchow). Lo Yeh's *Tsui-weng t'an-lu* (Tsui-weng's notebook), compiled most probably during the late Southern Sung period rather than the Yuan, is an even more important source. It classifies *hsiao-shuo* according to eight categories and lists over a hundred topics current among storytellers of his time. T'an Cheng-pi studies *Tsui-weng t'an-lu* in detail in *Hua-pen yü ku-chü* (*Hua-pen* and old Chinese drama). See also chap. 3, n. 17.

21. The titles and dates of the *San-yen* collections are given in the Appendix; see Bishop, *The Colloquial Short Story,* for fuller information. *Ch'ing-p'ing-shan-t'ang hua-pen* (Peking, Wen-hsüeh ku-chi k'an-hsing-

she, 1955) contains 27 stories which originally formed part of six individual collections of ten stories each printed by Hung P'ien, a bibliophile of the Chia-ching period (1522–66). *Pao-wen-t'ang shu-mu,* a catalogue of Ch'ao Li's private library, was compiled about 1560. Its listing
of over a hundred titles of *hua-pen* can be found in Sun K'ai-ti, *Chung-
kuo t'ung-su hsiao-shuo shu-mu.* For a study of this catalogue see T'an
Cheng-pi, *Hua-pen yü ku-chü,* pp. 38–60. André Lévy, "Études sur trois
recueils anciens de contes chinois," *T'oung Pao,* LII, contains a bibliographical study of *Ch'ing-p'ing-shan-t'ang hua-pen.*

22. To "Ts'ui tai-chao sheng-ssu yuan-chia," a story in *Ching-shih
t'ung-yen,* one of the *San-yen* collections, the editor Feng Meng-lung ap-
pends a headnote to the effect that it was a Sung tale originally bearing
the title "Nien-yü Kuan-yin." In 1920 the bibliophile Miao Ch'üan-sun
reprinted the story under that title as part of a fragmentary collection
supposedly dating from Yuan times, *Ching-pen t'ung-su hsiao-shuo.*
Though nearly every history of Chinese literature cites the latter as the
earliest extant anthology of colloquial stories, its spurious character has
been long suspected by discerning scholars. The latest attempt to expose
Miao's hoax is Ma Yau-Woon and Ma Tai-Loi, *"Ching-pen t'ung-su
hsiao-shuo ko-p'ien ti nien-tai chi ch'i chen-wei wen-t'i," Tsing Hua Journal of Chinese Studies* (new series), V, No. 1 (1965). The authenticity
of "Nien-yü Kuan-yin" as a Sung tale, however, is not affected by the
controversy. There are several English translations of the tale, including
the one entitled "The Jade Worker" in Yang Hsien-yi and Gladys Yang,
trs., *The Courtesan's Jewel Box.*

23. As a resident of Soochow and Shanghai in the thirties and forties,
I have heard the best Soochow storytellers of that time. For historical information on *t'an-tz'u* see Cheng Chen-to, *Chung-kuo su-wen-hsüeh
shih,* chap. 12.

24. Wang Shao-t'ang, narrator, *Yangchow p'ing-hua Shui-hu: Wu Sung.*

25. Cyril Birch has done an excellent translation of "The Pearl-sewn
Shirt" (*Chiang Hsing-ko ch'ung-hui chen-chu-shan*) in *Stories from a
Ming Collection.* The story is discussed in the Appendix. "The Oil
Peddler" (*Mai-yu-lang tu-chan hua-k'uei*) is available in English in
Yang and Yang, trs., *The Courtesan's Jewel Box,* and Chi-chen Wang,
tr., *Traditional Chinese Tales.*

26. In tracing the evolution of *San-kuo yen-i,* scholars who have had occasion to comment on this couplet (from the poem "Chiao-erh shih")
have unanimously regarded it as positive evidence that by the late T'ang
period the story-cycle of the Three Kingdoms had become so popular
that even children were well acquainted with the distinguishing features or characteristics of its heroes. Cf. *CWY,* I, 169, and *Chung-kuo*

wen-hsüeh shih (1962), III, 839. In *Chung-kuo ssu-ta hsiao-shuo chih yen-chiu,* p. 103, Chao Ts'ung further argues that, since the historian Ch'en Shou has not treated Chang Fei or Teng Ai as comic characters though he refers to the latter's stuttering, it must have been the storytellers who exploited the ludicrousness of their looks or speech.

The first line of this couplet reads in Chinese *Huo nüeh Chang Fei hu.* I am not certain of the meaning of the character *hu* in the present context. Feng Hao, annotator of the standard edition of Li Shang-yin's poems, takes it to mean the blackness or swarthiness of a barbarian, and I have followed his definition. But in *San-kuo yen-i shih-lun,* pp. 81–82, Tung Mei-k'an disagrees and takes *hu* to mean "big jaws" (*ta-han* or *yen-han*). Chao Ts'ung (p. 103) is undecided whether *hu* should mean "black" or "beard or whiskers." In the latter case, the character *hu* is taken to be identical with another character pronounced *hu* (*Mathews' Dictionary,* rev. ed., No. 2178). It may be noted that, while "Hei Chang Fei" (black Chang Fei) is a proverbial expression, the standard description of his features in the *p'ing-hua* and *yen-i* versions of *San-kuo* includes the phrase *yen-han hu-hsü* (big jaws and the tiger's whiskers).

27. *SK,* chap. 107, p. 652. Teng Ai's repartee was first recorded in the *Shih-shuo hsin-yü, chüan* 1, sec. 2: "yen-yü." However, in that source Teng's interrogator is not Ssu-ma I, but his younger son Ssu-ma Chao, posthumously honored as Chin Wen-ti. In Lo Kuan-chung's original version of *SKTSYI,* when Hsia-hou Pa informs Chiang Wei of the two brilliant young generals of the Wei, Teng Ai and Chung Hui, in the section corresponding to chap. 107 of the Mao Tsung-kang version, he makes no mention of Teng's stuttering (*ts'e* 22, pp. 30b–31a). It is in a later section (*ts'e* 23, p. 21a) that Hsia-hou Pa tells Chiang Wei about Teng's stutter: "Pa said, 'He is seven feet tall, has a broad face, big ears, big jaws, and a large mouth. But his speech is hesitant and hard to follow. People call him Stutterer Teng.'" In the *Shih chi* Ssu-ma Ch'ien makes one gallant attempt to reproduce a stutterer's speech, but as a role such speeches are impossible to duplicate in classical Chinese. From what I have observed of the Soochow storytellers, they delight in mimicking dialectal and defective speech for comic effect.

28. In its standard form, *Tung-Chou lieh-kuo chih* was compiled by Feng Meng-lung with a commentary by Ts'ai Yuan-fang. It is entirely faithful to such classical sources as the *Tso Commentary, Kuo yü, Chan-kuo ts'e,* and *Shih chi.*

29. Such as Li K'uei of the story-cycle about the Liangshan heroes and Chang Fei. It is interesting to note that Chang Fei is the only character in *San-kuo yen-i* whose speech approaches the vernacular. Eventually the coarse and quick-tempered hero becomes stereotyped in historical novels as an unlettered general lucky in battle but not without a trace

of child's cunning. The best-known examples of this comic type are Ch'eng Yao-chin in *Shuo T'ang ch'üan-chuan;* Niu Kao in *Shuo Yüeh ch'üan-chuan* (a novel about Yüeh Fei); and Chiao T'ing-kuei in *Wan-hua lou* and *Wu-hu p'ing-hsi* (novels about the Northern Sung general Ti Ch'ing).

30. *JLWS,* chap. 14.

31. Cf. *HLMC,* I, 64–65, 102, 271.

32. In the prefaces to his translations of *The Old Curiosity Shop* and *David Copperfield,* Lin Shu invokes both Ssu-ma Ch'ien and Ts'ao Hsüeh-ch'in to establish the greatness of Dickens. Cf. *HLMC,* I, 64–65.

33. Richard G. Irwin summarizes Chin Sheng-t'an's introduction to his edition of the novel partly as follows: "*Shui-hu-chuan . . .* surpasses *Shih-chi* because it is not reporting but pure creation. Here the author had a free hand, and making use of techniques derived from *Shih-chi,* he excelled his model in many respects" (*The Evolution of a Chinese Novel,* p. 93).

34. A prominent intellectual of his time affiliated with the T'ai-chou school of idealism, Li Chih (1527–1602) has enjoyed great esteem in modern China for the individualistic and libertarian strains of his thought. Ming publishers gave credit to Li as editor and commentator of many novels. His preface to *Shui-hu chuan* gives the novel the highest praise. See Irwin, pp. 75–86.

35. Cf. the sections on *Chin P'ing Mei* and *Hung-lou meng* in K'ung Ling-ching, ed., *Chung-kuo hsiao-shuo shih-liao.*

36. In China as elsewhere there are far more novels containing pornographic passages than novels of pornographic intent. By the latter I mean novels which have very little to offer besides a high concentration of scenes of explicit sexual description. *Chin P'ing Mei* is certainly a pornographic novel but it may not have been a work of pornographic intent since it has much more to offer. For obvious reasons novels of pornographic intent are usually short.

The sentimental novels about a scholar and a beauty or beauties (since he may end up with two wives) usually have a simple plot. Some villain or villains will cross their path, but the lovers are finally happily married, usually after the scholar has earned top honors at the examinations and the beauty has vindicated her honor. This type of novel arose toward the end of the Ming dynasty and achieved its greatest successes during the early Ch'ing period. Among its best-known titles, *Hao-ch'iu chuan* has 18 chapters, and both *Yü Chiao Li* and *P'ing Shan Leng Yen* have 20 chapters. These three novels have appeared in many Western-language translations; the earliest versions are listed in Bibliography, VIII.

37. Yang Hsien-yi and Gladys Yang, trs., *The Man Who Sold a Ghost: Chinese Tales of the 3rd–6th Centuries:* "The Old Man and the Devils," p. 33. This tale is taken from Kan Pao, *Sou-shen chi, chüan* 16.

38. Ming Neo-Confucianism was dominated by Wang Yang-ming and the many schools founded by his disciples. Though many late Ming intellectuals more or less influenced by Wang (I have mentioned Li Chih) showed a great interest in vernacular literature, it is hard to say whether any specific ideas of Neo-Confucian idealism were consciously reflected in the fiction of their time. All we can say is that in the late Ming certain novelists and certain thinkers not necessarily identified with the T'ai-chou school share a strong sympathy for sensuality and individual autonomy.

39. "Tragedy and the Whole Truth" is reprinted in Aldous Huxley's *Collected Essays* (New York, Harper, 1958). The quotation appears on p. 100.

40. Robert Penn Warren discusses this oft-quoted passage from *A Farewell to Arms* in his famous essay on Hemingway. Cf. John W. Aldridge, ed., *Critiques and Essays on Modern Fiction, 1920–1952* (New York, Ronald Press, 1952), pp. 460 ff.

41. *Shen-tu* is an important concept in the *Book of the Mean*. Though modern scholars tend to stress the Buddhist influence on Chinese fiction, its use of the Confucian ideology is actually more explicit and deliberate. In his stimulating essay "Chiu wen-hua yü hsin hsiao-shuo" (The old culture and the new fiction) (*Wen-hsüeh Tsa-chih,* III, No. 1, Taipei, 1957), my late brother Tsi-an Hsia suggests that even for the novelist of today a true depiction of Confucian character and sensibility should prove a challenge. This essay has been included in T. A. Hsia, ed., *Hsiao-shuo yü wen-hua* (Fiction and culture).

42. Modern scholars have rightly paid far more attention to the colloquial love stories of the *San-yen* tradition than to the conventionalized romances about a scholar and a beauty. But as a type of fiction cultivated by scholars, the latter represent far more of a deliberate extension of the romantic sentimentalism of classical literature. Though not strictly a *ts'ai-tzu chia-jen* romance, *Yen-shan wai-shih,* a delightful exercise composed by Ch'en Ch'iu *ca.* 1810, is the most self-consciously literary of all works of Chinese fiction. The whole book is a mellifluous flow of parallel sentences, each pair or quartet bristling with images and allusions borrowed from classical literature.

43. Li Chih was the prominent example of an intellectual defending sensuality. For the craze for erotic woodcuts and fiction, see R. H. van Gulik, *Erotic Colour Prints of the Ming Period, with an Essay on Chinese Sex Life from the Han to the Ch'ing Dynasty.*

44. Cf. Arthur F. Wright, "Sui Yang-ti: Personality and Stereotype," in Arthur F. Wright, ed., *The Confucian Persuasion* (Stanford University Press, 1960).

45. Among the novels available in English translation, read especially *The Travels of Lao Ts'an* for its many cases of injustice perpetrated by harsh officials. Unlike earlier novelists, the author Liu Ê was a humanitarian reformer under Western influence and he attacked these officials with a great deal of personal indignation.

46. For example, such Taoist canonical works as *T'ai-shang kan-ying p'ien* and *Yin-chih ching*. For excerpts see Wm. Theodore de Bary *et al.*, eds., *Sources of Chinese Tradition* (New York, Columbia University Press, 1960), pp. 632–38.

47. *Hsing-shih yin-yuan,* an early Ch'ing work about a shrew and her henpecked husband, is the best known of the Chinese novels fully illustrating the efficacy of moral retribution. In "*Hsing-shih yin-yuan* k'ao-cheng" (*HSWT,* IV, 329–95), Hu Shih ascribes the work to P'u Sung-ling, the author of *Liao-chai chih-i.* Few scholars today, however, would agree with his attribution.

48. Swordsmen and swordswomen with magic skill first appeared in the T'ang *ch'uan-ch'i* tales. Chi-chen Wang's *Traditional Chinese Tales* contains two such tales.

49. Most *aficionados* consider the postwar period to be the golden age of *wu-hsia hsiao-shuo* and the Hong Kong author Chin Yung to be the reigning practitioner of the genre. Many readers of cultivated taste compare him seriously to Alexandre Dumas, *père.* For a survey of Chinese chivalric fiction see James J. Y. Liu, *The Chinese Knight-Errant,* chap. 3.

50. For a study of Yüeh Fei as a type of Confucian hero see Hellmut Wilhelm, "From Myth to Myth: The Case of Yüeh Fei's Biography," in Arthur F. Wright and Denis Twitchett, eds., *Confucian Personalities* (Stanford University Press, 1962). Like Yüeh Fei, the early T'ang general Hsüeh Jen-kuei and the early Sung general Yang Yeh are historical figures, though novelists have depicted their careers and the careers of their descendants in a fictitious manner. The deeds of the Yang family are celebrated in Hsiung Ta-mu's *Pei-Sung-chih chuan* and another late Ming novel, *Yang-chia-fu t'ung-su yen-i.* Ch'ien Ts'ai and Chin Feng's *Shuo Yüeh ch'üan-chuan* is about Yüeh Fei while *Shuo T'ang hou-chuan* and *Shuo T'ang cheng-hsi chuan,* also of the early Ch'ing period, chronicle the adventures of the Hsüeh family. Hsüeh Jen-kuei, Yang Yeh, and Yüeh Fei all suffer unjustly at the hands of military commanders or ministers at court jealous of their merit.

51. *Chuang Tzu,* chap. 6: "Ta-tsung-shih." Aldous Huxley cites this passage and comments on it brilliantly in *The Perennial Philosophy* (New York, Harper, 1944), p. 91.

NOTES TO CHAPTER II: THE ROMANCE OF THE THREE KINGDOMS

1. W. P. Ker, *Epic and Romance: Essays on Medieval Literature* (London, Macmillan & Co., 1897) is now available as a paperback (New York, Dover Publications, 1957). See especially chaps. 1–2.

2. Chang Hsüeh-ch'eng maintains that "seventy percent of *San-kuo yen-i* is fact and thirty percent fiction." His comments on the novel, taken from *Ping-ch'en cha-chi,* are cited in K'ung Ling-ching, ed., *Chung-kuo hsiao-shuo shih-liao,* pp. 44–45. Hu Shih's preface to the novel, "*San-kuo-chih yen-i* hsü," appears in *HSWT,* II.

3. *San-kuo-chih p'ing-hua* constitutes one of the five titles in the series entitled *Hsin-k'an ch'üan-hsiang p'ing-hua* (Newly published, fully illustrated *p'ing-hua*), published during the Chih-chih reign of Yuan Ying-tsung (1321–23). It has been reprinted a few times in the recent decades, the latest printing being *Ch'üan-hsiang p'ing-hua wu-chung,* a photolithographic edition (1956). For a detailed description and analysis of *San-kuo-chih p'ing-hua,* see secs. 3–5 of "*San-kuo-chih yen-i* ti yen-hua," in *CWY,* I.

4. For Ssu-ma Ch'ien's biographies of these three generals see Burton Watson, tr., *Records of the Grand Historian of China,* I (New York, Columbia University Press, 1961), 189–232.

5. *SKTSYI, ts'e* 1, p. 1a of the main text. "Minister of Public Instruction" is my translation of the official title *ssu-t'u.* For the duties of a *ssu-t'u* during the Later Han dynasty see *Hou Han shu,* XII (Peking, Chung-hua shu-chü, 1965), 3560–61.

6. *Ch'üan-hsiang p'ing-hua wu-chung,* V, 355.

7. C. H. Brewitt-Taylor, tr., *Romance of the Three Kingdoms,* I (1959), 1. Since Mao Tsung-kang assumes final responsibility as editor, in my subsequent references to his version of the novel I shall not mention Mao Lun, whose editorial role was in all probability much smaller.

8. *SKTSYI, ts'e* 1: Preface by Chiang Ta-ch'i, pp. 2b–3a. All prefatory materials in *ts'e* 1 are paginated separately. Chiang's preface is dated 1494; hence the common designation of this version as the Hung-chih (1488–1505) edition. Miss Liu Hsiu-yeh has quoted the entire text of a preface by Hsiu-jan-tzu dated the year *jen-wu* of the Chia-ching reign (1522) in *Ku-tien hsiao-shuo hsi-ch'ü ts'ung-k'ao,* pp. 63–64. She accord-

ingly states that the novel was published in the same year. However, according to *Chung-kuo wen-hsüeh shih* (1962), III, 341, Hsiu-jan-tzu's preface was dated 1552 (the *jen-tzu* year of the Chia-ching reign). This preface is missing from the facsimile edition of *SKTSYI* published by the Commercial Press.

9. In "*San-kuo-chih yen-i* ti yen-hua," Cheng Chen-to lists ten different Ming editions of the novel published after the Chia-ching edition, and of these ten, four include in their full titles the phrase *an Chien*. For a brief discussion of some Ming publishers' exploitation of the prestige of *Tzu-chih t'ung-chien* to enhance the commercial value of their novels, see *CWY*, I, 216–18. See also Liu Hsiu-yeh, *Ku-tien hsiao-shuo hsi-ch'ü ts'ung-k'ao*, pp. 65–67.

10. *HSWT*, II, 473.

11. *SK*, chap. 5, pp. 27–28. The corresponding passage in *SKTSYI*, ts'e 1, pp. 78a–79b, is slightly fuller since the standard version is more classical in style. Unless important discrepancies are to be commented on, I shall not refer to *SKTSYI* in my subsequent citations from *SK*. In translating this and other passages from the novel, I have consulted Brewitt-Taylor's version.

12. Kuan Yü keeps night vigil (this episode is added by Mao Tsung-kang) and kills Yuan Shao's general Yen Liang in chap. 25, kills Ts'ao Ts'ao's general Ts'ai Yang in front of Chang Fei in chap. 28, and is operated on in chap. 75.

13. See chaps. 37–39.

14. *SK*, chap. 97, p. 582.

15. In a collective biography (*San kuo chih, chüan* 36) Ch'en Shou treats the lives of the five generals in the historic order of their importance: Kuan Yü, Chang Fei, Ma Ch'ao, Huang Chung, Chao Yün. In the section "Liu Pei ascends the throne as the king of Han-chung" in *SKTSYI* (ts'e 15, p. 36a), when the five are appointed "Tiger Generals," Chao Yün is ranked the last. In the next section (ts'e 15, p. 43b), however, when Fei Shih arrives in Ching-chou to inform Kuan Yü of the news, he names the five in the following order: Kuan, Chang, Ma, Chao, and Huang.

16. *SK*, chap. 78, p. 465.

17. Cf. the biography of Kuan Yü in the *San kuo chih, chüan* 36.

18. *SK*, chap. 63, pp. 377–78.

19. *SK*, chap. 65, p. 394. In chap. 73 Kuan Yü objects vehemently to the inclusion of Huang Chung among the "Tiger Generals." The emissary Fei Shih has to flatter him to put him in good humor.

20. C. H. Brewitt-Taylor, tr., *Romance of the Three Kingdoms*, Introduction by Roy Andrew Miller, I, v.

21. Cf. *HSWT*, II, 467.

22. *SK*, chap. 29, p. 177. The wording is slightly different in *Hou Han shu*: "Ma Yuan lieh-chuan," III, 830.

23. *SK*, chap. 19, p. 117. The corresponding passage in *SKTSYI*, *ts'e* 4, pp. 69a–70a, includes fuller dialogue between Ts'ao Ts'ao and Ch'en Kung.

24. *SK*, chap. 7, pp. 37–38.

25. *SK*, chap. 28, p. 171.

26. *SK*, chap 31, p. 189.

27. Ts'ao Ts'ao's death takes place in chap. 78.

28. *SK*, chap. 29, pp. 174–75.

29. In *chüan* 46 of the *San kuo chih*, V, 1109, Ch'en Shou writes of the fatal ambush by the retainers of Hsü Kung, whom Sun Ts'e has earlier killed. In a note P'ei Sung-chih cites from the *Sou-shen chi* the story of Sun Ts'e's unreasoned antagonism toward Yü Chi and its fatal consequences.

30. Offended by K'ung Yung's impiety and supposed malice, Ts'ao Ts'ao puts him and his family to death in chap. 40. Ni Heng, whose mockery of Ts'ao Ts'ao is cited below in the chapter, is sent by the latter as an emissary to Liu Piao. Liu, who likewise does not want to incur the reputation of being his executioner, sends Ni Heng to Huang Tsu, the governor of Chiang-hsia, who kills him in chap. 23. Yang Hsiu, a precocious intellectual serving under Ts'ao Ts'ao (Ni Heng refers to him rather fondly as his "little son"—*SK*, p. 140), eventually in chap. 60 meets his match in Chang Sung. Chang Sung is killed by his master Liu Chang for his treachery in chap. 62 while Yang Hsiu is put to death by Ts'ao Ts'ao in chap. 72 because he has repeatedly guessed Ts'ao's mind correctly. Noted for his literary talent and philosophical commentaries, Ho Yen is implicated in the *coup* of Ts'ao Shuang against Ssu-ma I and sentenced to death in chap. 107.

31. *SK*, chap. 23, p. 138. Confucius' meeting with Yang Huo is recorded in *The Analects*, Bk. XVII, chap. 1. Tsang Ts'ang maligns Mencius in *Mencius*, Bk. I, Pt. 2, chap. 16.

32. In the popular opera known as *Ta-ku ma-Ts'ao*.

33. *SK*, chap. 36, p. 218. The friend is Hsü Shu, who has served Liu Pei briefly. When an emissary from King Wei of Ch'u approaches Chuang Tzu with costly presents and the offer of a premiership, the philosopher replies, "Haven't you seen, sir, a bull about to be slaughtered at a sacri-

fice to heaven?" (Tzu tu-pu-chien chiao-chi chih hsi-niu hu)—*Shih chi,
chüan* 63, *lieh chuan* 3. In irony and grammatical structure, this is not
unlike Chu-ko's retort, "Chün i wo wei hsiang-chi chih hsi-sheng hu?"

34. *SK*, chap. 37, p. 221. Mao Tsung-kang has admirably shortened the
speech as given in *SKTSYI, ts'e* 8, pp. 20a–21b. The last two sentences
of that speech, however, are Mao's addition.

35. In Ch'en Shou's biography (*Shu shu, chüan* 5) Chu-ko Liang is
praised as a conscientious administrator who metes out rewards and
punishments in strict accordance with justice but is deplored for his
lack of success in military campaigns. Cf. *San kuo chih*, IV, 934. In his
preface to *SKTSYI* (I, "Hsü," p. 5a) Chiang Ta-ch'i especially praises
the loyalty (*chung*) of Chu-ko, which "shines like the sun and stars."

36. *SK*, chap. 83, p. 496.

37. *SK*, chap. 84, p. 498.

38. *SK*, chap. 1, p. 3.

39. *SK*, chap. 85, pp. 504–5. The saying of Tseng Tzu is recorded in *The
Analects,* Bk. VIII, chap. 4.

40. According to the novel, after Ma Shu has involved Chu-ko Liang in
a major defeat, the latter is forced to adopt the boldest stratagem of his
entire career for self-preservation, thereby scoring a great personal victory
over his enemy Ssu-ma I. This episode (chaps. 95–96) is the source of
a popular Peking opera called *K'ung-ch'eng chi.*

41. *SK*, chap. 18, p. 110

42. In his biography of Hsia-hou Tun (*San kuo chih, chüan* 9), Ch'en
Shou merely states that his left eye is blinded by an arrow during a
campaign against Lü Pu. According to *San-kuo-chih p'ing-hua* (*Ch'üan-
hsiang p'ing-hua wu-chung,* V, 396), it was Lü Pu who shot this arrow:
"Hsia-hou Tun fell from his horse and pulled the arrow out. Hsia-hou
[said], 'This is the essence of my father and blood of my mother: I
cannot throw it away (*Fu-ching mu-hsüeh pu-k'o ch'i-chih*).' He then
swallowed the eye, mounted the horse, and fought again. Lü Pu said,
'This is indeed an extraordinary man!' Lü Pu suffered a great defeat."
Lo Kuan-chung retains the speech but invents the circumstances of the
battle which we have seen reproduced in the translation (*SKTSYI, ts'e*
4, pp. 52a–52b). Mao Tsung-kang has substituted the particle *yeh* for
the last character in Hsia-hou's speech.

43. See Burton Watson, *Early Chinese Literature* (New York, Columbia
University Press, 1962), pp. 56–62.

44. *SK*, chap. 49, pp. 284–85. According to *SKTSYI, ts'e* 10, p. 28a,
Ts'ao Ts'ao gives the banquet on the fifteenth of the eleventh month,
the thirteenth year of Chien-an (A.D. 208). This is the logical date since

the Battle of Red Cliff takes place in the winter of that year. Mao Tsung-kang has unaccountably placed the banquet a year earlier. This error has been corrected in the one-volume edition of *San-kuo yen-i* prepared by Tso-chia ch'u-pan-she (1955), though it remained uncorrected in its initial, two-volume edition of 1953.

The song of Ts'ao Ts'ao is entitled "Tuan-ko hsing." Both Lo Kuan-chung and Mao Tsung-kang have quoted a popular version of the poem with lines 11–12 missing; the Tso-chia ch'u-pan-she edition has restored these lines. Lines 13–16 are a quotation from a poem in *Shih ching* entitled "Lu ming"; for a translation of this poem see Arthur Waley, *The Book of Songs* (New York, Grove Press, 1960), p. 192. I have deliberately mistranslated l. 26 (*Wu ch'üeh nan fei*) as "Black crows fly south" to suit the dramatic context. It ought to be rendered "Crows and magpies fly south." When detached from the present context, crows and magpies actually symbolize in the poem men of worth in quest of a lord under whom they can properly exercise their talents. Or, according to Yü Kuan-ying, they refer to the common people wandering in a homeless state. Cf. *Wei-Chin Nan-pei-ch'ao wen-hsüeh-shih ts'an-k'ao tzu-liao* (Peking, Chung-hua shu-chü, 1962), I, 17.

Judging by the Mao Tsung-kang version alone, it is difficult to tell whether only a single crow or many crows are flying south. I have rendered Ts'ao Ts'ao's question, *Tz'u-ya yuan-ho yeh-ming*, as "Why are the crows cawing at night?" though *tz'u* is a demonstrative adjective and pronoun equivalent in meaning to "this." However, the corresponding text of *SKTSYI* has earlier referred to *ch'ün-ya* (crows), and I have adopted the plural form accordingly.

45. But already in the Northern Sung period Su Shih links Ts'ao Ts'ao's song with the celebrated battle. In his first *fu* on the Red Cliff (*Ch'ien Ch'ih-pi fu*) he quotes lines 25–26 from the song and then goes on to lament Ts'ao Ts'ao's mortality: "Looking down on the river winecup in hand, composing his poem with lance slung crossways, truly he was the hero of his age, but where is he now?" Cf. A. C. Graham, tr., "The Red Cliff, I," in Cyril Birch, ed., *Anthology of Chinese Literature*, pp. 381–82. I strongly suspect that Su Shih was indebted to the professional storytellers of his time for this vivid portrayal of a statesman-poet "composing his poem with lance slung crossways." On another occasion Su Shih quotes a source testifying to the extreme popularity of the story-cycle of the Three Kingdoms among city children of his time; cf. K'ung Ling-ching, ed., *Chung-kuo hsiao-shuo shih-liao*, p. 39. On the other hand, Su Shih could have invented this little scene himself, and since the *p'ing-hua* version does not include the banquet scene, it is most likely that Lo Kuan-chung was directly inspired by Su Shih's *fu* when composing that scene.

46. Cf. chap. 44. Chu-ko Liang commits a slight anachronism in citing

this poem on the eve of the Battle of Red Cliff. The poem could not have been written before the completion of the Bronze Bird Tower, which took place in the 15th year of Chien-an (A.D. 210).

47. Cf. chap. 49. In actual history southeastern winds did blow against Ts'ao Ts'ao's ships and the fire strategy was carried out with complete success. P'ei Sung-chih quotes a passage from *Chiang-piao chuan* to that effect in his comentary on the biography of Chou Yü (*San kuo chih*, V, 1263). Ssu-ma Kuang has adapted this passage in his retelling of the naval encounter and made it official history. See *Tzu-chih t'ung-chien*, V (Peking, Chung-hua shu-chü, 1956), 2093.

48. *HSWT*, II, 474.

49. The battle of Kuan-tu takes place in chap. 30. But the preparations for the battle and the subsequent disintegration of Yuan Shao's forces and contention among his sons take up chaps. 24–26, 27, and 31–33.

50. *SK*, chap. 24, pp. 144–45. The corresponding passage in *SKTSYI* (*ts'e* 5, pp. 46a–47a) is much longer and less effective.

51. *San kuo chih* (*Wei shu, chüan* 6), I, 197.

52. *SK*, chap. 31, p. 185.

NOTES TO CHAPTER III: THE WATER MARGIN

1. See Richard G. Irwin, *The Evolution of a Chinese Novel: Shui-hu-chuan*, chap. 2: "Historical Foundations." Chao Ts'ung, *Chung-kuo ssu-ta hsiao-shuo chih yen-chiu*, contains a valuable appendix on Sung Chiang in history and legend, pp. 31–97.

2. Cf. Kao Yu-kung, "A Study of the Fang La Rebellion," *Harvard Journal of Asiatic Studies*, XXIV (1963), 17–63. According to Chao Ts'ung, Sung Chiang did not participate in any government campaign against Fang La.

3. The section of *Hsüan-ho i-shih* about Sung Chiang and his band has been translated in Irwin, pp. 26–31. Though this anonymous work has received scholarly attention primarily as the earliest source on the Liangshan band in the colloquial language, its literary-language sections containing material adapted or copied from such historical sources as *Nan-chin chi-wen* and *Ch'ieh-fen lu* strike me as more interesting.

4. Traditional plays about the Liangshan heroes have been collected in *Shui-hu hsi-ch'ü chi* (2 vols.). Vol. 1, edited by Fu Hsi-hua and others, contains fifteen *tsa-chü* of the Yuan, Ming, and Ch'ing periods; Vol. 2, edited by Fu Hsi-hua, contains six Ming *ch'uan-ch'i* plays. For a listing

of all known *tsa-chü* about the Liangshan heroes, including those whose titles alone have survived, see Ho Hsin, *Shui-hu yen-chiu,* chap. 1.

5. Cf. Ho Hsin, chap. 2, and sec. 4 of "*Shui-hu-chuan* ti yen-hua," in *CWY,* I.

6. The supposition that Shih Nai-an was the author of *Shui-hu-chuan* dies hard. In the thirties two biographical documents in support of Shih's authorship were discovered. On the strength of this evidence, Irwin tentatively ascribes the first written version of the novel to the joint authorship of Shih and Lo Kuan-chung (Irwin, p. 51). But in chap. 2 of his study Ho Hsin has conclusively demonstrated the spurious character of these documents. Even though Shih and Lo appear as co-authors on the title page of the variorum edition of *Shui-hu ch'üan-chuan* (1954), in his preface Cheng Chen-to refers only to the "original version by Shih Nai-an" and makes no mention of Lo. In nearly all other modern reprints of the novel Shih Nai-an appears as sole author.

7. Richard G. Irwin notes 230 instances in which the Kuo Hsün text differs from the 100-chapter edition with a preface by T'ien-tu wai-ch'en (the basic text reprinted in *Shui-hu ch'üan-chuan*) and believes that five other extant 100-chapter editions of the late Ming "derive, not direct from the Kuo Hsün text, but via the T'ien-tu wai-ch'en" ("Water Margin Revisited," *T'oung Pao,* XLVIII, 397). It is upon Cheng Chen-to's authority that the 5-chapter fragment is believed to be part of the Kuo Hsün edition. Sun K'ai-ti believes that the fragment is of slightly later date ("Water Margin Revisited," pp. 394–95), while Ho Hsin thinks that it represents a version older than the Kuo Hsün text—the prototype of the so-called shorter text. For his reasons see *Shui-hu yen-chiu,* pp. 29–32.

8. For an examination of Chin Sheng-t'an's motives and methods as editor, see Irwin, pp. 87–94. Chin has come under strong attack in Communist China for his truncation and revision of the novel as well as for his critical commentary. See especially Ho Man-tzu, *Lun Chin Sheng-t'an p'ing-kai Shui-hu-chuan.* For a listing of all important editions of the novel preceding that of Chin Sheng-t'an, see the section on *Shui-hu chuan* in Sun K'ai-ti, *Chung-kuo t'ung-su hsiao-shuo shu-mu* (rev. ed., 1958).

9. *CWY,* I, 139. Lu Hsün gives his views on the shorter text in *Chung-kuo hsiao-shuo shih-lüeh,* pp. 176, 182–83.

10. Hu Shih opposes Lu Hsün's view in his preface to *SH,* subsequently collected in *HSWT,* III. Sun K'ai-ti agrees with Hu Shih in his comments on various editions of the novel in *Jih-pen Tung-ching so-chien Chung-kuo hsiao-shuo shu-mu t'i-yao* and *Chung-kuo t'ung-su hsiao-shuo shu-mu.* In *Shui-hu yen-chiu,* chap. 3, Ho Hsin adduces proof to show

that the 115-chapter novel reproduces in the main an earlier text than the 100-chapter version; see also chaps. 4-5. In his review of Ho Hsin's book (*Tsing Hua Journal of Chinese Studies* [New Series] I, No. 2), Tien-yi Li lists many Ming editions of the shorter version available in the libraries of Japan which the author ought to have examined before claiming that the 115-chapter text represents the earliest version of the novel. Professor Li withholds judgment concerning Ho Hsin's claim but is on the whole more sympathetic to the majority opinion of Hu Shih, Sun K'ai-ti, *et al*. For Liu Ts'un-yan's works on *Hsi-yu chi,* see chap. 4, n. 16, and the accompanying main text.

11. Irwin, *The Evolution of a Chinese Novel,* p. 74.

12. See, for example, Irwin, pp. 72-74, and *CWY,* I, 123-37, 145-48.

13. I have examined a badly printed edition of *Hsiu-hsiang Han-Sung ch'i-shu* (Illustrated astounding chronicles of the Han and Sung) (n.d., but certainly of the Ch'ing period) available in the East Asian Library of Columbia University. Printed from woodblocks in the possession of Wei-ching-t'ang, it bears the additional title, *Ying-hsiung p'u,* and reproduces the texts of the Mao Tsung-kang version of *San kuo* and the 115-chapter *Chung-i shui-hu chuan.* Though it reprints Hsiung Fei's preface to *Ying-hsiung p'u,* its *Shui hu* text may or may not be identical with that of the Hsiung-fei-t'ang edition of *Ying-hsiung p'u* dating from the Ch'ung-chen period (1628-43).

While the edition which I consulted is full of misprints and cannot be used for serious textual study, a comparison of its *Shui-hu* text with the fuller version still proves revealing. For instance, in chapter 2 of the shorter version, after the military coach Wang Chin has been forced to leave the capital with his mother, they stay one night with the Shih family. They arrive late in the evening and meet only Shih the Elder. The next morning, when he is about to leave the place, Wang Chin sees a youth exercising with a staff and casually remarks about his inexpertness. The youth becomes enraged. Then Shih the Elder arrives on the scene, introduces his son Shih Chin to his guest, and persuades the latter to stay on to coach him. In the 100-chapter version, however, Wang Chin's mother becomes ill on the night she arrives at the Shih house, and Wang Chin has to remain for five or seven days to attend her. Then the author returns to the story that has been given above. But if Wang Chin had stayed in the house for a week or so, he would soon have been introduced to Shih Chin; in the fuller version, it appears odd, therefore, that they should have remained perfect strangers during all that time, while in the shorter version it is quite natural that they should have been introduced in this dramatic manner. If one believes the shorter version to be an earlier text traceable to Lo Kuan-chung, then it would seem quite natural for the compiler of the 100-chapter version to have elaborated on an episode to the detriment of logic. Cf. *Shui-hu ch'üan-chuan*, I, 22–24.

14. Ho Hsin, pp. 46–48, lists eleven such instances of discrepancy between the 115-chapter and the fuller versions. The most telling instance (no. 5) concerns Lin Ch'ung and his wife. Like Wang Chin, Lin Ch'ung is a military coach serving under the commander of the Imperial Bodyguard, Kao Ch'iu. Kao's adopted son covets Lin's wife but is repeatedly foiled in his attempt to seduce her. To facilitate his son's success, Kao Ch'iu sets a trap into which Lin Ch'ung duly falls. He is convicted of a serious crime and sentenced to exile. Before going to serve his term, Lin meets Mr. Chang, his father-in-law, in a tavern and tells of his decision to divorce his wife. According to the 115-chapter version, he writes a bill of divorcement forthwith (in the fuller version he dictates to a scribe). At that juncture (115-chapter version, chap. 7), Lin's wife arrives on the scene with her maid, cries bitterly over the news, asks her husband to take care of himself in a most solemn manner, and then departs. Soon afterwards, the maid returns to the tavern with the news that her mistress has hanged herself. Lin and Chang both cry until they faint away. Upon regaining consciousness, however, Lin immediately departs with two yamen officers to begin serving his term of exile, leaving Chang to take care of the burial of his daughter. In chap. 8 of the 120-chapter version, Lin's wife comes to the tavern, faints away upon seeing the bill of divorcement, and is taken home by her father. In chap. 20, after Lin Ch'ung has already become a chieftain at Liangshan, he sends two men to fetch his wife. They return two months later with the report that she has hanged herself six months earlier when forced to marry Kao's son. In view of the pronounced misogyny of the novel, a topic which I will take up later, it seems most likely that the story of Mrs. Lin's suicide as given in the 115-chapter novel represents the original Lo Kuan-chung version whereas the editor of the 100-chapter version has revised the episode to make Lin Ch'ung a more sympathetic character just as he has introduced small changes elsewhere to make Kao Ch'iu more villainous. Cf. Ho Hsin, pp. 66–67.

In *The Chinese Knight-Errant*, pp. 114–16, Professor James J. Y. Liu takes me to task for being over-moralistic in my dissection of the novel's sadism and misogyny in the paper "Comparative Approaches to *Water Margin*." I agree with Professor Liu that no critic should condemn a work of literature simply because it endorses a system of morals differing from his own, and I am sorry that my paper, liable to misunderstanding in its truncated form, has given my esteemed colleague the impression that I have ignored literary values to give vent to my "moral indignation against the *Water Margin* heroes" (p. 115). (The paper reproduces only the portions actually read at a literary conference sponsored by Indiana University in 1962. A Chinese translation of the original version, which is almost twice as long, has subsequently appeared in *Hsien-tai Wen-hsüeh*, No. 26, under the title "*Shui-hu-chuan ti tsai-p'ing-chia.*" It has regrettably escaped Professor Liu's attention.) However, even in the truncated paper, I stated unambiguously that one of my tasks is to "examine the moral substance of the novel as against its noble professions of morality" (*Yearbook of Comparative and General Literature*, No. 11, p. 124). In view of "the novel's unquestioned importance within its native tradition," it was also my intention "to seek a renewal of understanding in the context of world masterpieces" (*ibid.*, p. 121). While I may not have succeeded in my task, I should think that to examine the moral substance of a work in a comparative fashion constitutes a legitimate aim of literary criticism and is not quite the same thing as indulging in moral indignation. If my findings prove disturbing, it is probably because we (I am referring to readers like Professor Liu and myself, who have taken delight in the novel since childhood days) have been so accustomed to equate its moral worth with the Liangshan heroes' noble professions of morality that it is difficult for us to reconcile ourselves to an objective view of their actual atrocities.

To counterbalance the cumulative weight of sadism and misogyny in the novel, Professor Liu cites Lin Ch'ung as a shining example of humanity—the very antithesis of "a sadistic misogynist" (p. 116). However, in the original version of my paper, I have not ignored the case of Lin Ch'ung, admittedly the most sympathetic hero in the novel. I now quote the relevant paragraph; the Chinese text appears in *Hsien-tai Wen-hsüeh*, No. 26, p. 16:

"Lin Ch'ung may seem an exceptional case in that he does care for his wife and is aggrieved over assaults on her honor. Yet, prior to his exile as a convict, he does the unusual thing in demanding a divorce, which hurts his virtuous wife far more deeply than the insults from Kao Ch'iu's son. Ostensibly, this divorce is for her protection so that she may remarry rather than waste her youth pining for his return. But would a man truly in love with his wife subject her to the humiliation of a divorce? Wouldn't he hope for a reunion while hope remains? Doesn't the action rather indicate that, in his bitterness over his misfortune, Lin Ch'ung unconsciously blames his wife for all his troubles and, in doing so, acquires the callousness of a true *hao-han* (good fellow)? It is significant that in the 115-chapter version of the novel the wife immediately hangs herself after receiving the news, though in the 120-chapter version the compiler has managed to retain our sympathy for Lin Ch'ung by placing her suicide at a later date, as a consequence of increasing pressure from Kao Ch'iu's son. But the story in the 115-chapter version may be more faithful to the oral tradition because it is more consonant with the pervasive misogyny of the Liangshan legends."

15. In addition to *San kuo* and *Shui hu*, Lo Kuan-chung is also credited

with the authorship of several works of historical fiction, such as *Sui-T'ang-chih chuan, San-Sui p'ing-yao chuan,* and *Ts'an-T'ang wu-tai-shih yen-chuan.* With the possible exception of the last title, which survives in a crude version unworthy of Lo, all the others are no longer extant because they were revised or rewritten by later authors. Thus Ch'u Jen-hu's *Sui-T'ang yen-i,* an early Ch'ing work, is ultimately traceable to *Sui-T'ang-chih chuan;* for a succinct summary of the development of the novel see *HSWT,* IV, 413–16. Until chap. 69, the 100-chapter *Sui-T'ang yen-i* tells the absorbing story of Li Shih-min (T'ang T'ai-tsung) and his followers. Many of the latter are quite memorable; Ch'in Shu-pao, especially, is given far more psychological attention than any of the warrior heroes in either *San kuo* or *Shui hu.* For further information on Lo Kuan-chung see Irwin, *The Evolution of a Chinese Novel,* pp. 48–49, and the relevant notes.

16. Ch'ai Jung is a popular hero in the story-cycle about the Five Dynasties period, though the extant fragment of *Hsin-pien wu-tai-shih p'ing-hua* (Newly compiled *p'ing-hua* of the history of the Five Dynasties) has left his story in an incomplete state. Ch'ai Jung also figures importantly in *Fei-lung ch'üan-chuan,* a novel of Chao K'uang-yin, the founding emperor of the Sung. Hu-yen Tsan, the hero of the novel *Shuo Hu ch'üan-chuan,* also appears in the novels about the Yang family referred to in chap. 1, n. 50.

17. In *The Chinese Knight-Errant,* p. 115, Professor James J. Y. Liu questions my application of the term "pseudo history" to *Shui hu* mainly on the evidence that "stories about *Water Margin* heroes were clearly classified as 'fiction proper' (*hsiao-shuo*) and not 'popularization of history' (*chiang-shih*) in Sung times." His main authority is Lo Yeh's *Tsui-weng t'an-lu* (see chap. 1, n. 20), which names at least four Liangshan heroes—Sun Li, Yang Chih, Wu Sung, Lu Chih-shen—as subjects for professional reciters of short stories (*hsiao-shuo*). But *Tsui-weng t'an-lu,* most probably a Southern Sung compilation, refers to a much earlier stage in the development of the legend, when storytellers were able to recite only a relatively small number of independent tales about the Liangshan heroes. By the time Lo Kuan-chung composed his version of *Shui hu,* there must have existed a long oral story-cycle about the Liangshan heroes in which stories dating from the Southern Sung and classified by Lo Yeh under such labels as *kung-an* (crime cases), *p'u-tao* (swords), and *kan-pang* (clubs) were integrated with military episodes of later invention concerned with the collective deeds of the band. Thus, while the early chapters of *Shui hu* retain the picaresque form of individual sagas, the later chapters increasingly suggest a military romance written in imitation of other historical romances of a military character. From the band's open confrontation with government forces in chapter 52 to the completion of its expedition against Fang La,

the novel certainly moves in the realm of pseudo history and retains little of its earlier strength as picaresque fiction. Although, in both my paper "Comparative Approaches to *Water Margin*" and the present chapter, I have for convenience designated historical romances by the term *yen-i*, actually the term *chuan* is equally applicable. Thus, among the romances attributed to Lo Kuan-chung (see n. 15), we find *Shui-hu chuan, San-Sui p'ing-yao chuan*, and *Sui-T'ang-chih chuan*. Subsequent romances labeled *chuan* are too numerous to mention here. The absence of the label *yen-i* from the title of *Shui-hu chuan*, therefore, does not mean that its composition was not "conditioned by the 'unquestioned supremacy of the historical mode of storytelling,'" as Professor Liu would have us believe.

Moreover, unlike earlier Sung sources, *Tsui-weng t'an-lu* seems to have applied the term *hsiao-shuo* to all types of storytelling. In a headnote to his introductory section Lo Yeh states that what he has to say about reciters of *hsiao-shuo* applies also to narrators of history (*yen-shih*) and expounders of Buddhist sutras (*chiang-ching*). In the all-important second section entitled "Hsiao-shuo k'ai-p'i," he seems to have further blurred the distinction between *hsiao-shuo* and *yen-shih*. Thus, with reference to a storyteller's training, he says, "While young, he should study *T'ai-p'ing kuang-chi;* when older, he should apply himself to a perusal of the histories of successive dynasties." Cf. *Tsui-weng t'an-lu* (Taipei, Shih-chieh shu-chü, 1958), p. 3. To gain a comprehensive knowledge of history would seem to be as essential to his preparation as to memorize the contents of an immense story collection. Literary historians have understandably paid great attention to over a hundred topics listed under eight categories of short stories in the section, but Lo Yeh himself does not say that these topics are exclusively *hsiao-shuo* while the more historical topics—the Three Kingdoms and Six Dynasties periods, Liu Pang, Hsiang Yü, Huang Ch'ao, Ti Ch'ing, etc.—are not. It is only by reference to other sources that scholars have distinguished the eight types of *hsiao-shuo* from other types of storytelling mentioned in the section.

Several *hsiao-shuo* topics, however, were eventually written down as historical romances during the Ming. Thus "Fei-lung chi" (The story of the flying dragon) is most certainly about the founder of the Sung dynasty and may have been the prototype for the novel *Fei-lung ch'üan-chuan*, also about that emperor. Yang Yeh and his fifth son, both listed as *hsiao-shuo* topics, are celebrated in two Ming novels (see chap. 1, n. 50). Like the Liangshan legend, the legend of the Yang family must have begun as a series of independent short stories and eventually grown into a story-cycle of considerable size.

18. In chap. 98, Chang Ch'ing goes to the enemy camp in the guise of a physician's brother and marries Ch'iung-ying, the foster daughter

of Wu Li, the rebel T'ien Hu's uncle. Both Chang and Ch'iung-ying
throw pellets with deadly precision and their marriage is foretold in
dreams. In many historical romances a handsome young general marries
a beautiful female warrior of the enemy camp. Thus Hsüeh Ting-shan,
Hsüeh Jen-kuei's son, marries Fan Li-hua in *Shuo T'ang cheng-hsi
chuan* and Ti Ch'ing marries Princess Sai-hua in *Wu-hu p'ing-hsi*.

19. This episode takes place in chap. 18. Cf. Chin Sheng-t'an's general
commentary on chap. 17 in *Chin Sheng-t'an ch'i-shih-i-hui-pen Shui-hu-
chuan, ts'e 7, chüan* 22. From his point of view Sung Chiang's failure to
arrest Ch'ao Kai is of decisive relevance to our understanding of his character: "If Sung Chiang were really loyal and just, then he could not let
Ch'ao Kai go but, since he does, then he cannot be called loyal and just."

20. In chap. 46.

21. For instance, in chap. 32, after he has been captured by three highwaymen and is about to be disemboweled, Sung Chiang happens to
mention his name and he is immediately loosed and treated as an honored guest.

22. Wang Ying is one of the three highwaymen referred to in n. 21.
When informed of his weakness, Sung Chiang immediately remarks,
"I didn't know that Brother Wang lusts after women. This is not the
way of a *hao-han*" (*SH*, VI, p. 32). Wang Ying is married to Hu San-
niang in chap. 50.

23. This incident takes place at the end of chap. 38.

24. Translated from *SH*, II, chap. 4, pp. 17-20. The corresponding translation by Pearl S. Buck appears in *All Men Are Brothers*, I, 82–85.

25. Though fishermen by trade, the three Juan brothers also engage in
smuggling and gambling so that they are by no means law-abiding
peasants helpless under government oppression. When Wu Yung comes
to them to secure their assistance in the plot against the birthday convoy
in chap. 15, the brothers complain primarily of the gang of bad men at
Liang-shan-po who have blocked their access to the best fishing waters
and only secondarily of the government (because it would be too much
bother and, indeed, financially ruinous to try to regain their fishing
rights with governmental assistance). The episode of "The Plot Against
the Birthday Convoy" (chaps. 14–16) has been newly translated by Cyril
Birch in his *Anthology of Chinese Literature*, pp. 451–87.

26. *SH*, VII, chap. 34, p. 15.

27. This episode takes place in chap. 51.

28. The Liangshan band attacks Chu-chia-chuang in chaps. 46–50 and
Tseng-t'ou-shih in chaps. 60 and 68.

29. *SH*, VI, chap. 31, pp. 42–44. Cf. also *Shui-hu ch'üan-chuan*, II,

476–78, and the accompanying notes for minor textual discrepancies among various editions. In l. 7 (*SH*, VI, 44), the third character from the top, *huai* (*Mathews' Dictionary*, No. 2233), is obviously a misprint for the third form of *shuan* (*Mathews'*, No. 5914)—the form adopted in the 70-chapter version—and I have translated accordingly. When Wu Sung goes through the back door to get his sword, its location is not specified in the translated text. Earlier in the chapter we are informed that, before Wu Sung uses his dagger to push open the kitchen door, he has "leaned the sword" (*i-le p'u-tao*), most certainly against the outer wall by the kitchen door. Upon entering the kitchen, he forthwith kills the two maids there, and in his eagerness to get to his enemies in the Mandarin Duck Hall, he apparently forgets to take his sword with him.

30. *All Men Are Brothers*, I, 526.

31. *SH*, VIII, chap. 41, p. 48.

32. Burton Watson, tr., *Records of the Grand Historian of China*, I, 323.

33. *SH*, IX, chap. 46, pp. 48–49.

34. In view of Mao Tse-tung's high praise of Sung Chiang as a peasant rebel (see, for example, *Mao Tse-tung hsüan-chi*, II [Peking, Jen-min ch'u-pan-she, 1952], 595), it is little wonder that Communist critics have been obliged to acclaim *Shui hu* as a novel of peasant rebellion. For representative Communist criticism, see *Shui-hu yen-chiu lun-wen-chi* and Li Hsi-fan, "A Great Novel of Peasant Revolt," *Chinese Literature*, No. 12 (1959), pp. 62–71.

35. For Li Chih's appraisal of Sung Chiang see his preface to the novel in *Li-shih fen-shu* (Shanghai, Pei-yeh shan-fang, 1936), pp. 122–24. In *Shui-hu yen-chiu*, pp. 85–87, Ho Hsin gives instances of revision where Chin Sheng-t'an deliberately blackens Sung Chiang's character.

36. *SH*, VIII, chap. 41, pp. 54–55.

37. *SH*, XIII, chap. 71, pp. 58–59.

38. *Ibid.*, p. 59.

39. *SH*, XIX, chap. 110, pp. 9–10.

40. Of the four evil ministers, T'ung Kuan and Yang Chien were actually eunuchs. T'ung rose to the position of grand preceptor (*t'ai-shih*) after pacifying the Fang La Rebellion. Yang Chien ingratiated himself with Hui-tsung and rose to the position of grand tutor (*t'ai-fu*). Kao Ch'iu, a favorite of Hui-tsung while the latter was still a prince, stayed powerful during his reign. The best known of the four, Ts'ai Ching, was Hui-tsung's prime minister four times.

41. Accounts differ as to what happened to Li Shih-shih after the capital

was taken by the Chin forces. According to the Sung classical tale "Li Shih-shih wai-chuan," when the traitor Chang Pang-ch'ang sought her out with the object of presenting her to the Chin headquarters, Li Shih-shih reviled him. "And she snatched a golden hairpin from her head and thrust it violently through her throat. As she did not immediately die, she broke off the point and swallowed it. Thus she departed this life." Wolfgang Bauer and Herbert Franke, eds., *The Golden Casket,* p. 218.

42. *SH,* XX, chap. 120, pp. 86–87. The translation is by Irwin, pp. 197–98.

43. These events take place in chap. 119.

44. *SH,* XVI, chap. 93, pp. 84–85.

45. *SH,* XX, chap. 120, pp. 81–82.

NOTES TO CHAPTER IV: JOURNEY TO THE WEST

1. *"Hsi-yu-chi* k'ao-cheng" *(HSWT,* II), completed in February, 1923, combines two earlier essays on the novel. When writing the first essay in 1921, Hu Shih had not yet begun to investigate the problem of its authorship.

2. G. Dudbridge, *"Hsi-yu-chi* tsu-pen-k'ao ti tsai shang-chüeh," *Hsin-ya Hsüeh-pao,* VI, No. 2 (1964), p. 499.

3. Liu Hsiu-yeh, ed., *Wu Ch'eng-en shih-wen chi.*

4. Dudbridge *(Hsin-ya Hsüeh-pao,* VI, No. 2, p. 513) believes that an edition or editions of *Hsi yu chi* must have preceded the Shih-te-t'ang edition because in its preface Ch'en Yuan-chih refers to an "old preface" *(chiu-hsü).* But that preface may have existed only in manuscript form.

   The K'ang-hsi edition incorporating the legend of the young Tripitaka is entitled *Ku-pen Hsi-yu cheng-tao-shu.* It was prepared by Wang Tan-i, who also provides a commentary. Wang lifts the legend from the Ta-lüeh-t'ang edition of *[Hsi-yu] shih-o chuan* and redivides chaps. 9–11 of the Wu version as chaps. 10–11. While most scholars equate the Ta-lüeh-t'ang edition of *Shih-o chuan* with Chu Ting-ch'en, *T'ang San-tsang hsi-yu shih-o chuan* (see p. 122 ff), Dudbridge believes that it was an edition older than either the Shih-te-t'ang edition or the earliest extant Chu Ting-ch'en version dating from the Lung-ch'ing or Wan-li period. He further believes that the Chu version was an adaptation of the Ta-lüeh-t'ang edition but, since the latter has long been lost, he is not yet prepared to establish the exact nature of its relationship to the Shih-te-t'ang edition. Cf. *Hsin-ya Hsüeh-pao,* VI, No. 2, pp. 508-13.

5. Cf. *HYC:* "Ch'u-pan shuo-ming," pp. 1–7.

6. Arthur Waley gives an excellent biography of Hsüan-tsang in *The Real Tripitaka, and Other Pieces*. For a scholarly exposition of the Mere Ideation school, see Fung Yu-lan, *A History of Chinese Philosophy* (Princeton University Press, 1953), II, chap. 8.

7. Hsüan-tsang's account of his pilgrimage as recorded by Pien-chi is entitled *Ta-T'ang hsi-yü chi;* it has been translated in Thomas Watters, *On Yuan Chwang's Travels in India, 629–645 A.D.* (2 vols.; London, 1904–5). Hui-li depicts Hsüan-tsang's career prior to his return to Ch'ang-an in chaps. 1–5 of *Ta Tz'u-en-ssu San-tsang fa-shih chuan;* the monk Yen-ts'ung records his subsequent career in chaps. 6–10. This work is the main source for Waley, *The Real Tripitaka.*

8. Quoted in *"Hsi-yu-chi* k'ao-cheng," *HSWT,* II, 357.

9. Cf. "The Summons of the Soul" and "The Great Summons" in David Hawkes, tr., *Ch'u Tz'u: The Songs of the South* (Oxford, Clarendon Press, 1959).

10. Before Sun K'ai-ti identified the author of these plays as Yang Ching-hsien in 1939, scholars had for years accepted Hu Shih's ascription of their authorship to an earlier Yuan playwright, Wu Ch'ang-ling, whose *tsa-chü, T'ang San-tsang hsi-t'ien ch'ü-ching* (Tripitaka procures the scriptures from the western paradise), exists only in fragments. Sun's article on Yang Ching-hsien, "Wu Ch'ang-ling yü tsa-chü *Hsi-yu-chi,*" has been reprinted in *Ts'ang-chou chi,* II. Yang is known under other names, including Yang Ching-yen and ,Yang No; in *Yuan-ch'ü-hsüan wai-pien* (2 vols., Peking, Chung-hua shu-chü, 1959), a standard anthology which includes Yang's plays and all other Yuan *tsa-chü* not appearing in *Yuan-ch'ü hsüan,* however, the editor Sui Shu-sen adopts the form Yang Ching-hsien.

11. Cf. *Chung-kuo wen-hsüeh shih* (1962), III, 904–5. For additional information on *Pak t'ongsa önhae* see Yang Lien-sheng, "A Study of the Grammar and Vocabulary as Found in *Lao Ch'i-ta* and *P'u T'ung-shih,* Two Old Korean Textbooks on Colloquial Chinese," *Bulletin of the Institute of History and Philology,* XXIX (Taipei, Academia Sinica, 1957), 197–208.

12. Quoted in *CWY,* I, 270–71.

13. *Feng-shen yen-i* (Peking, Tso-chia ch'u-pan-she, 1955), I, chap. 23, p. 212. The Chinese have traditionally associated fishermen and woodcutters with an idyllic life of contemplation detached from worldly cares. The phrase *yü-ch'iao* occurs frequently in T'ang poetry. The Northern Sung philosopher Shao Yung wrote a short dialogue between a fisherman and a woodcutter entitled *Yü-ch'iao wen-tui.*

14. *HYC,* pp. 103–4.

15. *Ibid.*, pp. 104–5.

16. For learned opinions on this work, see Chao Ts'ung, *Chung-kuo ssu-ta hsiao-shuo chih yen-chiu,* chap. 3; Cheng Chen-to, "Hsi-yu-chi ti yen-hua," *CWY,* I; Dudbridge's article cited in n. 2; and the long appendix to Liu Ts'un-yan, "*Ssu-yu-chi* ti Ming k'o-pen" ("The Ming Editions of the 'Four Travels' "), *Hsin-ya Hsüeh-pao,* V, No. 2 (1963). Professor Liu's article in English, "The Prototypes of *Monkey (Hsi Yu Chi)*," *T'oung Pao,* LI, No. 1, pp. 55–71, makes the same points as his other article.

17. For information on this text, see the sources cited in n. 16. While *T'ang San-tsang hsi-yu shih-o chuan* remains a rare book (a microfilm copy is available at the Library of Congress), there have been two recent reprints of *Ssu-yu-chi* (Shanghai, 1956, and Taipei, 1958).

18. In 1931 Sun K'ai-ti located in the Cabinet Library a Ming copy of *Tung-yu chi,* with a preface by Yü Hsiang-tou. In 1957 Liu Ts'un-yan found in the British Museum a Ming copy of *Nan-yu-chih chuan* and one of *Pei-yu chi* (both compiled by Yü Hsiang-tou) as well as a fragmentary Ming copy of *Tung-yu chi.* For full bibliographical data on these editions see Liu's articles cited in n. 16. Miss Liu Hsiu-yeh had seen the British Museum copies of *Nan-yu-chih chuan* and *Pei-yu chi* before Professor Liu, but she describes them rather briefly in *Ku-tien hsiao-shuo hsi-ch'ü ts'ung-k'ao* (1958). Yü Hsiang-tou, who headed the long-established printing firm of the Yü house during the Wan-li period, also published the earliest extant shorter version of *Shui hu.*

19. *CWY,* I, 285–87.

20. Sun K'ai-ti comments on various editions of *Hsi yu chi* in *Jih-pen Tung-ching so-chien Chung-kuo hsiao-shuo shu-mu t'i-yao.* Both Liu Ts'un-yan and Dudbridge imply that Hu Shih's position is identical to Sun's in regard to the Yang and Chu texts. Hu Shih dismisses the Yang version as a careless condensation of the Wu version in his colophon to a modern reprint of that work (*HSWT,* IV), but neither in that piece nor in his longer article on *Hsi yu chi* does he mention the Chu version.

21. *Hsin-ya Hsüeh-pao,* VI (No. 2), "Abstracts in English," p. 8. I have referred to Dudbridge's article in n. 2 and Liu Ts'un-yan's articles in n. 16.

22. The immediate model for the Chu version could not have been the primitive Yuan version. In *CWY,* I, 282–83, Cheng Chen-to quotes a significant portion of the dialogue between Chang Shao and Li Ting as recorded in the Chu version. It is strikingly similar to the Wu version of the dialogue and bears no resemblance to the *Yung-lo ta-tien* version. Unless Chu was adapting Wu, we must postulate a pre-Wu version which was already highly developed and contains many passages later incorporated into the Wu text with little or no change.

23. Cf. Chao Ts'ung, *Chung-kuo ssu-ta hsiao-shuo chih yen-chiu*, pp. 172–77. See also n. 4 for fuller information on the Ta-lüeh-t'ang edition.

24. See *The Real Tripitaka*, pp. 27–29, 38-41.

25. Tripitaka's identity as the Elder Golden Cicada is repeatedly mentioned in the novel; see, for instance, chaps. 12 and 100. In chap. 27 we are for the first time informed that he has undergone ten incarnations of sexual purity.

26. Arthur Waley, *Monkey*, pp. 281-82. This passage occurs in chap. 98.

27. In his preface to *Monkey*, Waley says, "As regards the allegory, it is clear that Tripitaka stands for the ordinary man, blundering anxiously through the difficulties of life" (*Monkey*, p. 8). See also Yi-tse Mei Feuerwerker, "The Chinese Novel," in Wm. Theodore de Bary, ed., *Approaches to the Oriental Classics*, p. 178.

28. This episode takes place in chap. 19. Hsüan-tsang's translation of the Heart Sutra has superseded all earlier Chinese versions.

29. In *Buddhist Wisdom Books, Containing the Diamond Sutra and the Heart Sutra* (London, Allen and Unwin, 1958), the translator, Edward Conze, affirms the common Buddhist opinion that these two scriptures are "the holiest of the holy" among Prajnaparamita sutras. The Heart Sutra, especially, "sets out to formulate the very 'heart,' 'core' or 'essence' of perfect wisdom" (p. 10).

30. *The Real Tripitaka*, p. 98.

31. The heading for sec. 16 of *Ta-T'ang San-tsang ch'ü-ching shih-hua* is "Chuan-chih Hsiang-lin-ssu shou *Hsin-ching*" (Stopping by the fragrant grove temple to receive the Heart Sutra). In the second line of the main text, however, we are told that Tripitaka stopped by Hsiang-lin-shih (fragrant grove market). A photolithographic edition of this book was made in 1916 with a colophon by Lo Chen-yü.

32. *Ibid.*, sec. 16.

33. Cf. George Steiner, *Tolstoy or Dostoevsky: An Essay in the Old Criticism* (New York, Knopf, 1959), pp. 58–59, 300–5.

34. Conze, *Buddhist Wisdom Books*, p. 81.

35. *HYC*, chap. 43, pp. 494–95.

36. *HYC*, chap. 93, p. 1051.

37. This episode takes place in chap. 14. Cf. *Monkey*, pp. 131–37.

38. Cf. chaps. 27–28, 56–57.

39. *HSWT*, II, 370–72.

40. *CWY*, I, 290–93. One of the tales referred to by Cheng Chen-to is the T'ang *ch'uan-ch'i*, "Pu Chiang Tsung pai-yuan chuan," translated

under the title "The White Monkey" in Chi-chen Wang, *Traditional Chinese Tales*.

41. See, for example, Feng Yuan-chün, "P'i-p'an Hu Shih ti 'Hsi-yu-chi k'ao-cheng,'" in *Hu Shih ssu-hsiang p'i-p'an*, VII, pp. 332–43. This essay attacks Hu Shih for three things: 1) his theory of the Indian origin of Monkey; 2) his appraisal of *Hsi-yu-chi* as a book of playful humor little concerned with the social and political reality of its author's time; 3) his wrong attribution of *Hsi-yu-chi tsa-chü* to Wu Ch'ang-ling. The repudiation of Hu Shih is implicit in all the essays collected in *Hsi-yu-chi yen-chiu lun-wen chi*.

42. Wu Hsiao-ling, "'Hsi-yu-chi' ho 'Lo-mo-yen-shu'" (*Hsi-yu-chi* and *The Ramayana*), *Wen-hsüeh Yen-chiu* (Studies in literature) (No. 1, 1958), pp. 163–69.

43. *Monkey,* pp. 67–68 (*HYC,* chap. 6).

44. Richard F. Burton, tr., *The Arabian Nights' Entertainment* (New York, The Modern Library, 1932), p. 98.

45. In "Sun Wu-k'ung ho ch'i-shih-erh pien" (Monkey and his seventy-two transformations), an article published in the *Chung-yang Fu-k'an* page of the Taipei *Central Daily News*, June 13–14, 1965, Chou Yen-mou cites a few familiar instances of transformation from pre-T'ang literature but many more stories of this type from T'ang literature. The author is certainly right in believing that the greater influx of foreigners from Central Asia during the T'ang had enriched the Chinese imagination.

46. *Monkey,* p. 14 (*HYC,* chap. 1).

47. He tries to melt down Monkey in chap. 7.

48. Cf. Chang T'ien-i, "*Hsi-yu-chi* cha-chi" (Notes on *Hsi-yu-chi*), *Hsi-yu-chi yen-chiu lun-wen chi*. It originally appeared in *Jen-min Wen-hsüeh,* February, 1954.

49. Most essays collected in *Hsi-yu-chi yen-chiu lun-wen chi* express this view. In "Shih-lun 'Hsi-yu-chi' ti chu-t'i ssu-hsiang" (A tentative discussion of the central theme of *Hsi-yu-chi*), for instance, T'ung Ssu-kao maintains on p. 61, "The demons and monsters are not only subordinate to gods and Buddhas; they are their direct instruments for the oppression and control of the people."

50. These commentators were certainly influenced by the chapter headings of the novel, which repeatedly refer to Monkey as *hsin yuan* or Mind-Monkey. In his preface to the Shih-te-t'ang edition, Ch'en Yuan-chih refers to an older preface which expounds the allegorical meaning of the names of the pilgrims, including Tripitaka's horse, who is in reality a dragon prince. Cf. *CWY,* I, 274. In view of the early date of this

nonextant preface, modern scholars are certainly unjustified in maintaining that later commentators have arbitrarily read allegorical meanings into Wu's novel.

51. *HYC*, chap. 35, p. 409.

52. *HYC*, chap. 56, p. 649.

53. *HYC*, chap. 27, p. 313.

54. *HYC*, chaps. 27–28, pp. 313–15. Since I translated the passage, Yang Hsien-yi and Gladys Yang have published their complete translation of chap. 27 in *Chinese Literature*, No. 5 (1966). I have omitted from my translation a poem on the ocean and a few sentences serving to link the two chapters.

55. "Introduction to the American Edition," *Monkey*, p. 5.

56. Many essays in *Hsi-yu-chi yen-chiu lun-wen chi* stress Wu Ch'eng-en's role as a political satirist; see, for instance, Shen Jen-k'ang, " 'Hsi-yu-chi' shih-lun" (A tentative critique of *Hsi-yu-chi*). Among non-Communist critics, Li Ch'en-tung also adopts the political approach to the novel in "Hsi-yu-chi ti chia-chih" (The value of *Hsi-yu-chi*), which is one of the prefatory essays in *Hsi-yu-chi* (Taipei, Shih-chieh shu-chü, 1964). It is true that once an evil minister and his clique had suffered imperial punishment and fallen from power, it would have been possible for Ming storytellers and playwrights to excoriate their misdeeds. Thus the *ch'uan-ch'i* play, *Ming-feng chi,* attributed to Wang Shih-chen, and the *San-yen* story *Shen Hsiao-hsia hsiang-hui ch'u-shih-piao* (translated as "A Just Man Avenged" in Yang Hsien-yi and Gladys Yang, trs., *The Courtesan's Jewel Box*) alike celebrate upright men suffering persecution from and putting up resistance to Yen Sung and his son Yen Shih-fan, both evil ministers enjoying great power during the Chia-ching reign. But explicit denunciation of a deceased and discredited minister is something quite different from veiled satire of a minister or eunuch still enjoying imperial favor. The latter type of satire is extremely rare in Ming fiction.

57. For example, in chap. 47 Monkey advises the ruler of the Cart-Slow Kingdom to revere the three teachings, "Never again follow false doctrines nor follow foolish courses, but know that the Three Religions are one. Reverence priests, reverence Taoists too, and cultivate the faculties of man" (*Monkey*, p. 248).

58. Cf. William K. Wimsatt, Jr., and Cleanth Brooks, *Literary Criticism: A Short History* (New York, Knopf, 1957), chap. 31: "Myth and Archetype"; and Northrop Frye, *Anatomy of Criticism* (Princeton University Press, 1957).

59. *Feng-shen yen-i,* chaps. 12–14. Cf. Liu Ts'un-yan, *Buddhist and*

Taoist Influences on Chinese Novels. Vol. I. *The Authorship of the Feng Shen Yen I*, chap. 11: "The Story of Vaisravana and Nata."

60. *HYC*, chaps. 37–39; *Monkey*, chaps. 19–21.

61. *HYC*, chaps. 44–46; *Monkey*, chaps. 22–24.

62. *HYC*, chaps. 47–49; *Monkey*, chaps. 25–27. Hsi-men Pao of the Warring States period put a stop to the practice of sacrificing girls to Ho Po (Lord of the Yellow River) at Yeh. Cf. *Shih chi, chüan* 126.

63. This episode takes place in chaps. 78–79.

64. *HYC*, chap. 31, pp. 359–60.

65. *HYC*, chap. 30, pp. 340–41. My translation omits a poetic passage describing the fright of the palace girls.

66. *HYC*, chap. 60, p. 686.

67. *HYC*, chap. 79, p. 906.

68. *HYC*, chap. 64, p. 738.

69. *HYC*, chap. 64, p. 740.

70. *HYC*, chap. 77, pp. 888–89. The bird monster bears the name Yün-ch'eng wan-li-p'eng. But when he is reduced to his original shape by Buddha, he is described as a *ta-p'eng chin-ch'ih tiao*, which is the standard Chinese name for the bird-shaped creature in Hindu and Buddhist mythology known as the Garuda. Cf. Liu Ts'un-yan, *Buddhist and Taoist Influences on Chinese Novels*, I, 173–74.

71. Pigsy tells of his past in chaps. 8 and 19 (*HYC*, pp. 85, 212–13).

72. *HYC*, chap. 8, p. 83.

73. Cf. the essays "The Angelic Imagination" and "Our Cousin, Mr. Poe" in Allen Tate, *The Man of Letters in the Modern World* (New York, Meridian Books, 1955). "Poe's heroines—Berenice, Ligeia, Madeline, Morella, with the curious exception of the abstemious Eleanora—are ill-disguised vampires; his heroes become necromancers (in the root meaning of the word) whose wills, like the heroines' wills, defy the term of life to keep them equivocally 'alive'" (p. 115).

74. This quotation from Joseph Glanvill forms part of the epigraph to the story "Ligeia."

75. *HYC*, chap. 18, p. 210. The first four sentences are from *Monkey*, p. 151. The passage which I have translated as "enjoy fresh fruit all the four seasons" reads in Chinese *Ssu-shih yu hua-kuo hsiang-yung*. The editors of *HYC* have most probably adopted this reading from the Shih-te-t'ang edition since in the corresponding passage of other modern reprints of the novel the verb phrase *hsiang-yung* is replaced by *kuan-wan*. The passage should then be translated as "enjoy the view of flow-

ers and fruits all the four seasons." Presumably, Pigsy's wife could enjoy the view of flowers and fruits either in their natural state in the garden or after they have been picked and placed inside the house.

76. *Monkey*, p. 153.

77. *Monkey*, p. 158 (*HYC*, chap. 19).

78. *HYC*, chap. 75, p. 864. Pigsy is aware, of course, that the horse is a dragon prince in disguise (see n. 50) and understands human speech. To treat him as if he were a mere beast of burden adds another comic touch to Pigsy's speech.

79. *Monkey*, p. 253.

80. This episode takes place in chaps. 24–26.

81. *HYC*, chap. 67, pp. 768–69.

82. J. M. Cohen, tr., *The Histories of Gargantua and Pantagruel* (Baltimore, Penguin Books, 1955), p. 524.

83. *HYC*, chap. 95, p. 1076.

84. *HYC*, chap. 23, p. 260.

85. *Ch'ien-ma* (to lead a horse) also means "to act as a matchmaker, to bring about an assignation or liaison between a man and a woman." Cf. *HYC*, p. 268, n. 16.

86. To pelt the bed curtains (*sa-chang*) forms part of the traditional Chinese wedding ceremony. See "Marriage Songs" in Waley, *Ballads and Stories from Tun-huang*, pp. 189–201. However, according to the story "K'uai-tsui Li Ts'ui-lien chi" (The sharp-tongued Li Ts'ui-lien), which gives a detailed account of a wedding, the bed curtains are pelted with five kinds of grain rather than "coins and balls of colored silk." This story appears in *Ch'ing-p'ing-shan-t'ang hua-pen*.

87. *HYC*, chap. 23, pp. 261–66.

88. See H. C. Chang, *Allegory and Courtesy in Spenser* (Edinburgh University Press, 1955), chap. 3: "Allegory and the Theme of Temptation: A Comparative Study."

89. Pigsy shares a bath with seven spider-spirits in chap. 72.

NOTES TO CHAPTER V: CHIN P'ING MEI

1. On the dedication page Lao She (Lau Shaw) is given his real name C. C. Shu, which stands for Shu Ch'ing-ch'un. Egerton acknowledges his debt to Lao She in the translator's note.

2. Kuhn's version was first published in Leipzig in 1930. Bernard

Miall's retranslation entitled *Chin P'ing Mei: The Adventurous History of Hsi Men and His Six Wives* (1940) is now available as a paperback.

3. Among the special studies to which Hanan is indebted are Feng Yuan-chün, "*Chin P'ing Mei tz'u-hua* chung ti wen-hsüeh shih-liao," *Ku-chü shuo-hui,* and Wu Han, "*Chin P'ing Mei* ti chu-tso shih-tai chi ch'i she-hui pei-ching," *Tu-shih cha-chi.* Hanan has also contributed a critical article on *Chin P'ing Mei* to Douglas Grant and Millar Mac-Lure, eds., *The Far East: China and Japan.*

4. Cf. Cheng Chen-to's representative opinion in "T'an *Chin P'ing Mei tz'u-hua,*" *CWY,* I.

5. These are the so-called A editions. Cf. "Text," pp. 1–5.

6. See P'an K'ai-p'ei, "*Chin P'ing Mei* ti ch'an-sheng ho tso-che" (*Chin P'ing Mei:* its creation and authorship), in *Ming-Ch'ing hsiao-shuo yen-chiu lun-wen chi.* Hanan believes that P'an's hypothesis "has been adequately rebutted" by Hsü Meng-hsiang in an article appearing in the same volume ("Sources," p. 24, n. 2).

7. Cf. R. H. van Gulik, *Erotic Colour Prints of the Ming Period.*

8. Lung-chu K'e, "*Chin P'ing Mei* hsü," *CPM, ts'e* 1.

9. This story has been retold mainly for its entertainment value in nearly every textbook account of the novel. For original sources on differing accounts of the story see the section on *Chin P'ing Mei* in K'ung Ling-ching, ed., *Chung-kuo hsiao-shuo shih-liao.*

10. Arthur Waley's Introduction to Bernard Miall, tr., *Chin P'ing Mei,* pp. xviii-xix. The poet and playwright Li K'ai-hsien (1501–68) has also received serious consideration as a candidate for author; cf. *Chung-kuo wen-hsüeh shih,* III (1962), 949, n. 1. For Li's indubitable contributions to the novel see below, p. 177, and "Sources," pp. 50–55.

11. Cf. "Sources," pp. 39–49.

12. K'ung Ling-ching, p. 81. The original source for this passage is Yuan Chung-tao, *Yu-chü fei-lu.*

13. Of the sixteenth-century songbooks, *Sheng-shih hsin-sheng* and *Tz'u-lin chai-yen* have been reprinted in Peking in 1955 while *Yung-hsi yüeh-fu* is available in the Ssu-pu ts'ung-k'an series.

14. Cf. "Sources," pp. 55–63.

15. It is P'an K'ai-p'ei's contention (see n. 6) that the original story-tellers' version of the novel ends with the death of P'an Chin-lien in chap. 87. It is only in the continuation, which begins with chap. 88, that Ch'un-mei (Plum Blossom), who has hitherto played a minor role, emerges as a major heroine. Whatever the value of his theory, P'an is certainly right in sensing the inferiority of the last part of the novel. For

reasons to be discussed later, I believe that this part should properly include chaps. 80–87.

16. In "Text," Hanan lists ten of these B editions and compares them in detail with the A editions. Textually, the C editions of the Ch'ing period, designated by Sun K'ai-ti as *Chang Chu-p'o p'ing Chin P'ing Mei,* differ hardly at all from the B editions.

17. Moon Lady first encounters the monk P'u-ching in chap. 84. On that occasion he tells her that he will claim Hsiao-ko as a disciple fifteen years later (*kuo shih-wu-nien—CPM, ts'e* 18, chap. 84, p. 8a). In chap. 100, P'u-ching reminds Moon Lady that she has promised to give him her son ten years ago (*shih-nien ch'ien—CPM, ts'e* 21, chap. 100, p. 10a). That would make Hsiao-ko an eleven-year-old boy, but at the same time he is declared to be fifteen years of age. This is but one of many such inconsistencies in the novel.

18. *CPM, ts'e* 2, chap. 4, pp. 5b–6a; Egerton, *The Golden Lotus,* I, 71–72. Earlier in chap. 2, when Hsi-men Ch'ing sees P'an Chin-lien for the first time, the author immediately tells us that he is enraptured by her beauty and proceeds to give us a long catalogue of all her charms, even though Hsi-men could not have seen those parts of her body covered by clothing. This scene, however, is adapted from *Shui hu chuan.*

19. *CPM, ts'e* 21, chap. 100, p. 12a.

20. *CPM, ts'e* 12, chap. 55, pp. 6a–b. Egerton, III, 21, gives an incomplete list.

21. Hsi-men Ch'ing first meets Ts'ai Yün and gives him valuable presents in chap. 36. "A hundred taels of white gold" is Egerton's rendering of "pai-chin i-pai-liang" (II, 137). However, in accordance with traditional Chinese usage, the phrase "white gold" usually means "silver." The banquet takes place in chap. 49. "Ch'ien-liang chin-yin," which I have literally rendered as "one thousand taels of gold and silver," is an ambiguous phrase. Egerton is probably right in rendering it as "a thousand taels of silver" (II, 296), but even a thousand taels of silver is an enormous amount of money to spend for a banquet.

22. *CPM, ts'e* 17, chap. 80, p. 10a. For the term *jung-wa* (woolen socks), see Yao Ling-hsi, ed., *P'ing-wai chih-yen* (1962), p. 220. The editor has prepared a very useful glossary (pp. 100–240) for readers of *Chin P'ing Mei.*

23. This panegyric is recorded in chap. 80.

24. *CPM, ts'e* 13, chap. 61, p. 22b.

25. "Sources," p. 53. Hanan further comments, "As he [Dr. Chao] finishes the verse, altogether of some twenty-odd lines, we are told that

'everybody burst out laughing,' which was perhaps the hoped-for reaction of the theatre audience."

26. "It may be said, therefore, that the author's achievement has been to take popular songs and use them dramatically" ("Sources," p. 60).

27. One cannot make a clear-cut division between Parts I and II. Chap. 9 marks the arrival of Golden Lotus in the Hsi-men house, but it is not until chap. 11 that her new life there is given major attention. For the most part chaps. 9–10 continue with the Wu Sung saga and introduce us to the other heroine, Li P'ing-erh. So, judging strictly by style, one could with equal justice take chaps. 1–10 as Part I and chaps. 11–79 as Part II.

28. "Sources," pp. 57–58.

29. Li Chiao-erh is married in chap. 80 to Chang Erh-kuan-erh who serves briefly as Hsi-men's replacement in the novel, fawned upon by Hsi-men's friends. However, the novelist soon drops this character.

30. This episode takes place in chap. 91. The magistrate's son is surnamed Li.

31. This episode occurs in chap. 90. In chap. 25 Hsüeh-o informs Lai Wang of his wife Hui-lien's adultery with Hsi-men. But the reason given in chap. 90 for their elopement is that they are both sex-starved creatures (*k'uang-fu kua-nü, yü-hsin ju-huo*) not uninterested in thievery.

32. "Sources," pp. 29–31.

33. But even some of these scenes are disappointing. Moon Lady sells Plum Blossom in chap. 85, and in chap. 89 they confront each other again in a temple. Plum Blossom is now a fine lady and can afford to express her hatred for Moon Lady. Instead, we find her prostrating herself before the latter as if she were still a bond servant.

34. In *Chung-kuo wen-hsüeh fa-chan shih* (The development of Chinese literature) (Peking, Chung-hua shu-chü, 1963), III, 1064, Liu Ta-chieh gives Ting Yao-k'ang's dates as 1599–1670, though other literary historians consulted by me give only approximate dates. His 64-chapter novel, although erotic, demonstrates the workings of karma with didactic explicitness. Subsequently, an author with the studio name of Ssu-ch'iao Chü-shih condensed the work to 48 chapters, renamed all its characters, and gave it the new title *Ko-lien hua-ying*. The latter is available in a German translation by Franz Kuhn under the title *Blumenschatten hinter dem Vorhang* (Freiburg im Breisgau, 1956); Vladimir Kean, tr., *Flower Shadows Behind the Curtain* (New York, 1959) is a shortened translation of the German version. For further information on *Hsü Chin P'ing Mei* and *Ko-lien hua-ying* see Dr. Kuhn's introduction to Kean's translation. The author of *Chin P'ing Mei* is supposed to have written a sequel called *Yü chiao li* (not to be confused with *Yü*

Chiao Li, listed in Bibliography VIII), but this work, if it ever existed, has been long lost.

35. *CPM, ts'e* 16, chap. 75, p. 1b.

36. I have already mentioned P'u-ching, who claims Hsiao-ko at the end of the novel, and the mysterious Indian monk who gives Hsi-men the aphrodisiac pills and ointment in chap. 49. While the latter's fierce looks suggest "a veritable Lohan [Arhat]," (Egerton, II, 305), the former is supposed to be the incarnation of an ancient Buddha. In *Hsü Chin P'ing Mei* P'u-ching is definitely identified as an avatar of the Bodhisattva Kshitigarbha.

37. The story of Chiang Chu-shan is given in chaps. 17 and 19.

38. Wen Pi-ku is unmasked in chap. 76. His name puns with the phrase *wen p'i-ku* (warm the buttocks). Many of Hsi-men's sponging friends have such punning names.

39. A paramour of her brother-in-law, Wang VI enters into a liaison with Hsi-men with the connivance of her husband. Madame Lin's lewdness is known even among the local courtesans. It is Cheng Ai-yüeh-erh who informs Hsi-men of Madame Lin's availability in chap. 68. Hsi-men calls on the lady one afternoon in chap. 78, and they are in bed the same evening.

40. Hui-lien's past history is recounted in chap. 22. See Egerton, I, 349–50.

41. Cf. *Han shu, chüan* 30, *Yi-wen chih* (Essay on bibliography), which lists eight sex manuals.

42. In Part II, only the story of the servant Miao Ch'ing and his murdered master Miao T'ien-hsiu as given in chaps. 47–48 blocks the flow of the narrative. It is adapted from one of the crime-case stories in the collection known as *Lung-t'u kung-an* or *Pao kung-an.* Hanan believes that this borrowed tale "causes perhaps the only serious break in the *Chin P'ing Mei*'s continuity" ("Sources," p. 42).

43. Ou-yang Yü-ch'ien, noted for his varied activities in behalf of the modern Chinese theater, wrote *P'an Chin-lien,* a short play first published in *Hsin-yüeh Yüeh-k'an,* I, No. 4 (1928). Among the many popular historical novels by Nan-kung Po, a Hong Kong author now residing in Taiwan, is *P'an Chin-lien* (Taipei, Ta-fang shu-chü, 1965).

44. *CPM, ts'e* 17, chap. 78, p. 23a.

45. This episode takes place in chap. 8.

46. In chap. 11.

47. Egerton, I, 163 (*CPM, ts'e* 4, chap. 12, p. 8a).

48. *CPM, ts'e* 4, chap. 12, p. 9b.

49. This incident takes place in chap. 19.

50. In chap. 17 Vase is grateful to Hsi-men for his sexual attentions after being long neglected by her first husband. She tells her lover, "Who is ever like you in knowing how to please me? You are the medicine that cures my sickness. Night and day I can think only of you" (*CPM, ts'e* 5, chap. 17, p. 2b). Later, Vase marries Dr. Chiang to spite Hsi-men for his neglect. Following their reconciliation, however, she again praises him, using the same medical metaphor, "You are the medicine that cures me. Once treated by you, I could think only of you day and night" (*CPM, ts'e* 5, chap. 19, p. 15b).

51. In chap. 26.

52. In chap. 29.

53. *CPM, ts'e* 13, chap. 58, pp. 14b–15a.

54. *CPM, ts'e* 13, chap. 59, pp. 12a–b.

55. Vase dies in chap. 62 and Hsi-men takes his trip to the capital in chap. 70.

56. *CPM, ts'e* 16, chap. 72, pp. 10b–11a.

57. *Ibid.*, pp. 11a–b.

58. *CPM, ts'e* 16, chap. 75, pp. 1b–2b. The antecedents relevant to our understanding of this conversation are as follows. Early that morning, after a night of love-making, Lotus asked Hsi-men to give her the sable coat that used to belong to Vase. After getting up, he went straight to Ju-i's room to get the coat. To placate Ju-i, who complained of his neglect, Hsi-men gave her a few pieces of Vase's clothing and promised her to stay the coming night with her. Ju-i then personally took the sable coat to Lotus and kowtowed to her. In the afternoon Hsi-men entertained some important guests at home. After he had seen them off to their sedan-chairs, upon his return to the house he was intercepted at the side door by Lotus and taken to her room.

This excerpt contains at least two misprints. On page 2a, l.4, the period should be removed after the phrase *ch'en-tao* since it does not form a sentence with the preceding characters but begins a new sentence, *Ch'en-tao t'ou-li pu-shih ya-t'ou* . . . (That's why you didn't send a maid . . .). On the same page, l.6, the phrase *lung p'an-tzu* must have been a misprint for *lung la-tzu*, since the characters *p'an* (*Mathews'*, No. 4893) and *la* (No. 3757) look rather alike. For the meanings of *ch'en-tao* and *lung la-tzu*, see Lu Tan-an, *Hsiao-shuo tz'u-yü hui-shih* (A dictionary of phrases and idioms from traditional Chinese fiction), pp. 608, 253.

59. *Ibid.*, p. 17a.

60. *Ibid.*, pp. 17a–b.

61. Hsi-men first sees her in chap. 78.

62. *CPM, ts'e* 17, chap. 79, p. 9b.

63. *Ibid.*, pp. 9b–10a.

64. *Ibid.*, p. 13b.

65. *Ibid,* p. 16a.

66. However, as noted earlier, Lotus has had two miscarriages while living with Hsi-men. After his death, she cohabits with Ch'en Ching-chi and again becomes pregnant. In chap. 85 she undergoes an abortion.

67. The first such story is "Chao Fei-yen wai-chuan," most probably of the Han period; it is translated as "The Emperor and the Two Sisters" in Wolfgang Bauer and Herbert Franke, eds., *The Golden Casket.* Though scholars are not agreed about its date of composition, *Chin Hai-ling tsung-yü wang-shen* (King Hai-ling of the Chin dynasty destroys himself through unrestrained debauchery), the most blatant example of pornography in the *San-yen* collections and certainly one of the earliest such stories to employ the vernacular, adapts its salacious material partly from official history. Hanan traces *Chin P'ing Mei's* indebtedness to *Ju-i-chün chuan,* a Ming pornographic story in the literary language about Empress Wu and one of her favorites ("Sources," pp. 43–47).

68. Katherine Anne Porter, "A Wreath for the Gamekeeper," *Encounter,* XIV, No. 2 (1960), pp. 72–73.

69. *CPM, ts'e* 4, chap. 15, pp. 3b–4a.

NOTES TO CHAPTER VI: THE SCHOLARS

1. "Text," p. 54.

2. Thomas Percy, ed., *Hau Kiou Choaan, or The Pleasing History* (2d ed., 1761). Other versions in English, French, and German have appeared since.

3. Richard Martin has translated the Kuhn version (*Jou Pu Tuan,* Zürich, Verlag die Waage, 1959) into English as *Jou Pu Tuan (The Prayer Mat of Flesh).* See my review of the translation in the *Journal of Asian Studies,* XXIII, No. 2 (February, 1964).

4. Cf. C. T. Hsia and T. A. Hsia, "New Perspectives on Two Ming Novels: *Hsi-yu chi* and *Hsi-yu pu,*" in Chow Tse-tsung, ed., *Wen-lin: Studies in the Chinese Humanities.*

5. Cf. chap. 1, n. 47.

6. Cf. Ch'ien Hsüan-t'ung, "*Ju-lin wai-shih* hsin-hsü" (A new preface

to *The Scholars*), *Ju-lin wai-shih* (Shanghai, Ya-tung t'u-shu-kuan, publisher's note to 4th edition dated 1922).

7. P'u Sung-ling is famed for his *Liao-chai chih-i*, partially translated by Herbert A. Giles as *Strange Stories from a Chinese Studio*. Yuan Mei, *Tzu pu-yü*, and Chi Yün, *Yüeh-wei-ts'ao-t'ang pi-chi*, are still much read today.

8. Hu Shih, "Wu Ching-tzu nien-p'u" (A chronological biography of Wu Ching-tzu), *HSWT*, II, 328, quotes three such *tz'u* poems written in 1730. Though several Communist critics have attacked Hu Shih for his use of such sources to pinpoint Wu's libertinage, Ho Tse-han has cited poems by Wu's cousins to corroborate the autobiographical information given in the novelist's own poetry. See Ho, *Ju-lin wai-shih jen-wu pen-shih k'ao-lüeh*, pp. 164–73.

9. In the few places where I refer to Wu Ching-tzu's age, I have measured it according to Western custom. Thus, at twenty-two, Wu would be twenty-three years (*sui*) old in Chinese reckoning. For all characters in fiction, however, I have adopted the Chinese way of measuring age in order to be consistent with my sources. Ho Tse-han, pp. 169–71, cites a poem by the author's cousin Chin Liang-ming to prove that Wu received his *hsiu-ts'ai* degree in 1723, the year his father died. Hu Shih imprecisely dates the event at 1720, on the strength of one line of poetry (*HSWT*, II, 327). For other errors in Hu's biography, see Ho, pp. 197–200.

10. *HSWT*, II, 332–35. Among Communist critics opposing Hu Shih's view are Wang Huang, "Ch'ih Hu Shih tui *Ju-lin wai-shih* ti wu-mieh" (Repudiate Hu Shih's disparagement of *The Scholars*), *Hu Shih ssu-hsiang p'i-p'an*, III, 145–48, and Ho Chia-huai, "Hu Shih tui-yü Wu Ching-tzu ho *Ju-lin wai-shih* ti wu-mieh" (How Hu Shih maligned Wu Ching-tzu and disparaged *The Scholars*), *Ming-Ch'ing hsiao-shuo yen-chiu lun-wen chi*, pp. 332–40. To Ho, the supposition that Wu Ching-tzu did not take the special examination because of illness, though supported by autobiographical documents, betrays Hu Shih's malicious intent to defame the novelist.

11. *Shih shuo* was never printed. In *Ju-lin wai-shih*, chap. 34, it is cited as a work by the autobiographical hero, Tu Shao-ch'ing. Several comments on the *Shih ching* appearing in that chapter may have been paraphrased from the lost treatise. For a survey of Wu's extant and lost writings in classical verse and prose, see Ho Tse-han, pp. 175–80.

12. Chin Ho's postface is included in Ho Tse-han, pp. 202–5. For a quick guide to the names of some thirty persons and their fictional counterparts see Ho, pp. 131–36.

13. Cf. Ho, pp. 137–63.

14. Quoted in *HSWT*, II, 338.

15. Cf. *HSWT*, II, 351, and Liu Ts'un-yan, "Lun chin-jen yen-chiu Chung-kuo hsiao-shuo chih te-shih" (Amendments to earlier studies of Chinese fiction), *Lien-ho Shu-yuan Hsüeh-pao*, III, 15–16. The earliest extant edition of *Ju-lin wai-shih*, dated 1803, has 56 chapters, the last chapter obviously a forgery. As Liu sees it, the trouble with Hu Shih's theory lies in the impossibility of detaching any one episode from the 55-chapter novel without tearing its closely knit fabric. Stylistically, too, all the chapters are quite uniform.

16. Cf. the stories of Hsiao Yün-hsien in chap. 39–40 and of Brigade General T'ang Chou in chap. 43.

17. Several essays in *Ju-lin wai-shih yen-chiu lun-chi* (Studies in *The Scholars*) stress Wu's anti-Manchu nationalism. Wu Tsu-hsiang, for example, calls the novelist "an ardent patriot" (p. 12) and Yao Hsüeh-yin refers to his "intense nationalism and emotional patriotism" (p. 45). In his preface to *JLWS* entitled "*Ju-lin wai-shih* chih chia-chih" (The value of *The Scholars*), Li Ch'en-tung also stresses Wu's anti-Manchu and pro-Ming sentiments.

18. For a life of this great Ming poet see F. W. Mote, *The Poet Kao Ch'i, 1336–1375* (Princeton University Press, 1962). In chap. 8 of *Ju-lin wai-shih* the young scholar Ch'ü Kung-sun prints Kao Ch'i's Notes on Poetry (*Kao Ch'ing-ch'iu shih-hua*) from a manuscript copy in the poet's own hand. In chap. 35 Lu Hsin-hou is arrested for owning the works of Kao Ch'i, but through the good offices of his influential scholar-friend Chuang Shao-kuang he is soon released. Chin Ho in his postface states that the latter episode alludes to the case of Tai Ming-shih (1653–1713), a victim of literary inquisition under the K'ang-hsi Emperor. On the authority of Chin Ho, it has been further believed that Lu Hsin-hou was modeled after an unidentified friend of Wu Ching-tzu's brought to court for his illegal possession of Tai's works. But while the story of Lu reflects the fear of literary inquisition in the author's time, Ho Tse-han has proved beyond a doubt that it refers to a minor case of the Yung-cheng period. Lu Te, *tzu* Hsin-hou, was modeled after Liu Chu, *tzu* Yün-kung, a friend of Ch'eng T'ing-tso, who appears as Chuang Shao-kuang in the novel. In one of his essays Ch'eng tells of the harassment of Liu Chu by a man who coveted a manuscript copy of a book in his possession. The book, Ku Tsu-yü's *Tu-shih fang-yü chi-yao* (Essentials of historical geography), was actually nonsubversive, but, because officials then were overeager to punish owners of dangerous works, the man managed to involve Liu Chu in litigation over a number of years. He was not freed from mental torture until the accuser himself died in prison. If Wu Ching-tzu intends to convey through this brief episode his concern over literary inquisition, his criticism of the

government is nevertheless very mild since he has not referred to Tai Ming-shih or other notorious cases of persecution. See Ho, pp. 74–82.

19. In chap. 29 Tu Shen-ch'ing defends Emperor Ch'eng-tsu as follows, "If Yung Lo had not stirred up this dynasty, but left the government in the hands of that weakling Chien Wen, the empire would now be as weak as in the time of the Six Dynasties" (*TS*, p. 402).

20. One of the Lou brothers comments in chap. 8: "'I see very little difference between Prince Ning's rebellion and that of Emperor Yung Lo,' put in Lou Tsan. 'But luck was with the emperor, so now he is called sagacious and divine; whereas Prince Ning had no luck, so now he is considered a rebel and bandit. That is hardly fair'" (*TS*, p. 142).

21. *TS*, p. 39.

22. *TS*, p. 42.

23. Po-i and Shu-ch'i were princes of a minor feudal state who protested King Wu's overhasty conquest of the Shang house by starving themselves to death on a mountain.

24. Yen Kuang, *tzu* Tzu-ling, whose biography is recorded in *Hou Han shu*, *chüan* 113, *lieh-chuan* 73, is a beloved figure in Chinese literature.

25. *TS*, p. 45.

26. *TS*, pp. 45–46.

27. *TS*, p. 48. "Curiously enough" stands for *k'o-hsiao*, which could be more effectively rendered as "absurdly enough."

28. In the earlier chapters we have referred to such late Ming intellectuals as Li Chih, the Yuan brothers, and Chin Sheng-t'an. It is generally believed that Wu Ching-tzu typifies the trends of Ch'ing thought developed by Ku Yen-wu, Huang Tsung-hsi, Wang Fu-chih, Yen Yuan, and Tai Chen. Known for their earnest moral endeavor and concern with the Confucian classics, these men represent a strong reaction against extreme Ming individualism and idealism. See the essays by Wu Tsu-hsiang and Yao Hsüeh-yin referred to in n. 17; see also Ho Man-tzu, *Lun Ju-lin wai-shih* (On *The Scholars*), chap. 2.

29. *TS*, pp. 46–47.

30. *TS*, p. 35. This passage has been often cited by critics ever since Hu Shih singled it out for praise in "*Lao-ts'an yu-chi* hsü" (Preface to *The Travels of Lao Ts'an*, 1925), *HSWT*, III.

31. *TS*, chap. 2, pp. 49–51.

32. *TS*, chap. 2, p. 59.

33. *TS*, chap 3, pp. 62–63.

34. *TS*, chaps. 5–6, pp. 103–6. I have omitted a few sentences serving to link the two chapters.

35. Ho Ching-ming (1483–1521) was a leading classical writer of the middle Ming period, one of the so-called Seven Earlier Talents.

36. *TS*, pp. 120–21.

37. Ho Tse-han, pp. 140–41. In his biography of the poet Wang Tao-k'un, Ch'ien Ch'ien-i records an anecdote illustrative of Wang's conceit and contempt for Szechwanese. Twice before a commissioner of education for Szechwan he disparages the prose style of Su Shih, who was of course the greatest man of letters ever produced in that province. To humor his friend, the commissioner pretends ignorance of Su's identity and answers him the second time in much the same fashion as the commissioner for Szechwan answers Ho Ching-ming in *The Scholars*. In Ch'ien Ch'ien-i's biography, therefore, the joke is upon Wang Tao-k'un. Wu Ching-tzu has refashioned the joke by making the commissioner a literal ignoramus. Wang, incidentally, wrote a preface to the 1589 edition of the 100-chapter *Shui-hu chuan* under the pseudonym T'ien-tu wai-ch'en. See chap. 3, n. 7.

38. This takes place in chap. 14 (*TS*, p. 220).

39. However, the abundance of jokes and anecdotes in Ming and Ch'ing times about the ignorance of scholars does reflect social reality. In his book of miscellaneous notes, *Hsiang-tsu pi-chi* (1702), the poet and critic Wang Shih-chen writes of a scholar who has never heard of the *Shih chi* and its author. Recorded in Ho Man-tzu, *Lun Ju-lin wai-shih*, p. 35.

40. *TS*, chap. 10, p. 169.

41. Cf. Ho Tse-han, p. 144. This brief episode occurs in the biography of Liu Ching-hsüan, in *Nan shih, chüan* 17, *lieh-chuan* 7.

42. In chap. 8 Ch'ü Kung-sun prints a rare manuscript (see n. 18); in chaps. 11–13 the Lou brothers expose themselves to ridicule by cultivating three eccentrics pretending to virtue and chivalry; they also sponsor a poetic party on a lake. Tu Shen-ch'ing judges a contest of opera singers on the Mo-ch'ou Lake of Nanking in chap. 30.

43. His long speech is recorded in chap. 13 (*TS*, pp. 203–4).

44. In chap. 14.

45. *TS*, chap. 16, p. 244.

46. *TS*, chap. 20, pp. 290–91.

47. *JLWS*, chap. 17, p. 119. The corresponding passage in *TS* is on p. 251.

48. *TS*, chap. 21, p. 298.

49. Cf. Ho Man-tzu, pp. 48–49, and Ma Mao-yuan, "*Ju-lin wai-shih* ti hsien-shih chu-i" (Realism in *The Scholars*), in *Ming-Ch'ing hsiao-shuo yen-chiu lun-wen chi*, p. 272.

50. *TS*, chap. 31, p. 428.

51. *JLWS*, chap. 31, p. 220. The corresponding sentence in *TS*, p. 418, is "Yet he loves to act the patron."

52. *TS*, chap. 33, p. 449.

53. *TS*, chap. 34, pp. 457–58.

54. *TS*, chap. 34, p. 467. The translators have supplied a footnote on Lao Lai-tzu: "During the Spring and Autumn Period (722–481 B.C.) the king of Chu [Ch'u] invited Lao Lai-tzu to court, but his wife persuaded him that it would be undignified to accept an appointment."

55. *TS*, chap. 35, p. 475.

56. *TS*, chap. 33, pp. 455–56. The proposer of the scheme is Ch'ih Heng-shan. Since the author has failed to supply the name of the dynasty during which "the ancient ceremonies and music" flourished, in my subsequent comment on this passage I have equated them with those of the early Chou period, for which Confucius had the greatest admiration. My criticism of Wu's "bookish and antiquarian temper" still stands, however, even if the ritual and music adopted for the initial sacrifice at the temple are a hybrid sort of lesser antiquity.

57. *JLWS*, chap. 37, p. 265. The corresponding passage in *TS*, p. 499, is abridged. Ch'eng Chih-t'ing has singled out the ritual scene for adverse criticism in "Tu *Ju-lin wai-shih* sui-pi" (Random notes on *The Scholars*), *Wen-hsüeh Tsa-chih*, III, No. 6 (February, 1958).

58. *JLWS*, chap. 37, p. 268.

59. Yü Yü-te's biography is given in chap. 36.

60. *JLWS*, chap. 47, p. 336.

61. *JLWS*, chap. 44, p. 318. *TS*, p. 585, gives a toned-down version, "As regards both character and learning, the Yu brothers had rarely been equalled."

62. Ho Tse-han, pp. 102–14, gives detailed information on the brothers Chin Chü and Chin Liang-ming.

63. *TS*, pp. 713–14.

64. *TS*, p. 712.

65. Thus in traditional criticism such great poets as Ch'ü Yuan, T'ao Ch'ien, and Tu Fu are as much praised for their moral character as for their literary genius.

66. Her death takes place in chap. 48. Wang Yü-hui, who at first approved of his daughter's suicide, eventually undergoes pangs of remorse in one of the most deservedly praised scenes in the novel.

67. *TS*, chap. 27, p. 372.

68. *JLWS*, chap. 27, p. 190. The corresponding passage in *TS*, p. 373, is expurgated.

NOTES TO CHAPTER VII: DREAM OF THE RED CHAMBER

1. Lin Tai-yi has done an abridged translation of *Ching-hua yuan* in *Flowers in the Mirror*. For a translation and critique of the concluding chapters of the novel, see H. C. Chang, *Allegory and Courtesy in Spenser*, chaps. 1–3.

2. Professor Shen Kang-po of National Taiwan University, for one, asks that question in "Chung-kuø wen-hsüeh ti mo-lo" (The decline of Chinese literature), *Wen-hsüeh Tsa-chih*, III, No. 4 (December, 1957), p. 4.

3. Wang Kuo-wei, "*Hung-lou-meng* p'ing-lun" (A critique of *Hung-lou-meng*) is included in *HLMC*, I, 244–65. This compilation contains an ample selection of critical comments on the novel by Ch'ing and early Republican scholars.

4. *HLM*, chap. 1, p. 1. Although I have consulted many editions in preparing this chapter, including the variorum 4-volume edition *Hung-lou-meng pa-shih-hui chiao-pen*, collated by Yü P'ing-po with the assistance of Wang Hsi-shih, I have translated from the 1792 edition as prepared by Ch'eng Wei-yuan and Kao Ê (the so-called Ch'eng-Kao B Edition) because it is still the standard text in general use. *HLM* is a modern reprint of that edition.

5. In his 1921 essay "*Hung-lou-meng* k'ao-cheng" (A study of *Hou-lou-meng*), *HSWT*, I, Hu Shih appeared in his double pioneering role as critic and scholar. He not only demolished earlier theories concerning the novel in favor of his own autobiographical approach but unearthed an impressive body of data about the Ts'ao family, thus paving the way for further research by younger scholars. Among the latter, Chou Ju-ch'ang has deservedly earned the gratitude of all readers of the novel for the immense amount of material on the Ts'ao family presented in his major work, *Hung-lou-meng hsin-cheng* (New studies in *Hung-lou-meng*). More recently, Jonathan D. Spence published a valuable study on the novelist's grandfather entitled *Ts'ao Yin and the K'ang-hsi Emperor, Bondservant and Master*.

6. To determine Ts'ao Hsüeh-ch'in's age, we have first to establish the identity of his father. Soon after the death of Ts'ao Yin in 1712, his only son Ts'ao Yung, about nineteen years old, succeeded him as textile commissioner in Nanking. In the winter of 1714, however, Ts'ao Yung suddenly died, and the next year his widow gave birth to a posthumous son. By that time Ts'ao Fu, Ts'ao Yin's nephew, had been posthumously adopted as Yin's son and given imperial permission to succeed his late cousin as textile commissioner. Most scholars believe Ts'ao Fu to be Ts'ao Hsüeh-ch'in's father. The novelist's commentator Chih-yen Chai tells us that Ts'ao died on New Year's eve of the year *jen-wu* (February 12, 1763) and, since the other date proposed by Chou Ju-ch'ang—1764— has been effectively discredited by Chao Kang in *Hung-lou-meng k'ao-cheng shih-i* (Studies in problems connected with *Hung-lou-meng*), we have no choice but to accept 1763 as the year of Ts'ao's death. A poem by Ts'ao's good friend, Tun-ch'eng, states that the novelist died in his fortieth year (*ssu-shih nien-hua*) or in his forties (since a round figure in a Chinese poem is usually not to be taken literally). On the strength of this evidence, Chou Ju-ch'ang believes that Ts'ao was born in 1724. However, Chou has failed to consider a headnote to a poem by another friend of Ts'ao's, Chang I-ch'üan, which states that "he died at the age of not yet fifty." Both Chao Kang and Wu Shih-ch'ang, the author of *On The Red Chamber Dream,* give more weight to Chang I-ch'üan's statement mainly for the reason that, if Ts'ao had indeed died at the age of forty, then he would have been too young when he left for Peking with his parents in 1728. He could not have remembered much of his life in Nanking; since he was eventually to write a novel partially based upon his recollections of his home life in Nanking, he should have been at least ten to thirteen when he left for Peking. Hence Chao places the date of his birth between 1715 and 1718; Wu suggests the date 1715, and Hu Shih has proposed the date 1718.

In recent years, however, two eminent specialists, Yü P'ing-po and Wu En-yü, came forward with the hypothesis that the novelist was not Ts'ao Fu's son, but the posthumous son of Ts'ao Yung. The theory is very plausible in many ways and presents one definite advantage—at least we are sure that Ts'ao was born in 1715. Jonathan Spence agrees with Yü and Wu and presents the theory lucidly in *Ts'ao Yin and the K'ang-hsi Emperor,* pp. 301–3.

The main difficulty with this theory is that Chao Kang has already argued most cogently for his thesis that the posthumous son is to be identified with Chih-yen Chai rather than with Ts'ao Hsüeh-ch'in. Later I shall refer briefly to this thesis, but one must read Chao's brilliant long essay "Chih-yen Chai yü *Hung-lou-meng*" (Chih-yen Chai and *Hung-lou-meng*), included in his book, to be convinced of its soundness. Since we know from his comments that Chih-yen Chai was somewhat older than the novelist, I have placed the latter's birth between 1716 and 1718.

7. Tun-ch'eng and Tun-min are quoted in *HLMC*, I, 1–7; Yü-jui, *ibid.*, p. 14. Concerning the date of Ts'ao's death, see n. 6.

8. Cf. Wu Shih-ch'ang, *On The Red Chamber Dream,* Appendixes II and III. I must warn the reader, however, against Wu's subjective appraisal of these manuscript copies.

9. Hu Shih was the first modern scholar to accuse Kao Ê of forgery in his pioneer study referred to in n. 5. Yü P'ing-po carried forward the attack with great vehemence in *Hung-lou-meng pien* (Shanghai, Ya-tung t'u-shu-kuan, 1923). Chou Ju-ch'ang continued in the same vein in *Hung-lou-meng hsin-cheng.* The reaction set in with Lin Yutang's paper "P'ing-hsin lun Kao Ê" (Re-opening the question of authorship of "Red Chamber Dream"), *Bulletin of the Institute of History and Philology* (Taipei, Academia Sinica, 1958). While presenting no new facts, Lin sensibly exposes the subjective character of Yü's and Chou's arguments. In *Hou-lou-meng k'ao-cheng shih-i* Chao Kang has conclusively argued against the theory of Kao Ê's forgery. For a brief survey of the controversy over the authorship of the last forty chapters, see my review of Wu's book in the *Journal of Asian Studies,* XXI, No. 1 (November, 1961).

10. Published by Chung-hua shu-chü (Peking, 1963) with a postface by Fan Ning. The original MS. of the edition is in the keeping of the Literary Institute, the Chinese Academy of Sciences, Peking.

11. Yü P'ing-po, "T'an hsin-k'an *Ch'ien-lung ch'ao-pen pai-nien-hui Hung-lou-meng kao*" (On the newly published *Hung-lou-meng kao*) in *Chung-hua wen-shih lun-ts'ung* (Papers on Chinese literature and history), 5th Series, pp. 395–445.

12. *Hung-lou-meng pa-shih-hui chiao-pen,* I, pp. 30–31, n. 28.

13. Chang Wen-t'ao was a good friend of Kao Ê. His poem, "Ts'eng Kao Lan-shu t'ung-nien" (To Kao Ê, my fellow examinee) carries a headnote stating that all the chapters of *Hung-lou-meng* after chap. 80 were "repaired" by Kao Ê. The ambiguous character *pu* (repair) could mean either "to emend and redact" or "to complete." See *HLMC,* I, 20–21.

14. *Chung-hua wen-shih lun-ts'ung,* 5th Series, pp. 437–38.

15. See such book-length critical studies as Liu Ta-chieh, *Hung-lou-meng ti ssu-hsiang yü jen-wu* (*Hung-lou-meng:* a study of its thought and characters) and Chiang Ho-sen, *Hung-lou-meng lun-kao* (A tentative critique of *Hung-lou-meng*). See also Ho Ch'i-fang, "Lun *Hung-lou-meng*" (On *Hung-lou-meng*), *Wen-hsüeh yen-chiu chi-k'an* (Collec-

tion of literary studies), V, 28–148, and the critical essays included in *Hung-lou-meng yen-chiu lun-wen chi* (*Hung-lou-meng:* studies and critiques). The last volume also contains three research articles.

16. Lin Yutang, especially, adopts this approach in "P'ing-hsin lun Kao Ê."

17. Both Lin Yutang and Chao Kang stress this point. Wu Shih-ch'ang examines the Keng-ch'en manuscript in *On The Red Chamber Dream*, Pt. I. A translation of the note on chap. 75 appears on p. 29.

18. In the Keng-ch'en manuscript Chih-yen Chai comments on chap. 22 to that effect. Cf. Yü P'ing-po, comp., *Chih-yen Chai Hung-lou-meng chi-p'ing* (A compilation of all the comments in the Chih-yen Chai versions of *Hung-lou-meng*), p. 381. This most useful volume has Wang Erh as principal editor.

19. See Wu Shih-ch'ang, chap. 8: "The Identity of Chih-yen Chai." Chao Kang agrees with Wu on this point.

20. Chou Ju-ch'ang identifies Chih-yen Chai with the real-life counterpart of Shih Hsiang-yün in *Hung-lou-meng hsin-cheng,* pp. 547–65. Wu Shih-ch'ang identifies him with Ts'ao's uncle Ts'ao Chu-chien (Wu, pp. 97–98).

21. See n. 6, and Chao Kang, pp. 25–58. Chao refutes Wu Shih-ch'ang's arguments on pp. 190–94.

22. See the concluding comment on chap. 13 of the Chia-hsü manuscript, in *Chih-yen Chai Hung-lou-meng chi-p'ing,* p. 214. This unique fragment was reproduced in a limited collotype edition in 1961 with its owner Hu Shih as publisher and two Taiwan firms (Commercial Press; Ch'i-ming shu-chü) and a Hong Kong firm (Yu-lien ch'u-pan-she) as distributors. It has a postface by Hu Shih. Its full title is *Ch'ien-lung chia-hsü Chih-yen Chai ch'ung-p'ing Shih-t'ou-chi.*

23. Cf. Lin Yutang, pp. 378–82.

24. Cf. Chao Kang, pp. 88–124. On p. 82 Chao suggests that the relative could well have been Chih-yen Chai.

25. *Chih-yen Chai Hung-lou-meng chi-p'ing,* p. 33.

26. His name is Chia Ching. He dies in chap. 63.

27. His name is Chia Chu. His widow, nee Li Huan, lives in the Takuanyuan and rears her son Chia Lan for academic success.

28. *HLM,* chap. 54, p. 343.

29. Cf. Chao Kang, p. 34.

30. See Appendix: Society and Self in the Chinese Short Story.

31. *HLM,* chap. 2, p. 11.

32. *HLM*, chap. 120, p. 789.

33. In chap. 23, to choose a conspicuous example, both Pao-yü and Black Jade read *The Romance of the Western Chamber* (*Hsi-hsiang chi*) for the first time. Pao-yü teasingly compares himself to Chang Sheng and Black Jade to Ying-ying. Later, Black Jade listens with rapt attention to famous arias from *The Peony Pavilion* (*Mu-tan t'ing*) as sung by young female singers in the employ of the Chia house.

34. In the 80-chapter version the opening section of chap. 1 is much fuller and properly emphasizes the rock's active longing for the pleasures of the mundane world. In the abbreviated opening section of the 120-chapter version the rock is more passive and appears entirely at the mercy of the Buddhist monk and Taoist priest. Compare *Hung-lou-meng pa-shih-hui chiao-pen*, I, 2–3, with the corresponding passage in *HLM*, chap. 1, p. 1.

35. Chi-chen Wang, tr., *Dream of the Red Chamber*, pp. 58–59.

36. Chia Jui dies in chap. 12. We are told in chap. 1 that the novel is also known by the title *Feng-yüeh pao-chien*, which is the name of the magic mirror that hastens Chia Jui's death.

37. After a few trysts with a nun, Ch'in Chung falls ill and receives a beating from his father, who soon suffers from the recurrence of an old disease and dies. His condition aggravated by remorse, Ch'in Chung dies soon afterwards, in chap. 16. Chess is dismissed from service after her affair with her cousin P'an Yu-an is exposed. In chap. 92 both are reported to have committed suicide following her mother's refusal to grant them permission to marry. Yu San-chieh, in love with Liu Hsiang-lien, kills herself in chap. 66 after Liu has broken his promise to marry her.

38. Chen Shih-yin and Chia Yü-ts'un, with their obviously allegorical names, are introduced in chap. 1. By the end of that chapter Chen Shih-yin has received enlightenment and disappeared with the lame Taoist while Chia Yü-ts'un is beginning to rise in the official world. His successful career having ended in ignominy, Chia again meets Chen in chap. 120 but he falls asleep on the brink of enlightenment.

39. Golden Bracelet drowns herself in a well in chap. 32 after she has been harshly scolded by Madame Wang for her supposed flirtation with Pao-yü. Bright Cloud dies in chap. 77; her story will be taken up later.

40. Leng Tzu-hsing reports this saying in chap. 2.

41. See *HLMC*, I, *chüan* 3, for comments on the novel by Ch'ing critics. Feng Chia-sheng, pp. 232–35, is typical. He praises Black Jade most highly while condemning Precious Clasp as "the most venomous among the shrewd characters" (p. 234). He laments the fate of Bright Cloud

but deplores the character of Pervading Fragrance. See also Hsü Yeh-fen's contrasting study of the two major heroines on pp. 228–29. Precious Clasp and Pervading Fragrance were not without defenders by late Ch'ing and early Republican times, however; see *ibid.*, II, *chüan* 6.

42. See Liu Ta-chieh, *Hung-lou-meng ti ssu-hsiang yü jen-wu*, pp. 43–54,65–77; Chiang Ho-sen, *Hung-lou-meng lun-kao*, pp. 46–112.

43. Mark Van Doren's preface to Chi-chen Wang, tr., *Dream of the Red Chamber*, p. vi. Van Doren, however, is responding only to a partial translation.

44. *HLM*, chap. 27, p. 163.

45. Pao-yü asks Bright Cloud in chap. 34 to send two old handkerchiefs to Black Jade. In chap. 97, however, Black Jade asks her maids to fetch her only one such handkerchief and burns it forthwith. Franz Kuhn has justifiably revised chap. 97 so that we read in chap. 43 of his version that the dying heroine burns two handkerchiefs rather than one. Cf. Florence and Isabel McHugh, trs., *The Dream of the Red Chamber*, pp. 492–93.

46. *HLM*, chap. 82, pp. 547–48.

47. *Ibid.*, p. 549.

48. *Ibid.*, p. 550.

49. In chap. 107.

50. The story of Ch'iao-chieh is told in chaps. 118–20.

51. Miao-yü dreams that dream after spending part of an afternoon with Pao-yü in chap. 87. She is abducted in chap. 112.

52. *HLM*, chap. 74, p. 489. Bright Cloud had been the Matriarch's maid before she was assigned to Pao-yü's quarters. Cf. *ibid.*, p. 488.

53. *HLM*, chap. 77, pp. 513–15.

54. Cf. *Hung-lou-meng pa-shih-hui chiao-pen*, II, 878–81. In a talk given in Taipei on May 4, 1967, Lin Yutang made public his preposterous theory that it was Ts'ao Hsüeh-ch'in himself who made all the revisions in the manuscript now reprinted under the title *Ch'ien-lung ch'ao-pen pai-nien-hui Hung-lou-meng kao* (cf. n. 10). According to Lin, Ch'eng and Kao acquired this manuscript after they had published their first edition of *Hung-lou meng* and they hurriedly made corrections in that edition in the light of the manuscript and published their second edition, which, therefore, must be regarded as a faithful copy of the novel as Ts'ao wrote it, incorporating all the revisions in his handwriting. To prove his contention, Lin cites the farewell scene we have been considering. Who, he asked, could have taken so many pains to revise and

improve the scene as originally written down in the manuscript but Ts'ao Hsüeh-ch'in himself? Lin's talk is reproduced in the Taipei *Central Daily News* (May 5, 1967), p. 4.

55. *HLM*, chap. 79, p. 529. *Hung-lou-meng pa-shih-hui chiao-pen*, II, 909, has the identical passage.

56. The exception is Ch'ien Yün, "Kuan-yü Hsüeh Pao-ch'ai ti tien-hsing fen-hsi wen-t'i" (How to analyze Precious Clasp as a character type), in *Hung-lou-meng yen-chiu lun-wen chi*. His concluding remarks are especially corrective of the ideological slant of Communist criticism: "To vilify the character of Precious Clasp—perhaps this is done in order to manifest more fully the ideological character of the work? I beg to differ completely from those comrades who would favor this type of criticism. I maintain that, precisely because Ts'ao Hsüeh-ch'in has drawn Precious Clasp as a tragic type with many facets of beauty to her character and at the same time probed deeply into the disharmony and contradiction of her inner psyche, her character has gained greater meaning and depth as a type" (p. 138).

57. *HLM*, chap. 97, p. 642.

58. *HLM*, chap. 118, p. 774.

59. *HLM*, chap. 98, p. 652.

60. *HLM*, chap. 96, p. 639.

61. *Ibid.*, p. 640.

62. *HLM*, chap. 119, p. 778. Florence and Isabel McHugh, trs., *The Dream of the Red Chamber*, p. 576, include in slightly abridged form part of Pao-yü's earlier conversation with his mother, which has so saddened Precious Clasp:

> He knelt down before his mother and saluted her with a ceremonious kowtow, touching his forehead to the ground three times.
> "Up till now I have had no opportunity of repaying my mother for all the love that she has shown me since I came into the world," he said earnestly. "I will exert myself to pass the examination as well as I can and thereby make good my former negligence. If it is granted me to give my parents joy by a notable success, I shall regard my filial duty as fulfilled and the injustice which I have been doing my parents all my life as atoned for."
> How solemn that sounded! Like a parting for ever!
> "My good, good boy! If only your old grandmother had lived to see this hour!" sobbed [Madame Wang], deeply moved, as she raised him to his feet.

"Even though she is no longer bodily among us, her spirit will be our witness and will rejoice with us," he declared simply.

63. Anthony West, "Through a Glass, Darkly," *The New Yorker* (November 22, 1958), pp. 223–32. Weng T'ing-shu has translated this review into Chinese in *Wen-hsüeh Tsa-chih*, V, No. 6 (Taipei, 1959).

64. As has been earlier mentioned, both Chen Shih-yin (see n. 38) and Liu Hsiang-lien heed the call of the lame Taoist priest and receive complete enlightenment. Compassion Spring and Purple Cuckoo may be said to have reached partial enlightenment when they elect to become nuns towards the end of the novel.

NOTES TO APPENDIX

1. It is titled *K'an p'i-hsüeh tan-cheng Erh-lang-shen* (The impersonator of Erh-lang-shen is convicted upon the sole evidence of a leather shoe). Though *hsüeh* (*Mathews'*, No. 2902) is usually translated as "boots," the boots commonly seen in America are so unlike the traditional Chinese footwear called *hsüeh* that I have used the more common word "shoe" to render the term. The tale is highly praised in *CWY*, I, 402–3.

2. Yang Chien was a eunuch and could not have a wife. Cf. chap. 3, n. 40.

3. The T'ang beauty is also surnamed Han. The Sung author Chang Shih wrote about her providential marriage to the scholar Yü Yu in a *ch'uan-ch'i* tale entitled *Liu-hung chi*. It has been translated as "Red Leaves in the Waves" in Bauer and Franke, eds., *The Golden Casket*. It differs in important details from the summary retelling of the legend in the Ming story.

4. *Hsing-shih heng-yen*, I (Taipei, Shih-chieh shu-chü, 1959), *chüan* 13, p. 4b. This reprint is an enlargement of a microfilm copy (made by Tien-yi Li) of the 1627 edition.

5. *Ibid.*, p. 7b.

6. *Ibid.*, p. 9a.

7. For an illuminating study of this tale, see Erich Auerbach, *Mimesis: The Representation of Reality in Western Literature* (Princeton University Press, 1953), chap. 9: "Frate Alberto."

8. The two are often compared. See especially Arthur Waley's introduction to Harold Acton and Lee Yi-hsieh, trs., *Four Cautionary Tales*. I question, however, Dr. Waley's assertion on p. xi that "in complication, in poetic colouring, in elegance, the Chinese tales stand far above the *Decameron*, which represents the art of narrative at a very crude stage."

9. Acton and Lee have translated *Ch'en To-shou sheng-ssu fu-ch'i* (Ch'en To-shou and his wife: a couple through life and death) under this title in *Four Cautionary Tales*. However, in their earlier volume of translations, *Glue and Lacquer* (London, The Golden Cockerel Press, 1941), the tale was called "The Predestined Couple." In the table of contents for the 1627 edition of *Hsing-shih heng-yen* we find an alternative title, *Ch'en To-shou sheng-ssu yin-yuan*.

10. Acton and Lee, trs., *Four Cautionary Tales*, p. 80.

11. *Ibid.*, pp. 94–95. Both this and the preceding quotation appear in the form of parallel prose in the Chinese.

12. Lu Hsün, *Chung-kuo hsiao-shuo shih-lüeh*, pp. 245–48.

13. The best modern editions of the three sets are those prepared by Shih-chieh shu-chü, Taipei, from microfilm copies of the earliest Ming editions preserved in Japan: *Ku-chin hsiao-shuo*, 2 vols. (preface by Yang Chia-lo dated 1958); *Ching-shih t'ung-yen*, 2 vols. (1958); *Hsing-shih heng-yen*, 3 vols. (1959), to which I have already referred in n. 4. Professor Tien-yi Li microfilmed these rare editions in 1955–56 and made possible the republication of the *San-yen* stories in their original form. The full title for *Ku-chin hsiao-shuo* is *Ch'üan-hsiang ku-chin hsiao-shuo i-k'o* (Fully illustrated stories old and new, first series). Feng Meng-lung must have intended to use *Ku-chin hsiao-shuo* as a comprehensive title for all three series, but the earliest editions of *Ching-shih t'ung-yen* and *Hsing-shih heng-yen* do not carry that title.

14. The preface to the 1627 edition of *Hsing-shih heng-yen* already refers to the three collections as *San-yen*. No 40-*chüan* edition of *Yü-shih ming-yen* has survived. For the composite character of the earliest extant *Yü-shih ming-yen*, 24 *chüan*, see Yang Chia-lo's preface to *Ku-chin hsiao-shuo* and Tien-yi Li, "Notes on Chinese Short Story Collections Seen in Japan," *Tsing Hua Journal of Chinese Studies* (new series), I, No. 2, pp. 69–70.

15. Cyril Birch provides a life of Feng Meng-lung (1574–1646) in his introduction to *Stories from a Ming Collection*. Cf. also John L. Bishop, *The Colloquial Short Story in China*, pp. 16–17.

16. *Ch'ing-p'ing-shan-t'ang hua-pen* contains 27 stories, five of these incomplete. Two of the complete stories are in the classical style.

17. *Chin-ku ch'i-kuan*, which appeared sometime between 1633 and 1644, reprints stories from the *San-yen* collections, Ling Meng-ch'u's *P'o-an ching-ch'i* (1628), and *Erh-k'o p'o-an ching-ch'i* (1632). The latter two collections, which represent the most considerable achievement by an individual author writing in the *San-yen* style, ought to have contained 80 stories, though only 78 are extant. Tien-yi Li has prepared an excellent

2-volume edition of *P'o-an ching-ch'i* (Hong Kong, Yu-lien ch'u-pan-she, 1966) containing all 40 stories in the original Ming edition.

18. Since no manuscript promptbooks dating from the Sung, Yuan, or Ming have survived, none of the *San-yen* stories can actually be tested against its promptbook version or versions. Understandably, therefore, recent scholarly opinion has shied away from the view that every *San-yen* story is either a copy or a revision of its corresponding promptbook. Thus Patrick Hanan does not subscribe to "the unlikely proposition that every oral story had its own prompt-book and that all the extant stories are directly based on these prompt-books." (Cf. Hanan, "The Early Chinese Short Story: A Critical Theory in Outline," *Harvard Journal of Asiatic Studies,* XXVII, 180.) However, unless we endorse the hypothesis that Feng Meng-lung himself and other literary men were already composing colloquial stories of their own before the publication of the *San-yen,* it is difficult to account for the genesis of those stories in Feng's collections supposedly not based on promptbooks.

19. Cf. Birch, *Stories from a Ming Collection,* p. 10, and Bishop, *The Colloquial Short Story in China,* pp. 18–19. Scholars have not yet reached a consensus of opinion concerning the editorial role of Feng, however. According to literary histories prepared in Communist China, Feng not only revised many existing stories to enhance their literary quality but included his own compositions in the *San-yen.* Cf. *Chung-kuo wen-hsüeh shih* (1959), III, 302–10, and *Chung-kuo wen-hsüeh shih* (1962), III, 964.

20. Thus Bishop comments in *The Colloquial Short Story in China,* p. 39: "Yet pornography is never admitted as such and is presented under the guise of moral instruction, as advice to the young who are to take warning from these detailed accounts of vice and avoid the lures of sensual pleasure. The narrator's admonition and the hero's sick-bed speech in "Chin-nu Sells Love at Newbridge" illustrate an ostensible moral purpose; but the relish with which the hero's moral lapse is related tempers somewhat our belief in that purpose."

21. I refer to Tale 29 of *Hsing-shih heng-yen, Lu t'ai-hsüeh shih-chiu ao kung-hou* (Finding solace in poetry and wine, Lu Nan disdains the high and mighty). Lu Nan was a minor Ming poet whose biography is recorded in *Ming shih, chüan* 287.

22. The story is entitled *Kuan-yuan-sou wan-feng hsien-nü* (Late in his life, a gardener meets fairies) (*Hsing-shih heng-yen,* Tale 4). It has been translated as "The Flower Lover and the Fairies" in Chi-chen Wang, tr., *Traditional Chinese Tales,* and as "The Old Gardener" in Yang Hsien-yi and Gladys Yang, trs., *The Courtesan's Jewel Box.*

23. Of course, the Ch'eng-Chu school of Neo-Confucianism, which domi-

nated Chinese thought from the Sung to the early years of the Republic, opposes *li* (principle) to *yü* (desire). But the latter term describes a condition of biological necessity or moral evil and retains even today its negative connotations.

24. In chap. 1, I have referred to the intellectual and commercial climate of the late Ming period favoring the growth of an erotic literature. But even Li Chih was not Rousseau, a programmatic philosopher who compelled the intellectuals of his time to see the self and the world in a new light. Cf. chap. 1, n. 34.

25. For a fuller portrait of the prudential lover, see my review of *The Golden Casket* in *Saturday Review* (December 5, 1964), p. 63.

26. *Tu Shih-niang nu-ch'en pai-pao-hsiang* (Tu Shih-niang angrily drowns her jewel box), Tale 32 of *Ching-shih t'ung-yen,* is available, among other translations, as the title story in Yang Hsien-yi and Gladys Yang, trs., *The Courtesan's Jewel Box.* Liu Wu-chi discusses the story in detail in *An Introduction to Chinese Literature,* pp. 220–24.

27. This is Tale 15 of *Hsing-shih heng-yen,* entitled *Ho Ta-ch'ing i-hen yuan-yang-t'ao* (The mandarin-duck girdle—a clue to the regrettable death of Ho Ta-ch'ing). It has been translated into English as "The Mandarin-duck Girdle" in Acton and Lee, trs., *Four Cautionary Tales.*

28. This is Tale 35 of *Ching-shih t'ung-yen.* Its title is *K'uang t'ai-shou lu-tuan ssu-hai-erh.*

29. *Chiang Hsing-ko ch'ung-hui chen-chu-shan* (Chiang Hsing-ko twice encounters his pearl-sewn shirt), Tale 1 of *Ku-chin hsiao-shuo,* has been translated under this title in Cyril Birch, tr., *Stories from a Ming Collection.*

30. *Stories from a Ming Collection,* p. 53.

31. C. S. Lewis so describes the Criseyde of the first three books of Chaucer's poem in *The Allegory of Love* (Oxford University Press, 1936), p. 183.

32. *Troilus and Criseyde,* Bk. II, l. 757.

33. *Stories from a Ming Collection,* p. 82.

GLOSSARY

This glossary is divided into two parts. Part I lists characters from Chinese novels and stories mentioned in the text and appendix. With the exception of several emperors, whose temple-names and reign-titles are given in Chinese in *Mathews' Dictionary* and similar references, omissions are inconsequential, including a group of minor celebrants at the T'ai-po temple in *The Scholars*. Characters identified by such titles as "Dr.," "Madame," and "Magistrate" are entered by surname, but the names of a few characters such as Big Feet Shen and Old Ch'in are given in the form recorded in the text. Part II contains titles of traditional Chinese fiction (excluding those listed in Bibliography, Parts II-VII), names of their authors, compilers, editors, and publishers, and special terms given in romanized form in the text and notes. Terms of address and measurement like *t'ai-t'ai, ku-niang, li,* and *mou,* however, are not included.

I. CHARACTERS

An Fei 安妃
Apricot Fairy 杏仙
Avalokitesvara, *see* Kuan-yin

Bamboo Spirit 拂雲叟
Big Feet Shen 沈大脚
Black Jade, *see* Lin Tai-yü
Bright Cloud, *see* Ch'ing-wen
Bull Monster King 牛魔王

Cardinal Spring 賈元春

Cassia (Hsüeh P'an's wife) 夏金桂
Cassia (Li Kuei-chieh) 李桂姐
Ch'ai Chin 柴進
Chang, Commander 張都監
Chang, Sheriff 張團練
Chang Ch'ing 張清
Chang Fei (Yi-te) 張飛、翼德
Chang Jen 張任
Chang Kuo-lao 張果老
Chang Liao 張遼
Chang Shao 張稍 (梢)

Chang Sung 張松

Chang Ts'ing 張青

Chao, Dr. 趙太醫

Chao Yün (Tzu-lung) 趙雲、子龍

Ch'ao Kai 晁蓋

Ch'en Ching-chi 陳經濟

Ch'en Fan 陳蕃

Ch'en Ho-fu 陳和甫

Ch'en Kung (Kung-t'ai) 陳宮、公臺

Ch'en Ta-lang 陳大郎

Ch'en To-shou 陳多壽

Cheng, Butcher 鄭屠

Cheng, Old, see Old Cheng

Cheng Ai-yüeh-erh 鄭愛月兒

Chess 司棋

Chia Chen 賈珍

Chia Cheng 賈政

Chia Jui 賈瑞

Chia Lien 賈璉

Chia Pao-yü 賈寶玉

Chia She 賈赦

Chia Yü-ts'un 賈雨村

Chia Yung 賈蓉

Chiang (yamen clerk) 蔣刑房

Chiang, Dr. 蔣竹山

Chiang Hsing-ko 蔣興哥

Chiang the "Gate God" 蔣門神

Ch'iao-chieh 巧姐

Ch'iao Kung 喬公

Chien-mei 兼美

Chin Tung-yai 金東崖

Chin Yu-yü 金有餘

Ch'in, Old, see Old Ch'in

Ch'in Chü-po 秦巨伯

Ch'in Chung 秦鐘

Ch'in K'o-ch'ing (see also Chien-mei) 秦可卿

Ch'in Ming 秦明

Ch'in T'ung 琴童

Ch'ing-wen 晴雯

Ch'iu-wen 秋紋

Chou Chin 周進

Chou Hsiu 周秀

Chou Yü 周瑜

Chrysanthemum (Ch'iu-chü) 秋菊

Chu-ko Liang (K'ung-ming) 諸葛亮、孔明

Chu To-fu 朱多福

Chu T'ung 朱仝

Chu Wu-neng 豬悟能 (豬八戒)

Chu Yuan-chang 朱元璋

Ch'ü Ching-yü 瞿景玉

Ch'ü Kung-sun 瞿公孫

Chuang Shao-kuang 莊紹光

Compassion Spring 賈惜春

Crow Nest (Wu-ch'ao) 烏巢禪師

Cypress Spirit 孤直公

Dragon of the Ching River 涇河龍(王)

Embroidered Spring 繡春

Erh-lang Shen 二郎神

Fan Chin 范進

Fang La 方臘

Feng Chi 逢紀

Fortune (San-ch'iao-erh) 三巧兒

Garuda 雲程萬里鵬

Goddess of Disillusionment 警幻仙姑

Golden Bracelet 金釧兒

Golden Cicada 金蟬長老 (金蟬子)

Golden Lotus, see P'an Chin-lien

Han Hsin 韓信

Han Yü-ch'iao 韓玉翹

Ho, Captain 何千戶

Ho Yen 何晏

Hsi-men Ch'ing 西門慶

Hsia (village head) 夏總甲

Hsia-hou Tun 夏侯惇

Hsiang-ling (see also Ying-lien)· 香菱

Hsiao-ko 孝哥

Hsing, Madame 邢夫人

Hsü Huang 徐晃

Hsüan-tsang 玄奘

Hsüeh, Dame 薛婆

Hsüeh-o 孫雪娥

Hsüeh P'an 薛蟠

Hsüeh Pao-ch'ai 薛寶釵

Hsün (village squire) 荀老爹

Hsün Mei 荀玫

Hsün Yu 荀攸

Hu Kuang 胡廣

Hua Hsi-jen 花襲人

Hua Hsiung 華雄

Hua Jung 花榮

Hua T'o 華陀

Hua Tzu-hsü 花子虛

Huang, Bailiff 黃老爹

Huang Chung 黃忠

Huang Wen-ping 黃文炳

Hui-lien (Wistaria) 惠蓮

Hu-yen Cho 呼延灼

Jade Emperor 玉皇大天尊

Jade-Face Princess 玉面公主

Ju-i (Heart's Delight) 如意兒

Juan Brothers 阮小二、小五、小七

Juniper Spirit 凌空子

Kai K'uan 蓋寬

Kao (Pigsy's father-in-law) 高太公

Kao Ch'iu 高俅

Kao Shun 高順

Kuan-ko 官哥

Kuan P'ing 關平

Kuan Sheng 關勝

Kuan-yin 觀(世)音菩薩

Kuan Yü (Yün-ch'ang) 關羽、雲長

K'uang Ch'ao-jen 匡超人

Kung-sun Sheng 公孫勝

Kung-sun Tsan 公孫瓚

K'ung Yung 孔融

Lai Wang 來旺

Lao Tzu, see T'ai-shang Lao-chün

Leng Tzu-hsing 冷子興

Li, Magistrate 李本瑛

Li Chiao-erh 李嬌兒

Li Huan 李紈

Li K'uei 李逵

Li P'ing-erh 李瓶兒

Li-shan Lao-mu 梨山老母

Li Shih-shih 李師師

Li Ting 李定

Lin, Madame 林太太

Lin Ch'ung 林冲

Lin Tai-yü 林黛玉

Liu Ch'an 劉禪

Liu Chang 劉璋

Liu Fu (Yuan-ying) 劉馥、元穎

Liu Hsi 劉熙

Liu Hsiang-lien 柳湘蓮

Liu Hsiu (Wen-shu) 劉秀、文叔

Liu Lao-lao 劉老老

Liu Li 劉理

Liu Pei (Hsüan-te) 劉備、玄德

Liu Piao 劉表

Liu Yung (Liu Pei's son) 劉永

Lou, Old, see Old Lou

Lou Brothers 婁琫、婁瓚

Love 愛愛

Lu Chih-shen 魯智深

Lu Chün-i 盧俊義

Lu Hua-shih 盧華士

Lu Su 魯肅

Lu Sun 陸遜

Lü Meng 呂蒙

Lü Pu 呂布

Lü Tung-pin 呂洞賓

Ma Ch'ao (Meng-ch'i) 馬超、孟起

Ma Ch'un-shang 馬純上

Ma Liang 馬良

Ma Shu 馬謖

Magnolia 玉蘭

Mandarin Duck 鴛鴦

Maple Spirit 赤身鬼使

Matriarch 賈母

Meng Yü-lou 孟玉樓

Miao-yü 妙玉

Monkey, see Sun Wu-k'ung

Monster at the River that Leads to
　Heaven 靈感大王

Moon Lady (Yüeh-niang) 吳月娘

Moonbeam, see Cheng Ai-yüeh-erh

Ni Heng 禰衡

Niu Pu-yi 牛布衣

Niu P'u-lang 牛浦郎

No-cha 哪吒

Old Cheng 鄭老爹

Old Ch'in 秦老

Old Lou 婁煥文

P'an (Golden Lotus' mother) 潘姥姥

P'an (village head) 潘保正

P'an, Bailiff 潘三

P'an Ch'iao-yün 潘巧雲

P'an Chin-lien 潘金蓮

P'an Yu-an 潘又安

P'ang Te 龐德

P'ang T'ung 龐統

Pao, Mrs. 鮑老太

Pao T'ing-hsi 鮑廷璽

Pao Wen-ch'ing 鮑文卿

P'eng, Mr. 彭鄉紳

P'eng Yüeh 彭越

Pervading Fragrance, see Hua Hsi-jen

Phoenix, see Wang Hsi-feng

Pigsy, see Chu Wu-neng

Pine Spirit 十八公

Pity 憐憐

Plum Blossom (Ch'un-mei) 春梅

Pock-marked Ch'ien 錢麻子

Precious Clasp, see Hsüeh Pao-ch'ai

P'u-ching 普淨

Purple Cuckoo 紫鵑

Quest Spring 賈探春

Rakshas, Madame 羅剎女

Recluse of Divine Prophecy 神言山人

Red Boy 紅孩兒

Red-scaled Python 紅鱗大蟒

Sandy, see Sha Wu-ching

Sha Wu-ching 沙悟淨 (沙和尚)

Shen, Big Feet, see Big Feet Shen

Shen, Hsiang-fu 申祥甫

Shih, Magistrate 時知縣

Shih Chin 史進

Shih En 施恩

Shih Hsiang-yün 史湘雲

Shih Hsiu 石秀

Shih Wen-kung 史文恭

Snow Goose 雪雁

Ssu-ma Chung-hsiang 司馬仲相

Ssu-ma I (Chung-ta) 司馬懿、仲達

Star of the South Pole 壽星（南極老
　人星）

Subodhi 須菩提

Sun Ch'ien 孫乾

Sun Ch'üan 孫權

Sun Ts'e 孫策

Sun Wu-k'ung 孫悟空（孫行者）

Sung, Censor 宋御史

Sung Chiang 宋江

T'ai-shang Lao-chün 太上老君

T'ai-yin Hsing-chün 太陰星君

T'ang San-tsang 唐三藏

Teng Ai 鄧艾

T'ien Feng 田豐

T'ien Hu 田虎

Tiny Jade 小玉

Tou Wu 竇武

Tripitaka, see Hsüan-tsang; T'ang
　San-tsang; Golden Cicada

Truth 眞眞

Ts'ai Ching 蔡京

Ts'ai Yün 蔡蘊

Ts'ao Chieh 曹節

Ts'ao Hsing 曹性

Ts'ao P'i 曹丕

Ts'ao Ts'ao 曹操

Ts'ui Chou-p'ing 崔州平

Tu Shao-ch'ing 杜少卿

Tu Shen-ch'ing 杜慎卿

Tu Shih-niang 杜十娘

Tung Cho 董卓

T'ung Kuan 童貫

Vase, see Li P'ing-erh

Wang, Madame 王夫人

Wang, Magistrate 王知縣

Wang, Mrs. 王太太

Wang Ch'ing 王慶

Wang Fu 王甫

Wang Hsi-feng 王熙鳳

Wang Hui 王惠

Wang Mien 王冕

Wang Shan-pao's wife 王善保家的

Wang VI 王六兒

Wang Ying 王英

Wang Yü-hui 王玉輝

Wei Su 危素

Welcome Spring 賈迎春

Welcome Spring (Vase's maid)
　迎春

Wen Ch'ou 文醜

Wen Pi-ku 溫必古

White Deer 白鹿（比邱國史）

White-faced Fox 白面狐狸

Wu, Dowager 吳太夫人

Wu Shu 武書

Wu Sung 武松

Wu Yung 吳用

Yang Chien 楊戩

Yang Chih 楊志

Yang Hsiu 楊修

Yang Hsiung 楊雄

Yellow-robed Monster 黃袍怪

Yen Chih-ho 嚴致和

Yen Ch'ing 燕青

Yen Liang 顏良

Yen P'o-hsi 閻婆惜

Ying-erh 迎兒

Ying-lien 甄英蓮

Ying Po-chüeh 應伯爵

Ying Pu 英布

Yu Erh-chieh 尤二姐
Yu San-chieh 尤三姐
Yü Brothers, *see* Yü Yu-ta
Yü Chi 于吉
Yü Chin 于禁
Yü Hua-hsüan 虞華軒

Yü Yu-ta 余有達
Yü Yü-te 虞育德
Yuan Shao 袁紹
Yuan Shu 袁術
Yüeh Fei 岳飛

II. AUTHORS, TITLES, AND TERMS

an Chien 按鑑

*ch*ʻ*an* (*Zen*) 禪
*Chang Chu-p*ʻ*o p*ʻ*ing Chin P*ʻ*ing Mei* 張竹坡評金瓶梅
chang-hui hsiao-shuo 章回小說
Chang Yün 張勻
Chao Fei-yen wai-chuan 趙飛燕外傳
chen 真 (甄)
Chʻen Chʻiu 陳球
*Ch*ʻ*en To-shou sheng-ssu fu-ch*ʻ*i* 陳多壽生死夫妻
*cheng-ch*ʻ*iang* 爭強
Chʻeng Wei-yuan 程偉元
Chi Yün 紀昀
chia 假 (賈)
chiang-ching 講經
*Chiang Hsing-ko ch*ʻ*ung-hui chen-chu shan* 蔣興哥重會珍珠衫
chiang-shih 講史
chien-hsia 劍俠
Chʻien Tsʻan 錢彩
*ch*ʻ*ih-ch*ʻ*ing* 癡情
Chin Feng 金豐
Chin Hai-ling tsung-yü wang-shen 金海陵縱欲亡身
Chin Ho 金和
*Chin-ku ch*ʻ*i-kuan* 今古奇觀
Chin Sheng-tʻan 金聖歎

chin-shih 進士
*ch*ʻ*in ch*ʻ*i shu hua* 琴棋書畫
Ching-hua yuan 鏡花緣
*Ching-pen t*ʻ*ung-su hsiao-shuo* 京本通俗小說
*Ching-shih t*ʻ*ung-yen* 警世通言
*ch*ʻ*ing* 情
*Ch*ʻ*ing-p*ʻ*ing-shan-t*ʻ*ang hua-pen* 清平山堂話本
chiu hsiao-shuo 舊小說
Chu Ting-chʻen 朱鼎臣
Chʻu Jen-hu 褚人穫
chü-jen 舉人
*ch*ʻ*ü* 曲
chuan 傳
*ch*ʻ*uan-ch*ʻ*i* 傳奇
chuang-yuan 狀元
chung hsiao chieh i 忠孝節義
Chung-i shui-hu-chuan 忠義水滸傳
Chung-kuo ku-tien hsiao-shuo 中國古典小說

*Erh-k*ʻ*o p*ʻ*o-an ching-ch*ʻ*i* 二刻拍案驚奇

*Fei-lung ch*ʻ*üan-chuan* 飛龍全傳
Feng Meng-lung 馮夢龍
Feng-shen yen-i 封神演義
fu 賦
fu (a prefecture) 府

Hai-shang-hua lieh-chuan 海上花列傳

Hao-chʻiu chuan 好逑傳

hao han 好漢

Ho Ta-chʻing i-hen yuan-yang-tʻao 赫
　大卿遺恨鴛鴦絛

Hsi-yu-chi chuan 西遊記傳

Hsi-yu pu 西遊補

Hsiao-hsiao Sheng 笑笑生

hsiao-ling 小令

hsiao-shuo 小説

hsien 縣

Hsin Chung-kuo wei-lai chi 新中國未
　來記

hsin hsiao-shuo 新小説

Hsin-pien wu-tai-shih pʻing-hua 新編五
　代史平話

Hsing-shih heng-yen 醒世恒言

Hsing-shih yin-yuan 醒世姻緣

Hsiu-hsiang Han-Sung chʻi-shu 繡像漢
　宋奇書

hsiu-tsʻai 秀才

Hsiung Fei 熊飛

Hsiung Ta-mu 熊大木

Hsü Chin Pʻing Mei 續金瓶梅

hua-pen 話本

hua-shuo 話説

hui 回

Hung Pʻien 洪楩

i 義

Jou pʻu-tʻuan 肉蒲團

Ju-i-chün chuan 如意君傳

kan-pang 桿棒

Kan Pao 干寶

Kʻan pʻi-hsüeh tan-cheng Erh-lang Shen
　勘皮靴單證二郎神

kang erh tzu chin 剛而自矜

Kao Ê 高鶚

Ko-lien hua-ying 隔簾花影

Ku-chin hsiao-shuo 古今小説

Ku-pen hsi-yu cheng-tao shu 古本西
　遊證道書

ku-wen 古文

Kuan-yuan-sou wan-feng hsien-nü 灌園
　叟晚逢仙女

Kʻuang tʻai-shou lu-tuan ssu-hai-erh 況
　太守路斷死孩兒

kung-an 公案

kung-sheng 貢生

Kuo Hsün 郭勳

Kuo-yü 國語

Lao-tsʻan yu-chi 老殘遊記

Li Chih 李贄

Li Ju-chen 李汝珍

Li Pao-chia 李寶嘉

Ling Chʻi-chʻao 梁啓超

Liao-chai chih-i 聊齋志異

Ling Meng-chʻu 凌濛初

Liu Ê 劉鶚

Lo Kuan-chung 羅貫中

Lo Pen (*see also* Lo Kuan-chung) 羅本

Lu tʻai-hsüeh shih-chiu ao kung-hou 盧
　太學詩酒傲公侯

lü-shih 律詩

Lung-tʻu kung-an 龍圖公案

Mai-yu-lang tu-chan hua-kʻuei 賣油郎
　獨占花魁

Mao Lun 毛綸

Mao Tsung-kang 毛宗崗

ming-shih 名士

Nan-yu-chih chuan 南遊志傳

Nien-yü kuan-yin 碾玉觀音

pa-ku wen 八股文
p'ai-lü 排律
pao-chüan 寶卷
Pao kung-an 包公案
pao-ying 報應
Pei-Sung-chih chuan 北宋志傳
Pei-yu chi 北遊記
pien-wen 變文
p'in-hsiao 品簫
p'ing-hua 平(評)話
P'ing Shan Leng Yen 平山冷燕
P'o-an ching-ch'i 拍案驚奇
Pu Chiang Tsung pai-yuan chuan 補江
    總白猿傳
pu-jen 不忍
P'u Sung-ling 蒲松齡
p'u-tao 朴刀

san-chiao 三教
San-hsia wu-i 三俠五義
San-Sui p'ing-yao chuan 三遂平妖傳
san-t'ao 散套
San-yen 三言
Shen Hsiao-hsia hsiang-hui ch'u-shih-piao
    沈小霞相會出師表
shen-tu 慎獨
shih 詩
Shih Nai-an 施耐菴
Shih-shuo hsin-yü 世說新語
Shuo Hu ch'üan-chuan 說呼全傳
Shuo T'ang cheng-hsi chuan
    說唐征西傳
Shuo T'ang ch'üan-chuan 說唐全傳
Shuo T'ang hou-chuan 說唐後傳
Shuo Yüeh ch'üan-chuan 說岳全傳
Sou-shen chi 搜神記

Ssu-ch'iao Chü-shih 四橋居士
su 俗
Sui-T'ang-chih chuan 隋唐志傳
Sui T'ang yen-i 隋唐演義

ta-lao-kuan 大老官
T'ai-p'ing kuang-chi 太平廣記
t'an-tz'u 彈詞
T'ang San-tsang hsi-yu shih-o chuan 唐
    三藏西遊釋厄傳
tao 道
te-hsing 德行
Ting Yao-k'ang 丁耀亢
ts'ai-tzu chia-jen 才子佳人
Ts'ai Yuan-fang 蔡元放
Ts'an-T'ang wu-tai-shih yen-chuan 殘
    唐五代史演傳
Ts'ao Chan (see also *Ts'ao Hsüeh-
    ch'in*) 曹霑
Ts'ao Hsüeh-ch'in 曹雪芹
Ts'ui tai-chao sheng-ssu yuan-chia 崔
    待詔生死冤家
Tu Shih-niang nu-ch'en pai-pao-hsiang 杜
    十娘怒沉百寶箱
Tung-Chou lieh-kuo chih 東周列國志
Tung-yu chi 東遊記
Tung Yüeh 董說
Tzu pu-yü 子不語
tz'u 詞

Wan-hua lou 萬花樓
Wang Shih-chen 王世貞
Wang Tan-i 汪憺猗
Wu Ch'eng-en 吳承恩
Wu Ching-tzu 吳敬梓
wu-hsia hsiao-shuo 武俠小說
Wu Wo-yao 吳沃堯

ya 雅

Yang-chia-fu tᶜung-su yen-i 楊家府通
俗演義

Yang Chih-ho 楊志(致)和

yen-i 演義

Yen-shan wai-shih 燕山外史

yen-shih 演史

yin 淫

Ying-hsiung pᶜu 英雄譜

Yü chiao li 玉嬌李(麗)

Yü Chiao Li 玉嬌梨

yü-chᶜiao wen-ta 漁樵問答

Yü Hsiang-tou 余象斗

Yü-shih ming-yen 喻世明言

Yuan Mei 袁枚

yüeh 曰

Yüeh-wei-tsᶜao-tᶜang pi-chi 閱微草堂
筆記

BIBLIOGRAPHY

This bibliography includes all books and articles on traditional Chinese fiction mentioned in the text, appendix, and notes, with the exception of a few which are either of small interest or cited in support of minor points. Full bibliographical information concerning the latter, however, is given in the relevant notes. To the list of references culled from the text and notes I have added other titles of interest, though I am fully aware of the impossibility of providing in a few pages more than a modest bibliography on the subject. The specialist should consult Tien-yi Li, *Chinese Fiction: A Bibliography of Books and Articles in Chinese and English* (Yale University, Far Eastern Publications, 1968). It is to be hoped that Professor Li will soon prepare a sequel to the volume covering titles in Japanese, French, and German.

The bibliography is in eight parts. Part I contains books and articles of general interest to the student of traditional Chinese fiction. Parts II-VII are devoted to the six major novels. Each of these parts comprises two sections. Section A gives the more important texts of a novel and its antecedents (if such exist) as well as translations, while Section B lists monographic studies and other references of value. Part VIII contains Western-language versions of other classic novels listed in the Glossary as well as collections of traditional stories in English translation referred to in the notes, either new or based on standard collections listed in the Glossary. For fuller coverage of Chinese fiction in translation see Martha Davidson, comp., *A List of Published Translations from Chinese into English, French, and German*. Part I: *Literature, Exclusive of Poetry* (Ann Arbor, J. W. Edwards, 1952), and Tung-Li Yuan, comp., *China in Western Literature* (Yale University, Far Eastern Publications, 1958).

I. TRADITIONAL CHINESE FICTION

A Ying 阿英. *Wai-Ch'ing hsiao-shuo shih* 晚清小說史 (A history of late Ch'ing fiction). Rev. ed. Peking, Tso-chia ch'u-pan-she, 1955.

Birch, Cyril. "Feng Meng-lung and the *Ku chin hsiao shuo*," *Bulletin of the School of Oriental and African Studies*, XVIII, Pt. 1 (1956).

Bishop, John L. "Some Limitations of Chinese Fiction," in John L. Bishop, ed., *Studies in Chinese Literature*. Cambridge, Harvard University Press, 1965.

—— *The Colloquial Short Story in China: A Study of the San-Yen Collections*. Cambridge, Harvard University Press, 1956.

Chai, Ch'u, and Winberg Chai, trs. & eds. *A Treasury of Chinese Literature*. New York, Appleton-Century, 1965. Chapter 8 contains selections from the six major classic novels.

Chao Ts'ung 趙聰. *Chung-kuo ssu-ta hsiao-shuo chih yen-chiu* 中國四大小說之研究 (Studies in four great Chinese novels). Hong Kong, Yu-lien ch'u-pan-she, 1964.

Cheng Chen-to 鄭振鐸. *Chung-kuo su-wen-hsüeh shih* 中國俗文學史 (A history of Chinese popular literature). Peking, Wen-hsüeh ku-chi k'an-hsing-she, 1957.

—— *Chung-kuo wen-hsüeh yen-chiu* 中國文學研究 (Studies in Chinese literature). 3 vols. Peking, Tso-chia ch'u-pan-she, 1957.

Chiang Tsu-i 蔣祖怡. *Hsiao-shuo tsuan-yao* 小說纂要 (A handbook of Chinese fiction). Nanking, Cheng-chung shu-chü, 1948.

Ch'ien Ching-fang 錢靜方. *Hsiao-shuo ts'ung-k'ao* 小說叢考 (Historical sources for Chinese fiction and drama). Shanghai, Commercial Press, 1916.

Chung-kuo ku-tien hsiao-shuo p'ing-lun-chi 中國古典小說評論集 (Critical essays on classic Chinese novels). Peking, Peking ch'u-pan-she, 1957.

Chung-kuo wen-hsüeh shih 中國文學史 (A history of Chinese literature), prepared by the class of 1955, Chinese Department, Peking University. 4 vols. Peking, Jen-min-wen-hsüeh ch'u-pan-she, 1959.

Chung-kuo wen-hsüeh shih 中國文學史 (A history of Chinese literature), prepared by the Literary Institute, Academy of Sciences, Peking. 3 vols. Peking, Jen-min-wen-hsüeh ch'u-pan-she, 1962.

Feuerwerker, Yi-tse Mei. "The Chinese Novel," in Wm. Theodore de Bary, ed., *Approaches to the Oriental Classics*. New York, Columbia University Press, 1959.

Gulik, R. H. van. *Erotic Colour Prints of the Ming Period, with an Essay on Chinese Sex Life from the Han to the Ch'ing dynasty*. 3 vols. Tokyo, privately printed, 1951.

Hanan, Patrick. "The Development of Fiction and Drama," in Raymond Dawson, ed., *The Legacy of China*. Oxford University Press, 1964.

—— "The Early Chinese Short Story: A Critical Theory in Outline," *Harvard Journal of Asiatic Studies*, XXVII (1967).

Hsia, C. T. 夏志清. "Hsia Tsi-an tui Chung-kuo su-wen-hsüeh ti k‘an-fa 夏濟安對中國俗文學的看法" (T. A. Hsia on Chinese popular literature), *Hsien-tai Wen-hsüeh*, No. 25 (Taipei, 1965).

Hsia, T. A. 夏濟安, ed. *Hsiao-shuo yü wen-hua* 小說與文化 (Fiction and culture). Taipei, Ming-hua shu-chü, 1959.

Hsü Shih-nien 徐士年. *Ku-tien hsiao-shuo lun-chi* 古典小說論集 (Critiques of classic Chinese novels). Shanghai, Shanghai ch‘u-pan-kung-ssu, 1955.

Hu Shih 胡適. *Hu Shih wen-ts‘un* 胡適文存 (Collected essays of Hu Shih). 4 vols. Taipei, Yüan-tung t‘u-shu-kung-ssu, 1953.

—— *Chung-kuo chang-hui hsiao-shuo k‘ao-cheng* 中國章回小說考證 (Studies in traditional Chinese novels). Dairen, Shih-yeh yin-shu-kuan, 1943.

Hu Shih ssu-hsiang p‘i-p‘an 胡適思想批判 (Critiques of Hu Shih's thought). 8 vols. Peking, San-lien shu-tien, 1955–56.

K‘ung Ling-ching 孔另境, ed. *Chung-kuo hsiao-shuo shih-liao* 中國小說史料 (Source materials on Chinese fiction). Shanghai, Chung-hua shu-chü, 1936. Rev. ed. Shanghai, Ku-tien-wen-hsüeh ch‘u-pan-she, 1957.

Lévy, André. "Études sur trois recueils anciens de contes chinois," *T‘oung Pao*, LII, Nos. 1-3 (1963).

Li Ch‘en-tung 李辰冬. *San-kuo Shui-hu yü Hsi-yu* 三國水滸與西遊 (*San-kuo, Shui-hu,* and *Hsi-yu chi*). Chungking, Ta-tao ch‘u-pan-she, 1945.

Li Hsi-fan 李希凡. *Lun Chung-kuo ku-tien hsiao-shuo ti i-shu hsing-hsiang* 論中國古典小說的藝術形象 (Artistic aspects of classic Chinese novels). Shanghai, Shanghai wen-i ch‘u-pan-she, 1961.

Li, Tien-yi 李田意. "Notes on Chinese Short Story Collections Seen in Japan 日本所見中國短篇小說略記," *Tsing Hua Journal of Chinese Studies* (new series), I, No. 2 (1957).

Liu Hsiu-yeh 劉修業. *Ku-tien hsiao-shuo hsi-ch‘ü ts‘ung-k‘ao* 古典小說戲曲叢考 (Classic Chinese fiction and drama: biographical and bibliographical studies). Peking, Tso-chia ch‘u-pan-she, 1958.

Liu, James J. Y. *The Chinese Knight-Errant*. University of Chicago Press, 1967.

Liu K‘ai-jung 劉開榮. *T‘ang-tai hsiao-shuo yen-chiu* 唐代小說研究 (Studies in T‘ang fiction). Shanghai, Commercial Press, 1947.

Liu Ts‘un-yan. *Buddhist and Taoist Influences on Chinese Novels*. Vol. I: *The Authorship of the Feng Shen Yen I*. Wiesbaden, Otto Harrassowitz, 1962.

—— 柳存仁. "Lun chin-jen yen-chiu Chung-kuo hsiao-shuo chih te-shih 論近人研究中國小說之得失 (Amendments to Earlier Studies of Chinese Fiction)," *Lien-ho*

Shu-yuan Hsüeh-pao (*The United College Journal*), III (Hong Kong, 1964).

Liu Wu-chi. *An Introduction to Chinese Literature*. Bloomington and London, Indiana University Press, 1966.

Lo Yeh 羅燁. *Tsui-weng t'an-lu* 醉翁談錄 (Tsui-weng's notebook). Modern reprint: Taipei, Shih-chieh shu-chü, 1958.

Lu Hsün 魯迅. *Chung-kuo hsiao-shuo shih-lüeh* 中國小説史略. Rev. ed. Shanghai, Pei-hsin shu-chü, 1931.

——— Translation, under title *A Brief History of Chinese Fiction*, by Yang Hsien-yi and Gladys Yang. Peking, Foreign Languages Press, 1954.

Lu Tan-an 陸澹安, ed. *Hsiao-shuo tz'u-yü hui-shih* 小説詞語匯釋 (A dictionary of phrases and idioms from traditional Chinese fiction). Peking, Chung-hua shu-chü, 1964.

Meng Yao 孟瑤. *Chung-kuo hsiao-shuo shih* 中國小説史 (A history of Chinese fiction). 4 vols. Taipei, Wen-hsing shu-tien, 1966.

Meng Yuan-lao 孟元老, *et al. Tung-ching meng-hua lu (wai ssu-chung)* 東京夢華錄 (外四種) ("Reminiscences of Pien-liang" and four accounts of Hangchow). Modern reprint: Peking, Chung-hua shu-chü, 1962.

Ming Ch'ing hsiao-shuo yen-chiu lun-wen chi 明清小説研究論文集 (Studies in Ming and Ch'ing fiction). Peking, Jen-min-wen-hsüeh ch'u-pan-she, 1954.

Průšek, Jaroslav. "History and Epics in China and in the West," *Diogenes*, No. 42 (1963).

——— "The Narrators of Buddhist Scriptures and Religious Tales in the Sung Period," *Archiv Orientální*, X (Prague, 1938).

——— "New Studies of the Chinese Colloquial Short Story," *Archiv Orientální*, XXV (1957).

——— "The Realistic and Lyric Elements in the Chinese Medieval Story," *Archiv Orientální*, XXXII (1964).

——— "Researches into the Beginnings of the Chinese Popular Novel," *Archiv Orientální*, XI (1939); XXIII (1955).

Ruhlmann, Robert. "Traditional Heroes in Chinese Popular Fiction," in Arthur F. Wright, ed., *The Confucian Persuasion*. Stanford University Press, 1960.

Sun K'ai-ti 孫楷第. *Chung-kuo t'ung-su hsiao-shuo shu-mu* 中國通俗小説書目 (A catalogue of Chinese works of popular fiction). Peiping, National Peiping Library, 1932. Rev. ed. Peking, Tso-chia ch'u-pan-she, 1958.

——— *Jih-pen Tung-ching so-chien Chung-kuo hsiao-shuo shu-mu t'i-yao* 日本東京所見中國小説書目提要 (A descriptive bibliography of Chinese works of fiction seen in Tokyo). Peiping, National Peiping Library, 1932. The new edition (Shanghai, Shang-tsa ch'u-pan-she, 1953) deletes *t'i-yao* from the title.

——— *Lun Chung-kuo tuan-p'ien pai-hua hsiao-shuo* 論中國短篇白話小説 (On Chinese short stories). Shanghai, T'ang-ti ch'u-pan-she, 1935.

—— *Ts'ang-chou chi* 滄州集 (Collected essays of Sun K'ai-ti). 2 vols. Peking, Chung-hua shu-chü, 1965.

T'an Cheng-pi 譚正璧. *Chung-kuo hsiao-shuo fa-ta shih* 中國小說發達史 (The development of Chinese fiction). Shanghai, Kuang-ming shu-chü, 1935.

—— *Hua-pen yü ku-chü* 話本與古劇 (*Hua-pen* and old Chinese drama). Shanghai, Shanghai ku-tien-wen-hsüeh ch'u-pan-she, 1956.

Wang Chung-min 王重民, *et al.*, eds. *Tun-huang pien-wen chi* 敦煌變文集 (A collection of *pien-wen* from Tun-huang). 2 vols. Peking, Jen-min-wen-hsüeh ch'u-pan-she, 1957.

Wen-hsüeh i-ch'an hsüan-chi 文學遺產選集 (Selections from "Literary Heritage"). 3 vols. Peking, Tso-chia ch'u-pan-she (later, Chung-hua shu-chü), 1956–60.

Wen-hsüeh i-ch'an tseng-k'an 文學遺產增刊 (A supplement to "Literary Heritage"). 13 vols. Peking, Tso-chia ch'u-pan-she (later, Chung-hua shu-chü), 1955–63.

II. THE ROMANCE OF THE THREE KINGDOMS (San-kuo-chih yen-i)

A

Ch'en Shou 陳壽. *San-kuo chih* 三國志. Commentary by P'ei Sung-chih 裴松之. 5 vols. Peking, Chung-hua shu-chü, 1959.

"San-kuo-chih p'ing-hua 三國志平話," in *Ch'üan-hsiang p'ing-hua wu-chung* 全相平話五種 (Five fully illustrated *p'ing-hua*). 5 vols. Peking, Wen-hsüeh ku-chi k'an-hsing-she, 1956.

Lo Kuan-chung 羅貫中. *San-kuo-chih t'ung-su yen-i* 三國志通俗演義 (An explanation of the *San-kuo-chih*, done in the popular style). 24 vols. Shanghai, Han-fen-lou (a division of the Commercial Press), 1929. A photolithographic reprint of the Chia-ching edition.

Tsu-pen San-kuo yen-i 足本三國演義 (The full-text *San-kuo yen-i*). 2 vols. 19th ptg.: Taipei, Shih-chieh shu-chü, 1958. A reprint of the Mao Tsung-kang version.

San-kuo yen-i 三國演義. 2 vols. Peking, Tso-chia ch'u-pan-she, 1953; one-volume edition, 1955. An emended edition of the Mao Tsung-kang version.

Brewitt-Taylor, C. H., tr. *Romance of the Three Kingdoms* (*San Kuo Chih Yen-i*). 2 vols. Shanghai, Kelly and Walsh, 1925. Reprint with "Introduction" by Roy Andrew Miller: Rutland, Vt., Charles E. Tuttle, 1959.

Nghiêm Toan, and Louis Ricaud, trs. *Les Trois Royaumes*. 3 vols. Introduction by Robert Ruhlmann. Saigon, Société des Études Indochinoises, 1960–63. Chapters 1-45.

B

Chu Hsiu-hsia 祝秀俠. *San-kuo jen-wu hsin-lun* 三國人物新論 (New studies in the characters of the Three Kingdoms period). Shanghai, Kuo-chi wen-hua fu-wu-she, 1948.

Lü Ssu-mien 呂思勉. *San-kuo shih-hua* 三國史話 (On the history of the Three Kingdoms period). 1st Taipei ed., K'ai-ming shu-tien, 1954.

San-kuo yen-i yen-chiu lun-wen chi 三國演義研究論文集 (Studies in *San-kuo yen-i*). Peking, Tso-chia ch'u-pan-she, 1957.

Tung Mei-k'an 董每戡. *San-kuo yen-i shih-lun* 三國演義試論 (A tentative critique of *San-kuo yen-i*). Shanghai, Ku-tien-wen-hsüeh ch'u-pan-she, 1956.

III. THE WATER MARGIN (*Shui-hu chuan*)

A

Hsüan-ho i-shih 宣和遺事 (Events of the Hsüan-ho reign and after). Taipei, Shih-chieh shu-chü, 1958.

I-pai-erh-shih-hui ti Shui-hu 一百二十回的水滸 (The 120-chapter *Shui-hu*). Preface by Hu Shih. 20 vols. Shanghai, Commercial Press, 1929.

Chin Sheng-t'an ch'i-shih-i-hui-pen Shui-hu-chuan 金聖歎七十一回本水滸傳 (The Chin Sheng-t'an version of *Shui-hu-chuan* in 71 chapters). 24 vols. Shanghai, Chung-hua shu-chü, 1934. A photolithographic reprint, in reduced size, of the original Kuan-hua-t'ang edition.

Shih Nai-an 施耐菴, and Lo Kuan-chung 羅貫中. *Shui-hu ch'üan-chuan* 水滸全傳 (The complete *Shui-hu chuan*). Preface by Cheng Chen-to. 4 vols. Peking, Jen-min wen-hsüeh ch'u-pan-she, 1954. A variorum edition prepared by Cheng Chen-to, Wang Li-ch'i, *et al.*

Wang Shao-t'ang 王少堂, narrator. *Yangchow p'ing-hua Shui-hu: Wu Sung* 揚州評話 水滸: 武松 (The Wu Sung saga as retold in the Yangchow *p'ing-hua* version of *Shui-hu*). 2 vols. Nanking, Kiangsu wen-i ch'u-pan-she, 1959.

Birch, Cyril, tr. "The Plot Against the Birthday Convoy [*Shui hu chuan*, XIV–XVI]," in Cyril Birch, ed., *Anthology of Chinese Literature*. New York, Grove Press, 1965.

Buck, Pearl S., tr. *All Men Are Brothers*. 2 vols. New York, John Day, 1933. Reprint New York, Grove Press, 1957.

Jackson, J. H., tr. *Water Margin*. 2 vols. Shanghai, Commercial Press, 1937.

Kuhn, Franz, tr. *Die Räuber vom Liang Schan Moor*. Leipzig, Insel-Verlag, 1934.

Shapiro, Sidney, tr. "Outlaws of the Marshes (An Excerpt from the Novel)," *Chinese Literature*, No. 12 (1959). Chapter 6–9 of the 70-chapter version.

B

Ho Hsin 何心. *Shui-hu yen-chiu* 水滸研究 (Studies in *Shui-hu*). Rev. ed. Shanghai, Ku-tien-wen-hsüeh ch'u-pan-she, 1957.

Ho Man-tzu 何滿子. *Lun Chin Sheng-t'an p'ing-kai Shui-hu-chuan* 論金聖歎評改水滸傳 (A study of Chin Sheng-t'an's commentary on and revision of *Shui-hu chuan*). Shanghai, Shanghai ch'u-pan-she, 1954.

Hsia, C. T. "Comparative Approaches to *Water Margin*," *Yearbook of Comparative and General Literature*, No. 11 (1962).

———— "*Shui-hu-chuan* ti tsai-p'ing-chia 水滸傳的再評價" (*Shui-hu-chuan:* a revaluation), *Hsien-tai Wen-hsüeh*, No. 26 (1965).

Irwin, Richard G. *The Evolution of a Chinese Novel: Shui-hu-chuan*. Cambridge, Harvard University Press, 1953.

———— "Water Margin Revisited," *T'oung Pao*, XLVIII, Nos. 4-5 (1960).

Li Hsi-fan. "A Great Novel of Peasant Revolt," *Chinese Literature*, No. 12 (1959).

Sa Meng-wu 薩孟武. *Shui-hu-chuan yü Chung-kuo she-hui* 水滸傳與中國社會 (*Shui-hu-chuan* and Chinese society). Nanking, Cheng-chung shu-chü, 1946.

Shui-hu hsi-ch'ü chi 水滸戲曲集 (Traditional plays about Liangshan heroes), ed. by Fu Hsi-hua, *et al.* 2 vols. Shanghai, Chung-hua shu-chü, 1962.

Shui-hu yen-chiu lun-wen-chi 水滸研究論文集 (Studies and critiques in *Shui-hu*). Peking, Tso-chia ch'u-pan-she, 1957.

IV. JOURNEY TO THE WEST (*Hsi-yu chi*)

A

Ta-T'ang San-tsang ch'ü-ching shih-hua 大唐三藏取經詩話 (The *shih-hua* version of Tripitaka's quest for scriptures). Photolithographic ed., 1916. Colophon by Lo Chen-yü. Reprint without Lo's colophon: Taipei, Shih-chieh shu-chü, 1958.

Yü Hsiang-tou 余象斗, *et al. Ssu-yu-chi* 四遊記 (Four pilgrimages). Shanghai, Ku-tien-wen-hsüeh ch'u-pan-she, 1956; Taipei, Shih-chieh shu-chü, 1958.

Wu Ch'eng-en 吳承恩. *Hsi-yu chi* 西遊記. 2 vols. Peking, Tso-chia ch'u-pan-she, 1954.

Avenol, Louis. tr. *Si Yeou Ki, ou, Le voyage en Occident*. 2 vols. Paris, Editions du Seuil, 1957. A complete translation.

Waley, Arthur, tr. *Monkey*. New York, John Day, 1944; New York, Grove Press (Evergreen), 1958; Harmondsworth, Penguin Books, 1961.

Yang Hsien-yi, and Gladys Yang, trs. "Pilgrimage to the West: Chapter 27," *Chinese Literature*, No. 5 (1966).

B

Dudbridge, G. 杜德橋. "*Hsi-yu-chi* tsu-pen k'ao ti tsai-shang-chüeh 西遊記祖本考的再商榷 (The Problem of 'Hsi yu chi' and Its Early Versions: A Reappraisal)," *Hsin-ya Hsüeh-pao* (*The New Asia Journal*), VI, No. 2 (Hong Kong, 1964).

Hsi-yu-chi yen-chiu lun-wen-chi 西遊記研究論文集 (Studies in *Hsi-yu-chi*). Peking, Tso-chia ch'u-pan-she, 1957.

Hsia, C. T., and T. A. Hsia. "New Perspectives on Two Ming Novels: *Hsi-yu chi* and *Hsi-yu pu*," in Chow Tse-tsung, ed., *Wen-lin: Studies in the Chinese Humanities*. Madison, University of Wisconsin Press, in press.

Liu Hsiu-yeh 劉修業, ed. *Wu Ch'eng-en shih-wen chi* 吳承恩詩文集 (The poetry and prose of Wu Ch'eng-en). Shanghai, Ku-tien-wen-hsüeh ch'u-pan-she, 1958.

Liu Ts'un-yan 柳存仁. "*Ssu-yu-chi* ti Ming k'o-pen 四遊記的明刻本 (The Ming Editions of the 'Four Travels')," *Hsin-ya Hsüeh-pao*, V, No. 2 (1963).

——— "The Prototypes of *Monkey* (*Hsi Yu Chi*)," *T'oung Pao*, LI, No. 1 (1964).

Waley, Arthur. *The Real Tripitaka, and Other Pieces*. New York, Macmillan, 1952.

Wu Hsiao-ling 吳曉鈴. "'Hsi-yu-chi' ho 'Lo-mo-yen-shu' '西遊記' 與 '羅摩延書'" (*Hsi-yu-chi* and *The Ramayana*), *Wen-hsüeh Yen-chiu*, No. 1 (1958).

V. CHIN P'ING MEI

A

Chin P'ing Mei tz'u-hua 金瓶梅詞話. 21 vols., Peiping, Ku-i hsiao-shuo k'an-hsing-hui, 1933; 5 vols., Tokyo, Daian, 1963.

Hsin-k'o hsiu-hsiang p'i-p'ing Chin P'ing Mei 新刻繡像批評金瓶梅 (*Chin P'ing Mei*: a new block print edition with illustrations and notes). There are no satisfactory modern reprints of this Ch'ung-chen edition.

Egerton, Clement, tr. *The Golden Lotus*. 4 vols. London, Routledge, 1939; New York, Paragon Book Gallery, 1962.

Kuhn, Franz, tr. *Kin Ping Meh, oder, Die Abenteuerliche Geschichte von Hsi Men und seinen sechs Frauen*. Leipzig, Insel-Verlag, 1930.

Miall, Bernard, tr. *Chin P'ing Mei: The Adventurous History of Hsi Men and His Six Wives*. New York, Putnam, 1940; reprint: Capricorn Books, 1962. A translation of the Kuhn version.

B

Bishop, John L. "A Colloquial Short Story in the Novel *Chin P'ing Mei*," in Bishop, ed., *Studies in Chinese Literature*.

Feng Yuan-chün 馮沅君. "*Chin P'ing Mei tz'u-hua* chung ti wen-hsüeh shih-liao

金瓶梅詞話中的文學史料" (Materials for literary history in *Chin P'ing Mei*), in *Ku-chü shuo-hui* 古劇説彙 (Studies in old drama). Peking, Tso-chia ch'u-pan-she, 1956.

Hanan, P. D. "A Landmark of the Chinese Novel," in Douglas Grant and Millar MacLure, eds., *The Far East: China and Japan*. University of Toronto Press, 1961.

—— "The Text of the *Chin P'ing Mei*," *Asia Major* (new series), IX, Pt. 1 (1962).

—— "Sources of the *Chin P'ing Mei*," *Asia Major* (new series), X, Pt. 1 (1963).

Wu Han 吳晗. "*Chin P'ing Mei* ti chu-tso shih-tai chi ch'i she-hui pei-ching 金瓶梅的著作時代及其社會背景" (The age in which *Chin P'ing Mei* was written and its social background), in *Tu-shih cha-chi* 讀史劄記 (Notes on history). Peking, San-lien shu-tien, 1957.

Yao Ling-hsi 姚靈犀, ed. *P'ing-wai chih-yen* 瓶外卮言 (Papers and reference materials on *Chin P'ing Mei*). Tientsin, Tientsin shu-chü, 1940. Reprint: Nagoya, Saika shorin, 1962. Contains a valuable glossary by the editor.

VI. THE SCHOLARS (*Ju-lin wai-shih*)

A

Wu Ching-tzu 吳敬梓. *Tsu-pen Ju-lin wai-shih* 足本儒林外史 (The full-text *Ju-lin wai-shih*). 4th ptg.: Taipei, Shih-chieh shu-chü, 1957.

Yang Hsien-yi, and Gladys Yang, trs. *The Scholars*. Peking, Foreign Languages Press, 1957.

Wang, Chi-chen, tr. "Two Scholars Who Passed the Examinations," in George Kao, ed., *Chinese Wit and Humor*. New York, Coward-McCann, 1946.

B

Ch'eng Chih-t'ing 程芝亭. "Tu *Ju-lin wai-shih* sui-pi 讀儒林外史隨筆" (Random notes on *The Scholars*), *Wen-hsüeh Tsa-chih*, III, No. 6 (Taipei, 1958).

Ho Man-tzu 何滿子. *Lun Ju-lin wai-shih* 論儒林外史 (On *The Scholars*). Shanghai, Shanghai ch'u-pan-she, 1954.

Ho Tse-han 何澤翰. *Ju-lin wai-shih jen-wu pen-shih k'ao-lüeh* 儒林外史人物本事考畧 (The characters and stories in *The Scholars*: a source study). Shanghai, Ku-tien wen-hsüeh ch'u-pan-she, 1957.

Ju-lin wai-shih yen-chiu lun-chi 儒林外史研究論集 (Studies in *The Scholars*). Peking, Tso-chia ch'u-pan-she, 1955.

Král, Oldrich. "Several Artistic Methods in the Classic Chinese Novel *Ju-lin wai-shih*," *Archiv Orientální*, XXXII (1964).

VII. DREAM OF THE RED CHAMBER (*Hung-lou meng*)

A

Ch'ien-lung chia-hsü Chih-yen Chai ch'ung-p'ing Shih-t'ou-chi 乾隆甲戌脂硯齋重評石頭記 (Chih-yen Chai-annotated *Shih-t'ou chi:* a Ch'ien-lung manuscript mistakenly dated 1754). 2 vols. Taipei, Hu Shih, 1961. Postface by Hu Shih.

Ch'ien-lung ch'ao-pen pai-nien-hui Hung-lou-meng kao 乾隆抄本百廿回紅樓夢稿 (A draft copy of the 120-chapter *Hung-lou-meng* transcribed in the Ch'ien-lung period). 12 vols. Peking, Chung-hua shu-chü, 1963. Colophon by Fan Ning.

Ts'ao Hsüeh-ch'in 曹雪芹. *Hung-lou-meng pa-shih-hui chiao-pen* 紅樓夢八十回校本. 4 vols. Peking, Jen-min-wen-hsüeh ch'u-pan-she, 1958. A variorum edition prepared by Yü P'ing-po with the assistance of Wang Hsi-shih.

Tsu-pen Hung-lou meng 足本紅樓夢 (The full-text *Hung-lou meng*). 2 vols. 17th ptg.: Taipei, Shih-chieh shu-chü, 1957. A reprint of the Ch'eng-Kao B edition.

Kuhn, Franz, tr. *Der Traum der roten Kammer*. Leipzig, Insel-Verlag, 1932.

McHugh, Florence, and Isabel McHugh, trs. *The Dream of the Red Chamber*. New York, Pantheon Books, 1958. A translation of the Kuhn version.

Wang, Chi-chen, tr. *Dream of the Red Chamber*. New York, Twayne, 1958; abridged ed.: New York, Doubleday (Anchor), 1958.

Yang Hsien-yi, and Gladys Yang, trs. "Dream of the Red Chamber (An Excerpt from the Novel)," *Chinese Literature*, Nos. 6-8 (1964). Chapters 18-20, 32-34, 74-77.

B

Chao Kang 趙岡. *Hung-lou-meng k'ao-cheng shih-i* 紅樓夢考證拾遺 (Studies in problems connected with *Hung-lou-meng*). Hong Kong, Kao-yuan ch'u-pan-she, 1963.

Chiang Ho-sen 蔣和森. *Hung-lou-meng lun-kao* 紅樓夢論稿 (A tentative critique of *Hung-lou-meng*). Peking, Jen-min-wen-hsüeh ch'u-pan-she, 1959.

Chou Ju-ch'ang 周汝昌. *Hung-lou-meng hsin-cheng* 紅樓夢新證 (New studies in *Hung-lou-meng*). Shanghai, T'ang-ti ch'u-pan-she, 1953.

Chuang, Hsin-cheng. Themes of *Dream of the Red Chamber:* A Comparative Interpretation. Unpublished dissertation, Indiana University, 1966.

Gregory, Sister Mary, S. P. A Critical Analysis of "The Dream of the Red Chamber" in Terms of Western Novelistic Criteria. Unpublished dissertation, Indiana University, 1966.

Grieder, Jerome B. "The Communist Critique of *Hung Lou Meng*," *Papers on China*, X. Harvard University, East Asian Research Center, 1956.

Ho Chi-fang. "On 'The Dream of the Red Chamber,'" *Chinese Literature*, No. 1 (1963).

Hsia, C. T. "Love and Compassion in *Dream of the Red Chamber*," *Criticism*, v, No. 3 (1963).

Hung-lou-meng yen-chiu lun-wen chi 紅樓夢研究論文集 (*Hung-lou-meng*: studies and critiques). Peking, Jen-min-wen-hsüeh ch'u-pan-she, 1957.

I Su 一粟, comp. *Hou-lou-meng chüan* 紅樓夢卷 (Pre-1919 sources on *Hung-lou-meng*). 2 vols. Peking, Chung-hua shu-chü, 1963.

——— *Hung-lou-meng shu-lu* 紅樓夢書錄 (*Hung-lou-meng*: a descriptive bibliography). Shanghai, Ku-tien-wen-hsüeh ch'u-pan-she, 1958.

Li Ch'en-tung 李辰冬. *Hung-lou-meng yen-chiu* 紅樓夢研究 (Studies in *Hung-lou-meng*). Taipei, Hsin-hsing shu-chü, 1962.

Lin Yutang 林語堂. "P'ing-hsin lun Kao Ê 平心論高鶚 (Re-opening the Question of Authorship of 'Red Chamber Dream')," *Bulletin of the Institute of History and Philology* (Taipei, Academia Sinica, 1958). Reprinted with other essays on the novel in *P'ing-hsin lun Kao Ê* (Taipei, Wen-hsing shu-tien, 1966).

Liu Ta-chieh 劉大杰. *Hung-lou-meng ti ssu-hsiang yü jen-wu* 紅樓夢的思想與人物 (*Hung-lou-meng*: a study of its thought and characters). Shanghai, Shanghai ku-tien-wen-hsüeh ch'u-pan-she, 1956.

Spence, Jonathan D. *Ts'ao Yin and the K'ang-hsi Emperor, Bondservant and Master*. New Haven and London, Yale University Press, 1966.

Wen-hsüeh yen-chiu chi-k'an 文學研究集刊 (Collection of literary studies). Vol. 5, ed. by the Literary Institute, Peking University. Peking, Jen-min-wen-hsüeh ch'u-pan-she, 1957. Contains articles on the novel and its author by Ho Ch'i-fang, Ts'ao Tao-heng, and Wang P'ei-chang.

West, Anthony. "Through a Glass, Darkly," *The New Yorker* (November 22, 1958).

Wu En-yü 吳恩裕. *Yu-kuei Ts'ao Hsüeh-ch'in shih-chung* 有關曹雪芹十種 (Documents concerning Ts'ao Hsüeh-ch'in). Peking, Chung-hua shu-chü, 1963.

Wu Shih-ch'ang. *On The Red Chamber Dream: A Critical Study of Two Annotated Manuscripts of the XVIIIth Century*. Oxford University Press, 1961.

——— "History of 'The Red Chamber Dream,'" *Chinese Literature*, No. 1 (1963).

——— 吳世昌, et al. *San-lun Hung-lou-meng* 散論紅樓夢 (Essays on *Hung-lou-meng*). Hong Kong, Chien-wen shu-chü, 1963.

Yü P'ing-po 俞平伯. *Hung-lou-meng yen-chiu* 紅樓夢研究 (Studies in *Hung-lou-meng*). Shanghai, T'ang-ti ch'u-pan-she, 1953.

———, comp. *Chih-yen Chai Hung-lou-meng chi-p'ing* 脂硯齋紅樓夢輯評 (A compilation of all the comments in the Chih-yen Chai versions of *Hung-lou-meng*), ed. by Wang Erh. Shanghai, Shanghai wen-i lien-ho ch'u-pan-she, 1954.

——— "T'an hsin-k'an Ch'ien-lung ch'ao-pen pai-nien-hui Hung-lou-meng kao 談新刊乾隆抄本百廿回紅樓夢稿" (On the newly published *Hung-lou-meng kao*), in *Chung-hua wen-shih lun-tsᶜung* (Papers on Chinese literature and history), 5th series. Peking, Chung-hua shu-chü, 1964.

VIII.　OTHER TRANSLATIONS OF TRADITIONAL CHINESE FICTION

Bauer, Wolfgang, and Herbert Franke, eds. *The Golden Casket: Chinese Novellas of Two Millennia,* tr. by Christopher Levenson, mostly from Bauer and Franke, trs., *Die Goldene Truhe.* New York, Harcourt, Brace & World, 1964.

Chang Yün. *Yü Chiao Li.*

　Abel-Rémusat, J. P. *Iu-kiao-li, ou, les deux cousines.* 4 vols. Paris, Moutardier, 1826. Retranslated into English as *Iu-Kiao-li; or, The Two Fair Cousins.* 2 vols. London, Hunt and Clarke, 1827.

Hao-chᶜiu chuan.

　Percy, Thomas, ed. *Hau Kiou Choaan, or, The Pleasing History.* 4 vols. 2d ed. London, R. and J. Dodsley, 1761.

Hsing-shih heng-yen.

　Acton, Harold, and Lee Yi-hsieh. *Four Cautionary Tales.* London, Lehmann, 1947.

Jou pᶜu-tᶜuan.

　Martin, Richard. *Jou Pu Tuan (The Prayer Mat of Flesh),* tr. from the German version of Franz Kuhn. New York, Grove Press, 1963.

Ko-lien hua-ying.

　Kean, Vladimir. *Flower Shadows Behind the Curtain (Ko Lien Hua Ying),* tr. from the German version of Franz Kuhn. New York, Pantheon Books, 1959.

Ku-chin hsiao-shuo.

　Birch, Cyril. *Stories from a Ming Collection: Translations of Chinese Short Stories Published in the Seventeenth Century.* Bloomington, Indiana University Press, 1959.

Li Ju-chen. *Ching-hua yuan.*

　Lin Tai-yi. *Flowers in the Mirror.* Berkeley and Los Angeles, University of California Press, 1966. An abridged translation.

Liu Ê. *Lao-tsᶜan yu-chi.*

　Shadick, Harold. *The Travels of Lao Tsᶜan.* Ithaca, Cornell University Press, 1952; paperback reprint, 1966.

Pᶜing Shan Leng Yen.

　Julien, Stanislas. *Les Deux jeunes filles lettrées.* 2 vols. Paris, Didier, 1826.

Pᶜu Sung-ling. *Liao-chai chih-i.*

　Giles, Herbert A. *Strange Stories from a Chinese Studio.* 2 vols. London, Thomas de la Rue, 1880.

Waley, Arthur. *Ballads and Stories from Tun-huang*. New York, Macmillan, 1963.

Wang, Chi-chen. *Traditional Chinese Tales*. New York, Columbia University Press, 1944.

Yang Hsien-yi, and Gladys Yang. *The Courtesan's Jewel Box: Chinese Stories of the Xth-XVIIth Centuries*. Peking, Foreign Languages Press, 1957.

———— *The Man Who Sold a Ghost: Chinese Tales of the 3rd-6th Centuries*. Peking, Foreign Languages Press, 1958.

INDEX